International Journal on Advances in Networks and Services

ADVANCED TOPICS
mob comm
special topics on systems

2017 vol. 10 nr. 3&4

Printed from e-media with permission by:

Curran Associates, Inc.
57 Morehouse Lane
Red Hook, NY 12571

Some format issues inherent in the e-media version may also appear in this print version.

Printed by Curran Associates, Inc. (2018)

International Academy, Research, and Industry Association (IARIA)
412 Derby Way
Wilmington, DE 19810

Phone: (408) 893-6407
Fax: (408) 527-6351

petre@iaria.org

Additional copies of this publication are available from:

Curran Associates, Inc.
57 Morehouse Lane
Red Hook, NY 12571 USA
Phone: 845-758-0400
Fax: 845-758-2633
Email: curran@proceedings.com
Web: www.proceedings.com

The *International Journal on Advances in Networks and Services* is published by IARIA.
ISSN: 1942-2644
journals site: http://www.iariajournals.org
contact: petre@iaria.org

Sponsored by IARIA
www.iaria.org

International Journal on Advances in Networks and Services
Volume 10, Number 3 & 4, 2017

International Journal on Advances in Networks and Services
Volume 10, Numbers 3 & 4, 2017

CONTENTS

International Journal on Advances in Networks and Services, vol 10 no 3 & 4, year 2017, http://www.iariajournals.org/networks_and_services/

Flexible 5G Edge Server for Multi Industry Service Network

Carlo Vitucci
Technology Management
Ericsson AB
Stockholm, Sweden
carlo.vitucci@ericsson.com

Alf Larsson
Senior Specialist
Ericsson AB
Stockholm, Sweden
alf.larsson@ericsson.com

***Abstract*— The Telecom world is converging with IT rapidly in order to address users demands in a more agile and personalized way and is a once in a generation inflection point in the telecommunications industry. But how can a 5th generation wireless system architecture framework also conforms to the new demands from the major areas Internet of Things and Networked Society? The Software defined Network – Network Function Virtualization matches the 5th generation wireless system framework, it has the concepts and the key components for deploying a service at the edge of the Radio Access Network. But with a different approach: moving Software Defined Network-Network Function Virtualization into the Radio Access Network which is conceptually different than moving the Radio Access Network into the Cloud. This paper is an extension of Server at the Edge concept introduced recently and depicted with its key characterizations. Resources and meters handling are also considered fundamental for the new architecture using analytics feedback for a more efficient and autonomous deployment of new services. Business cases examples are added to highlight why the proposed components for the edge of the network are considered important.**

Keywords-component; 5G; IoT; SDN-NFV; Edge Network OS; SON; Analytics.

I. INTRODUCTION

The server at the edge concept has been presented as "SEED, a Server Platform for the Edge of the Network" [1]. Today, the Telecom realm is facing an epic moment, a technology step that will drive the evolution of the networked system in the future and, at the end of the day, the End User services and life style. The entire world of communication is driving the strong requirement for new services, where End User is at the center of the business case of a digital society (see Figure 1), and Telecom operators could make the difference. Mobility is dominating the area with significant smartphone penetration growth, it has changed the usage of connectivity [3][5]. With the emerging 5th Generation wireless system (5G) new great benefits opens up for the Telecom operators.

Figure 1. 5G is about digital society (source [2])

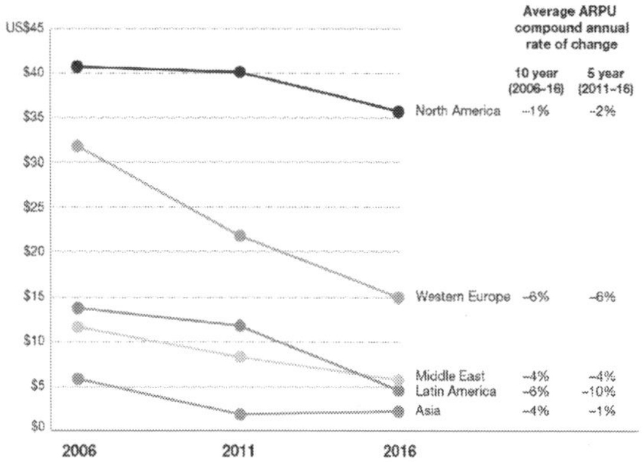

Figure 2. Average revenue per user in telecom industry (source [4])

In the last years, Telecom operators have seen an exponential growth of data traffic and, at the same time, a significant income reduction from the "golden eggs goose" voice and Short Message Service (SMS). Today the majority of the operators have most of their Average Revenue Per User (ARPU) coming from data traffic where voice and SMS is often offered at a very cheap price just to attract new customers and increase revenue from data traffic. The trend is not supposed to change in the next years. Ericsson prediction shows that, by 2021, there will be 28 billion connected devices around the world [3].

With that trend prediction, there are at least two aspects; The first is Mobile data offloading [6] and in this context for the operator a strive to find alternative for the backhaul and core network offloading. This not only affects the business model and the type of services provided. It would also require an interworking standardization between cellular and Wi-Fi to create a seamless user experience. The second would be for the operators to increase network capability and thereby increase income. But the picture is not complete, most mobile users are not prepared to spend too much for using their smartphones. However, it is not a case that the revenue from new subscriber dropped down dramatically in the last years, as reported in Figure 2. Such a condition would result in a significant reduction of operator margin in a way that some pessimistic vision [7] is predicting a possible "end of profitability" condition for their business. But it is a fact that even in a more optimistic prediction the current business model is not sustainable. Operators need a new direction where their margins can start to increase again [8].

A common understanding is that Software Defined Network – Network Function Virtualization (SDN-NFV) is a key to reduce Operating expenses (Opex) and Capital expenditures (Capex) and thereby increase margin for operators. But it looks like that statement is not enough to make operators change strategy. Just to avoid any misunderstanding, SDN-NFV architecture will reduce Opex and Capex, but it is not actually that huge of an incentive for the business of the operators. In fact, Opex and Capex have been reduced during the latest years. Mostly thanks to the cost reduction of technology, and the truth is that today total cost and revenue are so close that one can hardly imagine a new golden era thanks only to Opex and Capex reduction. It seems enough for surviving in the Telecom market battlefield, but surely not enough to justify a new infrastructure investment.

Eventually, let us consider the life cycle of a new Telecom technology: the delivery rate between a technology step (from 2G to 3G, from 3G to 4G and so on) has an aggressive pace, in most of the case "forcing" operators to make a new infrastructure investment. But reduced revenue and delivery interval is concurrently reducing the business case window. Thus operators are not actually too keen to join a new technology in such conditions and for sure they are looking at any new investment very carefully. So, what are the actual needs of the operators then?

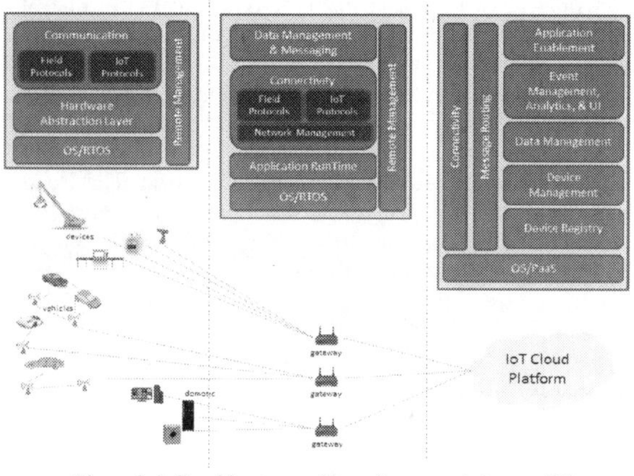

Figure 3. IoT architecture and its software stack (source [9])

So far, their effort has been focused on a market where improvement of capacity and quality of the connectivity has been enough. But the richest market today is fully in the hands of the Over-The-Top (OTT) content media delivery companies (Google, Facebook, Netflix, etc.). A real shift of business for the operators is the key to enter such a rich market. Eventually, that will be a win-win condition, since OTT is perfectly aware that reducing the end-to-end (E2E) data contents latency will improve their business. They are also aware that accessing User Metadata (very well known by Telecom operators) will increase even more such a market thanks to new business cases.

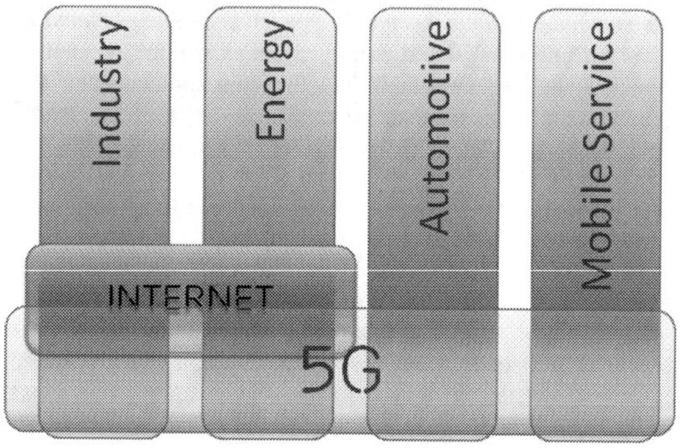

Figure 4. 5G is a common accelerator

II. IOT AND MACHINE TYPE COMMUNICATION

A clear huge opportunity for operators comes from the Internet Of Things (IoT). Telemetry, sensors and infrastructure monitoring have been visible for the last ten years, but cost reduction of semiconductors, system on chips, and new radio technology opens the door to smarter devices. Security, enhanced health, manufacturers fully connected, intelligent and with autonomous data handling are today very attractive business opportunities and promise great benefits for the consumers. The IoT is part of the Industry 4.0: an instrumented and data-driven world, a world where Data is the new oil. But a business is valid only if it is sensible. It is not realistic to expect operators investing and maintaining different infrastructures and limiting the operation agility. So the IoT infrastructure, as described in Figure 3, needs a system solution where IoT is considered as a vertical service more than a different infrastructure. This leads to the conclusion that the requirement for the next generation of mobile system is to concurrently support different areas of industry, from new End User services to IoT (Figure 4). Once devices and machines are connected, the traditional vision of data flow into centralized cloud repositories will not work any longer. The solution is to move intelligence close to those devices and machines. That will reduce latency in decision control loops for time-critical applications and

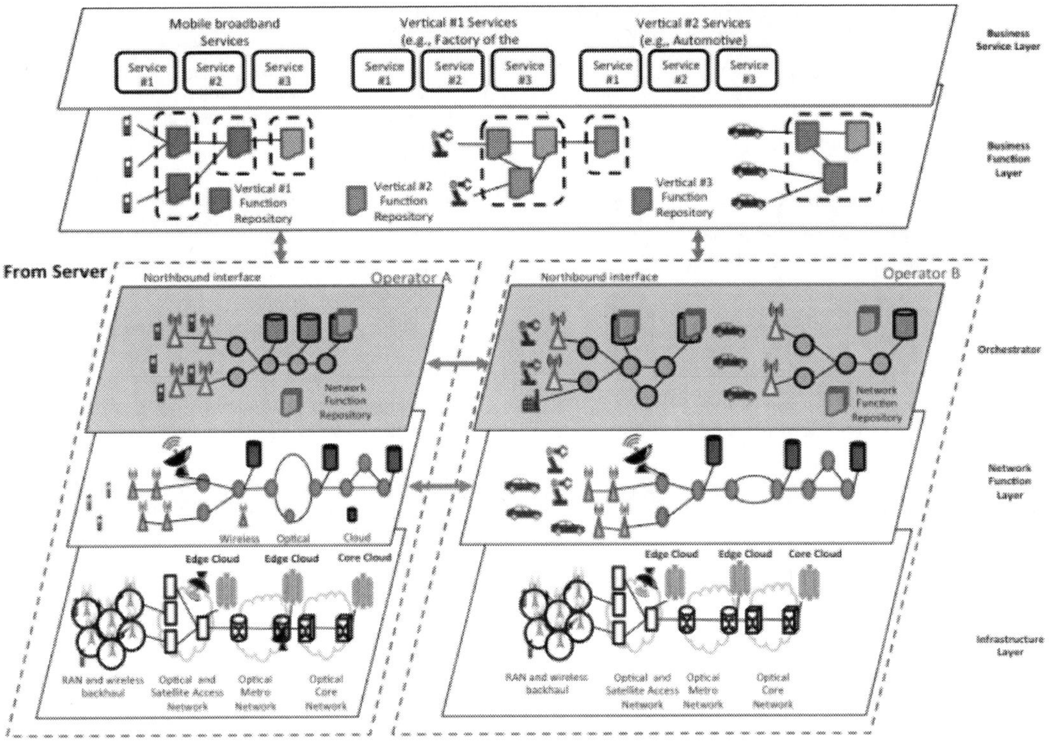

Figure 5. 5G Architecture (source [10])

the backhaul bandwidth drawback caused by that massive data flow.

III. 5G

5G is the answer. It is not a bare new radio technology. 5G has the ambition to be a new framework, covering the system architecture, the network management and the software deployment to act as the enabler of the new business opportunity mentioned. Massive broadband, machine-type communication and time-critical autonomous control are the three groups where to find 5G requirements, with the declared scope to offer an eco-system for business innovation. 5G solution wants to support vertical markets, such as IoT, automotive connectivity, Mobile broadband.

The vertical deployment approach is based on a complex integration of: distributed computing, storage, networking and spectrum capabilities. Slicing those underlying resources is fundamental. A vertical service deployment needs a system where it is possible to have: multi-tenancy and multi-service, respecting the Service Level Agreement (SLA), providing different Quality Of Service (QoS) level to achieve different Service characterization and different network policy. The diversity of that system needs an orchestrator responsible to allocate computing, storage and networking resources to the network functions. Then allocate those network functions to the vertical services.

Security, Reliability and Power Consumption efficiency are very challenging in this scenario and need special focus.

Automation of service deployment is also very important. In the traditional system, installation of a new service required months because it depended on a number of installation parameters. That traditional way of working is very expensive and often the root cause of performance drawback or bad reputation for infrastructure providers. The 5G system needs to be more autonomous, self-organizing resources when and where needed. These characterizations are important enablers to a successful system, but they explain very well the complexity of the new architecture too.

The 5G architecture is based on five pillars:

- Radio Technology: Massive Multiple Input, Multiple Output (MIMO);
- SDN/NFV Technology;
- Radio Protocol split: The Mobile Edge Computing;
- Management and Orchestration (MANO);
- Self-organizing Network (SON)

The concepts behind the 5G architecture are summarized in Figure 5. This paper is mainly focusing on the Mobile Edge Computing, identifying the critical technologies needed. For the other bullets above only a recall is provided though with an emphasis taken for Edge Analytic handling.

IV. SDN-NFV: A RECALL

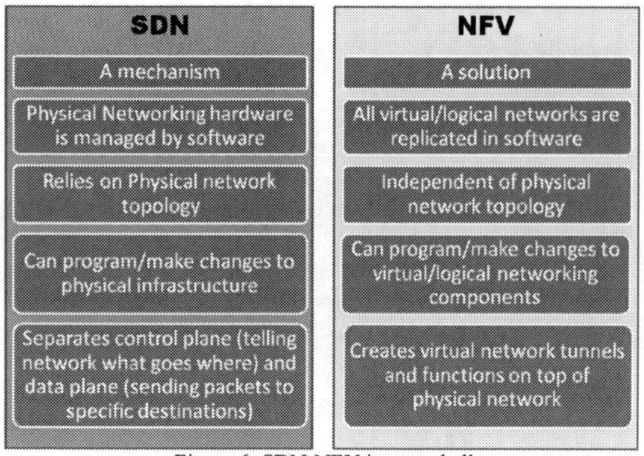

Figure 6: SDN-NFV in a nutshell

An SDN-NFV introduction should start from the reason behind the SDN-NFV architecture. In fact, following this approach, it will be clear why SDN-NFV is a pillar of 5G. SDN-NFV has been designed to cope with the reality that, in the next decades, enterprises will increasingly make their specific applications available on mobile devices. The next wave of mobile communication is to mobilize and automate industries and industry processes. This is widely referred to as Machine-Type Communication (MTC) and IoT. OTT players will move to deliver more and more applications that require higher quality, lower latency, and other service enhancing capabilities. The SDN-NFV target is to allow vertical multiservice deployment and, at the same time, reduce Opex and CapEx; thereby creating a more green-power environment and allows an easy deployment of a new technology in a shorter, safer and comfortable new way. The "core" promise of SDN-NFV is to guarantee a new "business environment" where telecom operators are a stakeholder in service creation. SDN-NFV architecture is built over three layers [16], as logically shown in Figure 7:

- Business Application Layer – where the enterprise business value model is defined
- Business Enablement Layer – where the enabling and capabilities value are defined
- Infrastructure Resources Layer – where the resources needed by the value are defined

The SDN-NFV layered vision is the most useful to understand the service oriented approach supported by the architecture itself. The comparison between Figure 5 and Figure 7 is self-explaining: it is the same concept. The European Telecommunications Standards Institute (ETSI) has set regulations and indications to design and define SDN-NFV architecture [12][13].

The Architecture Framework is showed in Figure 8 [11], where any block has specific role, briefly summarized below:

- Virtual Infrastructure Manager (VIM)
  - Manages life cycle of virtual resources in an Network Function Virtualitazion Infrastructure (NFVI) domain. That is, it creates, maintains and tears down virtual machines (VMs) from physical resources in an NFVI domain.
  - Keeps inventory of virtual machines (VMs) associated with physical resources.
  - Performance and fault management of hardware, software and virtual resources.
  - Keeps north bound Application Program Interfaces (APIs) and thus exposes physical and virtual resources to other management systems.

- Virtual Network Function (VNF) Manager (VNFM)
  - VNFM manages life cycle of VNFs. It creates, maintains and terminates VNF instances.

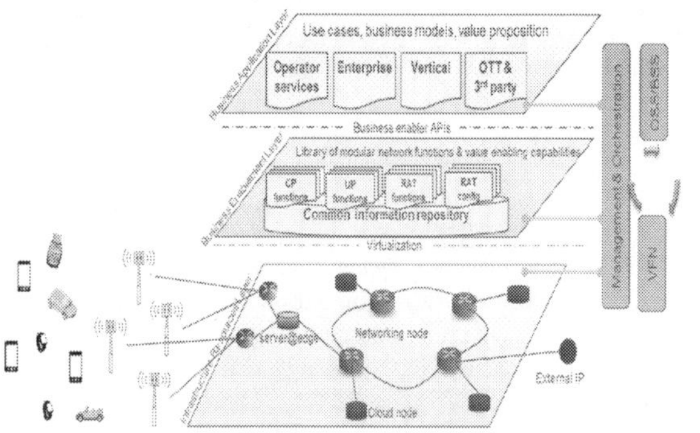

Figure 7. SDN-NFV: the Layered Architecture

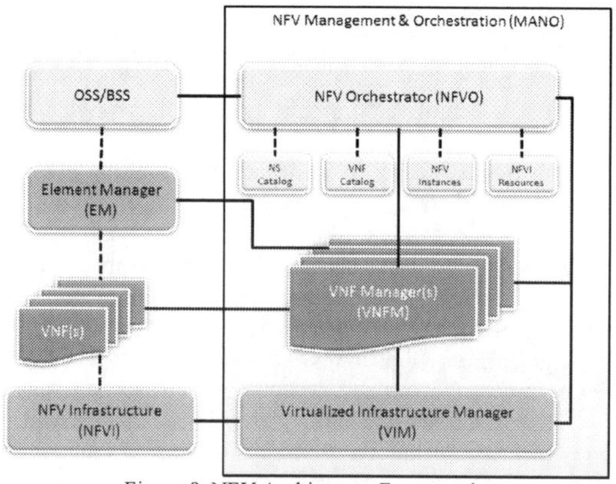

Figure 8. NFV Architecture Framework

(Which are installed on the VMs which the VIM creates and manages)

- It is responsible for the Fault, Configuration, Accounting, Performance and Security (FCAPS) of VNFs.
- It scales up/scales down VNFs which results in scaling up and scaling down of CPU usage.

- NFV Orchestrator (NFVO)
  - Resource Orchestration
  - NFVO coordinates, authorizes, releases and engages NFVI resources among different Point of Presence (PoPs) or within one PoP. This does so by engaging with the VIMs directly through their north bound APIs instead of engaging with the NFVI resources, directly
  - Service Orchestration
  - Service Orchestration creates end to end service between different VNFs. It achieves this by coordinating with the respective VNFMs so it does not need to talk to VNFs directly. Example would be creating a service between the base station VNFs of one vendor and core node VNFs of another vendor.
  - Service Orchestration can instantiate VNFMs, where applicable.
  - It does the topology management of the network services instances.

- NFV Catalogs
  - A VNF Catalog is a repository of all usable VNF Descriptors (VNFDs).
  - Network Services (NS) Catalog is the list of the usable Network services.
  - NFV Instances list holds all details about Network Services instances and related VNF Instances.
  - NFVI Resources is a repository of NFVI resources utilized for establishing NFV services.

- Element Management (EM)

EM is not part of the MANO but, if it is available, it needs to coordinate with VNFM so it is important to know about it. Element Management System is responsible for the FCAPS of VNF. If you recall, VNFM does the same job. But EM can do it through proprietary interface with the VNF in contrast to VNFM. However, EM needs to make sure that it exchanges information with VNFM through open reference point (Ve-Vnfm-em). The EM may be aware of virtualization and collaborate with VNFM to perform those functions that require exchange of information regarding the NFVI resources associated with VNF.

- Operations Support System (OSS)/Business Support System (BSS)

NFV is supposed to work in coordination with OSS/BSS.

It is useful to finish this recall for the SDN-NFV with a clarification: SDN and NFV are mentioned together because they need to be considered concurrently in the implementation of the architecture: the NFV system is the solution matching Figure 5 and Figure 7, while SDN is the tool used to deploy the NFV framework.

V. Radio Protocol Split And Mobile Edge Platform

Despite the effort done by ETSI, some parts are left for others to design. One of those parts is the so-called NFVI (see Figure 8), where the Radio Network vendors could play their significant role, both contributing to the SDN-NFV best deployment and improving their own business. The first discriminating condition to succeed in this challenge is their ability to integrate the traditional IT world with the Telecom (as explicitly required by the new business case), that is, their ability to provide full SDN-NFV architecture up to the edge of the network; into the Radio Access Network (RAN). ETSI group defined the deployment of the SDN-NFV for the mobile network in their Use Cases study report [11]. According to that scenario, the current base station is actually split into two main objects: the Remote Radio Header (RRH), that is antenna and eventually the basic Layer 1, and the virtualized Baseband Unit (vBBU) as a service housed in a specific server implementing Layer 2 and Layer 3 of mobile protocols. Then, from an infrastructure point of view, the challenge is to understand what SDN-NFV deployment into the RAN really means, identifying how the server at the edge of the network should look like. The questions that initially need to be answered are: what are the characterizations and technologies that must be considered as key components of the server itself, which hardware characteristics are matching the requirements, which functions are clearly new components (services) of the platform housed into the server@edge (SEED) and which ones need more attention and effort to remove possible obstacles and limitations?

It is a long journey where the infrastructure designers must remember the real needs behind the SDN-NFV. Moreover, the expectation of operators must be fulfilled and a more complete understanding of other opportunities, like footprint and energy consumption, play their important role. For these reasons, it is worth to focus on the SEED concept, identifying its characterization to cope with the radio function requirements.

In fact, the starting point of this paper is that it could be very difficult to move the RAN into the cloud and it is more suitable to port SDN-NFV into the RAN. This will give all the benefits of SDN-NFV described in the introduction, and at the same time answer the specific requirements needed at the edge of the network.

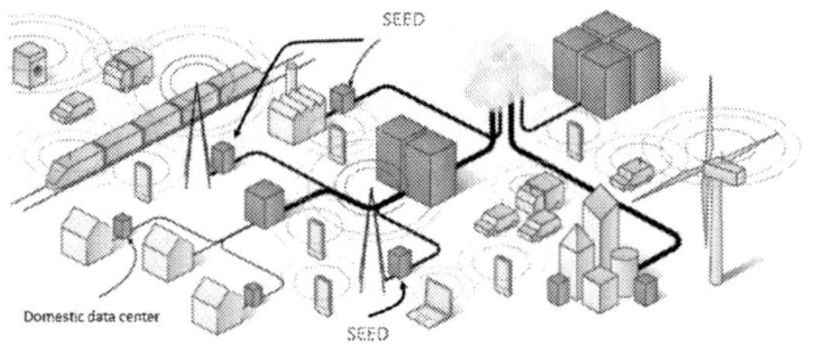

Figure 9. Distributed computing in the next infrastructure (source [17])

The reference deployment model has been described [14][15] and ETSI made some progress in the same area [12] introducing the so called Mobile-Edge Computing (MEC) server. It offers application developers and content providers cloud-computing capabilities and an IT service environment at the edge of the mobile network. The reference system architecture in this paper is depicted in Figure 9. Another aspect is to consider SDN-NFV as an overall system solution, an end-to-end solution and, from that perspective, to avoid not fulfilling the fundamental requirements.

There are also some concepts on the splitting of the current Base Station in RRH and vBBU and what it means for the current implementation of the Base Station Controller (BSC). As an example, one can refer to the Long Term Evolution (LTE) protocol deployment, to figure pros and cons out, while moving LTE function from RRH to the vBBU (see Figure 10).

The deployment of Radio Technology between RRH and BBU could be done in several ways; mostly by deciding the point in the protocol chain where the split is done and so defining the interface typology between RRH and BBU. Depending on the decision taken one can face different types of issues or constraints. An ETSI-based vBBU implementation, for example, might guarantee the highest possible service flexibility. Thus, also achieving the highest level of operational agility (indeed very useful for Telecom Infrastructure providers as well, since deployment of a new technology could be handled in the same shape as of a new service deployment), but it is challenged by very aggressive latency time requirement.

On the other hand, a "smooth" porting of the existing BSC solutions into the cloud could be attractive in term of legacy software or reduced latency time and would simply the first deployment. But it is a poor answer to the strong request of operation agility, because, in this case, the protocol splitting is done on the highest protocol layer only. In a similar way, splitting BSC between RRH and BBU could have important impacts by means of Fronthaul and Backhaul capacity demand [18].

There is not a common trend between proposed solutions of operators. For example, KT (Korea Telecom) has recently set its target for 2020 to Radio Link Control (RLC) [19], emphasizing the need of reducing the Fronthaul bandwidth requirement. However, SK Telecom is pointing to L2, so

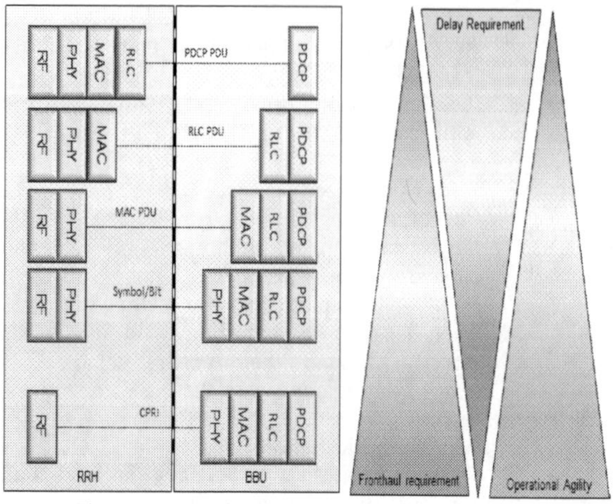

Figure 10. Pro and cons of splitting Radio Technology

somewhere between Medium Access Control (MAC) and RLC [20]. The uncertain trend is supposed to be fixed by 3GPP standardization group and it is out of the scope of this paper to point to any splitting point. Pro and cons have been listed before. For the nature of the radio technology, the design of the server at the edge of the network makes the difference; by means of feasibility and performance.

It is worth to mention that all network functions should be handled as a service, according to the layer architecture described in Figure 7. In SDN-NFV network, the deployment is based on Service Availability Concept: meaning, Radio Access must be a function deployed on the Business Enablement Layer and published to be used as component in a service chain at the Business Application Layer. The service chains capability [21] is considered a key accelerator of the SDN-NFV usage, since it is introducing a high level of operational agility, which is already mentioned as mandatory requirement. Note how the service chain is also a mindset in ETSI use case description of the BS [11] and it is at the very fundamental of SDN-NFV architecture description [22][23].

VI. SEED, A SDN-NFV SYSTEM ELEMENT

In order to understand the needs for the SEED, it is important to recall the vertical services concept as introduced in Figure 4. This is only possible if the system can define and handle "slices" of network that can be univocally assigned to different services. Slicing requires the capability to virtualize the underlying resources.

Virtualization is the core of the SDN-NFV architecture and there is no alternative to conform to such an architecture. All resources must be virtualized, with no exception. Functions are virtualized, and every single physical resource is virtualized as well. To downsize the virtualization is against the operational agility characterization, which has been already mentioned previously as the key incitement for the business model behind the SDN-NFV. Downsizing the virtualization means to downsize the operational agility. This affects the business capacity of the operators and eventually misses the expectation they have for the new business opportunity. Applications are services and handled as services into the new architecture. That means there is no software deployment as traditionally intended, but instances of services as VMs (or containers) deployed over the architecture to provide a network value. The MANO (see Figure 8) must concurrently be able to handle containers and VMs in a very elastic way. There will be services with strong real-time requirement that do not need any guest OS, and cannot accept the cost of non-OS based virtualization; among other services that will be deployed in the system as "standard" VMs. The SEED should be able to house both.

It would be convenient to use Common Off The Shelf hardware (COTS), but it should not be a restriction. There are cases where implementation of complex traffic protocols or functions in software has not acceptable performance drawback and requires usage of Hardware Accelerators (HA). Moreover, the cost of the virtualization could be significantly reduced if the server is armed by a full set of Hardware Assisted Virtualization (HAV) features. Sometimes, HAV is the only chance to reduce the virtualization layer drawback with an acceptable result, and they can help avoiding unwanted dependencies between services. Which hardware for the SEED should be used? It is a decision that is based on a few requirements:

- remove the latency obstacles to strengthen the operational agility, using HA and full set of HAV.
- improve connectivity and direct services communication bypassing the virtualization layer thanks to the HAV.
- structure a server to deploy both SDN-NFV objects, distributed computing capabilities, distributed storage and Radio interface.

For the edge of the network, there is also a non-hardware need to consider: design to ensure Quality of Service (QoS) resource usage for Service Level Agreement (SLA) handling. The above set of different capabilities is defining the SEED as described in Figure 11. The number of the capabilities for the SEED will define its size, which is a pure dimensioning calculation. The solution is fully aligned to the

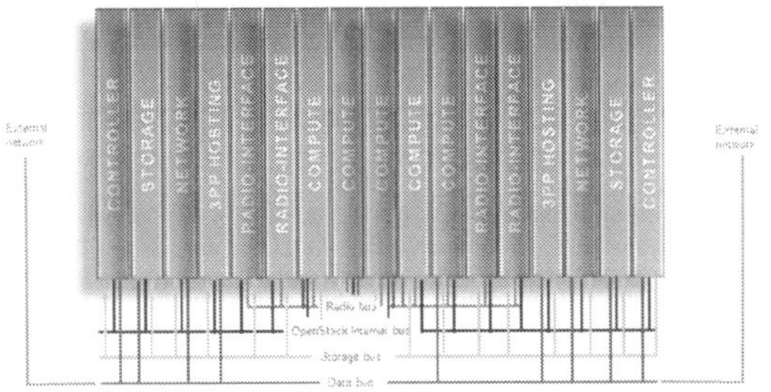

Figure 11. The SEED structured per function capabilities

most common cloud platform (ref. User's Guide indication [24][25]).

Traditional Data Center usage is considering slice allocation in computer domain, that is computation, storage and network capabilities. The SDN-NFV open source community created a solution with a data center way of working in mind and that drives the range and the "granularity" of resources while defining the slice. The characterization of applications running in a data center is on the opposite range of telecommunication applications: which are more sensitive to real-time constrains and, by definition, they need to have access to Radio Interfaces. Moreover, the distribution of computing into the system (see Figure 9) requires a more optimized usage of the resources, introducing the need of a different resource granularity definition. A better definition of resource slicing for the Radio Access is available in [26] and [37] and summarized in Figure 12.

The optimized usage of the resources will require a different computational granularity. By introducing a more flexible usage of scheduling policies [27] it is possible to achieve better resources utilization and still have strong temporal isolation. In such case, the guaranteed QoS based on SLA protects the business case of the operators. The above consideration, about the need of a slice approach to point to new requirements:

- The MANO should be able to manage resource allocation with a better elasticity, allowing the allocation of the resources per scheduling policies.
- Once using HA to cope with real-time constrains, the engines shall be designed to provide slice access to the services, without the need of software layers that create useless performance drawback.

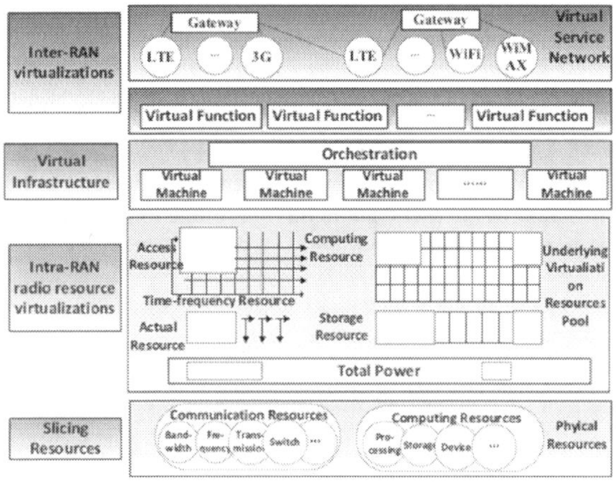

Figure 12. The slicing resource scheme for the Radio Access (source [26])

VII. STRUCTURING THE SEED

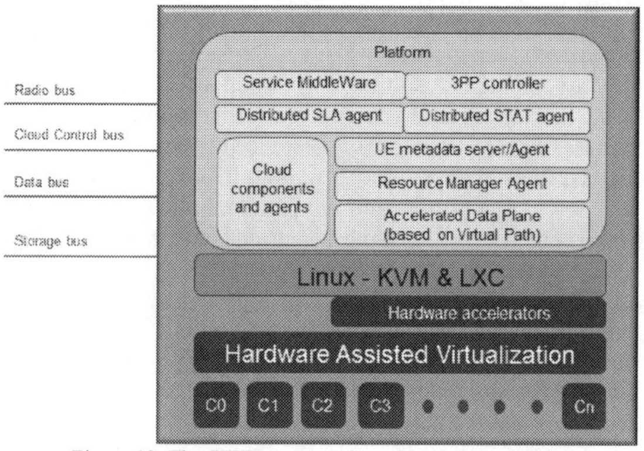

Figure 13. The SEED structured per function capabilities

Looking at the state of the art, Intel architecture seems to have better performance and virtualization features than other architectures: the management of virtualized objects requests less capability and introduce less latency in the system. Moreover, SDN-NFV implementation is strongly supported by the Open Software Community, and as a matter of fact a lot of functions and features in SDN-NFV are designed on Intel architecture first and then eventually ported to other targets. Though, power consumption needs to be considered, especially while referring to the edge of the network. Here power consumption really is a big issue and it seems that other hardware architectures would be more efficient. Figure 13 is summarizing the main objects housed in a SEED board, where differences are described in the next paragraphs.

A. Compute Platform for the Edge

The compute platform for the edge shall support Linux Containers (LXC) and be based on 64-bits Linux Operating system (OS). Both hardware and software support the virtualization layer, which points to a very specific set of needed features:

- reduce the cache pollution (e.g., Huge Page or Rapid Virtualization Indexing – RVI, depending on hardware architecture),
- support multi-core system,
- guarantee low power consumption,
- full set of hardware and software feature in order to speed up VM context switch,
- Virtual Interrupt Handling,
- hardware assisted trace & debug capability for a virtualized environment, and
- virtual path (Single Root Input/Output Virtualization, SR-IOV).

The OpenSoftware Cloud components and agents are obviously there (OpenStack, OpenDayLight, ONOS, M-CORD and whatever is requested by MANO). Accelerated Data Plane in User Space (virtual path, direct interrupt delivery, etc.) is needed to design an efficient connectivity solution. Security is a critical aspect for a computing distributed system and this requires HA for encryption/decryption, cryptography and data compression. A Resource Manager Agent is needed and must be able to handle the resources reference points as described in the SDN-NFV architecture. Distributed SLA and Statistics (STAT) agents are also needed and they shall interwork not only with each other, but according to higher hierarchical SLA and STAT objects in the architecture. This point will be discussed further in next session.

B. Third Party Product (3PP) Hosting Platform for the edge

The hardware board is just the same as the one for compute and likewise we can say about OS and virtualization layer, even if 3PP applications will be deployed as standard VMs. Platform components are the same; or agents of the same functions in the compute board. For example, User Equipment (UE) metadata agent interworks with its server in order to provide the complete list of metadata info. 3PP bridge is the active component of its controller, providing connectivity channel between 3PP application and external internet/radio channels and, for that reason: responsible for security check, registration, authorization and encryption/decryption. The available connectivity channels are not the same; 3PP hosting - for security reason - shall not have a possibility to use the radio bus directly. This will allow resource control according to the SLA in the compute board, thereby avoiding any possible malicious or faulty behavior of the 3PP applications themselves.

C. Radio-Interface Platform for the Edge

The board could be armed with dedicated hardware accelerators, needed to speed up the radio access protocols handling. It is not a limitation, as long as they are designed to be controlled as virtualized resource by the resource manager. With such differentiation, the board and the platform components/functions are not different from the components/functions mentioned so far for the SEED platform.

D. SEED Characterization

Connectivity and the efficient implementation of it is the critical key of the SEED. It is fundamental to avoid any bottleneck and additional overhead that will cost a lot for latency time. At the same time, the connectivity handling shall never be an obstacle for the service chain deployment concept (the operational agility is a mandatory requirement for the server at the edge of the network). Once one decides to share resources between different actors, it is crucial that they can access them without creating disturbances to each other and also acting according to the resource sharing agreement. It is like job scheduling where one wants threads continuously working and not starve them out. In case that happens, the thread may steal a job from someone else, and thereby maybe using another set of resources. The virtual path concept is trying to do the same with the connectivity access. Different running VMs should be able to access connectivity, based on the maximum available bandwidth defined in its SLA (the virtualized slice of connectivity assigned to it) and avoiding performance drawback due to system overhead (minimum or zero cost of virtualization layer, VM walkthrough data handling).

The nature of SEED sets a specific requirement for the platform; provide a wide range of computing characterization and also guarantee the agreed slice of computing resources, that should not be affected by other VMs running on a board. This is clear once one starts thinking on a platform where there are strong time constrains application types, like: radio services, relaxed time-constrains application types, video or audio services, no time-constrains application types, and general services. But that is not enough. If someone pays for a specific bandwidth and computing, the platform shall assure those resources. Again, the macro effect should be that, no matter if the VM is working alone or not, it can always count on the resource slices assigned by SLA. For that reason, the platform shall schedule VM jobs according to the following rules: a) Provide strong isolation for VMs with strong time-constrains; b) Provide maximum Central Processing Unit (CPU) utilization for VMs with relaxed time constrains using SCHED_DEADLINE policy.

VIII. SELF-ORGANIZING NETWORK – AN OBVIOUS SIMPLIFICATION?

The term "Self-Organizing" appears in many science fields, already in 1962 Ross Ashby a pioneer in cybernetics gave his first principles [39]. It might seem a little bit far-fetched when speaking about Self-Organizing Network which already was introduced by the Next Generation Mobile Networks (NGMN) [40] and now a part of the 3GPP standard [28]. But it gives a historical perspective of a trivial question; how do we know that the developed organization is "good"? The simple answer is; we must decide a criterion to distinguish between "good" and "bad" and then we must ensure that the appropriate selection is done!

As simple as it might sound the truth is that in a Self-Organizing Network we are heavily relying on an Operations Administration and Management (OAM) that in every selection makes the right decision. For that we need a Configuration Management with verified operations, Diagnostics capability with strict classification and a scalable Analytic infrastructure.

What is the rationale for Self-Organizing Network? From the 3GPP standard Technical Specification [41] it is stated as follows:

a) The number and structure of network parameters have become large and complex;
b) Quick evolution of wireless networks has led to parallel operation of 2G, 3G, Evolved Packet Core (EPC) infrastructures;
c) The rapidly expanding number of Base Stations needs to be configured and managed with the least possible human interaction;

Thus, the technical challenges. But the business target of SON is a transition from an operator controlled role to an autonomous operation environment to reduce the OPEX and shifts the management from an open loop to a close loop. The actions are taken by the SON functions and are dedicated of giving the best resource optimization, autonomous configuration and suitable setting of installation parameters. The ambitious target of the 5G framework, as shown in Figure 5, implies a higher network complexity and so a management overhead. If the target is to allow easy deployment of vertical service, it is mandatory to remove this management overhead from duties for operators. This means that SON in SDN-NFV is not only a simplification, but a crucial key technology to achieve the business purposes mentioned in the introduction of this paper.

To resolve the different optimization and deployment scenarios the SON architecture comes in three types (see Figure 14).

- Centralized – All SON functions are implemented close to the OAM;
- Distributed – All SON functions are implemented at the edge;
- Hybrid solution – The complex schemes are implemented close to OAM, and the simpler schemes are implemented at the edge;

There is nothing that prevents that all three scenarios can co-exists and varies over time too.

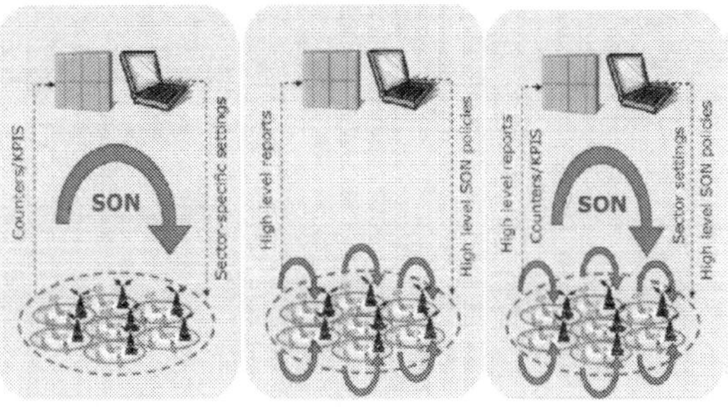

Figure 14. 3GPP, features delivery (source [44])

3GPP releases	Content	Type
Release 8	• Automatic Inventory • Automatic Software Download • Automatic Neighbor Relation (ANR) • Automatic Physical Cell ID (PCI) assignment	Procedures
Release 9	• Mobility Robustness/Handover optimization (MRO) • Random Access Channel (RACH) Optimization • Load Balancing Optimization • Inter-Cell Interference Coordination (ICIC)	Use cases
Release 10	• Coverage & Capacity Optimization (CCO) • Enhanced Inter-Cell Interference Coordination (eICIC) • Cell Outage Detection and Compensation • Self-healing Functions • Minimization of Drive Testing • Energy Savings	Use cases
Release 11	• Automatic Neighbor Relations • Load Balancing Optimization • Handover Optimization • Coverage and Capacity Optimization • Energy Savings • Coordination between various SON Functions • Minimization of Drive Tests	Features
Release 12	• Small cell and heterogeneous networks • Multi-antennas (e.g., MIMO and beam forming) • Proximity services • Procedures for supporting diverse traffic types	Features
Release 13	• Active Antenna Systems (AAS) • Enhancements for inter-site Coordinated Multi-Point Transmission and Reception (CoMP) • Support for up to 32 CA • DC enhancements • RAN sharing improvements • Indoor positioning enhancements • Downlink (DL) Multi-User Superposition Transmission (MUST) • LTE Wireless Local Area Network (WLAN) Aggregation (LWA) radio integration • Licensed Assisted Access (LAA)	Features

Figure 15. 3GPP, features delivery (source [44])

SON solutions can be divided into three categories: Self-Configuration, Self-Optimization and Self-Healing, each containing a wide range of decomposed use cases. When the 3GPP standardization work started it was with the respect to eNodeB and as such focused with releases on the first LTE network deployments. Thereafter the releases have followed the LTE evolution and the maturity of commercial networks (see Figure 15).

As the SON only have taken a half step forward so far (even though a vital step) basically an automatic configuration system, it needs to be extended to meet the 5G requirement. The relation to the "good" organization has to be concrete and should be based on the resources and its behavior which are controlled and formalized in the shape of SLA and guaranteed QoS. This will require a fully automated SON and functions that is more Self-oriented and able to make their own decisions. That means providing

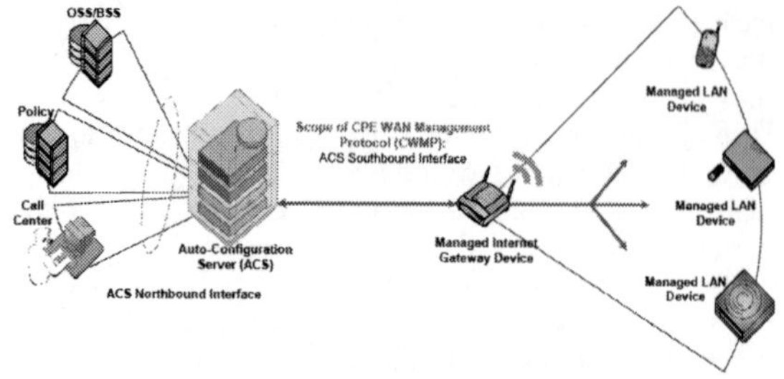

Figure 16. CPE WAN Management Protocol

intelligence in the network which opens up for technologies like Machine Learning (ML) and Artificial Intelligence (AI).

From standard point-of-view one of the crucial work is to identify the set of interfaces to support OAM and one of the important is TR-069 [42] defined by Broadband Forum.

TR-069 describes the CPE WAN Management Protocol (CWMP) (see Figure 16) which is intended for communication between a CPE (Customer Premises Equipment) and Auto-Configuration Server (ACS). The CPE WAN Management Protocol is intended to support a variety of functionalities to manage a collection of CPE, including the following primary capabilities:

- auto-configuration and dynamic service provisioning,
- software/firmware image management,
- software module management,
- status and performance monitoring, and
- diagnostics.

IX. The Correlation Between SON and SLA

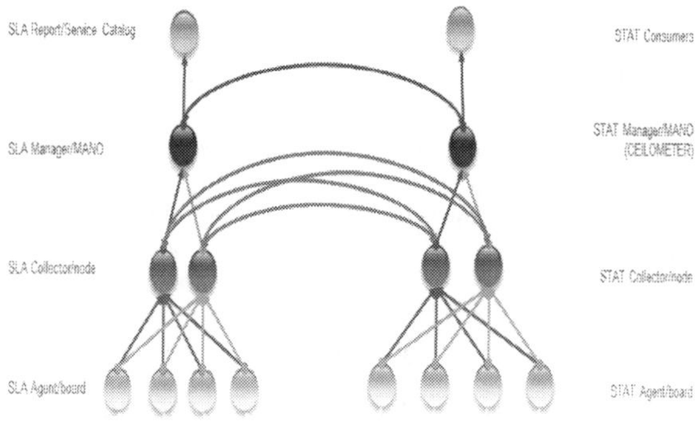

Figure 17. The hierarchical structure and co-relation of SLA and STAT

Concepts introduced in the previous two chapters, SLA and SON, are mutually inclusive. SLA and STATS are strictly correlated to each other and hierarchically spread all over the system (this concept is also emphasized in Figure 17).

Indeed, STATs are far from being a passive snapshot recording, they are actively interworking with SLA and resource manager to deploy the best resource utilization of the network. The hierarchical implementation of resources and metrics handling is fully devoted to simplifying the SON. SON brings a set of self-configuration and self-optimization use cases that allow a better control of the operational cost for the complex radio access technologies. Here, the role of the real-time data analysis makes the difference. It involves all resources of the system, removing the over-allocation, which today is dominating the dimensioning of RAN and causes a huge wasting of money in most of the operational time [29][30]. The hierarchical approach for meters and resources handling, as described in Figure 17, is crucial to avoid massive signaling. Moreover, the local resource-meters agents can by applying the right taxonomy create a resources relationship between different logical layers, from physical resources usage up to QoS, reducing the pressure of meters over the backhaul. This concept is further described in Figure 18 and the DPAC research program (Dependable Platforms for Autonomous System and Control) has designed a suitable framework for QoS control [31]. The model is suitable for debugging too, thanks to the centralized logs hosted as VNF, and it is integrated into the SDN-NFV solution (the so-called vProbe concept [32]).

Concepts like Real-Time and Run-Time are widely abused in literature due to the different domains where such terminologies are used. Radio Access Network is very sensitive to time constrains, considering deadline and latencies in the range of few milliseconds or even less. It is worth to explain the roles behind the different hierarchical analytics.

Real-time Analytics are responsible to collect, elaborate and act on the infrastructure resources usage, that, for the edge of the network, shall include the radio access too. The main target for real-time Analytics is the optimization of the resources allocation respecting the SLA. A function is described by its model, that is, characterization of inter-arrival triggering time (for example, the incoming packets), statistics distribution of computing and temporal constrains, like deadline and latency limitation. Resource reservation for that function could be based on prediction algorithms that identifies the opportunity of resources sharing between different functions, by considering statistics of distribution characterization, constraints and previous allocations. Thus , Real-time Analytics needs to be done as close as possible to the resources location and its data. Another important role for Real-time Analytics is mapping very low-level resources usage into function parameters/characterization, to decrease the pressure of the data into the backhaul. Real-time Analytics can create resources usage report for higher hierarchical Analytics and STATs agents, but in the form of statistical reports.

Run-Time Analytics collect, elaborate and act on the functions characterization. It is responsible to control the function slicing reservation and to scale in/out functions depending on the current usage and SLA. Run-Time Analytics could be based on prediction algorithms to be able to scale in/out function slicing and avoid resources conflicts. Depending on the outcomes of a prediction algorithm, Run-Time Analytics can set different SLA to the lower hierarchical Analytics and STATs agents. It will translate function slices reservation, usage and prediction into Key Performance Indicators (KPI) to higher hierarchical STATs. A special case is the trace&log control. In this case, the Run-Time Analytics will aggregate and correlate the data to set a contextual trace setting and thereby provide a "fault-detection" log. Trace&log can be supported with dedicated vProbe at NFVI level, dynamically set by the run-time analytics and collect important data on the fly. Note how different logs can be considered and aggregated to provide a layered view of the system covering more or less of the topology.

Statistics Analytics is probably the closest to data center analytics concept: there is not deadline of latency constrains and the analysis of the data can produce both Network statistics and new requests for the MANO.

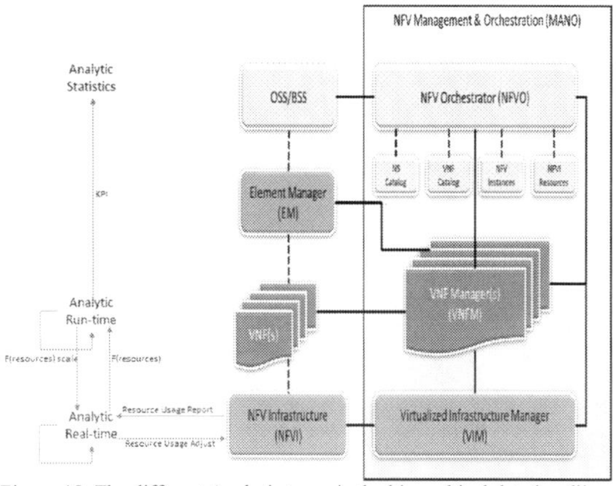

Figure 18. The different Analytic types in the hierarchical data handling

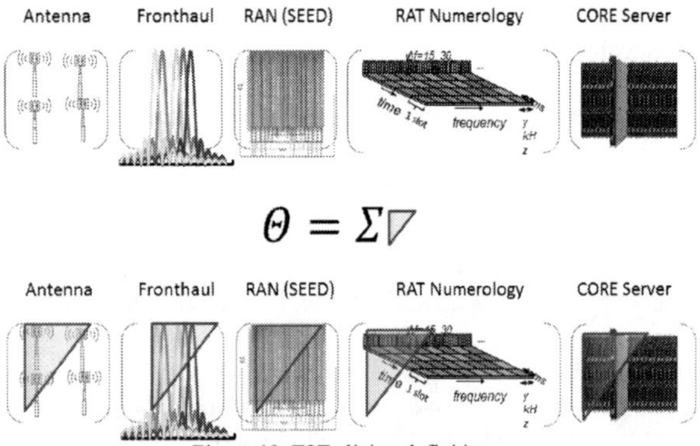

Figure 19. E2E slicing definition

Regardless which level of Analytic considered, a field that is emerging and attracts more attention is AI. Actually, it would be more suitable to talk of Machine Intelligence (MI), that stands for Machine Learning – Artificial Intelligence, in order to emphasize the active and pro-active usage of system data. MI is today one of the most active research topics, but it is important to identify where MI can effectively open new market opportunities rather than be a fascinating technology. In the RAN domain, the amount of data that can be generated is huge. Therefore, MI has become a key technology in the area of prediction models, classification, and optimization problems. The need to analyze large data sets is today actually one of the main obstacles on the strive to achieve efficiency. Machine learning and deep learning is probably the best way to consider MI. As it has been stated before, it is the ability to learn behaviors and anticipate both the system and the End User behaviors (to optimize the use of resources such as the quality of the experience), but also it is the technology to understand how to present the data to the operator, how to use the right data to characterize the system itself. Not least, how to use the data to locate a possible mistake automatically.

The dynamic resources handling as functional component of the network slicing is a critical enabler of the new services. For example, in Figure 12 it is shown how even spectrum is part of the slicing at the edge of the network and that is surely for optimal spectrum usage. But more focus should be put on its nature of E2E vertical deployment enabler, since it allows multiple services with multiple characterizations, from extreme bandwidths demand up to IoT (Figure 19).

Massive MIMO (M-MIMO) has already been addressed in the paper as a pillar of the 5G and probably the most complex part of spectrum dynamic control; like beamforming, cooperative multipoint coverage and swept beams, which are only possible in RRH so it is out of the scope for this paper. However, Figure 20 shows how consideration of spectrum involves hierarchically higher controller, so that spectrum handling and analytics connected is spread on different levels (note how this example is fully compliant to the concept described in Figure 17).

X. Business Case Opportunity Examples

The availability of distributed computing for the new system is the enabler for new business cases. Since 5G architecture is proposing itself as a new framework, it is the accelerator for new service products. This chapter wants to introduce two examples, already well-known.

The first one is based on the local storage availability. This concept has been mentioned at the beginning of the paper and already described. The second case is considering the high value of the End User metadata. In Figure 13 Agent/Server is considered a characteristic of the SEED. A service able to provide End User data is extremely attractive and valuable for enterprises and vertical services. Handling of such a service, however, shall be done in the proper way. Security, licenses, registration and publication of the service is fully involving MANO and most likely need a certification agreement between OTTs and operators. MANO is also

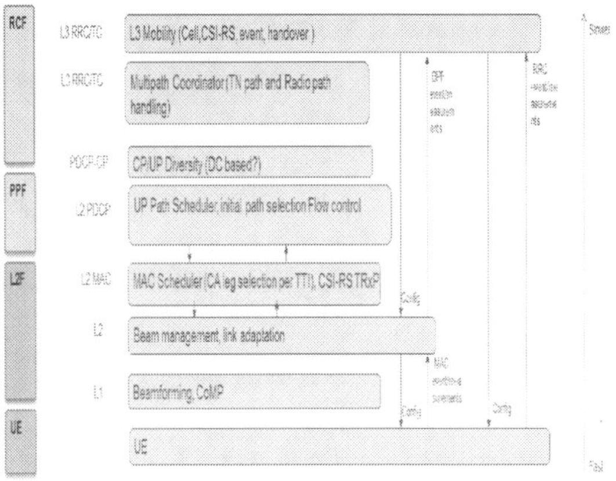

Figure 20. RAN Connected mobility

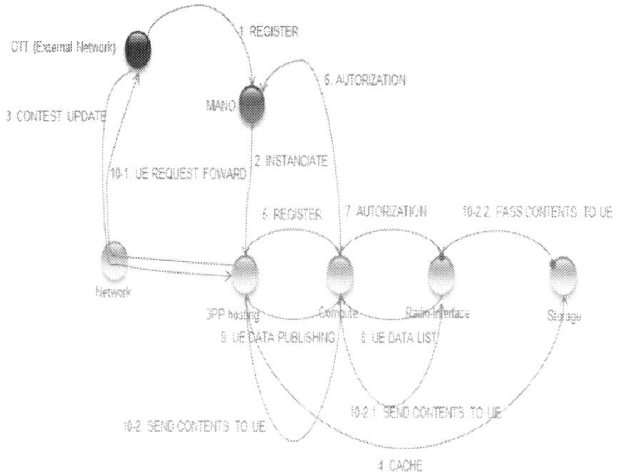

Figure 21. Ue Metadata publishing interwork example

responsible for authorization approval of the SEED 3PP controller, defining which level of End User metadata could be exposed for which 3PP application, as well as if the 3PP application is allowed to send data to the End User. Mainly, the SEED is the bridge between End User and OTTs providing a hierarchical service contents handling that will guarantee a better quality of experience to the consumers. For that reason, storage is a mandatory SEED capability, and one more time, the server dimensioning could be the differentiation of features while offering the solution to the operators (in telco vendors point of view) and while defining SLA to the OTTs (in the point of view of operators). Figure 21 is emphasizing the complexity of End User data publishing in a secure way by defining the different steps needed, from registration to usage.

XI. Conclusion

The opportunity to move SDN-NFV into the Radio Access Network is a crucial objective for the communication system in the next years. Fulfilling the needs of the customers means: to answer on the demand for the next generation mobile, create new business models for the operators and open new service market share for the infrastructure vendors. However, mobile cannot be handled as data center or networking nodes. Location, latency time, End User metadata are unique and added value for the radio access, which means an ad-hoc solution is the enabler for a successful and high performing product. A complete C-RAN solution is not considered suitable due to the fronthaul capacity explosion, the more flexible approach of the Radio Access Network as a Service (RANaaS) looks more promising. The ad-hoc solution is based on the implementation of the ETSI concept called MEC. This paper emphasizes the role of it as server@edge of the network, calling it SEED. SEED is a suitable set of heterogeneous hardware solution, designed to dramatically reduce the cost of virtualization. The engine of the SEED is the so-called C-mobile platform, a horizontal, per sever distributed, platform able to support the main functions characterizing the SEED: SDN-NFV controller, End User Metadata access service, Radio Access as Service solution, 3PP hosting and granted SLA. To be fully dynamic, SDN applications need to be responsive to their environment, therefore, triggers for network changes need to be state-driven. This automated management will be based on real-time network data analysis. Hierarchical Resource Manager and big data handling in the meaning of SON support is a key enabler together with the needed support.

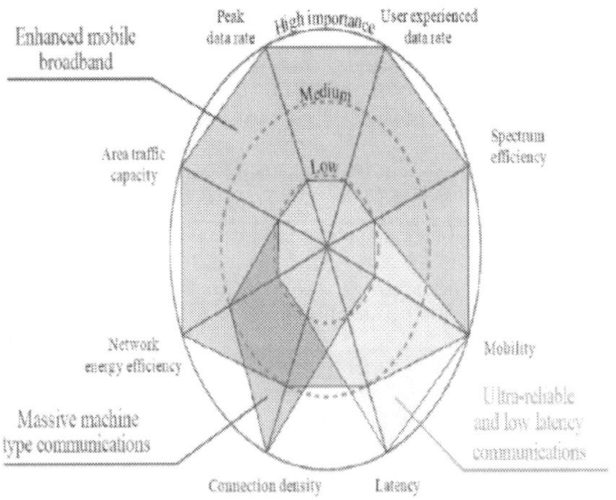

Figure 22. Key capabilities in different service domains (source: [33])

The International Telecommunication Union (ITU) standardization – network and service aspects – group, has set the 5G in that direction too, by emphasizing the diversification of service demands to be the key characterization of the 5G network for 2020 [33]. In fact, similarly as it has been done in the introduction of this paper, ITU identifies Enhanced Mobile Broadband (eMBB), Ultra-reliable and Low-Latency Communications (uRLLC) and Massive Machine Type Communications (mMTC) to be the service domains for 5G. Those services domains have a widely different set of performance and capabilities requirements (see Figure 22), that is only possible to achieve through the strengthening of the resource usage and SLA flexibility handling at the server of the edge.

XII. Future Works

All the concepts in the paper needs investigation and future study. For example, the usage of sched_deadline in a virtualized environment needs c-groups extension for a complete control of thread in containers. Moreover, a Greedy Reclamation of Unused Bandwidth (GRUB)-like mechanism implementation would decrease the Constant Bandwidth Server (CBS) effect of sched_deadline, providing a more performing latency time [34][35]. Usage of resources meters and statistics is a very interesting topic. One of the natural next steps is the evaluation of the taxonomy framework introduced in [36] for the characteristic resources of the Radio Access Network: network slices, load balancing, resource abstraction and resource control as defined in [37].

Similarly, the impacts on SDN-NFV MANO look significant. In fact, the same concept of Point Of Presence (PoP) as defined today is missing the elastic assignment of resources. In a future scenario where MTC and IoT begin accelerating 5G deployment, the slicing of computing, for example assigning different scheduling policies and fraction of a core, looks like a fundamental opportunity even to decrease the power consumption through the optimization of the resource usage. More should be done also in the domain of hardware accelerators. In Chapter VI, it has been stated how HAs, at the state of the art, are mandatory to meet protocols requirements and functions feasibility, but they should be designed in order to support the function slicing concept, that is, the vertical services introduced in Chapter III as fundamental characterization for the 5G system. HAs should provide SR-IOV-like virtualized access to the function as the enabler of needed intra-service resource sharing and isolation.

What has been considered only partially in this paper is the impact with respect to security requirements. Indeed, the strong temporal isolation introduced by the sched_deadline is in the security domain contents, but that is not enough. Even considering a fully slices based resources system, the intrusion avoidance is mandatory in order to protect sensitive data, like the End User data described in Chapter X. The real-time algorithms which are able to supervise, detect and lock unwanted threads are today under deployment [38].

REFERENCES

[1] C. Vitucci and A. Larsson, "SEED, A server platform for the edge of the network," IARIA 2017, Volume ICN 2017: the sixteenth conference on Networks (includes SOFTNETWORKING 2017), Mestre (Venice), 2017, pp. 118-123.

[2] DG Connect team, "Towards 5G," European commission, Digital Single Market Policies, February 2014. Available from https://ec.europa.eu/digital-single-market/en/policies/5g [retrivied: 06, 2017].

[3] Ericsson AB, "Ericsson mobility report on the pulse of the networked society," EAB-15:037849 Uen, 2015. Available from http://www.ericsson.com/res/docs/2015/mobility-report/ericsson-mobility-report-nov-2015.pdf [retrieved: 03, 2017].

[4] Bahjat el-Darwiche, Pierre Peladeau, Christine Rupp, and Florian Groene, "2017 telecommunications trends," Strategy& pwc, 2017. Available from https://www.strategyand.pwc.com/trend/2017-telecommunications-industry-trends [retrieved: 06, 2017].

[5] Ericsson AB, "Ericsson mobility report on the pulse of the networked society," EAB-15:026112 Uen, 2015. Available from http://www.ericsson.com/res/docs/2015/mobility-report/ericsson-mobility-report-june-2015.pdf [retrieved: 03, 2017].

[6] A Aijaz, H Aghvami, and M Amani, "A survey on mobile data offloading: technical and business perspectives," IEEE Wireless Communications 20(2):104-112 · April 2013

[7] T. Kridel, "The end of profitability," Tellabas Insight Q2, 2011, pp. 14-15.

[8] K. Shatzkamer, "Applying systems thinking to mobile networking," Brocade Communications Webinar, 2015. Available from http://docplayer.net/8990528-Applying-systems-thinking-to-mobile-networking.html [retrieved: 03, 2017].

[9] Eclipse IoT working group, "The three software stacks required for IoT architectures," Sept. 2016. Available from https://iot.eclipse.org/resources/white-papers/Eclipse%20IoT%20White%20Paper%20-%20The%20Three%20Software%20Stacks%20Required%20for%20IoT%20Architectures.pdf [retrivied: 06, 2017].

[10] 5G PPP architecture working group, "View on 5G architecture," EuCNC 2016. Available from https://5g-ppp.eu/wp-content/uploads/2014/02/5G-PPP-5G-Architecture-WP-July-2016.pdf [retrivied: 06, 2017].

[11] ETSI paper, "Network Functions Virtualisation (NFV); Use cases," ETSI GS NFV 001, v1.1.1, 2013. Available from http://www.etsi.org/deliver/etsi_gs/NFV/001_099/001/01.01.01_60/gs_NFV001v010101p.pdf [retrivied: 03, 2017].

[12] Y. C. Hu, M. Patel, D. Sabella, N. Sprecher and V. Young, "Mobile edge computing - A key technology towards 5G," Sept. 2015, availble from http://www.etsi.org/images/files/ETSIWhitePapers/etsi_wp11_mec_a_key_technology_towards_5g.pdf [retrieved: 03, 2017].

[13] ETSI paper, "Network Function Virtualisation (NFV); Network operator perspectives on industry progress," SDN & OpenFlow World Congress, Dusseldorf, 2014. Available from https://portal.etsi.org/Portals/0/TBpages/NFV/Docs/NFV_White_Paper3.pdf [retrivied: 03, 2017].

[14] G. Karagiannis et al, "Mobile cloud networking: virtualisation of cellular network," 21st International Conference on Telecommunications (ICT), 2014, pp. 410-415.

[15] C.Vitucci, J.Lelli, A.Pirri, and M.Marinoni, "A Linux-based virtualized solution providing computing quality of service to SDN-NFV telecommunication applications," In Proceeding of the 16th real time Linux workshop (RTLWS 2014), Dusseldorf, Germany, 2014, pp. 12-13.

[16] NGMN Alliance, "5G white paper," NGMN, 2015 J.S. Harrison, M.M. Do, "Mobile Network Architecture for 5G Era - New C-RAN Architecture and distributed 5G Core", Netmanias, 2015. Available from https://www.ngmn.org/uploads/media/NGMN_5G_White_Paper_V1_0.pdf [retrivied: 03, 2017].

[17] Karl-Erik Arzen et al, "WASP: autonomous Cloud," Lunds Universitet, 2017. Available from http://www.control.lth.se/Research/RealTimeComputing/autonomous-cloud.html [retrieved: 06, 2017].

[18] J.S. Harrison and M.M. Do, "Mobile network architecture for 5G era - New C-RAN architecture and distributed 5G core," Netmanias, 2015. Available from http://www.netmanias.com/en/post/blog/8153/5g-c-ran-fronthaul-kt-korea-sdn-nfv-sk-telecom/mobile-network-architecture-for-5g-era-new-c-ran-architecture-and-distributed-5g-core [retrivied: 03, 2017].

[19] Netmanias, "KT 5G network architecture," NMC Consulting Group, October 2015. Available from http://www.netmanias.com/en/post/oneshot/11146/5g-kt-sdn-nfv/kt-5g-network-architecture-update [retrivied: 06, 2017].

[20] SK telecom network technology R&D Center, "ATSCALE white paper," rev 1.0, 06/2016. Available from http://www.sktelecom.com/img/pds/press/SKT_5G%20White%20Paper_V1.0_Eng.pdf [retrivied: 06, 2017].

[21] G. Brown, "Service chaining in carrier networks," Heavy Reading, 2015. Available from http://www.qosmos.com/wp-content/uploads/2015/02/Service-Chaining-in-Carrier-Networks_WP_Heavy-Reading_Qosmos_Feb2015.pdf [retrivied: 03, 2017].

[22] T.A. Satria, M. Karimzadeh, and G. Karagiannis, "Performance evaluation of ICN/CCN based service migration approach in virtualized LTE systems," IEEE 3rd International Conference on Cloud Networking (CloudNet), 2014, pp. 461-467.

[23] M.J. McGrath, "Network functions as-a-service over virtualized infrastructures," Ref. Ares(2015)3376865, 2015. Available from http://cordis.europa.eu/docs/projects/cnect/0/619520/080/deliverables/001-TNOVAD32InfrastructureResourceRepositoryv10Ares20153376865.pdf [retrivied: 03, 2017].

[24] OpenStack, "OpenStack operations guide," OpenStack Foundation, 2014. Avaiable from https://docs.openstack.org/ops-guide/ [retrivied: 03, 2017].

[25] C. Dixon, "OpenDayLight: introduction, Lithium and beyond," available from http://colindixon.com/wp-content/uploads/2014/05/brighttalk-odl-webinar.pdf [retrivied: 03, 2017].

[26] N. Nikaein et al, "Network store: exploring slicing in future 5G network," in Proceeding of the 10th International Workshop on Mobility in the Evolving Internet Architecture, 2015-09, pp. 8-13.

[27] T. Cucinotta, M.Marinoni, A.Melani, A.Parri and C.Vitucci, "Temporal isolation among LTE/5G network functions by real-time scheduling," in Proceedings of the 7th IEEE International Conference on Cloud Computing and Services Science (CLOSER 2017), 2017.

[28] 3GPP TS 32.500, "3rd generation partnership project; technical specification group services and system aspects; telecommunication management; Self-Organizing Networks (SON); concepts and requirements (Release 11)," v11.1.0, 2011-12.

[29] K.Trichias, R.Litjens, A. Tall, Z. Altman, and P. Ramachandra, "Self-optimisation of vertical sectorisation in a realistic LTE network," Europen Conference on Networks and Communications, 2015, pp. 149-153.

[30] S. Fortes, A. Aguilar-Garcia, R. Barco, F. Barba, J.A. Fernandez-Luque, and A. Fernandez-Duran, "Management architecture for location-aware self-organizing LTE/LTE-A small cell networks," IEEE 53(1) Communications Magazine, 2015, pp. 294-302.

[31] M. Jägemar, A. Ermedahl, S. Eldh and M. Behnam, "A scheduling architecture for enforcing quality of service in multi-process system," (to appear in) Proceedings of Emerging Technologies and Factory Automation (ETFA), 09, 2017.

[32] G. Brown, "Virtual probes for NFVI monitoring," Heavy Reading, 2017. Available from https://builders.intel.com/docs/networkbuilders/virtual_probes_for_nfvi_monitoring.pdf [retrivied: 06, 2017].

[33] ITU-R, Recommendation ITU-R M.2083-0 (09/2015), "IMT vision - framework and overall objectives of the future of IMT for 2020 and beyond," M series, Mobile, radiodetermination, amateur and related satellite services, 2015.

[34] L. Abeni, J. Lelli, C. Scordino, and L. Palopoli, "Greedy CPU reclaiming for SCHED DEADLINE," in Proceedings of the Real-Time Linux Workshop (RTLWS), Dusseldorf, Germany, 2014.

[35] G.Lipari and S. Baruah, "Greedy reclaimation of unused bandwidth in constant bandwidth servers," in IEEE Proceedings of the 12th Euromicro Conference on Real-Time Systems, Stockholm, Sweden, 2000, pp. 193-200.

[36] S. Cai, B. Gallina, D. Nyström, and C. Seceleanu, "A taxonomy of data aggregation processes," IEEE DAGGERS project paper, 2016. Available from http://www.es.mdh.se/pdf_publications/4628.pdf [retrivied: 03, 2017].

[37] VG. Nguyen, TX. Do, and Y. Kim, "SDN and virtualization-based LTE mobile network architectures: A comprehensive survey," Wireless Personal Communications, 2016, Volume 86, Number 3, pp. 1401-1438.

[38] M. Fergurson, "Architecting a platform for big data analytics," 2nd Edition, Copyright © by Intelligent Business Strategies Limited, March 2016. Available from https://www-01.ibm.com/common/ssi/cgi-bin/ssialias?htmlfid=IML14333USEN [retrivied: 07, 2017].

[39] W.R. Ashby, "Principles of the self-organizing system," in Principles of Self-Organization: Transactions of the University of Illinois Symposiu, H. Von Foerster and G.W. Zopf, Jr. (eds.), Pergamon Press, London, UK, 1962, pp. 255-278.

[40] Frank Lehser, "NGMN recommendation on SON and O&M requirements," NGMN Alliance, December 2008. Available from https://www.ngmn.org/uploads/media/NGMN_Recommendation_on_SON_and_O_M_Requirements.pdf [retrivied: 10, 2017].

[41] Technical specification group services and system aspects, "SP-080064: New BB_Level WID on management of Self-Organizing Networks (SON)," 3GPP, 2008.

[42] William Lupton, John Blackford, Mike Digdon, and Tim Spets, "TR-069 CPE WAN management protocol v1.1", Broadand forum technical report, December 2007. Available from http://www.broadband-forum.org/technical/download/TR-069_Amendment-5.pdf [retrivied: 10, 2017].

[43] Magdalena Nohrborg, "SON," 3GPP, 2017. Available from http://www.3gpp.org/technologies/keywords-acronyms/105-son [retrivied: 10, 2017].

[44] 3GPP, "Release 13," 3GPP, 2017. Available from http://www.3gpp.org/release-13 [retrivied: 10, 2017].

An Integrated Data Model for Management and Mining of Social Big Data: Concepts and Applications

Hiroshi Ishikawa
Faculty of System Design
Tokyo Metropolitan University
Tokyo, Japan
e-mail: ishikawa-hiroshi@tmu.ac.jp

Richard Chbeir
LIUPPA Lab.
University of Pau and Adour Countries
Anglet, France
e-mail: richard.chbeir@univ-pau.fr

Abstract— **Big data typically include three kinds of data such as IoT (Internet of Things) data, social data, and open data. However, there exists no integrated analytic methodology as to big data applications involving different kinds of data sources. Furthermore, big data applications inherently involve data management and data mining. We propose an integrated analytic methodology by taking a data model approach. We propose an abstract data model for seamlessly describing both data management and data mining cooccurring in big data applications, based on mathematical concepts of families, that is, collections of sets. Our model also facilitates reproducibility and accountability required for promoting social big data researches and developments. We have validated our proposal by adapting our model to a variety of real case studies in social big data.**

Keywords-social data; big data; data model; data management; data mining; tourism; disaster prevention.

I. INTRODUCTION

In the present age, large amounts of data are produced continuously in science, on the Internet, and in physical systems. Such phenomena are collectively called data deluge. And needs for analytic methodologies dedicated to data deluge have emerged [1].

According to some researches carried by International Data Corporation, or IDC [2][3] for short, the size of data which are generated and reproduced all over the world every year is estimated to be 161 Exabytes as of the published year. The total amount of data produced in 2011 exceeded 10 or more times the storage capacity of the storage media available in that year. The size is forecasted to grow to 40, 000 Exabytes by 2020. Experts in scientific and engineering fields produce a large amount of data by observing and analyzing the target phenomena. Even ordinary people voluntarily post a vast amount of data via various social media on the Internet. Furthermore, people unconsciously produce data via various actions detected by physical systems, such as sensors and Global Positioning System, or GPS for short, in the real world. It is expected that such data can generate various values. In the above-mentioned research report of IDC, data produced in science, the Internet, and in physical systems are collectively called big data. The features of big data can be summarized as follows:

- The quantity (Volume) of data is extraordinary, as the name denotes.
- The kinds (Variety) of data have expanded into unstructured texts, semi-structured data, such as XML, and graphs (i.e., networks).
- As is often the case with Twitter and sensor data streams, the speed (Velocity) at which data are generated is very high.

Therefore, big data is often characterized as V^3 by taking the initial letters of these three terms Volume, Variety, and Velocity. Big data are expected to create not only knowledge in science but also derive values in various commercial ventures. "Volume" and "velocity" require more computing power than ever before. "Variety" implies that big data appear in a wide variety of applications and then data have a wide variety of structures.

Further, big data inherently contain "vagueness," such as inconsistency and deficiency. Such vagueness must be resolved in order to obtain quality analysis results. Moreover, a recent survey done in Japan has made it clear that a lot of users have other "vague" concerns as to the securities and mechanisms of big data applications [4]. In other words, service providers deploying big data have accountability for explaining to generic users among stake holders how relevant big data are used. The resolution of such concerns is one of the keys to successful diffusion of big data applications. In the sense that "vagueness" is a fourth V, V^4 should be used to characterize big data, instead of V^3.

Big data typically include three kinds of data: *IoT (Internet of Things) data* collected by a variety of networked sensors and mobile gadgets in real physical worlds, *social data* posted at social media sites, such as Twitter and Flickr, and *open data* published for everyone to access.

To our knowledge, however, there exists no analytic methodology as to applications involving different sources of big data. Furthermore, such big data applications are often mixed of data management and data mining from our observations. This integration is also needed for describing such applications.

Section II introduces concepts of social big data as an integrated analysis methodology to big data and describes rationales for a data model approach to it. Section III introduces our data model for social big data. Section IV explains case studies by adapting the model to them in order to verify the validity of the model.

II. RATIONALES FOR DATA MODEL

A. Social Big Data

In big data applications, especially, cases where two or more data sources including at least one social data source are involved, are more interesting from a viewpoint of usefulness to businesses [4]. If more than one data source can be analyzed by relating them to each other, and by paying attention to the interactions between them, it may be possible to understand what cannot be understood, by analysis of only either of them. For example, even if only sales data are deeply analyzed, reasons for a sudden increase in sales, that is, what has made customers purchase more products suddenly, cannot be known. By analysis of only social data, it is impossible to know how much they contributed to sales, if any. However, if both sales data and social data can be analyzed by relating them to each other, it is possible to discover why items have begun to sell suddenly, and to predict how much they will sell in the future, based on the results. In a word, such integrated analysis is expected to produce bigger values than otherwise. While big data simply imply data with V^3 or V^4 features, we would like to call such an integrated analytic methodology with respect to big data *Social Big Data*, or *SBD* for short. Throughout this paper, we use SBD instead of social big data.

Even if only one social data source, such as Twitter articles and Flickr images is available and if such articles and images have geo-tags (i.e., location information), as well, social big data mining is useful. That is, by collecting those articles and images based on conditions specified with respect to locations and time intervals and counting them for each grid (i.e., unit location), probabilities that users post such data at the locations can be basically computed. By using such probabilities, human activities can be analyzed, such as probabilities of foreigners staying at specific spots or those moving from one spot to another. The results will be applied to tourism and marketing.

Of course, locations and time can also be used in joining different sources of data in SBD applications. Further, a certain level of location can be represented as a collection of lower levels of locations. Similarly, a time interval can be divided into a collection of shorter time intervals. As such, locations and time have hierarchical structures inherently.

Furthermore, from observations of SBD applications as described later in this paper, they are hybrid processes consisting of data management and data management. In SBD applications, more time is often observed to be spent on development and execution of data management including preprocessing and postprocessing in addition to data mining than on data management.

B. Reproducibility

In general, the validity of published results of scientific researches has recently been judged based on not only traditional peer reviews but also reproducibility [5]. Reproducibility means that the same results with reported ones can be obtained by independent researchers. Success of reproduction hinges on detailed descriptions of methods and procedures, as well as data which have led to the published results.

At an extreme end of reproducibility spectrum [6] [7] is repeatability. Repeatability in computer science means that independent researchers can obtain exactly the same results by using the same data and the same codes that the reporters used. However, it is not always possible to use the same data and programming codes due to several reasons, such as limited space for publishing research results and lack or delayed spread of related standardization. Rex [8] is among ambitious attempts to facilitate repeatability. Rather, reproduction is done in order to make certain the essence of the experiments. All this is true of SBD researches and developments.

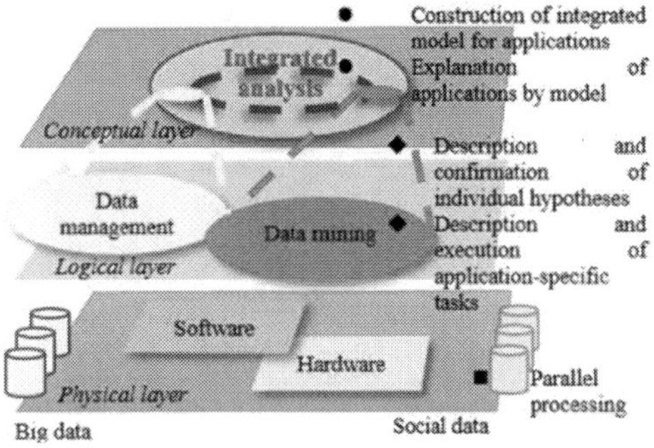

Figure 1. The reference architecture for social big data.

C. Data Model Approach

Reproducibility in researches and developments of SBD applications requires at least the following requirements.

- Description of SBD applications must be as independent from individual programming languages and frameworks as possible. It is not always possible for all researchers to access the same data and tools that the authors have used. However, reproducibility can be realized by enabling mappings from description of applications by an *SBD model* proposed in this paper to individual tools available for the other researchers even if the tools are not the same with the original one. Therefore, an SBD model (i.e., at conceptual level) must be more abstract than programming codes (i.e., at logical level). Such an abstract model is also expected to reduce the amount of description. In addition, the descriptions must be even as independent from programing models, such as parallel computing as possible. This *SBD model* approach can lead to increase of accountability of SDB applications to stake holders including generic users as a solution to the fourth V (i.e., vagueness).
- Both data management and data mining must be described in an integrated manner. Further, data management and data mining cannot be always separated in a crisp manner. Rather, in most SBD applications data mining is intermingled with data management. Later, such examples will be described in case studies. Therefore, an SBD model must be able to describe data management and data mining seamlessly.

We propose an integrated data model for describing SBD applications as hybrid processes of data management and data mining. And we describe applications using the model as case studies for the validation of the proposed model. The reference architecture for SBD is illustrated in Figure 1.

D. Relation with Other Work

This paper extends our previous work [1] to enhance the validation of the proposed model with respect to a variety of case studies. To our knowledge, there are no abstract data models that can handle data management and data mining. Relational models [9] and object models [10] are dedicated data models solely for data management. Indeed, there exist a lot of programming languages and frameworks that can host data management and data mining, such as Spark [11] and MLI [12]. However, such language interfaces have different levels of abstraction from those of our data model, which is proposed in this paper. Rather, those are among candidate targets to which our abstract model can be translated.

III. DATA MODEL FOR SBD

A. Overview

We propose an abstract data model as an approach to reinforcing both reproducibility and accountability of SBD. Our SBD model aims to satisfy the following requirements:

- Enable to describe data management and data mining in an integrated fashion or seamlessly.
- Be independent enough from existing programming languages and frameworks and easy enough to translate into executable programming languages, as well.

First, we extend relational model [9] prevalent in data management fields as our approach to SBD model. The Relational model is based on a mathematical concept of a *set*. On the other hand, data mining includes clustering, classification, and association rules [4]. Clustering partitions a given set of data into a collection of sets, each of which has elements similar to each other. Classification divides a given set of data into pre-scribed categories or classes, that is, a collection of sets by using supervised learning. Association rule mining discovers a collection of frequent itemsets collocating in transactional data. Unlike the relational model, all these data mining techniques handle a *collection of sets* instead of a set. In other words, we must bridge gaps between data management and data mining with respect to levels of granularity.

Second, we would like to adopt abstractness comparable to those that relational models [9] and object models [10] have because such abstractness hides unnecessary details from the stakeholders and helps them to understand how the related data are used. We would also like to keep our model more abstract than individual programming languages and frameworks and to make the former translatable into the latter. In other words, our model is independent of programming models such as SQL (i.e., relational model) and NoSQL (e.g., Hadoop [13] and Crouchbase [14]). It is relatively easy to translate our model into SQL commands by facilitating conversions between families and sets (e.g., adding special columns representing indices to relations). Similarly, our model can be straightforwardly translated into NoSQL commands via SQL-like interfaces available for NoSQL, such as Hive [15] and N1QL [16].

We propose our SBD data model consisting of data structures and operations in the following subsections.

B. SBD Data Structures

Our SBD model uses a mathematical concept of a *family* [17], a collection of sets, as a basis for data structures. Family can be used as an apparatus for bridging the gaps between data management operations and data analysis operations.

Basically, our database is a *Family*. A Family is divided into *Indexed family* and *Non-Indexed family*. A Non-Indexed family is a collection of sets.

An Indexed family is defined as follows:

- {*Set*} is a Non-Indexed family with *Set* as its element.
- {Set_i} is an Indexed family with Set_i as its *i-th* element. Here *i: Index* is called *indexing set* and *i* is an element of Index.
- *Set* is {<*time space object*>}.
- Set_i is {<*time space object*>}$_i$. Here, *object* is an identifier to arbitrary identifiable user-provided data, e.g., record, object, and multimedia data appearing in social big data. *Time* and *space* are universal keys across multiple sources of social big data.
- {*Indexed family*$_i$} is also an Indexed family with *Indexed family*$_i$ as its *i-th* element. In other words, Indexed family can constitute a hierarchy of sets.

Please note that the following concepts are interchangeably used in this paper.

- Singleton family ⇔ set
- Singleton set ⇔ element

In addition, Index of Indexed family can be used for implementing popular data structures such as array, vector, and matrix. In turn, matrix can represent graphs or networks frequently used for analyzing structures of social media such as Twitter [18].

As described later in Section IV, we can often observe that SBD applications contain families as well as sets and they involve both data mining and data management. Please note that a family is also suitable for representing hierarchical structures inherent in time and locations associated with social big data.

If operations constructing a family out of a collection of sets and those deconstructing a family into a collection of sets are provided in addition to both family-dedicated and set-dedicated operations, SBD applications will be described in an integrated fashion by our proposed model.

C. SBD Operations

SBD model constitutes an algebra with respect to Family as follows.

SBD is consisted of Family data management operations and Family data mining operations. Further, Family data management operations are divided into Intra Family operations and Inter Family operations.

1) *Intra Family Data Management Operations*

a) Intra Indexed Intersect (*i:Index Db p*(*i*)) returns a singleton family (i.e., set) intersecting sets which satisfy the predicate *p*(*i*). Database *Db* is a Family, which will not be mentioned hereafter.

b) Intra Indexed Union (*i:Index Db p*(*i*)) returns a singleton family union-ing sets which satisfy *p*(*i*).

c) Intra Indexed Difference (*i:Index Db p*(*i*)) returns a singleton family, that is, the first set satisfying *p*(*i*) minus all the rest of sets satisfying *p*(*i*)

d) Indexed Select (*i:Index Db p1*(*i*) *p2*(*i*)) returns an Indexed family with respect to *i* (preserved) where the element sets satisfy the predicate *p1*(*i*) and the elements of the sets satisfy the predicate *p2*(*i*). As a special case of true as *p1*(*i*), this operation returns the whole indexed family. In a special case of a singleton family, Indexed Select is reduced to Select (a relational operation).

e) Indexed Project (*i:Index Db p*(*i*) *a*(*i*)) returns an Indexed family where the element sets satisfy *p*(*i*) and the elements of the sets are projected according to *a*(*i*), attribute specification. This also extends also relational Project.

f) Intra Indexed cross product (*i:Index Db p*(*i*)) returns a singleton family obtained by product-ing sets which satisfy *p*(*i*). This is extension of Cartesian product, one of relational operators.

g) Intra Indexed Join (*i:Index Db p1*(*i*) *p2*(*i*)) returns a singleton family obtained by joining sets which satisfy *p1*(*i*) based on the join predicate *p2*(*i*). This is extension of join, one of relational operators.

h) Sort (*i:Index Db p*(*i*) *o*()) returns indexed family where the element sets satisfy *p*(*i*) and the elements of the sets are ordered according to the compare function *o*() with respect to two elements.

i) Indexed Sort (*i:Index Db p*(*i*) *o*()) returns an indexed family where the element sets satisfy *p*(*i*) and the sets are ordered according to *o*(), the compare function with respect to two sets.

j) Select-Index (*i:Index Db p*(*i*)) returns *i:Index* of set_i which satisfy *p*(*i*). As a special case of true as *p*(*i*), it returns all index.

k) Make-indexed family (*Index Non-Indexed Family*) returns an indexed Family. This operator requires *order-compatibility*, that is, that *i* corresponds to *i-th set of Non-Indexed Family*.

l) Partition (*i:Index Db p*(*i*)) returns an Indexed family. Partition makes an Indexed family out of a given set (i.e. singleton family either w/ or w/o index) by grouping elements with respect to *p* (*i:Index*). This is extension of "groupby" as a relational operator.

m) ApplyFunction (*i:Index Db f*(*i*)) applies *f*(*i*) to *i-th* set of DB, where *f*(*i*) takes a set as a whole and gives another set including a singleton set (i.e., Aggregate function). This returns an indexed family. *f*(*i*) can be defined by users.

2) *Inter Family Data Management Operations Index-Compatible*

a) Indexed Intersect (*i:Index Db1 Db2 p*(*i*)) union-compatible

b) Indexed Union (*i:Index Db1 Db2 p*(*i*)) union-compatible

c) Indexed Difference (*i:Index Db1 Db2 p*(*i*)) union-compatible

d) Indexed Join (*i:Index Db1 Db2 p1*(*i*) *p2*(*i*))

e) Indexed cross product (*i:Index Db1 Db2 p*(*i*))

Indexed (*) operation is extension of its corresponding relational operation. It preserves an Indexed Family. For example, Indexed Intersect returns an Indexed Family whose element is intersection of corresponding sets of two indexed families *Db1* and *Db2*, which satisfy *p*(*i*). At this time, we impose *union-compatibility*. Further, in case both *Db1* and *Db2* are singleton families and *p*(*i*) is constantly true, Indexed Intersect is reduced to Intersect, which returns intersection of two sets (a relational operation). Indexed Union and Indexed Difference are also similarly interpreted.

3) *Family Data Mining Operations*

a) Cluster (*Family method similarity* {*par*}) returns a Family as default, where Index is automatically produced. This is an unsupervised learner. In *hierarchical agglomerative clustering* or HAC, as well as similar methods, such as some spatial, temporal, and spatio-temporal clustering, index is merged into new index as clustering progresses. *method* includes k-means, HAC, spatial, temporal, etc. *similarity/distance* includes Euclidean, Cosine measure, etc. *par* (ammeters) depend on *method*.

b) Make-classifier (*i:Index set:Family learnMethod* {*par*}) returns a classifier (Classify) with its accuracy. This is a supervised learner. In this case *index* denotes classes (i.e., predefined categories). Sample *set* includes both training set and test set. *learnMethod* specifies methods, such as decision tree, SVM, deep learning. *par* (ammeters) depend on *learnMethod*. This operation itself is out of range of our algebra. In other words, it is a *meta*-operation.

c) Classify (*Index/class set*) returns an indexed family with class as its index.

d) Make-frequent itemset (*Db supportMin*) returns an Indexed Family as frequent itemsets, which satisfy *supportMin*.

e) Make-association-rule (*Db confidenceMin*) creates association rules based on frequent itemsets *Db*, which satisfy *confidenceMin*. This is out of range of our algebra, too.

The predicates and functions used in the above operations can be defined by the users in addition to the system-defined ones such as Count.

IV. CASE STUDY

A. Case One

We have validated our model by applying it to social big data applications consisting of data management and datamining, such as tourism and disaster prevention.

We use the following background colors and bounding box for each category of SBD operations for illustration:

- Relational (set) data management operation
- Family data management operation
- Data mining operation

First, we describe a case study, analysis of behaviors of foreigners (visitors or residents) in Japan [19]. This case is classified as analysis based on a single source of social data.

To classify foreign users as *residents* or *visitors*, we will classify the length of the stay in the country of interest as *long* and *short*, respectively. We assume the target country (i.e., the country of interest) uses one language dominantly. We first obtain the tweets that a user posted in Japan. We detect the principal language of the user in order to extract only foreign Twitter users. We define the *principal language* of a user as the language that meets the following two conditions.

- The language must be used in more than half of all the user's tweets. Since the Language-Detection toolkit [20] is over 99% precision according to their claim in detecting the tweet language, we used this toolkit in the experiment.
- The language must be selected by the user in his/her account settings. This means that the user claims that they use that language.

If the resultant principal language for a Twitter user is a language other than the one dominantly used in the target country, we regard the user as a foreign Twitter user and then classify the user as residents or visitors.

First, we sort a user's tweets posted in the target country in chronological order, where t_i denotes *i*-th tweet. Next, we set parameters *start date* and *stop date*, which specify the start and end date of interest, respectively. We define the oldest tweet between *start date* and *stop date* as T_{old} and define the parameter *travel period* as the maximum length of the stay. We define the newest tweet between T_{old} and T_{old} + *travel period* as T_{new}. Also, we set parameter *j*, a margin that ensures the foreign user is out of the target country. We identify a foreign user's tweets during a visit, if and only if all his/her tweets satisfy the following conditions:

- The foreign user posts more than T_{min} tweets between T_{old} and T_{new} and the user posts no tweets during the period from *j* days before to T_{old} to and the period from T_{new} to *j* days after T_{new}.

Here, T_{min} is the minimum number of tweets to prevent misclassification owing to a small number of tweets. The tweets posted between T_{old} and T_{new} are identified as the tweets during the visit. Since some users repeatedly visit the target country, we repeat the identification of tweets during a visit after T_{new}.

A foreign user is identified as a *visitor* to the target country, if and only if all his/her tweets between *start date* and *stop date* are tweets during visits. Foreign users who are not visitors are identified as *residents*. Here, we excluded foreign users who *tweeted* equal to or less than T_{min} times between *start date* and *stop date* as *unrecognizable*.

We obtained 72, 059, 720 geo-tagged tweets posted in Japan from Jun. 11, 2014 to Dec. 20, 2014 and used them as the dataset.

First, Classify$_{\text{foreign/domestic}}$ ({*Foreign Domestic*} DB_{tweet}) binarily splits into foreign and domestic sets as *AccountOrigin* (i.e., index class).

This classifier is based on a heuristic (i.e., manually-coded) rule for deciding foreigner as follows:

if Count (*t:tweet t.AccountId=AccountId* & *t.DetectedLanguage()=t.AccountLanguage* & *t.AccountLanguage*<>"Japanese") >=0.5*Count (t:tweet *t.AccountId=id*) then return foreign else domestic

The following fragment of descriptions collects only tweets posted by foreigners ("←" is the assignment operator):

DB_t ← **Sort** (**Select** (DB_{tweet} *Time of Interest* & Within "*Japan*") *compare-time*()) ; singleton family (i.e., set).

$DB_{foreign}$ ← **Indexed-Select** (Classify$_{\text{foreign/domestic}}$ ({*Foreign Domestic*} DB_t) *AccountOrigin="foreign"*); singleton family.

Next, Classify$_{\text{visitor/resident}}$ ({*Visitor Resident*} DB_{tweet}) , a data mining operator, binarily splits into visitor and resident sets as *AccountStatus* (i.e., index class).

This is based on a heuristic rule for deciding inbound visitor as follows:

if Count (*t.tweet t.AccountId=AccountId* & T_{old}=<*t.time*=<T_{new})>=C_{min} & *Count* (*t.tweet t.AccountId=id* & T_{old}-*j*<=*t.time*<T_{old})=0 & Count (*t.tweet t.AccountId=id* & T_{new}<*t.time*<=T_{new}+*j*)=0 then return visitor else resident

The following fragment classifies tweets by foreigners into ones by inbound visitors and ones by foreign residents:

$DB_{foreignVisitorOrResident}$ ← Classify$_{\text{visitor/resident}}$ ({*Visitor Resident*} $DB_{foreign}$); This returns an indexed family.

$DB_{visitor}$ ← **Indexed-Select** ($DB_{foreignerVisitorOrResident}$ *AccountStatus*="*visitor*") ; This returns a singleton family.

$DB_{resident}$ ← **Indexed-Select** ($DB_{foreignerVisitorOrResident}$ *AccountStatus*="*resident*"); This returns a singleton family.

B. Case Two

Next, we describe another case study, finding candidate access spots for accessible Free Wi-Fi in Japan [21]. This case is classified as integrated analysis based on two kinds of social data.

This section describes our proposed method of detecting attractive tourist areas where users cannot connect to accessible Free Wi-Fi by using posts by foreign travelers on social media.

Our method uses differences in the characteristics of two types of social media:

Real-time: Immediate posts, e.g., Twitter

Batch-time: Data stored to devices for later posts, e.g., Flickr

Twitter users can only post tweets when they can connect devices to Wi-Fi or wired networks. Therefore, travelers can post tweets in areas with Free Wi-Fi for inbound tourism or when they have mobile communications. In other words, we can obtain only tweets with geo-tags posted by foreign travelers from such places. Therefore, areas where we can obtain huge numbers of tweets posted by foreign travelers are identified as places where they can connect to accessible Free Wi-Fi and /or that are attractive for them to sightsee.

Flickr users, on the other hand, take many photographs by using digital devices regardless of networks, but whether they can upload photographs on-site depends on the conditions of the network. As a result, almost all users can upload photographs after returning to their hotels or home countries. However, geo-tags annotated to photographs can indicate when they were taken. Therefore, although it is difficult to obtain detailed information (activities, destinations, or routes) on foreign travelers from Twitter, Flickr can be used to observe such information. In this study, we are based on our hypothesis of "A place that has a lot of Flickr posts, but few Twitter posts must have a critical lack of accessible Free Wi-Fi." We extracted areas that were tourist attractions for foreign travelers, but from which they could not connect to accessible Free Wi-Fi by using these characteristics of social media. What our method aims to find is places currently without accessible Free Wi-Fi.

There are two main reasons for areas from where foreign travelers cannot connect to Free Wi-Fi. The first is areas where there are no Wi-Fi spots. The second is areas where users can use Wi-Fi but it is not accessible. We treat them both the same as inaccessible Free Wi-Fi because both areas are unavailable to foreign travelers. Since we conducted experiments focused on foreign travelers, we could detect actual areas without accessible Free Wi-Fi. In addition, our method extracted areas with accessible Free Wi-Fi, and then other locations were regarded as regions currently without accessible Free Wi-Fi.

This subsection describes a method of extracting foreign travelers using Twitter and Flickr. We obtained and analyzed tweets posted in Japan from Twitter using Twitter's Streaming application programming interface (API) [18]. We used the method introduced in Case One to extract foreign travelers.

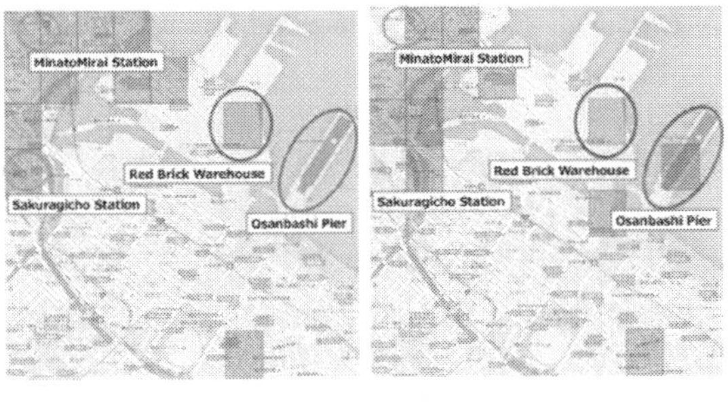

Figure 2. High density areas of tweets (left) and of Flickr photos (right).

We obtained photographs with geo-tags taken in Japan from Flickr using Flickr's API [22]. We extracted foreign travelers who had taken photographs in Japan. We regard Flickr users who had set their profiles of habitation on Flickr as Japan or associated geographical regions as the users *living* in Japan; otherwise, they are regarded as foreign *visitors*. We used the tweets and photographs that foreign visitors had created in Japan in the analysis that followed. Our method envisaged places that met the following two conditions as candidate access spots for accessible free Wi-Fi:

- Spots where there was no accessible Free Wi-Fi
- Spots that many foreign visitors visited

We use the number of photographs taken at locations to extract tourist spots. Many people might take photographs of subjects, such as landscapes based on their own interests. They might then upload those photographs to Flickr. As these were locations at which many photographs had been taken, these places might also be interesting places for many other people to sightsee or visit. We have defined such places as tourist spots. We specifically examined the number of photographic locations to identify tourist spots to find locations where photographs had been taken by a lot of people. We mapped photographs that had a photographic location onto a two-dimensional grid based on the location at which a photograph had been taken to achieve this. Here, we created individual cells in a grid that was 30 square meters. Consequently, all cells in the grid that was obtained included photographs taken in a range. We then counted the number of users in each cell. We regarded cells with greater numbers of users than the threshold as tourist spots.

The fragment collects attractive tourist spots for foreign visitors but without accessible free Wi-Fi currently (See Figure 2):

$DB_{t/visitor}$ ← Tweet DB of foreign visitors obtained by similar procedures like case one (i.e., hybrid processes consisting of data management and data mining);

$DB_{f/visitor}$ ← Flickr photo DB of foreign visitors obtained by similar procedures like case one;

T ← Partition (*i:Index grid* $DB_{t/visitor}$ $p(i)$); This partitions foreign visitors tweets into grids based on geo-tags; This operation returns a indexed family.

F ← Partition (*j:Index grid* $DB_{f/visitor}$ $p(j)$); This partitions foreign visitors photos into grids based on geo-tags; This operation returns a indexed family.

Index1 ← Select-Index (*i:Index T Density*(i) >= *th1*); *th1* is a threshold. This operation returns a singleton family.

Index2 ← Select-Index (*j:Index F Density*(i) >= *th2*); *th2* is a threshold. This operation returns a singleton family.

Index3 ← Difference (*Index2 Index1*); This operation returns a singleton family.

We collected more than 4.7 million data items with geo-tags from July 1, 2014 to February 28, 2015 in Japan. We detected tweets tweeted by foreign visitors by using the method proposed by Saeki *et al.* [19]. The number of tweets that was tweeted by foreign visitors was more than 1.9 million. The number of tweets that was tweeted by foreign visitors in the Yokohama area was more than 7,500. We collected more than 5,600 photos with geo-tags from July 1, 2014 to February 28, 2015 in Japan. We detected photos that had been posted by foreign visitors to Yokohama by using our proposed method. Foreign visitors posted 2,132 photos. For example, grids indexed by *Index3* contain "Osanbashi Pier." Please note that the above description doesn't take unique users into consideration.

C. Case Three

We use another tourism-related work [23] for a third case, which is classified as integrated analysis based on both social data and open data.

Tourists want real-time information and local unique seasonal information posted on web sites, according to a survey study of IT tourism and services to attract customers by the Ministry of Economy, Trade and Industry (METI) [24].

Current web sites provide related information in the form of guide books. Nevertheless, the information update frequency is usually low. Because local governments, tourism associations, and travel companies provide information about travel destination independently, it is difficult for tourists to collect "now" information for tourist spots.

Therefore, providing current, useful, real-world information for travelers by capturing the change of information in accordance with the season and time zone of the tourism region is important for the travel industry. We define "now" information as information for tourism and disaster prevention necessary for travelers during travel, such as best flower-viewing times, festivals, and local heavy rains.

We propose a method to estimate the best time for phenological observations for tourism such as the best-time viewing cherry blossoms ("Sakura" in Japanese) and autumn leaves in each region by particularly addressing phenological observations assumed for "now" information in the real world. Tourist information for the best time requires a peak period to view blooming flowers. Furthermore, the best times differ depending on regions and locations. Therefore, it is necessary to estimate a best time of phenological observation for each region and location. Estimating the best-time viewing requires the collection of a lot of information having real-time properties. For this research, we use Twitter data obtained for many users throughout Japan.

Preprocessing includes reverse geocoding and morphological analysis, as well as database storage for collected data.

Reverse geocoding identifies prefectures and municipalities by town name from latitude and longitude information of the collected tweets. We use a simple reverse geocoding service [25] available from the National Agriculture and Food Research Organization in this process: e.g., (latitude, longitude) = (35.7384446, 139.460910) by reverse geocoding becomes (Tokyo, Kodaira, City, Ogawanishi-cho 2-chome).

The standard lengths of time we used for the simple moving average were a seven-day moving average and one-year moving average. Since geo-tagged tweets tend to be more frequent at weekends than on weekdays, a moving average of seven days (one-week periodicity) is taken as one of estimation criteria. And the phenomenological observation is based on the one-year moving average as the estimation criterion since there are many "viewing" events every year, such as "viewing of cherry blossoms", "viewing of autumn leaves" and "harvesting period."

Table I: Examples of the target word.

Items	Target Words	In English
さくら	桜, さくら, サクラ	Cherry blossoms
かえで	楓, かえで, カエデ	Maple
いちょう	銀杏, いちょう, イチョウ	Ginkgo
こうよう	紅葉, 黄葉, こうよう, もみじ, コウヨウ, モミジ	Autumn leaves

Morphological analysis divides the collected geo-tagged tweet into morphemes. We use the *Mecab* morphological analyzer [26]. For example, the text "桜は美しいです" ("Cherry blossoms are beautiful" in English) is divided into morphemes ("桜 cherry blossom" / noun), ("は -" / particle), ("美しい beautiful" / adjective), ("です is" / auxiliary verb), and ("。 ." / symbol).

We use the simple moving average calculated by the formula (1) using the number of data going back to the past from the day before the estimated date of the best-time viewing.

$$X(Y) = \frac{P_1 + P_2 + \cdots + P_Y}{Y} \quad (1)$$

$X(Y)$: Y day moving average
P_n: Number of data of n days ago
Y: Calculation target period

Our method for estimating the best-time viewing processes the target number of extracted data and calculates a simple moving average, yielding an inference of the best flower-viewing time. The method defines a word related to the best-time viewing, estimated as the target word. The target word can include Chinese characters, hiragana, and katakana, which represents an organism name and seasonal change, as shown in Table I.

Next, we calculate a moving average for the best-time viewing judgment. The method calculates a simple moving average using data aggregated on a daily basis by the target number of extraction data. Figure 3 presents an overview of the simple moving average of the number of days.

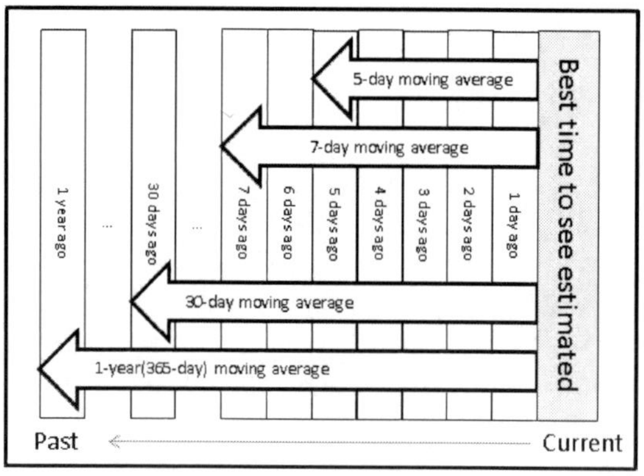

Figure 3. Number of days simple moving average.

In addition to the seven-day moving average and the one-year moving average, we also use the moving average of the number of days depending on each phenological target. In this study, we set the number of days of moving average from specified biological period of phenological target.

As an example, we describe cherry blossoms. The Japan Meteorological Agency (JMA) carries out phenological observations of Sakura, which yields two output the flowering date and the full bloom date of observation target [27]. JMA uses one specimen tree for observations in each target area, which produces open data. The flowering date of Sakura is the first day of blooming 5–6 or more wheels of flowers of a specimen tree. The full bloom date of Sakura is the first day of a state in which about 80% or more of the buds are open in the specimen tree. In addition, for Sakura the number of days from flowering until full bloom is about 5 days. Therefore, Sakura in this study uses a five-day moving average as a standard.

If the number of tweets on each day exceeds the one-year moving average, the Condition 1 holds as follows.

$$P_1 \geqq X(365) \tag{2}$$

For the Condition 2, we use the following inequation with respect to both biological moving average dependent on species and seven-day moving average for one-week periodicity.

$$X(A) \geqq X(B) \tag{3}$$

In case of cherry blossoms, we set A and B to five days and seven days, respectively. This inequation determines the date on which the moving average of a short number of days exceeds the moving average of a long number of days.

The Condition 2 holds if the inequality 3 continuously holds for the number of days, which is made equal to or more than half of the moving average of a short number of days. In the case of cherry blossoms, 5 days / 2 = 2.5 days≒ 3 days is the consecutive number of days. That is, if the 5-day moving average exceeds the seven-day moving average by 3 days or more, it shall be the date satisfying the Condition 2.

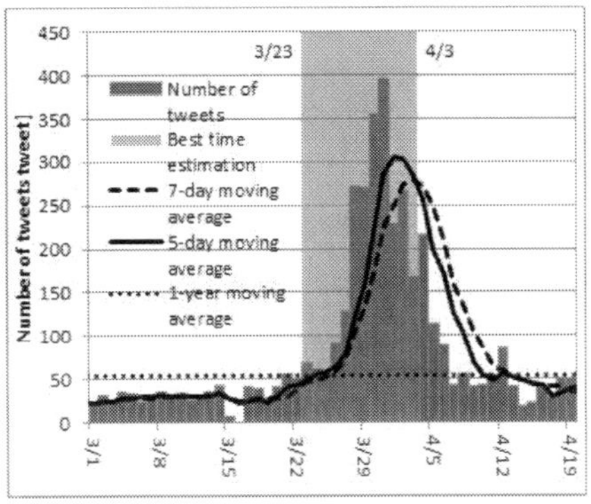

Figure 4. Results of the best time to see, as estimated for Tokyo in 2015.

We collected geo-tagged tweets posted in Japan from 2015/2/17 to 2016/6/30. The data include about 30 million items. We conducted the estimation experiment to ascertain the best-time viewing cherry blossoms uses the target word in Table I: "Sakura" or "cherry blossom," which has a variety of spellings such as "桜", "さくら" and "サクラ" in Japanese. The experimental target area is Tokyo. Our proposed method determines the best-time viewing duration in 2015.

The Condition 1 holds on the day when a dark gray bar exceeds the dotted line, one-year average (See Figure 4). The Condition 2 holds on the day when the solid line five-day average exceeds the broken line seven-day average for more than 3 days. Therefore, we estimated the duration 3/23 – 4/3 each of which satisfies both the Condition 1 and the Condition 2 as best-time viewing indicated by light gray area according to the following method:

ApplyFunction (ApplyFunction (Partition
(Select DB_{tweet} *Date* (2014, 2015) Within *"Tokyo" MorphologicalAnalyzer* (*Text*) contains (*Sakura*))
Date) Count) *Best-time-viewing-time* sequential

Here the function *Best-time-viewing-time* determines the duration as a temporal data mining operator, which is applied to one element of the set of counts of tweets per day after another as specified by the option *sequential*.

D. Case Four

We explain another case for integrated analysis based on both social data and open data.

For example, what in Osaka is equivalent to Tokyo Tower in Tokyo? Or what in Kobe corresponds to the Bay Bridge in Yokohama? Quantitatively answering these questions would be useful for applications such as destination management, which promotes travelers' visits to multiple touring spots in a region. In order to extract features of touristic resource names such as Tokyo Tower, we use Word2Vec [28] as a machine learning operator, which is suitable for natural language processing.

So we made an integrated hypothesis as follows.

Integrated hypothesis: By learning the vocabulary from corpus consisting of texts appearing in tweets (social data) containing a lot of touristic resource names such open data provided by the Ministry of Land, Infrastructure and Transport (MLIT) of Japan in consideration of the proximity of each other on the text, features of such names can be extracted. Furthermore, arithmetic operations such as plus and minus can be done over touristic resource names.

To this end, we collected geo-tagged tweets posted in Japan from March 11th to October 28th, 2015. Please note that we do not use location information in this case.

First, we create a list of touristic resource names by referring touristic resource data including open data of MLIT, and data obtained from TripAdvisor [29]. From the collected tweets, we selected about 115,610,000 tweets with touristic resource names on the list and the same number of tweets without them. Further we chose 500 tweets with touristic resource names and the same number of tweets without them to learn word semantics by Word2Vec as follows:

ApplyFunction (Union
(Select DB_{tweet} *MorphologicalAnalyzer*(*text*) contains (*touristic_resource_name*) fetch (500))
(Select DB_{tweet} *MorphologicalAnalyzer*(*text*) not contains (*touristic_resource_name*) fetch (500)))
Word2Vec

Here the user-defined function MorphologicalAnalyzer creates a bag of words from each text. Then ApplyFunction produces an indexed family. Word2Vec is based on a simple neural network (See Figure 5). It consists of three layers: input, hidden, and output. Each weight vector in the hidden layer represents a representation of its corresponding word. The analyst specifies the dimension of the middle layer. The dimension corresponds to the number of neurons. In learning, in the output corresponding to the input of a word, the weight of the middle layer is calculated so that the probability of a word appearing near the input word becomes high. We consider this weight as a feature vector of each word. Linear operations such plus, minus can be made between feature vectors. In the experiment, we set parameters for Word2Vec such as a dimension of 400, Skip-gram, Hierarchical Soft Max, and a window size of 5. For the similarity of word vectors, cosine similarity is used in our experiments.

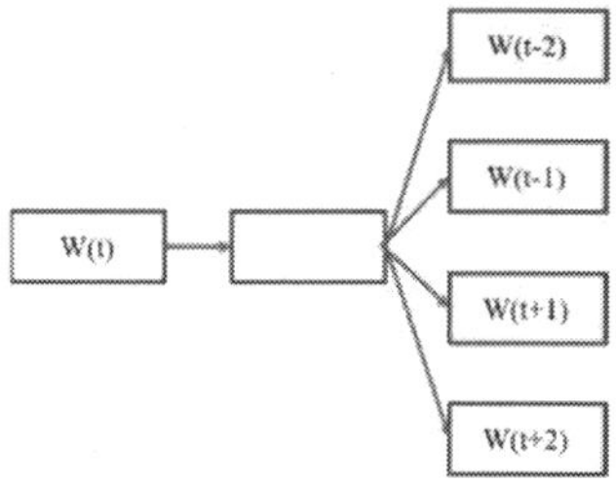

Figure 5. A neural network as Skip-gram model.

For example, we could calculate "Nankincho" by setting X = "Yokohama Chinatown" in the expression X - "Yokohama" + "Kobe."

Similarly, we could find "Akashi Kaikyo Bridge" by setting X = "Yokohama Bay Bridge" in the same expression. We have successfully confirmed the validity of the results by using relevant web pages.

E. Case Five

The last case is classified as integrated analysis based on a single source of social data and several sources of open data.

The 2011 Tohoku earthquake and tsunami showed the importance of smooth evacuation to nearest safe places. Smooth evacuation from crowded areas like train stations is difficult because people facing disaster often cannot find good paths to the nearest safe places and their evacuation may create congestion, which again hinders smooth evacuation. For smooth evacuation, the safety of roads used for evacuation needs to be evaluated. This evaluation requires 1) geographical characteristics of roads such as the collapse risk of neighboring buildings and road width and 2) crowdedness of roads at the moment of disaster. While previous studies considered the former, the latter information has not been well studied because the crowdedness depends on the demographics of a city, which is quite dynamic and difficult to measure. For example, daytime and nighttime populations of a city differ greatly. Our relevant work [30] proposes a method that measures demographics snapshot of a city from time and geo-stamped micro-blog posts and visualizes high-risk evacuation roads based on geographical characteristics and the demographics. Our method enabled visualization of high-risk evacuation roads on a per-hour basis. We also qualitatively analyze and discuss the visualization results.

Even though evacuees' first safe destinations are determined, we need to enable them to safely reach the destinations. To this end, local governments also specify evacuation roads, that is, roads considered to be safe and preferable for evacuation and recommended to be used. These roads are determined by considering three factors: 1) toughness of adjacent buildings to consider the risk of their collapse, 2) road width to consider the amount of people the roads can transport, and 3) population of adjacent areas to consider how crowded the roads become in the case of earthquakes. Evacuation roads and sites are manually revised about every five years.

Among the three factors, however, population of areas adjacent to roads is difficult to investigate because the actual population of a large city bearing millions of commuters is dynamic. For example, while the city center is densely populated during daytime, it is sparsely populated during nighttime. We thus need to take snapshots of dynamic demographics of a city. To tackle this problem, local governments currently use the Person Trip investigation [31] for determining evacuation roads. This is a government-led investigation by means of sending and gathering questionnaires to and from randomly sampled postal addresses. The questionnaire asks respondents where and how they usually go. However, these investigations are too costly to perform frequently, and the last one was performed in 1999 in Tokyo. In addition, they investigate only small samples of the whole population. Thus, infrequent and small samples in population snapshots make evaluation of crowdedness unreliable.

To determine roads preferable for evacuation, far more fine-grained demographics of areas of a city is needed considering the relative positions of each area and evacuation sites. Therefore, we propose a method for discovering high-risk paths (the roads for which evacuation risk is high), considering the number of people and geographical characteristics. To extract the number of people in each region, we use Twitter because it has many users and is a typical micro-blog, and we can understand "when" and "where" users upload tweets because they are tagged with time and location.

For example, people evacuating from crowded areas to evacuation sites are more likely to suffer fatal accidents such as stampedes and become confused than those evacuating from uncrowded areas. This means that evacuation from crowded areas is difficult. In addition, evacuation from crowded areas makes other roads crowded. Orange broken arrows in Figure 6 show crowded roads. Here we consider two types of crowded roads as depicted in Figure 6: Pattern A roads are made when people gather from two or more crowded areas, and Pattern B roads are made when a road is on the paths from a crowded area to multiple evacuation sites. We assume that crowded areas and crowded roads make evacuation difficult. In addition, geographical characteristics, such as many wooden buildings and many narrow roads located in the areas or along the roads, also make evacuation difficult.

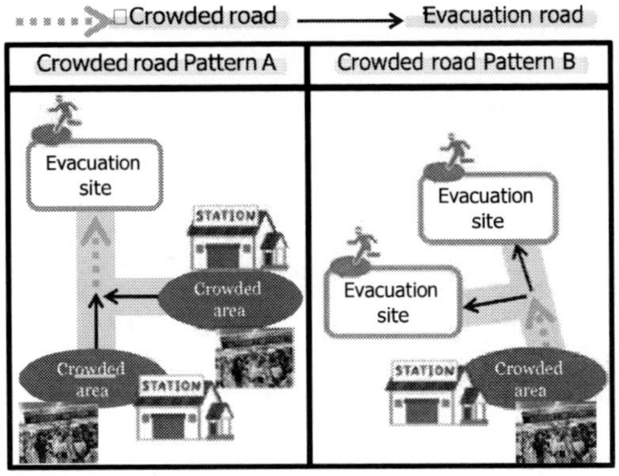

Figure 6. Examples of crowded roads.

1) Extraction of Crowded Areas and Evacuation Sites

When disasters occur, the situations in crowded areas are expected to be greatly influenced by people's behavior, which depends on the time of day. Therefore, we extract crowded areas using tweets with geo-tag every hour. First, we map tweets with geo-tag into two dimensional grids whose resolution is around 500 meters. Then, we adjust parameters for the extraction. Consequently, each cell in the grids includes tweets taken in the range. Then, using the grids, we calculate the number of tweets in each cell and normalize those numbers within a cell using the Gaussian Filter. The motivation of using a Gaussian filter here is to capture the fact that Twitter users move around after posting tweets and to allow the positioning errors of latitudes and longitudes obtained from GPS.

After the filtering, we extract cells in which tweets including photographs exceed the pre-determined threshold.

We make an index consisting of a crowded area *c* and an evacuation area *e* by using the dedicated function as follows:

$INDEX_{(c,\ e)}$ ← *Make-crowded-evacuation-area* (DB_{tweet}, *Gaussian*)

2) Extraction of Multiple Paths

We search multiple paths between evacuation sites and crowded areas extracted in the previous step. A path is defined as a route between an evacuation site and a crowded area. Road data consisting of routes are obtained from Open Street Map (OSM) [32]. In this work, we use pgRouting [33] to extract multiple paths for a crowded area *c* and a specified evacuation site *e*.

We extract paths from *c* to *e* as follows:

$FAMILY_{path}$ ← Make-indexed family ($INDEX_{(c,\ e)}$ *pgRouting*)

3) Extraction of High-Risk Path

We describe the method to extract high-risk paths from the paths obtained in the previous step. Our approach extracts high risk paths based on congestion degree and Emergency Response Difficulty Assessment (ERDA) degree. Congestion degree is considered as the weight of a crowded road and area as described below. ERDA degree is calculated based on geographical characteristics such as road width, possible degree of collapse of buildings, and fire risk. Finally, we calculate Risk degree using these measures. We define path *l* whose Risk degree is high as a High-Risk path.

a) Calculation of congestion degree

We calculate Congestion degree using crowded roads and the weight of a crowded area. We calculate betweenness centrality at target evacuation in 3km. We define the node located nearest to the median point of crowded areas on the network as node *i* (Origin) and define the node located nearest to each evacuation site as node *j* (Destination). Let g_{ij} be the number of paths between node *i* and node *j*. Also, we define $g_{ij}(l)$ as the number of occurrences of path *l* between node *i* and node *j*. Here, betweenness centrality $B(l)$ of path *l* can be written in the following Formula (4).

$$B(l) = \sum_{i \neq j} \sum_{j \in V_i, j \neq i} \frac{g_{ij}(l)}{g_{ij}} \quad (4)$$

V_i is the set of nodes of the evacuation sites that can be reached in less than 3km from node *i*.

Next, we describe a method for incorporating the weight of the crowded area into the calculation. Here, a weight is the estimated number of people passing through the path *l*. We incorporated the number of people extracted in the crowded area *C*, which is defined as R_C; the total number of evacuation sites from crowded area *C* within 3km, which is defined as $S(C)$; and the number of paths from crowded area *C* to evacuation site *S*, which is defined as $k(CS)$. After searching paths connected to crowded area *C* and evacuation site *S*, if path *l* is contained in the resulting paths, we calculate the weight of a crowded area, $W(l)$, using Formula (5).

$$W(l) = \sum_{C=1,N} \sum_{S=1,V(s)} \frac{R_C}{S(C) \cdot k(CS)} \quad (5)$$

Here, $V(S)$ is the set of nodes of evacuation sites that can be reached from the crowded area *C* within 3km. *N* is the total number of crowded areas extracted in the specified hour. Here, Congestion degree of path *l* can be written as Formula (6) by normalizing the results of Formula (4) and Formula (5).

$$Congestion(l) = Normalized(B(l)) + Normalized(W(l)) \quad (6)$$

b) Calculation of emergency response difficulty assessment degree

We describe a method for calculating Emergency Response Difficulty Assessment (ERDA) degree, another measure of risk of high-risk paths. ERDA degree is determined by the Bureau of Urban Development, Tokyo Metropolitan Government. The degree can be used as a measure of the difficulty of people's activities in disaster situations, and it comprehensively considers the building collapse probability, fire probability, and road width. The measure gives each district of each town of Tokyo in five-scale ranks. The lower ranks mean that people can more smoothly evacuate from the district during disasters.

When calculating the ERDA degree, we first find the rank values of the districts with which path l overlaps. Then, we calculate the length of the path l within each district. Finally, we calculate the resulting assessment by multiplying the rank and the length of the path. This can be formally written as follows. Let path l have total length L and l overlap with the district whose stage is *Rank*. Let the total length of path l within the districts whose stage is *Rank* be L_{Rank}. Then, we define ERDA(l) as follows.

$$ERDA(l) = Normalized\left(\sum_{Rank=1}^{5} Rank \cdot L_{Rank}\right) \quad (7)$$

c) Calculation of risk degree

Finally, we describe a method for calculating Risk degree. Risk degree of path l, namely *Risk*(l), is defined as follows by using Formula (6) and Formula (7).

$$Risk(l) = Congestion(l) + ERDA(l) \quad (8)$$

The higher *Risk*(l) means that path l is more dangerous at the time of disasters.

We obtain Risk of paths $FAMILY_{path}$ by calculating the formulas (4)-(8) sequentiallly.

4) Experiments

We describe the data set used in this study. We collected 5,769,800 geo-tagged tweets posted in Tokyo's 23 wards, the center of Tokyo. We collected tweets from April 1, 2015 to December 31, 2015. The number of Twitter users that were identified was 235,942. Rather than directly using the number of people tweeting, we performed smoothing of the people's distribution using a Gaussian Filter and manually identified 250 unique twitter users per grid as a crowded area because the number of people per grid abruptly change on that boundary.

We also used road network data of Tokyo collected from OpenStreetMap [32]. Roads in this network data are tagged with types of roads. We excluded data tagged as *motorway*, *motorway_link*, and *motorway_junction* because we are focusing on people evacuating on foot, and people cannot walk those roads safely during a disaster. As a result, 205,930 nodes and 302,141 edges remain.

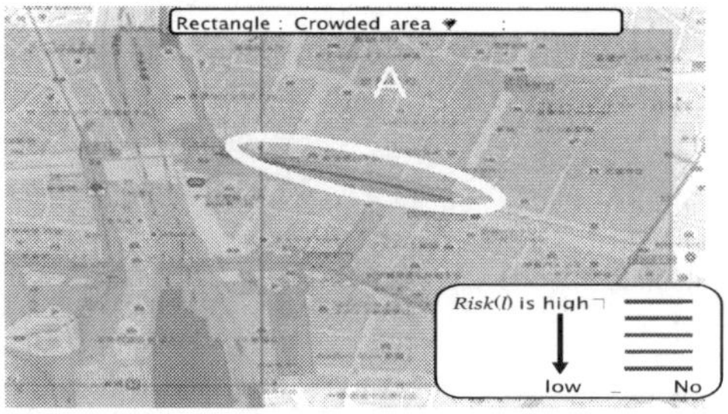

Figure 7. Visualization of high-risk paths Results from 5:00 am to 6:00 am.

a) Results from 5:00am to 6:00am

We describe high-risk paths extracted from 5:00am to 6:00am. All top-five high-risk paths extracted were parts of Yasukuni street within Shinjuku-Ward as shown by the red line within the yellow oval (A) in Figure 7.

From Figure 7, we can see that few lines are drawn around the oval (A) other than the straight red line. This result matches geographical characteristics of this area. While this area has many evacuation sites such as Shinjuku High School, Shinjuku Junior High School, and Tenjin Elementary School, evacuees can reach these sites without passing through narrow roads because this area is a city center where old narrow roads became obsolete and were demolished.

b) Results from 6:00pm to 7:00pm

We describe high-risk path extracted from 6:00pm to 7:00pm. The red line surrounded by the yellow circle and oval (B) of Figure 8 indicates 1st, 3rd, 4th, and 5th rankings. While the extracted areas from 5:00am to 6:00am and those from 6:00pm to 7:00pm share the same pattern (the areas around Shinjuku stations are detected to be crowded), our system successfully captured the difference in the overall patterns and different paths were extracted as high-risk paths.

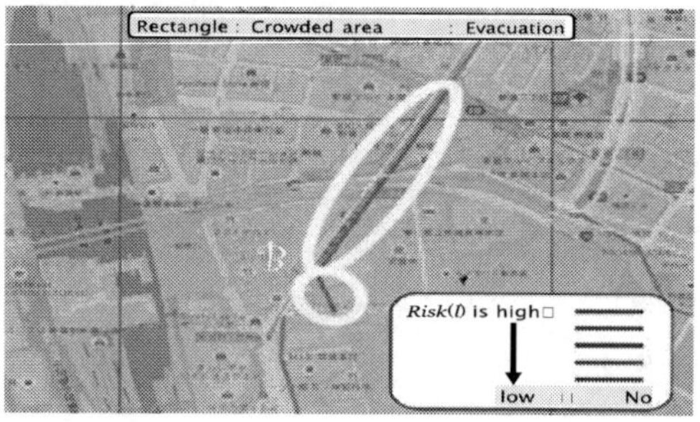

Figure 8. Visualization of high-risk paths Results from 6:00 pm to 7:00 pm.

V. CONCLUSION

We have proposed an abstract data model for integrating data management and data mining by using mathematical concepts of families, collections of sets. Our model facilitates reproducibility and accountability required for SBD researches and developments. We have partially validated our proposal by adapting our model to real case studies. Especially, we have illustrated that SBD applications are inherently mixed of data management and data mining and that integrated analysis based on different sources of data is effective in SBD applications. Technically, however, there still remain rooms to describe mappings from our model to existing programming tools, such as Spark. Further, we must devise some kinds of optimization comparable to query optimization of SQL. Empirically, we would like to validate our proposed model more thoroughly by adapting it to different kinds of applications.

ACKNOWLEDGMENT

This work was supported by JSPS KAKENHI Grant Number 16K00157, 16K16158, and Tokyo Metropolitan University Grant-in-Aid for Research on Priority Areas Research on social big data.

REFERENCES

[1] H. Ishikawa and R. Chbeir, "A data model for integrating data management and data mining in social big data," Proceedings of 9th IARIA International Conference on Advances in Multimedia (MMEDIA 2017), April 2017.

[2] IDC, *The Diverse and Exploding Digital Universe* (white paper, 2008). http:// www.emc.com/collateral/analyst-reports/diverse-exploding-digital-universe.pdf Accessed November 2017.

[3] IDC, *The Digital Universe In 2020: Big Data, Bigger Digital Shadows, and Biggest Growth in the Far East* (2012). http://www.emc.com/leadership/digital-universe/iview/index.htm Accessed November 2017.

[4] H. Ishikawa, Social Big Data Mining, CRC Press, 2015.

[5] T. C. Südhof, "Truth in Science Publishing: A Personal Perspective," PLOS August 26, 2016.

[6] D. G. Feitelson, "From Repeatability to Reproducibility and Corroboration," ACM SIGOPS Operating Systems Review - Special Issue on Repeatability and Sharing of Experimental Artifacts, Volume 49, Issue 1, pp. 3-11, January 2015.

[7] R. D. Peng, "Reproducible Research in Computational Science," SCIENCE, VOL 334, 2, December 2011.

[8] S. Perianayagam, G. R. Andrews, and J. H. Hartman, "Rex: A toolset for reproducing software experiments," Proceedings of IEEE International Conference on Bioinformatics and Biomedicine (BIBM) 2010, pp. 613-617, 2010.

[9] R. Ramakrishnan and J. Gehrke, Database Management Systems, 3rd Edition, McGraw-Hill Professional, 2002.

[10] H. Ishikawa, Y. Yamane, Y. Izumida, and N. Kawato, "An Object-Oriented Database System Jasmine: Implementation, Application, and Extension," IEEE Trans. on Knowl. and Data Eng. 8, 2, pp. 285-304, April 1996.

[11] M. Zaharia, R. S. Xin, P. Wendell, T. Das, M. Armbrust, A. Dave, X. Meng, J. Rosen, S. Venkataraman, M. J. Franklin, A. Ghodsi, J. Gonzalez, S. Shenker, and I. Stoica, "Apache Spark: a unified engine for big data processing," Com. ACM, 59, 11, pp. 56-65, October 2016.

[12] E. R. Sparks, A. Talwalkar, V. Smith, J. Kottalam, X. Pan, J. E. Gonzalez, M. J. Franklin, M. I. Jordan, and T. Kraska, "MLI: An API for distributed machine learning," Proceedings of the IEEE ICDM International Conference on Data Mining (Dallas, TX, Dec. 7–10). IEEE Press, 2013.

[13] Apache Hadoop. http://hadoop.apache.org/ Accessed November 2017.

[14] Crouchbase. https://www.couchbase.com/ Accessed November 2017.

[15] Apache Hive. http://hive.apache.org/index.html Accessed November 2017.

[16] N1QL. https://www.couchbase.com/products/n1ql Accessed August 2017.

[17] D. Smith, R. St. Andre, and M. Eggen, A Transition to Advanced Mathematics, Brooks/Cole Pub Co., 2014.

[18] Twitter, *Twitter Developer Documentation.* https://dev.twitter.com/streaming/overview Accessed November 2017.

[19] M. Hirota, K. Saeki, Y. Ehara, and H. Ishikawa, "Live or Stay?: Classifying Twitter Users into Residents and Visitors," Proceedings of International Conference on Knowledge Engineering and Semantic Web (KESW 2016), 2016.

[20] GitHub, Language Detection. https://github.com/shuyo/language-detection Accessed November 2017.

[21] K. Mitomi, M. Endo, M. Hirota, S. Yokoyama, Y. Shoji, and H. Ishikawa, "How to Find Accessible Free Wi-Fi at Tourist Spots in Japan," Volume 10046 of Lecture Notes in Computer Science, pp. 389-403, 2016.

[22] Flickr, *The App Garden.* https://www.flickr.com/services/api/ Accessed November 2017.

[23] M. Endo, S. Ohno, M. Hirota, Y. Shoji, and H. Ishikawa, "Examination of Best-time Estimation Using Interpolation for Geotagged Tweets," Proceedings of 9th IARIA International Conference on Advances in Multimedia (MMEDIA 2017), April 2017.

[24] Ministry of Economy, Trade and Industry, *study of landing type IT tourism and attract customers service*, http://www.meti.go.jp/report/downloadfiles/g70629a01j.pdf Accessed November 2017 (in Japanese).

[25] National Agriculture and Food Research Organization, *simple reverse geocoding service*, https://www.finds.jp/rgeocode/index.html.en Accessed November 2017.

[26] MeCab, *Yet Another Part-of-Speech and Morphological Analyzer.* http://taku910.github.io/mecab/ Accessed November 2017 (in Japanese).

[27] Japan Meteorological Agency, *Disaster prevention information XML format providing information page.* http://xml.kishou.go.jp/ Accessed November 2017 (in Japanese).

[28] T. Mikolov, I. Sutskever, K. Chen, G. S. Corrado, and J. Dean, "Distributed representations of words and phrases and their compositionality," *Advances in neural information processing systems.* 2013.

[29] TripAdvisor, *Read Reviews, Compare Prices & Book* http://tripadvisor.com Accessed November 2017.

[30] M. Kanno, Y. Ehara, M. Hirota, S. Yokoyama, and H. Ishikawa. "Visualizing High-Risk paths using Geo-tagged Social Data for Disaster Mitigation," 9th ACM SIGSPATIAL International Workshop on Location-Based Social Networks (LBSN '16), November 2016.

[31] Ministry of Land, Infrastructure, Transport and Tourism, *Results from the 4th Nationwide Person Trip Survey* http://www.mlit.go.jp/crd/tosiko/zpt/pdf/zenkokupt_gaiyoban_english.pdf Accessed November 2017.

[32] OpenStreetMap Contributors, *OpenStreetMap.* http://www.openstreetmap.org/ Accessed August 2017.

[33] pgRouting Community, *pgRouting.* http://pgrouting.org/ Accessed November 2017.

A Graph Partitioning Approach for Efficient Dependency Analysis using a Graph Database System

Kazuma Kusu
Graduate School of Culture and Information Science,
Doshisha University
1-3 Tatara-Miyakodani, Kyotanabe,
Kyoto 610-0394, Japan
Email: kusu@ilab.doshisha.ac.jp

Izuru Kume
Graduate School of Information Science,
Nara Institute of Science and Technology
8916-5 Takayama, Ikoma,
Nara 630-0192, Japan
Email: kume@is.naist.jp

Kenji Hatano
Faculty of Culture and Information Science,
Doshisha University
1-3 Tatara-Miyakodani, Kyotanabe,
Kyoto 610-0394, Japan
Email: khatano@mail.doshisha.ac.jp

***Abstract*—Program execution traces, which include data/control dependency information, are indispensable for new types of debugging such as back-in-time techniques. In this study, we implement a dependency environment for the Java programming language focusing on tracing the relationships in dependency analyses, using the graph database (Neo4j) optimized for tracing graph edges. In the dependency analysis environment, we propose an efficient approach for handling the traces on a graph database system by evaluating memory usage and analysis time. Traces of practical programs are prone to have vast complex data, making it difficult to develop practical back-in-time debuggers. To address this challenge, our dependency environment enables an efficient analysis of the traces. The trace in our dependency analysis environment has a graph structure whose nodes denote executed Java bytecode instructions, and edge that represent data/control dependencies between the nodes. By a simple implementation of our dependency analysis environment, we confirm the existence of bottlenecks through evaluation experiments, which are then remedied in order to improve the performance of the technique's memory usage and analysis time. As a result, our environment enabled efficient process dependency analysis, reducing memory usage by 43.1% and analysis time by 4.3%.**

Keywords–Dependency Analysis; Back-in-time Debugger; Debugging Support; Graph Database; Graph Search; Java.

I. INTRODUCTION

The examination of runtime states and their dependencies are indispensable to program debugging [2] [3]. Debuggers that are currently in use allow maintainers to suspend program execution at specified break points and examine the runtime states at these points. However, such debuggers do not have a provision for maintainers to examine states prior to the designated points for the suspension of execution. Therefore, they cannot trace backwards to detect causes of erroneous states by following the dependency of statements [4].

In the last decade, so-called *back-in-time debuggers* have emerged as a new kind of debugging support tools. These debuggers use traces containing dependency information [5] [6] [7]. Such debuggers analyze dependencies to determine the operation that assigns value to a referenced variable [5], to examine the reasons why a given statement is or is not executed [6], and what happens during the execution of a method that has already been successfully invoked [7]. This kind of dependency analysis is useful for the examination of a particular instruction.

The scalability of process traces containing dependency information has been discussed in the literature [4]. We believe that the recent, rapid developments in hardware and software technologies have made it possible to process the traces of a certain scale of software products. In previous work [8], we demonstrated two kinds of dependency analysis that detect symptoms of a malfunction caused by defects in the application of the Java framework application [9].

Although our previous study raised the prospect of a solution to the scalability problem, the implementation of our dependency analysis remained inefficient. The main cause of this was the richness of the data in the model of our traces. The design of our trace proposed here aims not only at the requirements of symptom detection [8], but also at the analysis of other aspects of program execution. Therefore, our trace design incorporates the richness of data to enable various kinds of dependency analysis instead of reducing the amount of data, such as in the approach proposed by Wang et al. [10].

In addition to back-in-time Debuggers [5] [6] [7], which aim at a microscopic perspective for the dependency analysis of a specific statement, our previous study [8] dealt with all-state updates via *persistent variables* and their value dependency across the entire trace. A persistent variable is either a class variable, an instance variable, or an array component. It implements a state that persists after the invocation of a method is completed [11]. This macroscopic nature of our dependency analysis renders it inefficient, although the algorithm works in practice. In order to solve this problem, an approach is needed to support the efficient analysis of dependency in a large trace.

In this paper, we implement an efficient dependency analysis environment to perform out the trace studies as done previously [8]. Moreover, we clarify the inefficiency factor in our dependency analysis environment, and suggest an approach to address this factor. Furthermore, we evaluate our approach for improving the processing of analysis results after applying our approach. According to this, we clarify bottlenecks in our dependency analysis environment that need to be resolved. Previously, we identified the factors affecting efficiency in our dependency analysis environment and expanded a trace-partitioning approach for use in our study [1]. Moreover, we proposed an extension of a previous approach [12] for partitioning trace. We reduced memory consumption in a dependency analysis, but did not reduce the processing time.

Therefore, we propose an approach for efficiently traversing our trace in this paper. Finally, we conduct an experiment characterizing the effectiveness of our approach.

We introduce concepts related to dependency analysis, and describe demands for dependency analysis environments in Section II. Then, in Section III, we illustrate our implementation of a dependency analysis environment that consists of trace generation and a trace processing parts using a graph database system (GDB). In Section IV, we propose a naïve trace-partitioning approach based on the characteristics of the GDB for efficient dependency analysis. We conduct a preliminary experiment for evaluating dependency analysis performance on our environment in Section V. In Section VI, we reconsider a trace-partitioning approach guided by an analysis of the bottleneck in our dependency analysis environment clarified during the preliminary experiment. In Section VII, we conduct an evaluation of the efficiency and scalability of our expanded approach. Finally, in Section VIII, we consider our contribution for efficient dependency analysis as indicated by the experiment.

II. RELATED WORK

Debuggers widely used in software development projects support a common feature to suspend program execution at a specified *break point* and show the runtime state at that point. They do not record the execution and, thus, have the common drawback that there is no way to examine the execution of a method whose invocation has been already completed. This is a serious problem because defects and infections are often found in methods that have been completed before the program fails [7]. A defect is an error in program code while an infection, in software engineering, is a runtime error caused by the execution of a defect [2].

Maintainers using a debugger must repeat a task to specify a breakpoint, as it is usually very difficult to find a suitable breakpoint in the program code, and re-execute the program to examine the executions of methods that have been completed. Such a debugging style, forced by the common limitation in current of existing debuggers, leads to inefficient debugging [4].

Using traces for debugging support is a natural idea to overcome the above limitation in existing debuggers [5] [6] [13]. An omniscient debugger [5] examined assignment operations with set values referenced from variables. If a maintainer wanted to determine why a statement has or has not been executed, Whyline [6] analyzed related dependencies and generated the results of the analysis using sophisticated Graphical User Interfaces (GUI).

Dynamic Object Flow Analysis [13] aims to understand program execution from the aspect of object references. Its area of application ranges from dependency analysis of methods for software testing [14] to performance engineering for a back-in-time debugger [7].

To the best of our knowledge, no existing dependency analysis approaches to debugging support are aimed at macroscopic dependency analysis except for our previous proposal [8]. An omniscient debugger deals with only the correspondence between the value of a variable and the assignment operation that has set this value. Whyline navigated

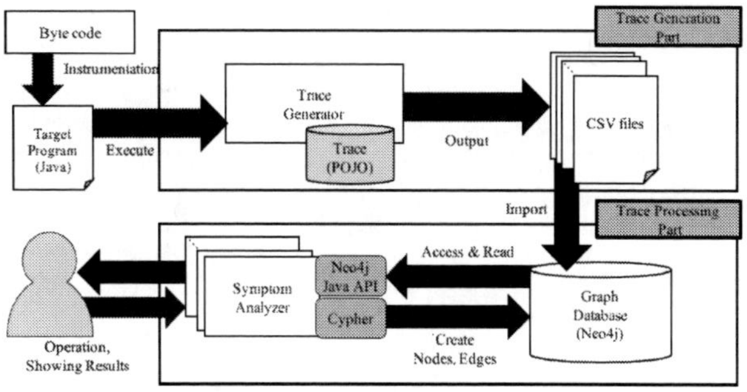

Figure 1. Our dependency analysis environment

a maintainer to the dependencies among statements to the extent of his/her manual examination. Dynamic object flow analysis performs macroscopic analysis but only deals with object references.

The above approaches to microscopic dependency analysis provide useful debugging aids. However, understanding a program from a macroscopic viewpoint is necessary for debugging [15]; therefore, maintainers have to spend time and effort to obtain this perspective through manual dependency analysis.

We studied several kinds of macroscopic dependency analysis in this context in our last study [8]. Of these, *outdated-state* analysis aims to identify symptoms to suggest possible infections incurred by the accidental use of an old value of a field or array component along with its updated value.

III. IMPLEMENTATION OF DEPENDENCY ANALYSIS ENVIRONMENT

Debugging a program requires various analyses of statement dependencies. Therefore, we developed two kinds of techniques for analyzing the relevant symptoms in our previous study [8]. The proposed trace was designed to execute such dependency analyses. For this reason, our trace tended to be large and complex, and to be usually led to inefficient processing of dependency analysis. In order to conduct an efficient dependency analysis, an analysis environment is needed that enable to handle our trace efficiently.

Figure 1 illustrates the entire process, which involves the execution of a Java program under instrumentation and several sub-processes of symptom analysis in our dependency analysis environment. In the trace generation portion, our system generates a trace using Java byte-code instrumentation technologies. The trace processing portion, on the other hand, stores the generated trace in a GDB and supports its efficient processing of various kinds of dependency analysis.

A. Trace Data Model

Dependency analysis approaches from various aspects of execution are necessary for practical debugging support. In previous work, we developed two kinds of dependency analysis algorithms to detect symptoms that indicate infections in a failed execution [8].

Both of the proposed algorithms process control data dependency across the entire extent of an execution. One

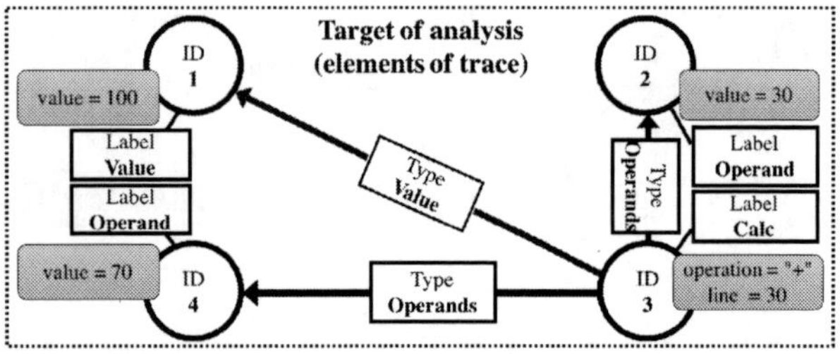

Nodes

Node ID	Attribute Key	Attribute Value
1	value	100
2	value	30
3	operation	"+"
	line	30
4	value	70

Relationships

Start Node ID	End Node ID	Attribute Key	Attribute Value
3	1	-	-
3	2	-	-
3	4	-	-

Figure 2. Property graph model

algorithm checks a complex condition that specifies data flow to associate operations in a class instance caused by the invocation of a certain kind of method. The other algorithm keeps track of side effects via fields and array components. We propose a new kind of dependency analysis that aims to abstract the effects of methods and operations on objects based on inputs by the debugger users.

In order to satisfy the above requirements, we defined our trace model as the following basic elements of program executions:

- Method execution
- Execution of abstracted byte code instructions to represent statements.
- Creation and reference of values by instructions.
- Values to be created or referenced.

Some abstracted instructions represent "control statements," such as conditional statements, method invocations, and throw and catch. Abstracted instructions contain assignment operations on local variables, fields, and array components. The instruction set also contains constants, instance creations, and array creations, as well as various calculation operations. Values created, calculated, and assigned are referenced by the instructions that use them.

For each instruction in an execution, its trace records the control instruction under which it is executed. If the instruction references a value, the trace records from the instruction from which the value originates. In this way, we can obtain control and data dependency information among instructions, including a method invocation structure.

A trace generated by our approach enables to first be represented using the property graph model shown in Figure 2. This is a data model defined in the TinkerPop project in Apache [16]. This data model features good descriptive capability, and hence can represent various kinds of data.

Our trace model allows programs to check data/control dependency for a large number of instructions in order to examine state changes on some objects or to find the cause of an infection. Algorithms to check such dependencies, represented by links among graph nodes, should be efficient.

B. Trace Processing

The requirements stated in Section III-A make it difficult to reduce trace size. Traces are needed not for a particular dependency analysis, but for various kinds of analysis dealing with the conditions of such program elements as classes, fields, and methods related to the four elements described in Section III-A. Therefore, rich data is required for the proposed trace model for such additional information.

For dependency analysis purposes, the instructions between, which the analysis is performed cannot be predicted. Therefore, for a failed execution, the trace of the entire extent of execution is first needed. Our algorithms then search for instructions that are the targets of dependency analysis.

Dependency analysis usually requires checking of complex conditions for the above four kinds of elements one by one along with their dependency relationships. Furthermore, the results of past condition checks must be stored for reference.

A situation sometimes arises where the Java virtual machine is quite inefficient, or even runs out of memory when applying dependency analysis to the execution of a software. Hence, data engineering approaches are needed to build a framework that enables efficient access to and processing of massive traces.

In this study, we develop a dependency analysis environment on the GDB to improve analysis performance. This paper uses a GDB called Neo4j following the property graph model [17] because it is suitable for storing traces with complex data structures. Moreover, Neo4j have considered the best for handling graph data for existing GDBs [18] [19].

In order to handle our trace, our dependency analysis environment was implemented using the native Java Application Program Interface(API) of Neo4j and its query language named Cypher.

IV. A Trace-partitioning Approach for Efficient Dependency Analysis

In Section III, we described how to store and process our trace on our dependency analysis environment using Neo4j. Our trace is expressed as graph data, which consists of nodes and edges. Therefore, the nodes and the edges unrelated to the graph data trace are not loaded into main memory when the dependency analysis is conducted. In short, memory efficiency of our dependency analysis environment is high. However, the size of the properties of a node or an edge that is loaded in main memory is large, this may likely to become a bottleneck of our dependency analysis environment. Especially, it goes double for becoming the bottleneck if the attribute is not related to dependency analysis. Therefore, we propose an approach for fixing this bottleneck.

A. Characteristics of Graph Database System

Initially, Neo4j manages graph data on hard disk drives until a query is issued. Once, a query is issued, Neo4j accesses the hard disk drive to load nodes and edges related to the query, into the main memory. Usually, nodes and edges not related to the query are not loaded.

If the nodes and the edges are loaded into main memory, their properties are also automatically loaded. Therefore, loading the properties into main memory is not efficient if the property is not related to an issued query. Moreover, this problem becomes a factor to produce useless disk access.

B. A Naïve Trace-partitioning Approach for Memory Reduction

As we described in Section IV-A, loading properties unrelated to an issued query leads to the potential for memory inefficiency of GDB. Nodes and properties, which are not the target of dependency analysis, will not be loaded in the main memory while conducting the analysis. This is the characteristic of GDB, which is supported by the native graph engine.

We deal with this bottleneck by simply storing an extra node in GDB. The extra node is to store properties of node, which is the target of the dependency analysis. In this way, it is possible to load only nodes and its properties, which are targets of dependency analysis, and eliminate the unnecessary ones from the dependency analysis. We believe that this is the best way as it is more frequent to distinguish the kind of a node than to acquire properties of nodes.

We illustrate our proposed approach in Figure 3. At first, it is necessary to create a node and an edge. A node plays the role of storing properties of node (node ID is 5, 6, 7, 8 in Figure 3.), which is trace elements (node ID is 1, 2, 3, 4 in shown Figure 3.) An edge plays the role of distinguishing certain node, which is an extra node for storing properties. We describe this node as a property-node, and this edge as a property-edge in this paper. Therefore, a change of the following graph structure occurs.

1) The number of nodes stored in a graph database system doubles.
2) One edge connecting with each nodes of the trace increases.

We assume that the time required for import processing of our trace increases by 1. However, graph traversal performance is influenced by the increase of the nodes, such as 1), intended only for the node where the graph traversal is connected to a certain node on the native GDB such as Neo4j [20] [21]. Then, instead of being able to reduce the loading of the properties of a node that is unnecessary for dependency analysis, one property-edge comes to is loaded with change 2). The specifications of Neo4j have a bigger fixed-length data size of the edge than the node on the disk [20] [21]. However, we assume that a data size of edges loaded in the memory is low, because the number of edges such as references and dependencies is less than that of nodes. In addition, the time for confirming edges with the need to follow in the graph traversal by 2) increases once in all nodes and we predict that it makes the performance of graph traversal inefficient. Since our approach has a factor that can promote and not promote efficiency of dependency analysis as described above.

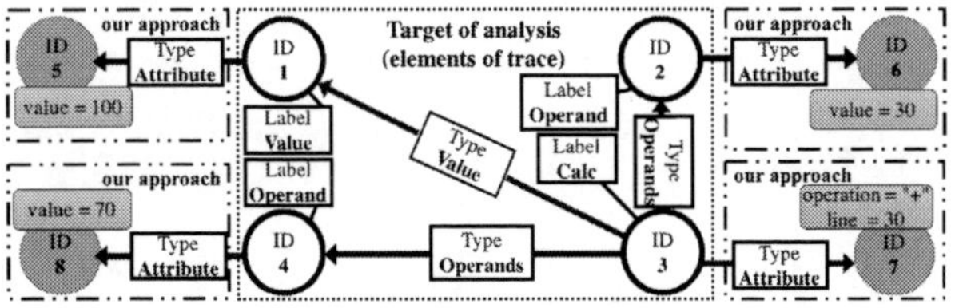

Nodes

Node ID	Attribut Key	Attribute Value
1	-	-
2	-	-
3	-	-
4	-	-
5	value	100
6	value	30
7	operation	"+"
	line	30
8	value	70

Relationships

Start Node ID	End Node ID	Attribute Key	Attribute Value
1	5	-	-
2	6	-	-
3	1	-	-
3	2	-	-
3	4	-	-
3	7	-	-
4	8	-	-

Figure 3. Graph partitioning approach for proposed trace.

V. Preliminary Experiment

We propose a trace-partitioning approach for efficient dependency analysis in Section IV. In this section, we conduct a preliminary experiment for confirming the change of the analysis performance for an approximate application of our approach. We conduct this preliminary experiment on a kernel-based virtual machine with 64 GB RAM and the Cent OS 7 operating system.

A. Unified Modeling Language Editor "GEFDemo"

We used our trace for the execution of the demonstration program on the Graph Editing Framework (GEFDemo) [9] for dependency analysis in Section V-B. GEFDemo is a simple Unified Modeling Language (UML) editor program that uses the application framework as shown in Figure 4(a). A flaw, such as in Figure 4(b), is known to occur during the delete operation, a ternary association, which is a defect in implementation of the GEFDemo.

Accurate inspection of the analysis program was possible because the cause of the defect shown in Figure 4 was manually confirmed. The trace used in this experiment recorded the execution process of GEFDemo that intentionally produced an exception, as shown in Figure 4 in the following procedure:

1) Creating three classes on the editor.
2) Creating an association for other classes from one class.
3) Creating an association for another association from the class that does not create an association.
4) A diamond object expressing the occurrence of a ternary connection occurs.
5) Deleting the diamond object.

The number of nodes in this trace was 510,370 and the number of relationships 4,437,367. Moreover, the trace into the GEFDemo contained 45 kinds of labels for nodes and 22 kinds of relationships. Furthermore, the amount of this trace was 292.63 MB.

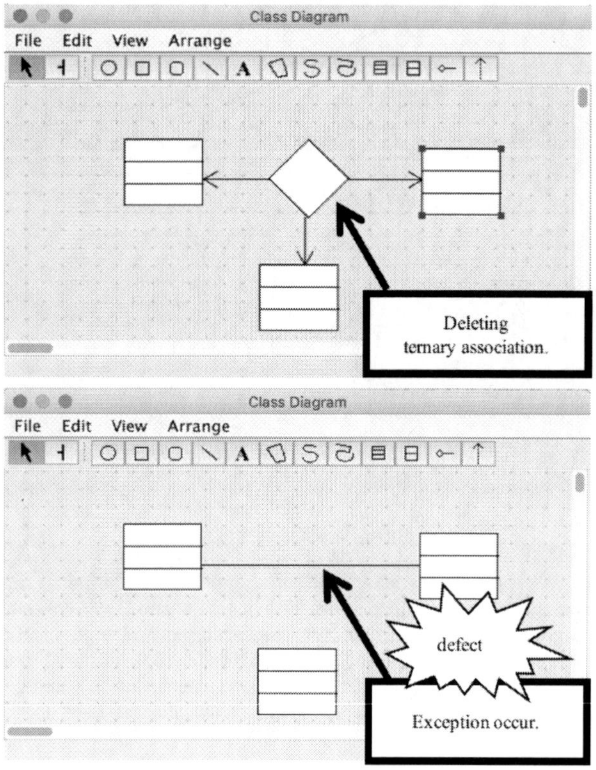

(b) Deleting a Ternary Association.

Figure 4. Operating the GEFDemo Program

B. Outdated-state Analysis

As described in Section V-A, a defect of the GEFDemo was caused by changes in the process of execution of the program during the collection state, which is an object of Java. We used an outdated-state analysis, which is the approach of dependency analysis proposed by Kume et al. [8]. It can detect instructions that use different states of a specified object.

We executed the outdated-state analysis in a dependency analysis environment as described below:

1) Investigating method called in execution order one by one.
2) Investigating dependencies with state of objects with many instructions occurring in each method.
3) When analyzing an instrument concerning the change in the state of the object, a node was created to record the frequency of change of the object for a GDB.
4) Investigating instructions dependence on the combination of a new state and old states of the same object from nodes that we created by Procedure 3).

In Procedure 1), the outdated-state analysis consumed a large amount of memory because it was necessary to analyze instruments and values in a trace. Moreover, outdated-state analysis is a two-step process: (1) analyzing the trace, (2) creating the nodes and edges to record the status of objects (data generated during dependency analysis) on GDB in Procedure 1). Finally, it analyzes data generated in Procedure 3).

C. Measurement of Effects on Entire Dependency Analysis

In this section, we measured the method's time and memory consumption in order to evaluate the effectiveness of our approach for efficient dependency analysis in Section IV. Memory consumptions per second were recorded using vmstat, which is a UNIX command that can report information related to memory, paging, CPU activity, and so on, and can calculate the basic statistics of memory consumption. We conducted dependency analysis ten times as we described above.

Figure 5 shows the results of two trace formats as the following:

NON: a non-transformational trace
ALL: a trace partitioned properties of each node in our trace using IV

Figures 5(a) and Figure 8(b) show the average of memory consumption in the dependency analysis. In these figures, NON represents our previously approach proposed in literature [8]. ALL refers to the naïve approach proposed in Section IV and literature [12].

We conduct an independent t-test in order to confirm whether there are significant differences between average of the time consumption and average of the memory consumption. We calculate a t-value by Formula (1):

$$t = \frac{\bar{x}_{NON} - \bar{x}_{ALL}}{s\sqrt{\frac{1}{n_1} + \frac{1}{n_2}}} \tag{1}$$

where x_{NON} denotes ten values of time consumption or memory consumption in a case of NON, $\bar{x}_{NON}$ denotes the mean of x_{NON}, x_{ALL} denotes ten values of time consumption or memory consumption in a case of ALL, $\bar{x}_{ALL}$ denotes the mean of x_{ALL}, n_{NON} and n_{ALL} are sample size of x_{NON} and x_{ALL}, and s is pooled variance with x_{NON} and x_{ALL}.

The two p-values in Figure 5 indicated that ALL could not reduce time consumption and memory consumption for dependency analysis compared with those of NON. On the contrary, our naïve approach worsen this performance.

D. Inefficient Processing in our Approach

We assume that the time required for importing a trace increases due to the above sorting 1). However, graph traversal performance is not influenced by the increase in the number of nodes; it is intended only for the node where graph traversal is connected to a certain node in Neo4j. On the other hand, instead of preventing the loading of property of a node that is unnecessary for analysis, a property-relationship is loaded with sorting 2). The fixed-length data size of edge on the Neo4j is larger than that of the node. However, we can assume that the data size of edges loaded in the memory is small because the size of a property of the edges, such as references and dependencies, is less than that of the nodes. The time needed to confirm the edges needed to traverse the graph traversal by sorting 2) increases in all nodes, and we predict that it leads to inefficient graph traversal performance.

Moreover, if it is necessary to access a property, the property-relationship is traversed during dependency analysis. Since traversing property-relationship is not necessary in the

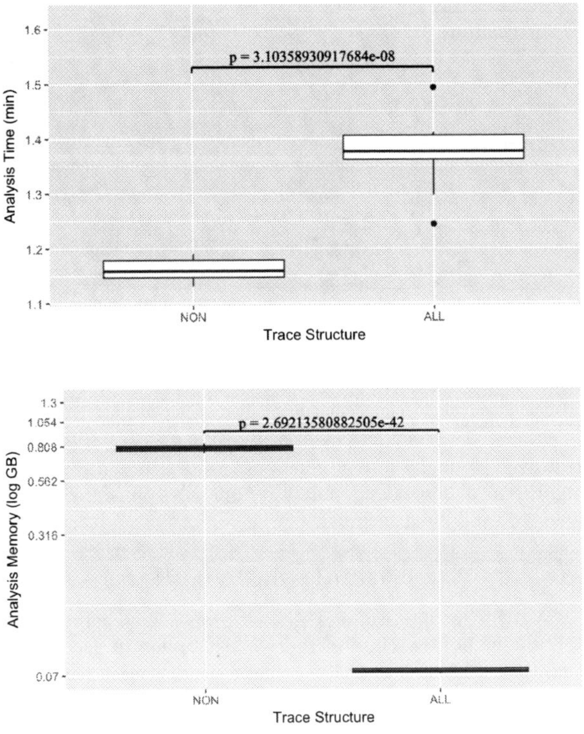

(b) Memory consumption.

Figure 5. Dependency analysis performance.

case of an original trace, as the number of processes increases, efficiency worsens.

Furthermore, there are difference instructions referred same object, same variable, and same element of array in runtime program. In this case, the trace has many pair of nodes; one is different two node implied instructions, other is same node implied object. Then, it is inefficient to traverse same node many times during dependency analysis.

VI. Improving and Extending our Approach

The loading nodes, the edges, and their properties used for dependency analysis are very important for the efficient use of the main memory. Neo4j supported on-disk-database, which loads the properties of node and edge when the nodes and edges are loaded. However, not all of the loaded properties are used for all dependency analyses. Therefore, we focused on the selection of loading properties.

In the previous study [12], we proposed an approach for partitioning our trace that can load properties as needed. However, this did not help improve the dependency analysis performance. Therefore, we formulate a rule in this section to determine whether a given property should be loaded for a given trace in literature [1].

Moreover, we extend our approach to enable rapid access to a node, which is accessed once during dependency analysis.

Require: N_{node}, N_{attr}, N_{trav}
  for each $l \in L$ **do**
    {Not applying proposed approach to all labels of the node.}
    {Initializing $\boldsymbol{f}$ of the dictionary type.}
    {The key of $\boldsymbol{f}$ is $l \in L$, and let the value be **false**.}
    $\boldsymbol{f}[l] \leftarrow$ **false**
  end for
  for each $l \in L$ **do**
    $before \leftarrow S_{attr}(\boldsymbol{f}, N_{attr}, N_{node})$
    $\boldsymbol{f}[l] \leftarrow$ **true** {Applying our approach to l.}
    $after \leftarrow S_{attr}(\boldsymbol{f}, N_{attr}, N_{node})$
    $traversal \leftarrow S_{trav}(\boldsymbol{f}, N_{trav}, N_{node})$
    if $before > after$ **and** $traversal = 0$ **then**
      continue
    else
      $\boldsymbol{f}[l] \leftarrow$ **false** {Not applying our approach to l.}
    end if
  end for
  return $\boldsymbol{f}$

Figure 6. Optimization algorithm for the proposed approach.

A. Optimization Algorithm for our Approach

The purpose of this approach is to reduce the memory consumed by the properties of the nodes to improve the efficiency of graph traversal. However, our previous approach [12] has been unable to improve the effectiveness of traversing the proposed trace because we had not considered the situation where the properties of each node are loaded into the main memory. As a result, the previous approach made additional traversals to analyze property-relationships. The traversal of property-relationships does not occur in the original structure of the trace; hence, we propose an algorithm to automatically determine the node needed for the approach in order to avoid creating properties over and above those that are required. If a minimum number of such properties can be loaded into the main memory, the effectiveness of the proposed approach will improve.

To automatically determine the node in this approach, the analytical algorithm of our dependency analysis environment needs to be recognized. That is to say, one needs to understand that the algorithm traverses nodes and loads their properties in the trace using our approach. In this case, our approach requires knowing the number of properties loaded from all nodes, with each node labeled as N_{trav}. At the same time, it also requires knowing the number of properties denoted by N_{attr}.

However, we cannot correctly estimate N_{trav} because the dependency analysis is dynamically executed depending on the value of the property in the trace. Hence, we assume that all nodes of the trace can be traversed, and the maximum number of loading properties of nodes is N_{trav}. In short, we decide to partition the properties of node into extra node when a loading property has the potential to obtain the property of node.

We developed an algorithm for the automatic application of our approach, as stated above. This algorithm is shown in Figure 6. Given a set of labels of nodes as L, every node is labelled $l \in L$ as $N_{node}(l)$ in Figure 6, and every property is labelled as N_{attr}. We also represent the frequency of the properties of loading nodes with label $m \in L$ when reaching label $l \in L$ of a node. Note that we take into account the identification of these labels ($l = m$).

We now introduce criteria for applying the proposed approach. S_{attr} is the sum of the number of loading properties while conducting dependency analysis, and S_{trav} is the sum of the number of traversing property-relationships. We can estimate these criteria using N_{node}, N_{attr} and N_{trav}, respectively. $S_{attr}(L)$ and $S_{trav}(L)$ can be calculated as Formula (2), Formula (3):

$$S_{attr}(L) = \sum_{l \in L} s_{attr}(l, \boldsymbol{f}[\boldsymbol{l}]) \quad (2)$$

$$\begin{aligned} &where: \\ &s_{attr}(l, \boldsymbol{f}[\boldsymbol{l}]) = \\ &\begin{cases} N_{attr}(l) \cdot N_{node}(l) & if\ \boldsymbol{f}[l] = false \\ 0 & otherwise \end{cases} \end{aligned}$$

$$S_{trav}(L) = \sum_{l \in L} s_{trav}(l, \boldsymbol{f}) \quad (3)$$

$$\begin{aligned} &where: \\ &s_{trav}(l, \boldsymbol{f}) = \\ &\begin{cases} \sum_{m \in L} N_{trav}(l, m) \cdot N_{node}(m) & if\ \boldsymbol{f}[m] = true \\ 0 & otherwise \end{cases} \end{aligned}$$

In Formula (2), $s_{attr}(l, \boldsymbol{f}[l])$ is calculated to multiply the number of loading properties of nodes labeled l by the number of nodes labeled l in GDB. In Formula (3), we also calculate $s_{trav}(l, \boldsymbol{f})$ to multiply the number of traversing property-relationships connected with nodes labeled m when reaching nodes labeled l. Note that the value of $s_{attr}(l, \boldsymbol{f}[l])$ is zero if the label l is applied because it does not obtain the traversal of a property-relationship.

Finally, our algorithm produces $\boldsymbol{f}$, which is a combination of whether the proposed approach is applied. This $\boldsymbol{f}$ allows for dependency analysis without traversing property-relationships and minimizes the sum of loading properties S_{attr}.

B. A Method for Reducing to Traverse Same Node

In a trace, there are many instructions, which refer to the same variables and objects. As described above, a trace have many-to-one relationships between instructions and object. For example, instructions 1 and 2 refer and use same object in Figure 7. Our dependency analysis environment traverses nodes and relationships one by one as we described in Section III-B. Thus, our environment loads the same node many times during dependency analysis when traversing many-to-one relationships. We have to solve this inefficiency of our environment as a way to keep loading nodes, which have many-to-one relationships when the node are loading to main memory in the first time.

In this paper, therefore, we solve the problem as described above by loading a pair of nodes, which have many-to-one relationship if traversed in the algorithm of dependency analysis. For example, our environment keep loading combination of instruction and object such as instruction 1 to object a, 2 to a, 3 to d, 4 to d, and 5 to d, to main memory in the case of Figure 7. However, if many-to-one relationships are not traversed in algorithm of dependency analysis, our environment does not load it to the main memory.

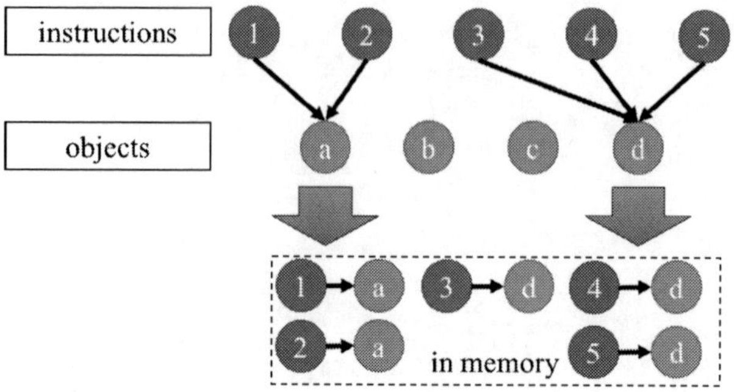

Figure 7. Target combinations of instruction and object in this approach

VII. Experimental Evaluations

As described in Section IV-B, we proposed an approach for solving the bottleneck in memory consumption in dependency analysis environments. In this section, we report an experiment to verify the effectiveness of our approach. For the assessment of macroscopic dependency analysis, not only is it necessary that memory consumption be evaluated, the time consumed for it is also a crucial factor to bear in mind. We assessed the improvement in analysis performance using the proposed approach by measuring the memory consumption and analysis time needed for dependency analysis.

We compared the experimental results with the following trace conditions:

- NON: a non-transformational trace
- ALL: a trace partitioned properties of each node in our trace using our previous approach as we described in Section IV
- OPT: a trace employed partitioning approach for a few nodes selected by the rule as we described in Section VI-A.

We conducted experimental evaluations on same machine in Section V.

A. Comparing our Approach with our Previous Approach

We conducted same experimental evaluation with NON, ALL, and OPT in Section VII-A.

As a result, our approach employed proposed rules in Section VI-A labeled OPT worsen the memory efficiency compared with naïve approach for partitioning property of all nodes labeled ALL as suspected. However, OPT enables to massively reduce 43.1% of memory consumption compared with original trace format as NON. The six p-values in Figure 8 indicated that OPT could reduce time consumption and memory consumption of dependency analysis compared with those of ALL; however, we could not find any difference in traversal times for dependency analysis. In short, OPT can conduct dependency analysis with the same efficiency

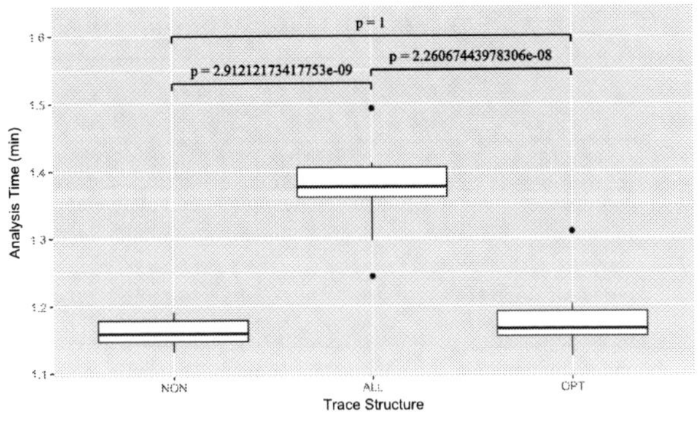

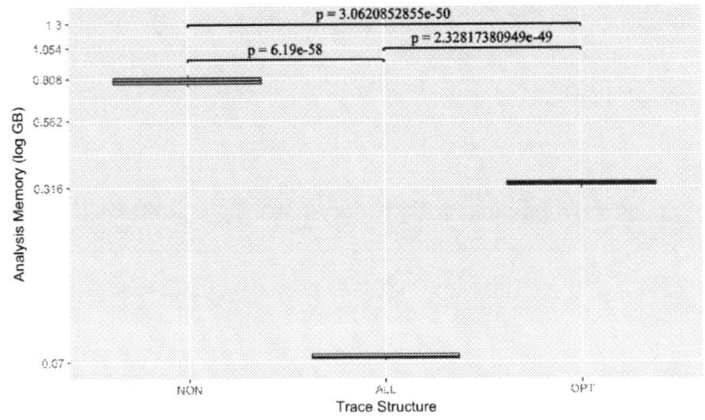

(b) Memory consumption.

Figure 8. Dependency analysis performance compared with NON, ALL, and OPT.

as NON but consumes less memory using Figure 6. On the other hand, ALL could not conduct dependency analysis with the same efficiency and memory consumption as NON and OPT. Therefore, it can be concluded that Figure 6 can help considerably to improve memory consumption for dependency analysis with the same efficiency as NON.

B. Evaluation for Scalability and Analysis Speed

In this experiment, we evaluate the scalability and analysis speed of our approach as described in Section VI. We prepare four programs of Ashes2 [22] as the following list:

- BiSort: a program to conduct Bitonic Sort [23]
- Em3d: an integrated software application designed to facilitate the analysis and visualization of electron microscope tomography data [24]
- MST: a program to find Minimum Spanning Tree
- TreeAdd: a program to recursively traverse a tree by depth-first

These programs enable us to set a few options for adjusting the amount of calculation. We set up options of each program as shown TABLE I in order to prepare traces in various data amount. In this experiment, we conduct dependency analysis with six situations; this is combination of three types trace format and two cases whether or not our approach is employed. We label six situations as "NON non-approach", "NON approach", "ALL non-approach", "ALL approach", "OPT non-approach", and "OPT approach". We conducted dependency

TABLE I. A LIST OF PROGRAMS IN ASHES2

program	options	data amount [MB]
BiSort	-s 0025	2.0
	-s 0100	12.0
	-s 0250	31.0
	-s 0400	68.0
	-s 0550	141.0
	-s 0700	150.0
	-s 0850	163.0
Em3d	-n 0050 -d 005	23.0
	-n 0100 -d 005	46.0
	-n 0150 -d 005	69.0
	-n 0200 -d 005	93.0
	-n 0250 -d 005	117.0
	-n 0300 -d 005	141.0
	-n 0350 -d 005	166.0
Mst	-v 0016	7.0
	-v 0024	15.0
	-v 0032	28.0
	-v 0040	44.0
	-v 0048	63.0
	-v 0064	113.0
TreeAdd	-l 05	0.3
	-l 10	7.6
	-l 11	16.0
	-l 12	33.0
	-l 13	69.0
	-l 14	142.0

analysis 20 times with these traces in TABLE I.

We show the result of this experiment TABLE II, TABLE III, and TABLE IV. TABLE II shows the averages of time consumption in the case of a trace formatted NON, TABLE III shows one in the case of a trace formatted ALL, and TABLE IV shows one in the case of a trace formatted OPT.

Moreover, we conducted a paired t-test with the result of experimental evaluation as shown TABLE II, TABLE III, and TABLE IV. We calculated a t-value by Formula (4):

$$t = \frac{\bar{d} - \mu}{\frac{s}{\sqrt{n}}} \tag{4}$$

where $\bar{d}$ denotes the mean of differences among two samples, μ denotes the population mean value, s denotes variance of d, and n denotes a sample size, in short, $n = 20$.

As a result, our approach labeled "OPT approach" enables reduce nine seconds on average compared with the situation labeled "NON non-approach". The sum of time consumptions in the situation labeled "OPT approach" was 4.3% lower than the situation labeled "NON non-approach". Moreover, the result of paired t-test shows there is significant difference of time consumption between "NON non-approach" and "OPT approach" as shown TABLE V. Furthermore, the situation labeled "OPT approach" has the best performance in all situations.

Then, we draw two line graphs as shown Figure 9(a) and Figure 9(b). Figure 9(a) shows the result in the situation labeled "NON non-approach", and Figure 9(b) shows the result in the situation labeled "OPT approach". As shown Figure 9(a) and Figure 9(b), we can reduce the time consumed for processing dependency analysis. However, in every situation, there is big difference of the time consumption for processing of dependency analysis even if there is a the difference in the trace.

TABLE II. THE AVERAGE OF ANALYSIS TIME WITH NON

trace	NON non-approach mean (± SD) [msec.]	NON approach mean (± SD) [msec.]
bisort-s0025	0.17 (± 0.03)	0.17 (± 0.03)
bisort-s0250	0.96 (±0.04)	0.93 (± 0.03)
bisort-s0550	3.85 (±0.12)	3.81 (± 0.09)
bisort-s0700	4.03 (±0.12)	3.93 (± 0.11)
bisort-s0850	4.15 (± 0.09)	4.02 (± 0.10)
em3d-n0050d005	0.96 (± 0.03)	0.93 (± 0.04)
em3d-n0100d005	2.17 (± 0.16)	2.05 (± 0.13)
em3d-n0150d005	3.78 (± 0.34)	3.69 (± 0.22)
em3d-n0200d005	6.39 (± 0.55)	5.99 (± 0.47)
em3d-n0250d005	9.59 (± 0.40)	9.22 (± 0.45)
em3d-n0300d005	12.46 (± 0.67)	12.44 (± 0.61)
em3d-n0350d005	16.72 (± 0.59)	16.74 (± 0.80)
mst-v0016	0.48 (± 0.02)	0.45 (± 0.05)
mst-v0024	0.86 (± 0.03)	0.85 (± 0.03)
mst-v0032	1.59 (± 0.09)	1.51 (± 0.05)
mst-v0040	2.65 (± 0.08)	2.56 (± 0.12)
mst-v0048	4.21 (± 0.09)	4.04 (± 0.09)
mst-v0064	9.80 (± 0.37)	9.89 (± 0.26)
treeadd-l05	0.12 (± 0.01)	0.11 (± 0.01)
treeadd-l10	0.47 (± 0.03)	0.39 (± 0.04)
treeadd-l11	0.70 (± 0.02)	0.68 (± 0.03)
treeadd-l12	1.14 (± 0.03)	1.14 (± 0.06)
treeadd-l13	2.14 (± 0.08)	2.15 (± 0.09)
treeadd-l14	4.33 (± 0.21)	4.27 (± 0.12)

SD: standard deviation

TABLE III. THE RESULT OF ANALYSIS TIME WITH ALL

trace	ALL non-approach mean (± SD) [msec.]	ALL approach mean (± SD) [msec.]
bisort-s0025	0.08 (± 0.01)	0.09 (± 0.01)
bisort-s0250	0.97 (± 0.03)	0.95 (± 0.05)
bisort-s0550	4.11 (± 0.17)	4.10 (± 0.10)
bisort-s0700	4.51 (± 0.17)	4.37 (± 0.15)
bisort-s0850	4.69 (± 0.14)	4.68 (± 0.23)
em3d-n0050d005	0.90 (± 0.06)	0.99 (± 0.05)
em3d-n0100d005	2.19 (± 0.13)	2.18 (± 0.15)
em3d-n0150d005	3.90 (± 0.23)	3.84 (± 0.24)
em3d-n0200d005	6.73 (± 0.63)	6.56 (± 0.47)
em3d-n0250d005	9.71 (± 0.60)	9.73 (± 0.52)
em3d-n0300d005	13.41 (± 0.63)	12.91 (± 0.68)
em3d-n0350d005	17.49 (± 0.71)	16.69 (± 0.95)
mst-v0016	0.32 (± 0.01)	0.32 (± 0.01)
mst-v0024	0.76 (± 0.04)	0.74 (± 0.04)
mst-v0032	1.59 (± 0.07)	1.56 (± 0.05)
mst-v0040	2.84 (± 0.14)	2.78 (± 0.17)
mst-v0048	4.53 (± 0.15)	4.39 (± 0.13)
mst-v0064	10.39 (± 0.22)	10.37 (± 0.22)
treeadd-l05	0.02 (± 0.00)	0.02 (± 0.00)
treeadd-l10	0.30 (± 0.01)	0.30 (± 0.02)
treeadd-l11	0.63 (± 0.04)	0.62 (± 0.04)
treeadd-l12	1.23 (± 0.06)	1.17 (± 0.05)
treeadd-l13	2.33 (± 0.09)	2.30 (± 0.08)
treeadd-l14	4.87 (± 0.09)	4.80 (± 0.13)

VIII. CONSIDERATION

In this section, we consider the performance and the scalability of our approach. Our approach labeled "OPT approach" is the best performance in six situations from the aspect of the memory consumption and the time consumption for processing dependency analysis. Our approach in Section VI-A avoids loading properties of the accessed node, leading to reduced memory consumption for processing dependency analysis. However, we cannot reduce time consumption for processing dependency analysis because it is less time-consuming to access a property of node. On the other hand, our expanded approach as described in Section VI-B enables to reduce the time consumption for processing dependency analysis. The

TABLE IV. THE RESULT OF ANALYSIS TIME WITH OPT

trace	OPT non-approach mean (± SD) [msec.]	OPT approach mean (± SD) [msec.]
bisort-s0025	0.07 (± 0.00)	0.07 (± 0.01)
bisort-s0250	0.79 (± 0.05)	0.76 (± 0.05)
bisort-s0550	3.88 (± 0.12)	3.81 (± 0.12)
bisort-s0700	4.14 (± 0.13)	3.90 (± 0.18)
bisort-s0850	4.14 (± 0.13)	4.09 (± 0.17)
em3d-n0050d005	0.73 (± 0.06)	0.71 (± 0.06)
em3d-n0100d005	2.06 (± 0.16)	2.02 (± 0.15)
em3d-n0150d005	3.86 (± 0.25)	3.63 (± 0.33)
em3d-n0200d005	6.18 (± 0.51)	6.11 (± 0.45)
em3d-n0250d005	9.85 (± 0.53)	9.48 (± 0.54)
em3d-n0300d005	12.38 (± 0.90)	12.40 (± 0.90)
em3d-n0350d005	16.49 (± 0.81)	16.19 (± 0.64)
mst-v0016	0.29 (± 0.01)	0.28 (± 0.01)
mst-v0024	0.65 (± 0.04)	0.63 (± 0.03)
mst-v0032	1.36 (± 0.05)	1.32 (± 0.05)
mst-v0040	2.52 (± 0.07)	2.53 (± 0.09)
mst-v0048	4.09 (± 0.10)	4.09 (± 0.22)
mst-v0064	9.79 (± 0.22)	9.72 (± 0.23)
treeadd-l05	0.02 (± 0.00)	0.02 (± 0.00)
treeadd-l10	0.27 (± 0.02)	0.26 (± 0.01)
treeadd-l11	0.50 (± 0.01)	0.49 (± 0.03)
treeadd-l12	0.99 (± 0.03)	0.95 (± 0.04)
treeadd-l13	2.11 (± 0.07)	2.09 (± 0.10)
treeadd-l14	4.47 (± 0.10)	4.37 (± 0.09)

TABLE V. THE MEAN OF DIFFERENCE CALCULATED BY PAIRED T-TEST [SEC.]

	2)	3)	4)	5)	6)
1) NON non-approach	** 4.41	** -11.33	* 5.66	-0.74	** 9.55
2) NON approach	–	** -15.73	-5.15	1.25	** 5.14
3) ALL non-approach	–	–	* 10.59	** 16.99	** 20.88
4) ALL approach	–	–	–	6.40	10.29
5) OPT non-approach	–	–	–	–	** 3.89
6) OPT approach	–	–	–	–	–

*: five percent level of significance
**: one percent level of significance

reason is that accessing to main memory is more efficient than accessing to GDB after all.

However, our approach was better but by no means great. Our approach enabled to improve the efficiency of graph traverse, but our approach did not reduce the number of graph traversal during dependency analysis. Moreover, our approach did not account for the difference of characteristic of program. Therefore, it led to a major difference in time consumed even if traces are same amount as described in Section . In order to close the difference among different traces, we have to take in to account the structure of programs.

IX. CONCLUSION

In this paper, we developed a prototype dependency analysis environment for efficient dependency analysis of large traces using complex graph structures. Our analysis environment is built on a graph database system that can efficiently traverse large and complex graph data. For efficient dependency analysis, moreover, we proposed trace partitioning based on the graph structure, and introduced a policy to restrict the number of loading operations on a node's properties to the main memory in order to improve the effect of our approach.

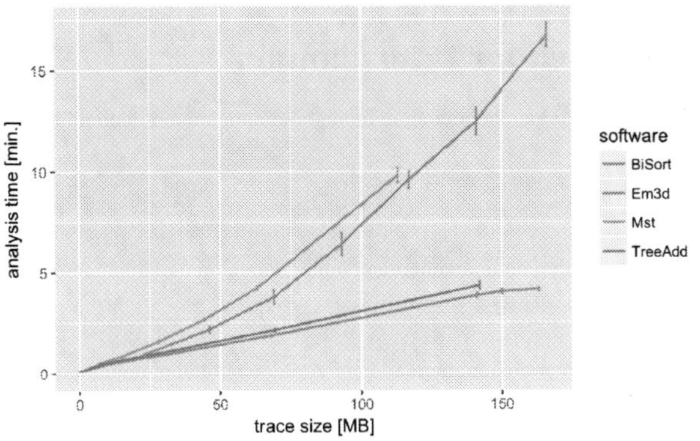

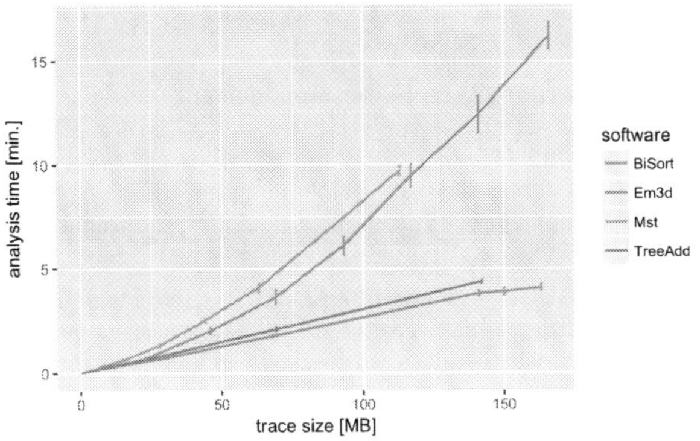

(b) Our approach with trace formatted OPT

Figure 9. Dependency analysis performance.

Furthermore, we proposed an approach to reduce loading the same node to main memory during dependency analysis.

In an experimental evaluation, our approach performed best in all situations. Our approach reduced time consumption 4.3% for processing dependency analysis compared to techniques not employing our approach.

In future work, we will account for the difference of program characteristics such as the number of each type of instruction, the number of each type of objects, and programming patterns.

Acknowledgment

This work was partially supported by a MEXT-Supported Program for the Strategic Research Foundation at Private Universities (#S1411030), JSPS KAKENHI [Grant-in-Aid for Challenging Exploratory Research (#15K12009), and Scientific Research (B) (#26280115)], the Artificial Intelligence Research Promotion Foundation, and the Kayamori Foundation of Informational Science Advancement.

References

[1] K. Kusu, I. Kume, and K. Hatano, "A node access frequency based graph partitioning technique for efficient dynamic dependency analysis," in Proceedings of The Ninth International Conferences on Advances in Multimedia, 2017, pp. 73 – 78.

[2] A. Zeller, Why Programs Fail, Second Edition: A Guide to Systematic Debugging. Morgan Kaufmann, 2009.

[3] M. Weiser, "Program slicing," in International Conference on Software Engineering. IEEE, 1981, pp. 439–449.

[4] J. Ressia, A. Bergel, and O. Nierstrasz, "Object-centric debugging," in International Conference on Software Engineering. IEEE, 2012, pp. 485–495.

[5] B. Lewis, "Debugging backwards in time," in Proceedings of the Fifth International Workshop on Automated Debugging, 2003, pp. 225–235.

[6] A. J. Ko and B. A. Myers, "Designing the whyline: a debugging interface for asking questions about program behavior," in SIGCHI Conference on Human Factors in Computing Systems. ACM, 2004, pp. 151–158.

[7] A. Lienhard, T. Gîrba, and O. Nierstrasz, Practical Object-Oriented Back-in-Time Debugging. Berlin, Heidelberg: Springer Berlin Heidelberg, 2008, pp. 592–615.

[8] I. Kume, M. Nakamura, N. Nitta, and E. Shibayama, "A Case Study of Dynamic Analysis to Locate Unexpected Side Effects Inside of Frameworks," International Journal of Software Innovation, vol. 3, no. 3, 2015, pp. 26–40.

[9] "gefdemo project," http://gefdemo.tigris.org/, [retrieved: 1 Mar. 2017].

[10] T. Wang and A. Roychoudhury, "Using compressed bytecode traces for slicing java programs," in International Conference on Software Engineering. IEEE, 2004, pp. 512–521.

[11] J. Hogg, "Islands: Aliasing protection in object-oriented languages," in OOPSLA, 1991, pp. 271–285.

[12] ——, "A trace partitioning approach for efficient trace analysis," in Proceedings of the 4th International Conference on Applied Computing & Information Technology, 2016 4th Intl Conf on Applied Computing and Information Technology / 3rd Intl Conf on Computational Science/Intelligence and Applied Informatics / 1st Intl Conf on Big Data, Cloud Computing, Data Science & Engineering, 2016, pp. 133 – 140.

[13] A. Lienhard, Dynamic Object Flow Analysis. Lulu.com, 2008.

[14] A. Lienhard, T. Gîrba, O. Greevy, and O. Nierstrasz, "Exposing side effects in execution traces," in International Workshop on Program Comprehension through Dynamic Analysis, 2007, pp. 11–17.

[15] D. J. Agans, Debugging: the 9 Indispensable Rules for Finding Even the Most Elusive Software and Hardware Problems. AMACOM, 2002.

[16] "The property graph model," http://github.com/tinkerpop/blueprints/wiki/Property-Graph-Model, [retrieved: March 2017].

[17] "Graph database neo4j," http://neo4j.com/, [retrieved: 1 Mar. 2017].

[18] V. Kolomičenko, M. Svoboda, and I. H. Mlýnková, "Experimental comparison of graph databases," in Proceedings of International Conference on Information Integration and Web-based Applications & Services, ser. IIWAS '13. ACM, 2013, pp. 115:115–115:124.

[19] S. Jouili and V. Vansteenberghe, "An empirical comparison of graph databases," in Proceedings of the 2013 International Conference on Social Computing, ser. SOCIALCOM '13. IEEE Computer Society, 2013, pp. 708–715.

[20] I. Robinson, J. Webber, and E. Eifrem, Graph Databases. O'Reilly Media, Inc., 2015.

[21] S. Raj, Neo4J High Performance. Packt Publishing, 2015.

[22] "Benchmark programs named ashes2," http://www.sable.mcgill.ca/~bdufou1/ashes2/, [retrieved: September 2017].

[23] K. E. Batcher, "Sorting networks and their applications," in Proceedings of the April 30–May 2, 1968, Spring Joint Computer Conference, ser. AFIPS'68. ACM, 1968, pp. 307–314.

[24] "Em3d," http://em3d.stanford.edu/about.html, [retrieved: September 2017].

A Low-Cost and Low-Latency Approach for Inter-domain Mobility Management

Nivia Cruz Quental and Paulo André da Silva Gonçalves
Department of Computer Science, Centro de Informática (CIn)
Universidade Federal de Pernambuco (UFPE)
Recife, Brazil
Email: ncq@cin.ufpe.br, pasg@cin.ufpe.br

Abstract—**Providing an inter-domain handover solution for PMIPv6 that achieves a low signaling overhead and a low handover latency remains a major challenge. In this paper, we respond to this challenge by proposing the Clustered Inter-domain PMIPv6 (CI-PMIPv6). CI-PMIPv6 takes advantage of the following: the use of Peer-to-Peer (P2P) techniques; the use of a clustering technique; and the execution of inter-domain handover-related operations in parallel with the execution of intra-domain handover-related operations. By doing so, CI-PMIPv6 allows the fast spread of Mobile Node (MN) information among Local Mobility Anchors (LMAs) from different domains during intra-domain handovers, thereby avoiding the need for extra signaling to request and obtain such information during inter-domain handovers. CI-PMIPv6 boosts the performance of inter-domain handovers. We support this statement by providing a comparative study of the performance of CI-PMIPv6 and related work. Additionally, we apply the design concepts of CI-PMIPv6 to Fast handovers for Proxy Mobile IPv6 (FPMIPv6). This results in a new proposed protocol, namely CI-FPMIPv6 (Clustered Inter-domain FPMIPv6), which also achieves a notable performance.**

Keywords–CI-PMIPv6; CI-FPMIPv6; P2P; Mobility; Inter-domain.

I. INTRODUCTION

The Proxy Mobile Internet Protocol version 6 (PMIPv6) is an IETF standard for network-based mobility management. PMIPv6 is mainly designed to overcome issues encountered in Mobile IPv6 (MIPv6) related to energy consumption of the Mobile Node (MN) and the latency incurred in intra-domain handovers. PMIPv6 introduces two types of network entities: the Mobile Access Gateway (MAG), which tracks the current location of the MN; and the Local Mobility Anchor (LMA), which plays a similar role as the MIP's Home Agent in a local domain. Signaling between MAG and LMA is responsible for updating the binding of the MN. A downside of PMIPv6 is that it has no support for inter-domain mobility. This occurs because it relies on a non-mobile entity to keep track of the MN.

There have been many contributions to the problem of giving inter-domain mobility support to PMIPv6 (e.g., [1],[2],[3],[4],[5]). Recently, the Clustered Inter-domain PMIPv6 (CI-PMIPv6) [1] has emerged as a low cost and a low latency intra- and inter-domain handover solution. CI-PMIPv6 makes an inter-domain handover possible because it spreads information on MNs among LMAs from different domains. However, the information spreading is anticipated and happens during intra-domain handovers. In this manner, this information will be rapidly available to those LMAs in subsequent inter-domain handovers. This, in turn, greatly saves inter-domain handover costs and latency. The main characteristics of CI-PMIPv6 are:

- **Distributed mobility management** - LMAs from each domain form a cluster, which is a Kademlia-based DHT [6] so as to spread information efficiently; this avoids the use of global entities and, thus, avoids creating single points of failure and performance bottlenecks;
- **Network-based handover** - CI-PMIPv6 maintains the PMIPv6 advantage of reducing MNs' consumption of energy by avoiding host-based handover signaling and processing overheads;
- **Reuse of existing PMIPv6 entities to exchange inter-domain information** - the compatibility with PMIPv6 legacy systems is achieved; no new entity needs to be added to the system;
- **Anticipation of MN information for future handovers** - during the MN's ongoing handover, its current LMA proactively spreads the MN information to neighbor LMAs in the cluster; this information is needed for future inter-domain handovers and is rapidly available to neighbor LMAs, thereby avoiding wasting time during such handovers due to the extra signaling needed to request and obtain such information.

Previous research in inter-domain support for PMIPv6 focuses on different strategies. Joe *et al.* [2] propose modifying the MAG function at the boundary region between two domains to reduce inter-domain signaling overhead. In the proposal of Neumann *et al.* [3], the LMA continues to manage the MN until the end of the session, even if the MN visits a new domain and relies on a centralized entity to keep track of the location of the MN. Zhong *et al.* [4] propose a solution that relies on a centralized entity to store and update the information of the MNs while they visit other domains. Park *et al.* [5] present a scheme that forwards all PMIPv6 signaling messages from a LMA in the local domain to an LMA in another domain in order to accomplish inter-domain handover. These proposals exhibit one or more issues such as: a high cost of signaling; the lacking of inter-working capability with legacy systems; high handover latency; and the use of centralized entities. CI-PMIPv6 is designed to add inter-domain handover capability to PMIPv6 and overcome these issues.

This paper is an extended version of the study presented in [1]. We present the CI-PMIPv6 protocol in a more detailed fashion. In particular, our motivation for using a Kademlia-based protocol for cluster management is discussed and a more detailed description of the cluster behavior is provided. We also apply the concepts of CI-PMIPv6 to Fast handover for Proxy Mobile IPv6 (FPMIPv6). This allows us to introduce a new protocol, namely Clustered Inter-domain FPMIPv6 (CI-FPMIPv6). We also improve the study presented in [1] to include a performance evaluation of CI-FPMIPv6. The remainder of this paper is organized as follows: Section II presents the PMIPv6 protocol and some of its most known extensions. Section III presents the state of the art on inter-domain mobility in PMIPv6-based networks. Section IV presents in detail the CI-PMIPv6 and CI-FPMIPv6. Section V presents a theoretical comparison among CI-PMIPv6, CI-FPMIPv6 and other solutions found in the literature. Section VI compares the performance of both CI-PMIPv6 and CI-FPMIPv6 with that of other proposals. Section VII presents the conclusions of this paper. Future research is presented in Section VIII.

II. *Proxy Mobile* IPv6 (PMIPv6) AND EXTENSIONS

One of the main challenges in IP mobility management is to achieve seamless and low-latency inter-domain handover. Mobile IP (MIP) is the best-known IP mobility standard ever released by IETF, in which an MN maintains its original IP address while it moves beyond its *Home Network*. MIP has versions for IPv4 and IPv6. Since MIP assumes that MNs must have the MIP protocol implemented in their operational systems and communicate with the *Home Network* whenever a handover occurs, high energy consumption and high latency are noteworthy issues.

PMIPv6 is mainly conceived by IETF in order to surmount these issues. PMIPv6 introduces two local entities: a MAG and an LMA. Signaling exchanged between the MAG and the LMA is responsible for the binding update of the MN. Thus, the LMAs and MAGs from the corresponding domain are responsible for mobility management instead of the MNs. Figure 1 presents the PMIPv6 architecture. The MAG tracks the current MN location. The LMA is responsible for the binding updates and assigns IP prefixes to the MNs in its domain.

Figure 2 presents the signaling flow for a PMIPv6 handover. When the MN moves away from an area managed by a previous MAG (PMAG) and enters an area managed by a new MAG (NMAG), a handover in the IP layer takes place. The MN sends the `Rtr Sol` message, which comes from the Internet Control Message Protocol (ICMP), to ask the closest NMAG for a route to the external network. The NMAG sends a *Proxy Binding Update* (`PBU`) message to its LMA that sends the *Proxy Binding Acknowledgment* `PBA` message to the PMAG. Finally, the NMAG announce a new route sending the ICMP message `Rtr Adv` to the MN.

The *Fast handovers for Proxy Mobile IPv6* (FPMIPv6) [7] protocol is an extension for PMIPv6 that aims to reduce packet loss. It adds a buffering scheme and a tunnel set up between the PMAG and the NMAG while signaling is exchanged. FPMIPv6 can operate in two modes: reactive or predictive. Figure 3 presents the reactive mode. After the MN enters in the new network, the NMAG and the PMAG send, respectively, the `HI` (*Handover Indication*) and `HACK` (*Handover Acknowledgment*) messages to set up a tunnel. The packets stored in the NMAG's buffer must be forwarded to the MN when the handover is complete. Then, the NMAG and the LMA exchange the `PBU` and `PBA` messages as in PMIPv6.

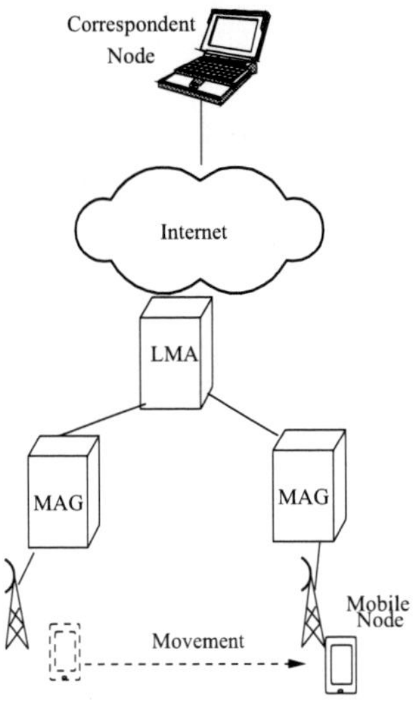

Figure 1. Architecture of PMIPv6.

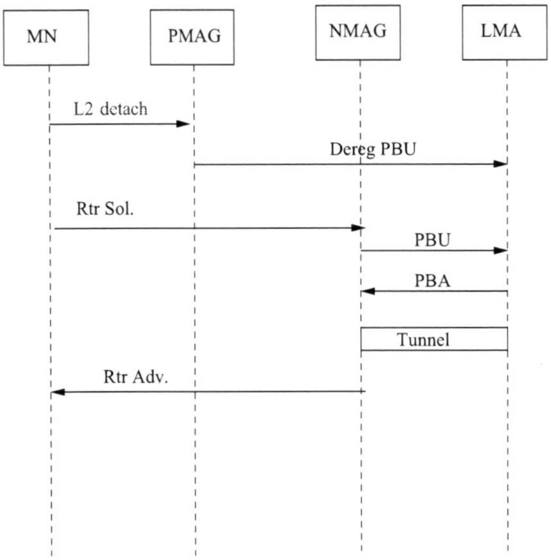

Figure 2. Signaling flow for PMIPv6.

In the predictive mode of the FPMIPv6, the tunnel between the PMAG and the NMAG is set up before the MN enters the new network as depicted in Figure 4. In that case, the PMAG sends the `HI` message to initiate a tunnel set up. Then, the NMAG responds with the `HACK` message. The PMAG can locate the chosen NMAG using a table that maps the address of Points of Attachment (PoA) - provided by the MN - to the corresponding MAG. The rest of the signaling is similar to that of the PMIPv6.

According to the RFC 5949 [7], the FPMIPv6 is designed to minimize packet loss during handover in comparison to PMIPv6. However, because of the increase of the signaling

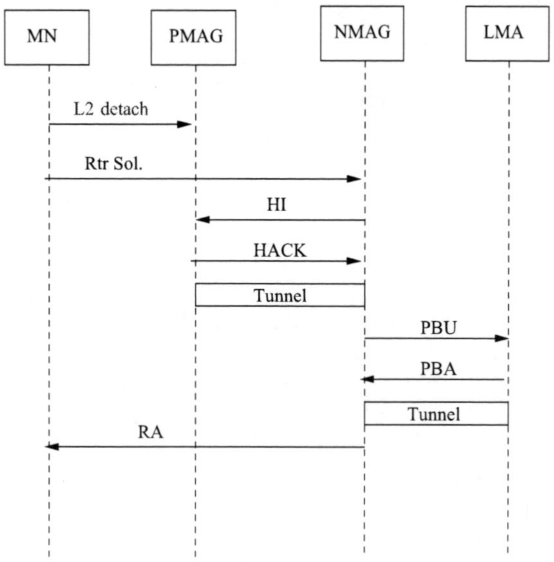

Figure 3. Signaling flow for the FPMIPv6 in the reactive mode.

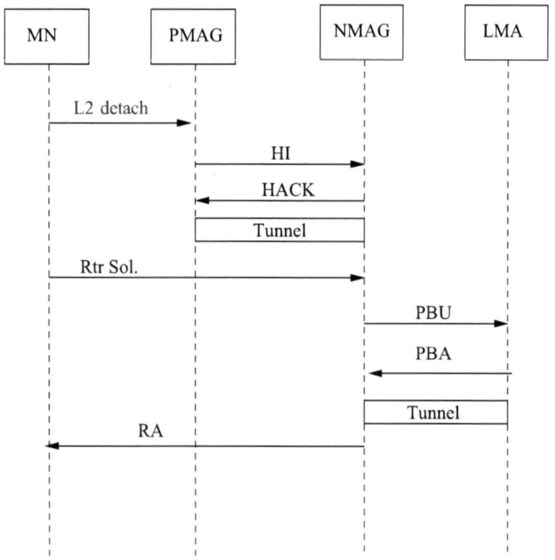

Figure 4. Signaling flow for the FPMIPv6 in the predictive mode.

overhead, the handover latency may become greater. The main advantage of the reactive mode is that it is not necessary to get the PoA information, since the handover in the link layer has already happened. On the other hand, the predictive mode can lead to a lower packet loss.

III. State of the Art on Inter-domain Mobility

A wireless domain can be defined as the logical representation of a wireless access network [8]. It is related to a coverage area where the same company controls the authentication and reliability of the network entities. Unlike MIPv6, PMIPv6 and its extensions do not have knowledge about other networks outside their domains, as a MIP's Home Agent would. The MIP's Home Agent can access other domains thanks to the MN, which informs about its new location to its home network. In PMIPv6 the MN does not have this responsibility, thus, it is not possible to keep track of the node outside its domain. Providing inter-domain mobility for PMIPv6-based systems has been the object of ongoing research. In the following sections, the main approaches for inter-domain mobility are presented.

A. Decentralized approach

Park *et al.* [5] present a scheme where the LMA from a domain forwards the handover signaling to the LMA in another domain to achieve inter-domain handover. There are neither protocol modifications nor additional entities. Figure 5 shows the signaling flow. The MN is responsible for requesting the authentication. Each domain has its own Authentication, Authorization, and Account (AAA) service. There must be an extra tunnel between those LMAs. The signaling messages of PMIPv6 are replicated in communication with PLMA, NLMA, and AAA serves, which increases signaling cost. Additionally, the extra header in IP-in-IP tunneling increases the packet delivery overhead.

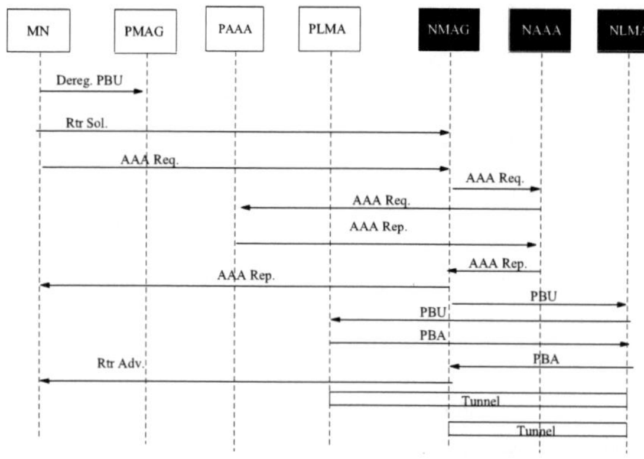

Figure 5. Inter-domain handover in the decentralized approach.

Simulations with QualNET [9] evaluate packet loss and latency in comparison with those of a scheme in which PMIPv6/MIPv6 inter-works. The authors state that the proposal is better suited for scenarios where handover is frequent.

B. LMA as session anchor

In I-PMIP [3], the original LMA keeps managing the node until the end of the session and exchanges signaling with the MAG in the new domain during inter-domain handover. That LMA is called the Session Mobility Anchor (SMA). It is assumed that LMAs from different domains already know each other and are physically close to each other. To locate the MAG in the new domain, the original LMA relies on a centralized entity called the Virtual Mobility Anchor (VMA), which undertakes location updates whenever a handover takes place. Hence, that solution faces a single point of failure issue. The authors state that I-PMIP sees to it that the policies of different domains remain transparent since there is no direct connection between MAGs from different domains.

Figure 6 presents the signaling flow for I-PMIP. When a MN moves to a new domain, the NMAG detects its presence and sends a PBU message to the new LMA. Then, the new LMA forwards the request to the VMA, which is updated whenever a MN moves to a new domain. The SMA forwards the data to the new LMA, which creates a tunnel to the new MAG.

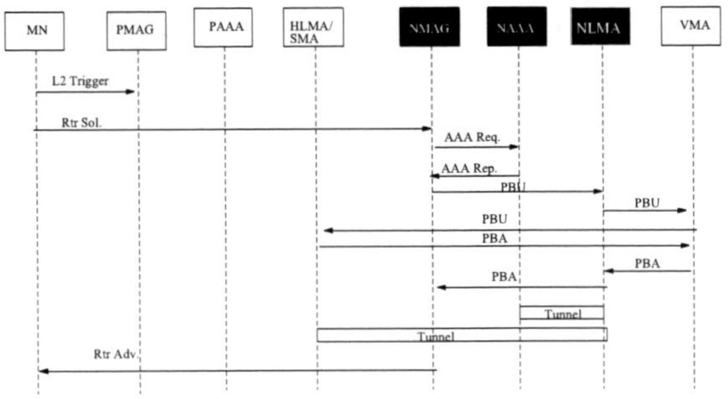

Figure 6. Inter-domain handover in I-PMIP.

The authors evaluate the performance of I-PMIP through a theoretical analysis that compares the latency of I-PMIP with that of MIP, PMIP and a hierarchical approach that uses MIP. According to [3], I-PMIP has proven to be more efficient in the scenarios studied. In addition, the authors state that I-PMIP has lower handover latency. However, we should take into consideration that the VMA introduces a single point of failure and an additional tunnel increases the packet delivery overhead. Nyguyen and Bonnet propose a similar solution in [10] focusing on routing optimizations.

C. Centralized entity

Zhong *et al.* propose the Enabling Inter PMIPv6 Domain Handover (EIPMH) [4]. The authors introduce the Traffic Distributor (TD), which is an entity that redirects data to the LMA while the MN is out of the original domain. The TDs are statically configured and have knowledge about other TDs, their IP prefixes, and mapping to the LMAs. In that proposal, the TD is responsible for assigning prefixes to its MNs instead of the LMA. The NLMA must send a query PBU_Forwarding to the PLMA to find additional information about the MN and the TD responsible for communicating with the Internet. The TD also creates a tunnel to the NLMA. Also, there are tunnels between LMAs and between the NLMA and the MAG. The authors acknowledge that there may be more than one distributor, each of which is responsible for a coverage area. Nevertheless, the handover between distributors is not covered by the authors.

Figure 7 presents the signaling flow for EIPMH. After the NMAG registers the MN using the PBU message, the NLMA queries the previous LMA using a PBU_Forwading message in order to get additional information about the MN and the TD that connects the network to the Internet. The PLMA replies with a PBA message. Then, the NLMA forwards the received MN information to the NMAG. A tunnel is set up between the TD and the NLMA. Another tunnel is set up between the PLMA and the NLMA.

The NS-2 simulation tool is used to evaluate performance. Latency and throughput are compared to those of I-PMIP.

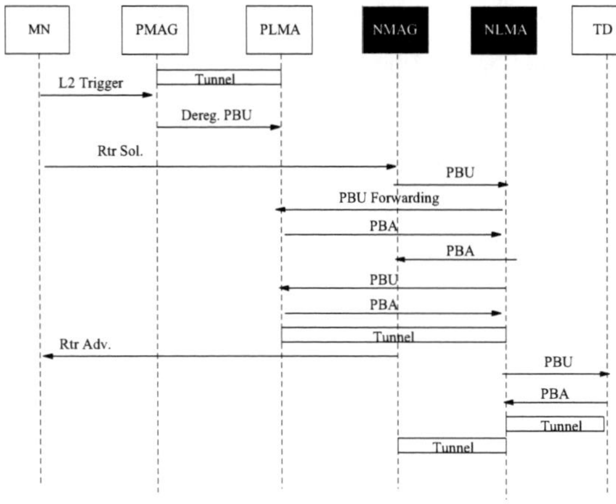

Figure 7. Inter-domain hanover in the EIMHP scheme.

However, the evaluation does not consider the extra overhead derived from the tunnel between the TD and the NLMA. The process of finding the PLMA, the lookup for the NLMA, and the change of MAGs are not considered.

Since EIPMH introduces two extra tunnels to the PMIPv6, it is expected an increase in the packet delivery overhead. A similar proposal can be found in [11], in which the solution is called GPMIP.

D. MAG Specialization

Joe *et al.* [2] present an inter-domain approach based on an architecture that considers special types of MAG: the Boundary and Overlapping MAG (BMAG and OMAG, respectively). The BMAG is associated with only one LMA, while the OMAG is associated with more than one domain. Both are found in regions where a domain ends and another domain begins. Also, only one authentication entity for all domains is considered. The presence of a gateway guarantees maintenance of the IP address. The authors propose two solutions: Reactive and No-Gap. In the Reactive solution, a path is created between CN and PLMA and NLMA. The BMAG discovers a NLMA by geographically locating it. The authors do not specify how the lookup is done. The functionality of the BMAG is shared with edge routers. A tunnel must be created between the gateway and the NLMA, between LMAs, and between the PLMA and the NMAG. In the No-Gap approach, the OMAG has information from both domains and creates two simultaneous paths as the MN enters its area. Thus, the MN receives redundant information from both LMAs. Besides the PMIPv6 messages, extra signaling is exchanged between the NLMA and the gateway to confirm and obtain additional information about the MN. Additionally, the NLMA must authenticate the MN. A tunnel must be created between the gateway and the NLMA, and between the NLMA and the OMAG. The No-Gap approach requires changes in legacy border routers and generates redundant data packets in the same MAG, coming from different LMAs.

Figure 8 presents the signaling flow for the *no-gap* approach. Beside the traditional PMIPv6 signaling, the messages FBD and FBDA are exchanged between the NLMA and the gateway to request and retrieve additional information about the MN. Additionally, the NLMA is responsible for requesting the authentication on behalf of the MN. A tunnel between the gateway and the NLMA is set up in addition to the tunnel between the NLMA and the OMAG. It is worth to notice that the same OMAG is shared by both the previous and the new domains.

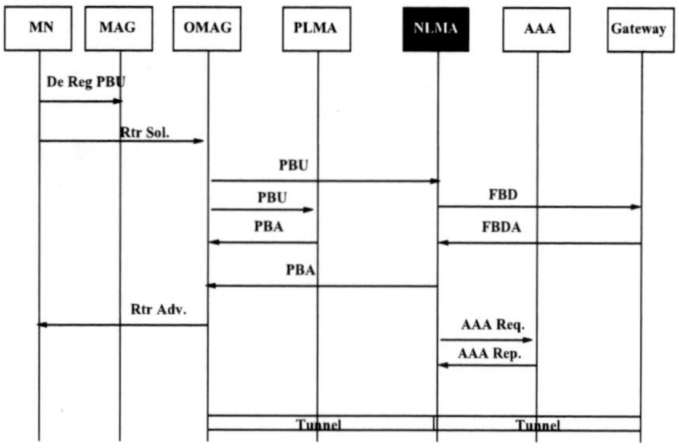

Figure 8. Inter-domain handover in the No-Gap scheme.

The evaluation of the performance compares the solution with MIPv6, Fast Handovers for MIPv6, I.PMIPv6, and EIPMH by measuring handover latency. What may well be noticed is that the Reactive mode leads to greater overheads because of an additional tunnel in comparison to the No-Gap model. According to the authors, the No-Gap model is the most efficient model. This is why this paper gives more focus to the No-Gap solution, which has a counterpart in [12].

IV. CI-PMIPv6 Overview

The architecture of CI-PIMIPv6 is depicted in Figure 9. This architecture makes the communication among LMAs from different domains possible. CI-PMIPv6 organizes LMAs in a structure called *cluster*, which is a P2P network. The data structures shared in the cluster represent the up-to-date information of the MNs. This allows LMAs to know the previous location of the MNs before the next handover takes place. This is possible since the cluster is updated at the moment of the MN registration and the execution of intra and inter-domain handovers.

The P2P protocol, which is used for the communication among LMAs, is Kademlia [13]. In the following sections, the Kademlia standard, the *cluster* management, and the main signaling flows of CI-PMIPv6 are described in detail.

A. Kademlia

Kademlia is a fault-tolerant Distributed Hash Table (DHT) with a logarithmic performance in lookup procedures. DHTs are the latest generation of P2P networks, in which resources are available through a relation between <key,value> pairs and the peers where they are stored. In a DHT, each peer has a unique identifier, namely *nodeID*. The resources are stored in the peers whose *nodeIDs* have a mapping function to their corresponding keys. Among the most widely known DHTs [14] [15] [16] [17], Kademlia [13] distinguishes itself because of its arrival/departure process of peers, and its performance in the access of keys, values, and routing table entries. A <key,value> pair is stored in peers whose *nodeID* is the

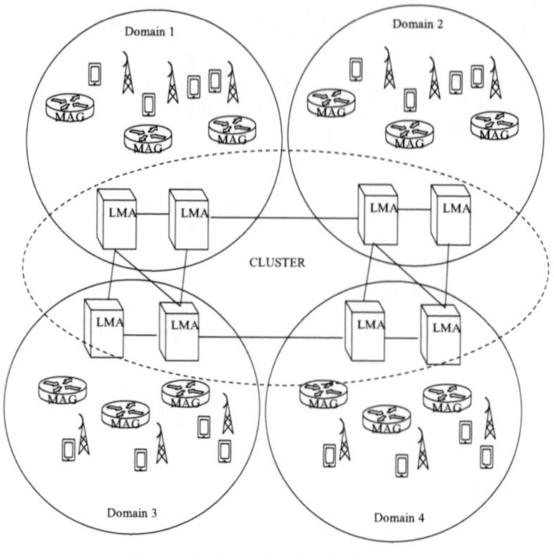

Figure 9. Domains in CI-PMIPv6.

TABLE I. Example of a routing table for the peer "110" using 3 k-buckets.

Peers dist. 1(2^0) to 2 (2^1)	[(IP, port,"111")]
Peers dist. (2^1) to (2^2)	[(IP, port,"100"),(IP, port,"101")]
Peers dist. (2^2) to (2^3)	[(IP, port,"000"), (IP, port,"001"), (IP, port,"010")]

closest to that key. The XOR operation is used for distance measurement between a key and a *nodeID*. The use of XOR simplifies the formal analysis due to its simple arithmetic. Figure 10 shows an example of a Kademlia-based network. In this example, the distance between the peers "110" and "100" is 2 ("10" in binary), which is the result of the XOR operation between their *nodeIDs*. Thus, for a given key, it is possible to find in the Kademlia routing table which peer has that particular key and its corresponding value by checking the peers with the smallest "distance". By default, keys and *nodeIDs* are in the 160-bit space. When a peer enters a Kademlia network, its *nodeID* is generated. Each peer has its own routing table with a set of 160 *k-buckets* (the same value of the key/*nodeID* size in bits), where k is a parameter that represents the maximum size of what is considered a "neighborhood". Depending on the distributions of the *nodeIDs* in the network, a *k-bucket* may never be entirely filled. Table I shows an example of a routing table in Kademlia. For simplification purposes, a 3-bit space is considered. The peer "011" does not appear in the table because it is not in the network at the moment. Each entry in a *bucket* is a <IP address, UDP port, *nodeID*> tuple. As new peers enter the Kademlia network, they are added to the respective *buckets*. A peer is added to the *bucket* i of another peer if the distance between them is between 2^i and 2^{i+1}, where $0 < i < \#buckets$.

Kademlia has four main primitives:

- `PING` - to check if a peer is online;
- `STORE` - instructs a peer to store a <key, value> pair;
- `FIND_NODE` - receives a 160-bit *nodeID* as parameter. The recipient must send a list of the k closest peers to the *nodeID* in the format <IP, UDP port, ID>;

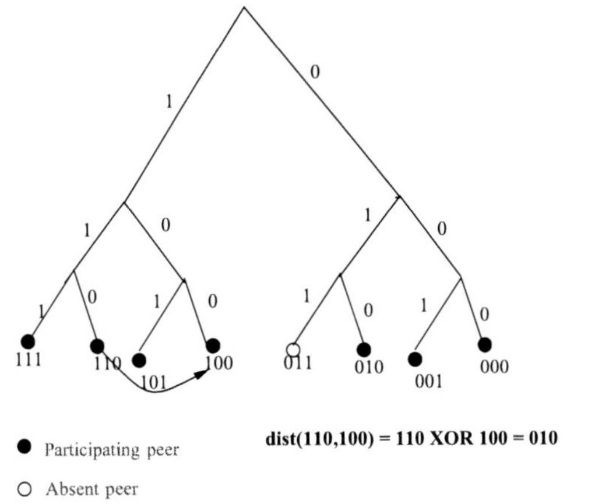

Figure 10. Example of a Kademlia network with a 3-bit key space

- `FIND_VALUE` - returns a similar result to `FIND_NODE`, however, the parameter is a 160-bit key. If the recipient peer has the key, then it responds with the corresponding value, otherwise, it returns the k closest peers in a list of tuples <IP, UDP port, ID>.

A very important operation in Kademlia is the *lookup*. This operation is used whenever a peer needs to find the k closest peers to a key or to another peer (represented by its *nodeID*). The search begins when the seeker peer selects α peers from its closest *k-bucket* and sends them a request of the type `FIND_NODE` or `FIND_VALUE`, depending on the context of the search. The α parameter is a parallelism parameter and its default value is 3. When these α peers respond to their requests, the seeker peer updates its *k-buckets* with the information that came in the responses. The seeker peer selects α more peers and continues doing so until its *k-buckets* stop growing. The bootstrap process of a peer involves a *lookup* operation in which the peer searches for itself. To enter the network, at least one neighbor must be known. This helps the new peer to discover the other neighbors and, therefore, fill its *k-buckets*. The Kademlia standard states that peers must republish their keys every hour and seeder peers must republish their keys every 24 hours. A peer is considered expired if it has not done any operation in the previous 24 hours. These peers may be removed from *k-buckets* and will be replaced by other peers.

B. *Cluster Management*

In the context of the CI-PMIPv6, the *cluster* is a Kademlia-based network where the peers are the LMAs from the different existing domains. The <key, value> pairs are stored in the *cluster* following the same logic as in Kademlia, where:

- The key is the prefix of the MN's IP address in its original domain;
- The value is a data structure containing the corresponding MAG's IP address, the current LMA's address, an identifier for the MN in its original network, an identifier of the link between the MN and its original network, and the prefix of the MN's IP address in its original domain, the International Mobile Subscriber Identity (IMSI) when applicable, and the list of all MAC addresses of the MN;
- The *nodeID* of an LMA in the *cluster* is its IP address;
- Keys and *nodeIDs* are in the 128-bit key space since it is the size of an IPv6 address instead of the 160-bit key space from the Kademlia standard.

TABLE II. KADEMLIA'S ROUTING TABLE FOR AN LMA - 128 K-BUCKETS.

Peers with distance $1(2^0)$ to $2\ (2^1)$	List of k LMAs
...	...
Peers with distance (2^i) to (2^{i+1})	List of k LMAs
Peers with distance (2^{127}) to (2^{128})	List of k LMAs

Following the logic in the Kademlia's original implementation, the <key, value> pairs are stored in the LMAs with the IPs closest to the MN's original IP prefix. Each LMA must have a local storage for its *k-buckets*. Each *bucket* has the IP addresses of the k LMAs whose distance to it is n, where n varies from 1 to 128. Table II presents an example of a Kademlia routing table for 128 *k-buckets*.

The `PING`, `STORE`, `FIND_NODE`, and `FIND_VALUE` primitives and the *lookup* procedure work in the same way as in the original implementation of Kademlia. An LMA in the *cluster* is registered during the deploy process of the CI-PMIPv6, following agreements among the related telecommunication companies. LMAs are not mobile entities and the departure of an LMA from the *cluster* during a call would be a very unlikely event. Therefore, the *cluster* can be considered a trusted area and the authentication services of the original PMIPv6 implementation remains unchanged.

The benefits of a solution based on a P2P architecture include:

- LMAs can communicate without there being a hierarchy among them;
- Mobility management is accomplished without centralized entities, which reduces the probability of bottlenecks in the network;
- MAGs can ignore the existence of the *cluster*, and therefore be out of the path of the core network;
- The spread of the `STORE` message during *handover* makes it unnecessary further communication to obtain the MN information in the next handover; in case of an eventual failure in *cluster* communication, the *lookup* process could be done in $\log(n)$ steps, where n is the size of the *cluster*.

CI-PMIPv6 introduces the new primitives `UPDATE` and `DELETE` to, respectively, update and remove keys during MNs handover and de-registration. These primitives follow the same logic as in `STORE`.

C. *CI-PMIPv6 signaling*

CI-PMIPv6 allows intra- and inter-domain handover with minor changes in the signaling flow of PMIPv6. For this purpose, CI-PMIPv6 assumes that:

- MAGs are physically reachable from a nearby LMA of another domain;

- LMAs work as Internet *gateways* - as in PMIPv6;
- Each domain has its own Authentication, Authorization and Accounting (AAA) service - as in PMIPv6.

Figure 11 shows the signaling flow for the MN registration in its original domain. The MN sends the `Rtr Sol` message to request the nearest MAG for a route to the external network. Initially, the MAG authenticates the MN with the corresponding AAA service of its domain. After authorization, the MAG sends a `PBU` message to its LMA. Until this point, the flow is exactly the same as in PMIPv6. Then, the LMA sends the `STORE` asynchronous message to the *cluster* according to its Kademlia routing table. The other LMAs in the *cluster* receive the MN information. Since the `STORE` message is asynchronous, the LMA does not have to wait for the responses from the LMAs in the *cluster* to proceed with the handover. The LMA sends the `PBA` message to the MAG. The MN is then registered and the MAG announces a new route sending to the MN the `Rtr Adv` ICMP message.

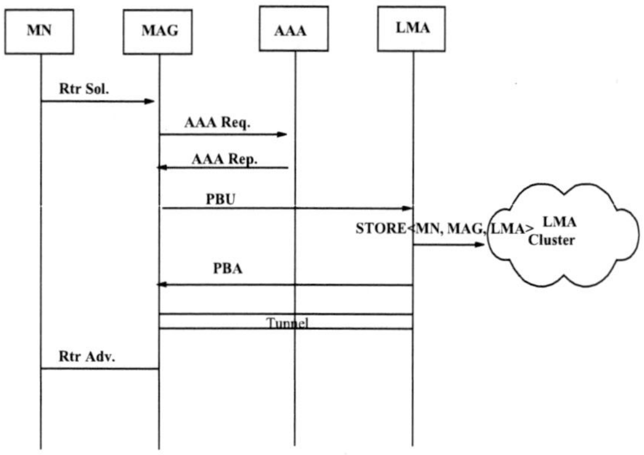

Figure 11. Registration of an MN in CI-PMIPv6.

Figure 12 presents the de-registration process for an MN. Initially, the signaling is the same as in PMIPv6. After detecting the MN's detachment event, the MAG sends the `PBU` message to the LMA. The LMA waits for a fixed amount of time named `INITIAL_BINDACK_TIMEOUT` [18] before deleting the MN information from its records. Then, the LMA sends the `DELETE` message to the *cluster*. As for the `STORE` message, the `DELETE` message is sent in an asynchronous manner. The LMA sends the `PBA` message to the MAG and finishs the de-registration process.

Figure 13 presents the signaling flow for the intra-domain handover. It is similar to that of the PMIPv6, except for the addition of the `UPDATE` message to update the *cluster* after the LMA acknowledges that the MN is associated to the new MAG. We assume that the LMA runs both the update operation and the rest of the intra-domain handover operation in parallel, e.g., the LMA runs both of the operations simultaneously on different cores. These two operations do not block each other. This is possible since the spread of binding information in the cluster is not useful for concluding the current intra-domain handover. MAGs do not need to interact with the cluster and may proceed with the handover normally. We further assume to be negligible the amount of time spent performing a system call for starting the update operation during intra-domain handovers. We also assume that traffic from the LMA to the cluster and traffic from the LMA to the MAGs can be kept isolated from each other. For instance, each LMA might have exclusive network interfaces and paths for communicating with MAGs. In this manner, update messages flowing from the LMA to the cluster during intra-domain handovers cannot block (e.g., head-of-the-line blocking in network interfaces) or affect (e.g., increasing queuing delay) messages flowing to the MAGs. The MN information is proactively spread in the cluster. The information will be necessary if there is ever an inter-domain handover executed by the MN. The MN information is rapidly available to neighbors LMAs in the cluster, thereby avoiding the need for the extra signaling to request and obtain such information during inter-domain handovers. Notice that CI-PMIPv6 takes advantage of the execution of inter-domain handover-related operations in parallel with the execution of intra-domain handover-related operations.

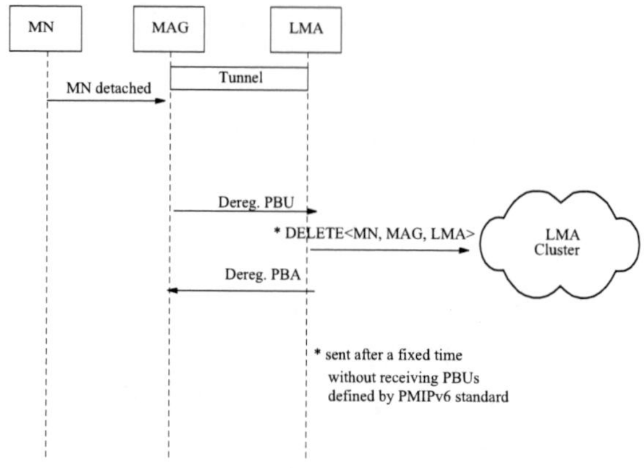

Figure 12. De-registration in CI-PMIPv6.

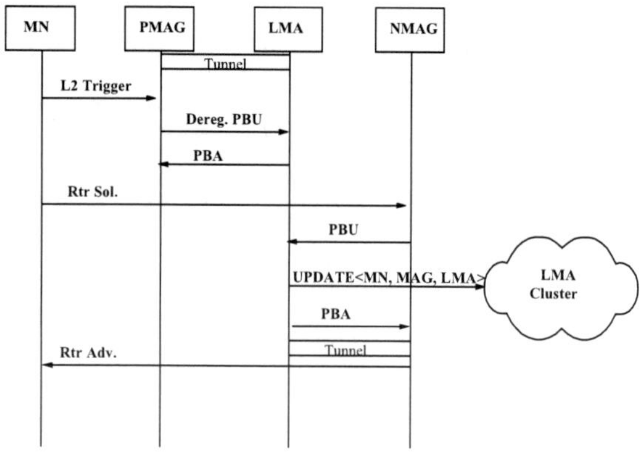

Figure 13. Intra-domain handover in CI-PMIPv6.

Figure 14 presents the signaling for the inter-domain handover. The PMAG sends the `PBU` to the previous LMA (PLMA) as the MN is about to leave the network. When the MN enters a new domain and requests the NMAG for a new route (`Rtr Sol`), the NMAG sends the `PBUNoProf` message to the new LMA (NLMA). This is because the NMAG cannot identify the MN in its records. The NLMA finds the MN's IP address in its records, which came from previous interactions with the *cluster*. The NLMA sends the PLMA the `PBUInter` message in order to inform it that the MN is doing an inter-domain handover. It is important to notice that the PLMA must receive this message before the `INITIAL_BINDACK_TIMEOUT` expires, so that it does not remove the MN record. The value of `INITIAL_BINDACK_TIMEOUT` must be adjusted depending on the network conditions so as to avoid the unnecessary removal of MN records. The PLMA sends the `UPDATE` asynchronous message to the *cluster* and, in parallel, sends the `PBAinter-domain` message to the NLMA. Finally, the NLMA sends the `PBAProf` message to the NMAG with the MN information, so that a tunnel between the NMAG and the PLMA can be set up. The PLMA remains responsible for the data delivery until the end of the session.

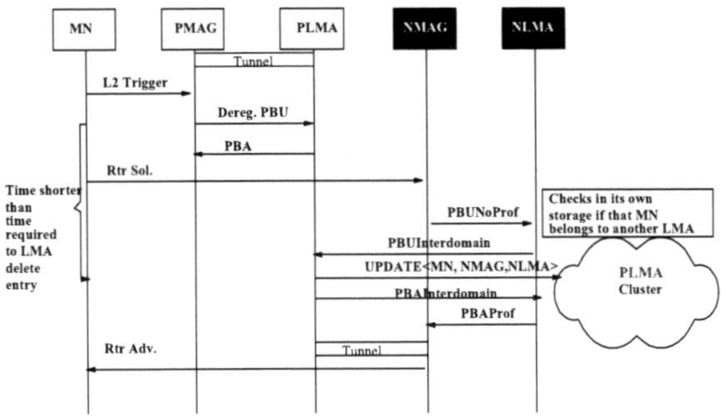

Figure 14. Inter-domain handover in CI-PMIPv6.

The greatest benefit of our approach to manage inter-domain handovers comes from the fact that LMAs have anticipated knowledge of MNs information. It is not necessary to wait for responses for messages sent to the *cluster* in order to finish the current handover since messages are asynchronous. Additionally, the messages exchanged in the *cluster* do not add signaling costs to the current intra-handover. It is important to notice that our approach does not remove any behavior from the original implementation of PMIPv6. Thus, a CI-PMIPv6 network can co-exist with legacy PMIPv6 networks. In such a case, the legacy LMA would not belong to any cluster and would manage only intra-domain handovers as is expected in PMIPv6.

D. CI-FPMIPv6

The design concepts of CI-PMIPv6 are generic and can be applied to other variants of PMIPv6 that has no support to inter-domain handover such as FPMIPv6. In this paper, we apply these concepts to FPMIPv6 as another case study. This results in a new proposed protocol, namely CI-FPMIPv6 (Clustered Inter-domain FPMIPv6). The inter-domain handover of the CI-FPMIPv6 in the reactive mode is straightforward and is depicted in Figure 15. As soon as the MN arrives in the new domain, the NMAG sends the `PBUNoProf` message to the NLMA in order to request the MN information. After receiving the `PBAProf` response, the NMAG sets up the tunnel and the buffer with the PMAG using the FPMIPv6 `HI` and `HACK` messages. After that, the NMAG sends a `PBU` message to inform the NLMA that the handover is happening and the NLMA informs the PLMA about the ongoing inter-domain handover. To do this, the PLMA sends the `PBUinter-domain` message. The PLMA, then, updates the *cluster* with the `UPDATE` asynchronous message and responds to the NLMA with the `PBAinter-domain` message. Thus, the data tunnel is created between the NMAG and the PLMA.

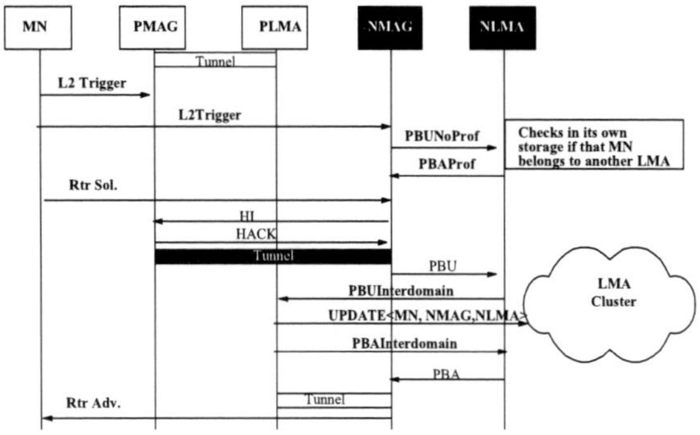

Figure 15. Inter-domain handover in CI-FPMIPv6 using the reactive mode.

In order to accomplish the inter-domain handover by considering the predictive mode of FPMIPv6, a new piece of information needs to be added to the tuple stored in the cluster: the IP address of the latest PoA associated to the MN. This information is important for the predictive mode since it is the only way a PLMA can find the NMAG that manages this PoA and then, it gives to its PMAG the NMAG address so that they can exchange tunnel information before the IP handover takes place. The `UPDATE` asynchronous message must now be sent not only during every intra-domain handover but also during every intra-MAG handover (when the MN changes the PoA without changing the MAG). This is important for the LMA to feed the mapping between PoAs and their corresponding MAGs. Figure 16 presents the signaling flow for an inter-domain handover considering the predictive mode in CI-FPMIPv6. After the link-layer handover, the PMAG sends the `FindNMAG` message to the PLMA since it could not find in its internal entries the NMAG that manages the new PoA. The PLMA, which has this information thanks to the *cluster* messages exchanged in previous handovers, replies with the `NMAGInfo` message. The PMAG then exchanges with the NMAG the `HI` and `HACK` messages. Thus the tunnel and buffering are initiated. When the MN finally arrives at the new network, the NMAG does not know that node, and, therefore, must send the `PBUNoProf` message to the NLMA. The NLMA checks for its records fed by the interactions with the *cluster* and informs the PLMA that an inter-domain handover is taking place by sending the `PBUinter-domain` message. The PLMA sends the `UPDATE` asynchronous message to the cluster and replies with the `PBAinter-domain` message. Finally, the NLMA sends the `PBAProf` message to the NMAG and the data tunnel is created between the NMAG and the PLMA.

E. CI-PMIPv6 and CI-FPMIPv6 Messages Format

In this section, the signaling messages used by CI-PMIPv6 and CI-FPMIPv6 are detailed. Some of the messages are inherited from PMIPv6 and FPMIPv6 protocols, respectively. Tables III to XIX show the fields of each signaling message.

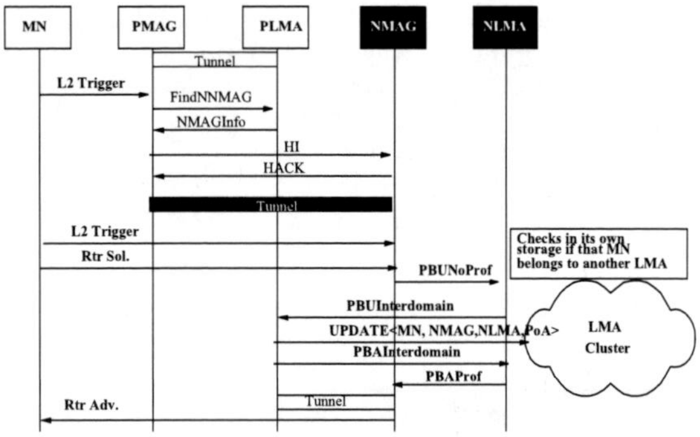

Figure 16. Inter-domain handover in CI-FPMIPv6 using the predictive mode.

Tables III to XIX shows the fields of each signaling message.

V. PRELIMINARY ANALYSIS

Table XX summarizes the differences among CI-PMIPv6, CI-FPMIPv6, and other inter-domain solutions. The extra signaling during an intra-domain handover is calculated in comparison with the original implementation of PMIPv6. FPMIPv6 has 2 more signaling messages than PMIPv6. Thus, CI-FPMIPv6 introduces 2 signaling messages with respect to FPMIPv6 but has 4+2 additional signaling messages with respect to PMIPv6. Notice that it is not the fault of our approach since it inherits the 2 extra signaling messages from FPMIPv6. The decentralized approach [5] has one of the greatest increase in extra signaling in comparison with the other approaches. Additionally, there might be an overhead related to the addition of one more IP header because of the need for the extra tunnel. It is expected that these factors cause a noteworthy increase in latency during the inter-domain handover.

CI-PMIPv6 and CI-FPMIPv6 appear as the best solutions. The reason is as follows: the extra signaling needed for inter-domain handover is one of the lowest; they do not require extra tunnels; and they can inter-work with legacy systems. The cluster messages do not add extra signaling costs to the ongoing handover because they are asynchronous and are necessary only in future inter-domain handovers. Thus, it is expected CI-PMIPv6 and CI-FPMIPv6 to exhibit a smaller handover cost, lower latency - as a consequence, less packet loss - and a higher useful traffic rate than the other proposals.

VI. PERFORMANCE EVALUATION AND RESULTS

In this section, the performance of the CI-PMIPv6 and CI-FPMIPv6 are compared to that of the decentralized, No-Gap, I-PMIP, and EIPMH solutions. The evaluation is based on the analytical modeling presented in [8] [23] [24]. This allows the cost of handover signaling in a session, latency and the packet loss of one handover, and the goodput in a session to be measured. It is considered that mobile devices are attached to vehicles in a highway during a voice call (e.g., Skype). Inter-domain handover takes place as the MN arrives at a new domain. The mobility pattern follows the Fluid-Flow model [25]. That model considers average velocity (v), the subnet and domain coverage areas (A_M and A_D,

TABLE III. PBU FORMAT [19].

Field name	Field size (bytes)	Data type	Comments
Sequence	2	integer	Identify the order of signaling messages
A	1	bool	Asks for an acknowledgment (from MIP [18])
H	1	bool	Home registration (from MIP [18])
L	1	bool	Link-Local Address Compatibility (from MIP [18])
K	1	bool	Key Management Mobility Capability (from MIP [18])
M	1	bool	Register to a Mobility Anchor Point (from Hierarchical MIP [20])
R	1	bool	Mobile Router (from NEMO Basic Support Protocol [21])
P	1	bool	Indicates that it is a proxy in behalf of the MN
Reserved	2	byte	
Lifetime	2	integer	The granted lifetime (from MIP [18])
Mobility Options	variable	byte	Optional information about prefix, handover, among others

TABLE IV. PBA FORMAT [19].

Field name	Field size (bytes)	Data type	Comments
Status	1	integer	Indicates the disposition of the binding update (from MIP [18])
K	1	bool	Key Management Mobility Capability (from MIP [18])
R	1	bool	Mobile Router (from NEMO Basic Support Protocol [21])
Reserved	2	byte	
Sequence	2	integer	Same value as in PBU
Lifetime	2	integer	The granted lifetime (from MIP [18])

TABLE V. PBU NO PROFILE FORMAT.

Field name	Field size (bytes)	Data type	Comments
Same fields from PBU	-	-	-
Mac address	6	byte	Indicates the MN's MAC address came from L2 handover-if it is using Wi-Fi
Imsi	8	byte	Indicates the MN's IMSI - if it is using 3GPP

TABLE VI. PBA PROFILE FORMAT.

Field name	Field size (bytes)	Data type	Comments
Same fields from PBA	-	-	-
Value	variable	byte	The information about the MN queried (see SectionIV-B)

TABLE VII. PBU INTERDOMAIN FORMAT.

Field name	Field size (bytes)	Data type	Comments
Same fields from PBU	-	-	- -

TABLE VIII. PBA INTERDOMAIN FORMAT.

Field name	Field size (bytes)	Data type	Comments
Same Same fields from PBA	-	-	-

TABLE IX. HI FORMAT [7].

Field name	Field size (bytes)	Data type	Comments
Sequence	2	integer	Identify the order of signaling messages (from PMIPv6 [19])
S	1	bool	Assigned address configuration flag (from Fast Handovers for MIP [22])
U	1	bool	Buffer flag (from Fast Handovers for MIP [22])
P	1	bool	Proxy flag (from PMIPv6 [19])
F	1	bool	Request to forward the packets for the mobile node
Reserved	-	-	
Code	1	bool	May indicate completion of forwarding, or context transferred (from Fast Handovers for MIP [22])
Mobility options	variable	byte	May indicate an alternative CoA or binding authorization data(from MIP [18])

TABLE X. HACK FORMAT [7].

Field name	Field size (bytes)	Data type	Comments
Sequence	2	integer	Identify the order of signaling messages (from PMIPv6 [19])
U	1	bool	Buffer flag (from Fast Handovers for MIP [22])
P	1	bool	Proxy flag (from PMIPv6 [19])
F	1	bool	Request to forward the packets for the mobile node
Reserved	-	-	
Code	1	byte	May indicate handover status - success, or failure
Mobility options	variable	byte	May indicate an alternative CoA or binding authorization data (from MIP [18])

TABLE XI. FIND NMAG FORMAT.

Field name	Field size (bytes)	Data type	Comments
PoA address	16	byte	IP address of the target PoA in the MN's handover

TABLE XII. NMAGINFO FORMAT.

Field name	Field size (bytes)	Data type	Comments
NMAG address	16	byte	IP address of the NMAG corresponding to the target PoA in the MN's handover

TABLE XIII. STORE FORMAT.

Field name	Field size (bytes)	Data type	Comments
Sender ID	16	byte	Node ID of Sender
Key	16	byte	Key for the content
Value	variable	byte	Information about the MN to be stored (see SectionIV-B)

TABLE XIV. UPDATE FORMAT.

Field name	Field size (bytes)	Data type	Comments
Sender ID	16	byte	Node ID of Sender
Key	16	byte	Key for the content
Value	variable	byte	Information about the MN to be stored (see SectionIV-B)

TABLE XV. DELETE FORMAT.

Field name	Field size (bytes)	Data type	Comments
Key	16	byte	Key for the content

TABLE XVI. FIND NODE FORMAT.

Field name	Field size (bytes)	Data type	Comments
Sender ID	16	byte	Node ID of Sender
Node ID	16	byte	The Node ID to be searched
Lookup	1	bool	Identifies if it is a lookup operation

TABLE XVII. FIND NODE RESPONSE FORMAT.

Field name	Field size (bytes)	Data type	Comments
Closest peers	variable	byte	A list of the closest peers to the key

TABLE XVIII. FIND VALUE FORMAT.

Field name	Field size (bytes)	Data type	Comments
Sender ID	16	byte	Node ID of Sender
Key	16	byte	Key for the content

TABLE XIX. FIND VALUE RESPONSE FORMAT.

Field name	Field size (bytes)	Data type	Comments
Key	16	byte	Key for the content
Found	1	bool	Tells if the search was successful
Value	variable	byte	The tuple of information about the MN in case of success (see SectionIV-B)
Closest peers	variable	byte	A list of the closest peers to the key in case of failure in search

TABLE XX. Comparison of the different proposals.

Solution	# extra messages in inter-domain handover	# extra tunnels	Infrastructure maintenance	Compatibility with legacy systems
decentralized [5]	8	1	Yes	Yes
EIPMH [4]	6	2	No	No
I-PMIP [3]	6	1	No	No
No-Gap [2]	4	1	No	Yes
CI-PMIPv6	2	0	Yes	Yes
CI-FPMIPv6 reac.	4+2	0	Yes	Yes
CI-FPMIPv6 pred.	4+2	0	Yes	Yes

respectively) and the subnet and domain perimeters (L_M and L_D, respectively) as parameters. The direction of movement is uniformly distributed in a range of 0 to 2π. Since this experiment is interested in a vehicular scenario, the choice of this model is very appropriate.

Two variables determine the dynamics of the MN: the domain crossing rate (μ_D) and the subnet crossing rate (μ_M). The former is the rate at which the node switches from one domain to another. It is equivalent to the inter-domain handover rate (Ng). The latter is the rate at which the node switches from one subnet to another. The intra-domain handover rate (Nl) considers a subnet crossing when this does not imply a domain crossing. That is, Nl is the difference between μ_M and μ_D. Their equations are as follows [8] [24]:

$$\mu_M = \frac{vL_M}{\pi A_M}, \quad (1)$$

$$Ng = \mu_D = \frac{vL_D}{\pi A_D}, \quad (2)$$

$$Nl = \mu_M - \mu_D. \quad (3)$$

Another important parameter to describe mobility of a node is the Session-to-Mobility Ratio (SMR), which relates session arrival rate and the subnet crossing rate as follows [8]:

$$SMR = \frac{\lambda_S}{\mu_M}. \quad (4)$$

If SMR is near zero, this means that the node has high mobility. The higher the SMR, the more static the node.

The signaling cost is the number of handover signaling messages, taking into consideration the distance in hops between two entities x and y, namely $H_{(x-y)}$, the underlying media, and the processing cost. For each protocol message sent, the signaling cost is (see [8])

$$C_{x-y} = \alpha(H_{(x-y)}) - \beta + PC_y, \quad (5)$$
$$PC_y = \varsigma \log N^y_{MN}, \quad (6)$$

where the parameters α and β represent the coefficients of unity transmission costs (in messages/hop) in wired and wireless links, respectively. The cost of processing at one end is represented by PC_y. It is measured based on a logarithmic search in a data structure with the size of the number of MN entries and a normalizing constant ς equivalent to the bandwidth allocation. If the reception of a message at one end does not imply searching a local storage, PC_y is considered zero. Additionally, if the node that sends or receives the message is not an MN, the β factor is excluded. The handover signaling cost is the sum of the cost of all messages exchanged during a handover. The average cost is measured as a weighted sum of the intra-domain and inter-domain counterparts. It depends on Ng and Nl rates. The average cost [8] is presented as

$$cost = \frac{intraDHO\ cost \times Nl + interDHO\ cost \times Ng}{Nl + Ng}. \quad (7)$$

The inter-domain signaling cost for a session is the cost of one inter-domain handover multiplied by both Ng and the session duration:

$$cost\ in\ session = interDHO\ cost \times Ng \times session\ duration. \quad (8)$$

Handover latency is measured as the handover duration, i.e., the time a node spends without effective communication. The latency equation for a message exchanged between two nodes x and y is (see [24])

$$T_{x-y} = \frac{1+q}{1-q}\left(\frac{M_{size}}{B_{wl}} + L_{wl}\right) + H_{x-y}\left(\frac{M_{size}}{B_w} + L_w + T_q\right). \quad (9)$$

The first part of the sum is the wireless overhead and it must be excluded if neither x nor y is a wireless device. The second part is the overhead in the wired medium. The parameter q is the probability of failure of the wireless link, M_{size} is the average length of a message, and B_{wl} and B_w are the wireless and wired bandwidths, respectively. The propagation delay in wireless and wired media are L_{wl} and L_w, respectively. The average queuing delay in each router is represented by T_q. Handover latency is the sum of the latency of all signaling messages exchanged during a handover, plus the link-layer handover latency. In the case of CI-PMIPv6 predictive mode, the link-layer handover latency is not considered, since it occurs nearly in parallel with the handover in the network layer. As in the signaling cost, the average latency is measured as a weighted sum of the intra-domain and inter-domain counterparts as follows [8]:

$$latency = \frac{intraDHO\ lat \times Nl + interDHO\ lat \times Ng}{Nl + Ng}. \quad (10)$$

The average packet loss in a handover is the average number of packages not sent/received during handover. The packet loss (PL) is the product of the handover latency (T) and the packet arrival rate (λ_p) [8], i.e.,

$$PL = T\lambda_p. \quad (11)$$

For the case of FPMIPv6-based protocols, the Equation (11) must be adapted to consider the packet buffering during handover. In the reactive mode, the average packet loss (PL_{reac}) is the average number of packets not sent/received during both the link-layer handover and the exchange of the HI and HACK messages (cf. [24]), i.e.,

$$PL_{reac} = (T_{L2} + T_{HI} + T_{HACK}) \times \lambda_p. \quad (12)$$

In the predictive mode, the link-layer handover starts nearly in parallel with the network-layer handover. Thus, we assume that in this mode the average packet loss is the average number of packets not sent/received during the tunnel setup, excluding the time interval ($T_{L2trig-L2HOexec}$) while link-layer handover has triggered but not yet executed (cf. [24]). In this manner, the packet loss under the preditive mode is defined as

$$PL_{pred} = ((T_{HI} + T_{HACK}) - (T_{L2trig-L2HOexec})) \times \lambda_p. \quad (13)$$

Finally, the goodput is a measure that relates the useful data traffic during a session and the total traffic (TOT), which is the total number of bytes transmitted during a session. The goodput is determined as follows (cf. [8]):

$$Goodput = \frac{TOT - (P_{size} \times PL_{session} + TOT \times PD)}{session\ duration}, \quad (14)$$

$$TOT = session\ duration \times \lambda_p \times P_{size}, \quad (15)$$

$$PD = \frac{40 \times H_{tunnel}}{(40 + P_{size}) \times H_{MN-CN}}. \quad (16)$$

Goodput additionally depends on the packet loss and the packet delivery (PD) overhead. PD overhead is the cost of tunneling the IP-in-IP extra 40-byte header along the path between an MN and its correspondent node (H_{MN-CN}). Packet size (P_{size}) and the PMIPv6 tunnel size in hops (H_{tunnel}) are parameters for the PD.

Now, let us turn our attention to the evaluation of the performance of CI-PMIPv6. The signaling cost in a session is measured as a function of SMR. Latency and packet loss in one handover are measured as a function of the probability of failure of the link in the wireless network. The goodput in a session is measured as a function of SMR.

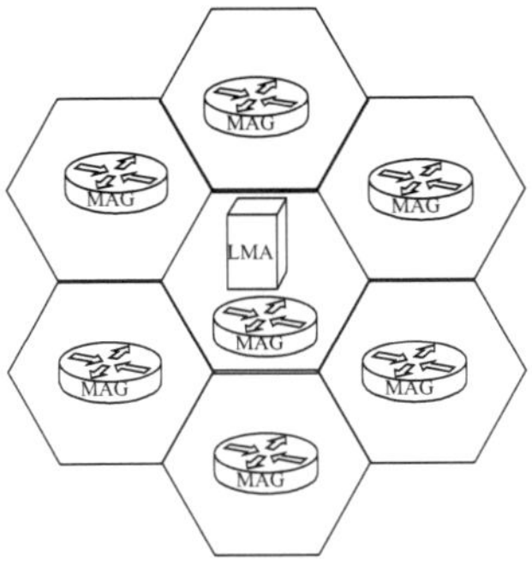

Figure 17. A domain with 7 subnets.

In these evaluations, a domain has 7 subnets. Each subnet follows a hexagonal model, has one PoA and one MAG. There is a central subnet that is managed by a single LMA. The other subnets surround the central subnet. The coverage area of each subnet is equal to 1.87 km^2 and the perimeter is equal to 5 km.

TABLE XXI. EVALUATION PARAMETERS.

Parameter	Default value
Number of subnets per domain	7
Coverage area of each subnet (A_M)	1.87 km^2
Kademlia's constant (k)	10
MN velocity (v)	15 m/s
Prob. of failure of the wireless link (q)	0.5 (range 0-0.8)
Coefficient of cost in wired medium (α)	1 message/hop
Coefficient of cost in wireless medium (β)	10 messages/hop
Normalizing constant (ς)	0.01
Queuing time (T_q)	5 ms
Subnet residency time ($1/\mu_M$)	300 s
Prop. delay (wired link) (L_w)	0.75 μs
Prop. delay (wireless link) (L_{wl})	10 ms
Packet arrival rate (λ_p)	38 packets/s (100 kbps)
Session arrival rate (λ_S)	0.001 sessions/s
Average data packet size (P_{size})	300 bytes
Average signaling packet size (M_{size})	160 bytes
Link-layer handover latency (T_{L2})	50 ms

Table XXI summarizes the values of the parameters used for performance evaluation. The Kademlia parameter k used in CI-PMIPv6, which represents the size of the neighborhood, is set to 10. This value is chosen based on a scenario where nodes have an average speed of 15 m/s (60 km/h) and may cross 10 domains during a session. The probability of failure of the wireless link ranges from 0 to 0.8 in experiments to consider the radio channel under different quality conditions during handover. The greater this probability is, the more link-layer retransmissions are necessary. The value of α is equal to 1 message/hop and β is equal to 10 messages/hop, since wireless links tend to cost more than wired links. The average queue time is a typical value of 5 ms. The average residency time of an MN is considered equal to 300 s, which corresponds to a mean speed of 15 m/s. The theoretical latency across a 4G LTE interface is in the order of 10 ms. It is assumed that the wireless link has a propagation delay of 10 ms in order to capture such behavior. The propagation delay of wired links are assumed to be a typical value for Fast Ethernet. The arrival rate of packets corresponds to a voice call (e.g., Skype) and the session arrival rate allows consecutive voice calls that are 13 minutes long each. The average data packet size considered is 300 bytes long [26]. The average packet size used for handover signaling is 160 bytes long. In our evaluation of the CI-FPMIPv6 operating in the predictive mode, we consider the contribution of the term $T_{L2trig-L2HOexec}$ in Equation (13) to be negligible.

Figure 18 presents the influence of SMR on the overall cost during a session. If SMR is near zero, there is a high mobility scenario. If SMR is high, this means that the network mobility is low. Therefore, the cost tends to be lower with higher values of SMR for all proposals. When SMR tends to zero, there is a high number of handovers during a session. In this case, the number of messages exchanged during handover plays an important role in the overall cost. Additionally, the presence of a cluster that exchanges proactively domain information and in parallel with the current binding update simplifies communication during future inter-domain handovers, which require less interaction between core network entities. CI-

PMIPv6 has a cost 20% lower than the cost in No-Gap when the SMR is equal to 0.01. The decentralized scheme has the worst performance. CI-PMIPv6 always exhibits the lowest cost since it requires fewer messages to accomplish handover, as shown in Table XX. CI-FPMIPv6 follows as the second best in performance along with the No-Gap solution. Both the predictive and reactive modes have the same number of additional messages. Although the same can be said about I-PMIPv6, it has a greater cost due to the signaling of de-registration between the MN and the previous domain, which is not necessary in FPMIPv6-based protocols.

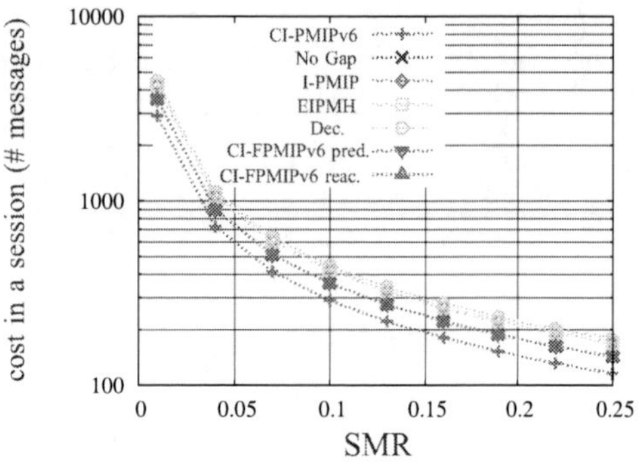

Figure 18. Overall cost *versus* SMR.

Figure 19 presents the average handover latency as a function of the probability of failure of the wireless link. This probability represents the reliability of the wireless channel and may degrade performance due to retransmissions in the link layer. The EIPMH results are influenced by the high number of interactions in the core network. It has the highest latency until the probability of failure reaches 0.65. From this point on, the decentralized scheme has greater latency. This is due to the fact that it has more messages involving the MN, thus making the scheme more sensitive to the wireless media. I-PMIP presents results with values close to the those of No Gap. It is important to notice that CI-PMIPv6 and CI-FPMIPv6 (predictive) present the smallest results for latency. In particular, CI-PMIPv6 latency is 16% smaller than the latency in I-PMIP when the probability of failure is 0.8. CI-PMIPv6 performs better because unnecessary interactions in both the core network and the wireless network were eliminated. CI-FPMIPv6 (predictive) performs similar because although it has 2 additional signaling messages than CI-PMIPv6, the handover starts as soon as the link-layer triggers the handover, which contributes to reduce the overall latency. The reactive mode of CI-FPMIPv6 has bigger latency than the predictive mode, despite having the same number of signaling messages in the inter-domain handover. Nevertheless, since the buffer setup is done after the handover in the link layer, the reactive mode of CI-FPMIPv6 finishes the overall process later than the predictive mode.

Figure 20 presents the number of lost packets based on the probability of failure of the wireless link. For those schemes that does not involve buffering, the packet loss is directly related to the handover latency. Considering that in this scenario the arrival rate is 38 packets/s, there is a significant loss of quality in the worst case. The number of lost data

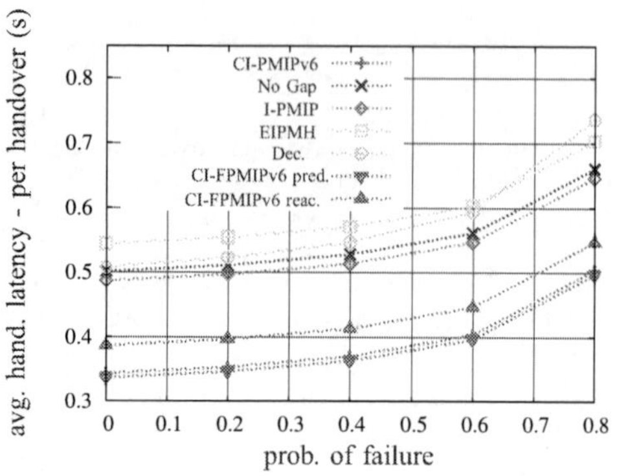

Figure 19. Overall latency *versus* prob. of failure of the wireless link.

packets for CI-FPMIPv6 (predictive) is the smallest, in all cases studied, and followed by CI-FPMIPv6 (reactive). This is due to the FPMIPv6's buffering of packets while the handover takes place. These packets are preserved and sent after the handover is finished, which reduces the packet loss during this process. CI-PMIPv6 loses a smaller number of packets in comparison to the other non-buffering schemes since the interval of time when handover takes place and the data path is "broken" is smaller. In particular, it is 16% smaller than the value observed for No-Gap when the failure probability is 0.8.

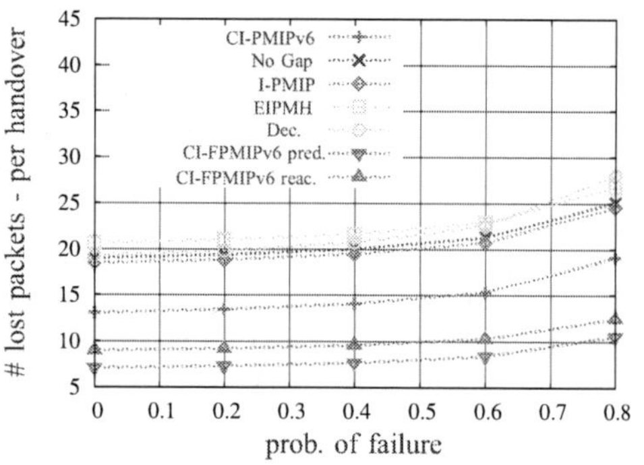

Figure 20. Packet loss *versus* prob. of failure of the wireless link.

Figure 21 presents the goodput *versus* the SMR. If SMR is high, it means that the network mobility is low. Thus, goodput tends to be more stable as SMR grows. CI-PMIPv6 and CI-FPMIPv6 have the highest goodput for all SMR values. This means that our approach makes both protocols capable of sending more useful data during a session. They maintain the same number of tunnels created in PMIPv6. This avoids the PD overhead due to headers in IP-in-IP tunneling. For a small SMR, the CI-FPMIPv6 in the predictive mode has slightly greater values, followed by CI-FPMIPv6 in reactive mode and CI-PMIPv6. This is due to the predictive CI-FPMIPv6's lower packet loss. When the SMR is greater, there is less mobility and less handovers. Thus, in this case, the difference in the goodput values among them is negligible. EIPMH has the worst goodput because it requires the creation of two extra tunnels, besides the pre-existing PMIPv6 tunnel. The

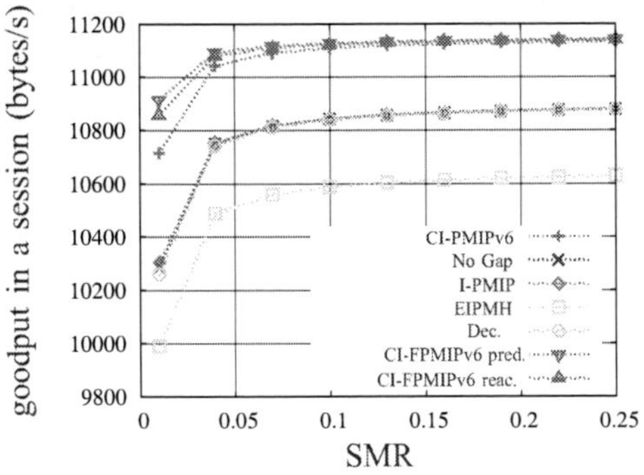

Figure 21. Goodput *versus* SMR.

decentralized solution as weel as I-PMIP and No-Gap have similar results, since they introduce just one extra tunnel in comparison to PMIPv6.

VII. CONCLUSION

This paper presented CI-PMIPv6 as distributed solutions for inter-domain IP mobility in PMIPv6-based systems. CI-PMIPv6 has a distributed design, which organizes LMAs from different domains in a cluster as Kademlia peers. In the cluster, information on MNs is spread proactively and in parallel with the current binding update, thereby simplifying future inter-domain handover processes. We have shown that CI-PMIPv6 significantly boosts the performance of inter-domain handovers. The design concepts of CI-PMIPv6 are generic and can be applied to other variants of PMIPv6 that have no support to inter-domain handover such as FPMIPv6. We applied these concepts to FPMIPv6 as another case study and showed that the performance can also be significantly boosted. Plain CI-PMIPv6 and its reactive and predictive modes were compared to several inter-domain approaches and results have shown that when CI-PMIPv6 is used, the cost, the latency, and the packet loss in the studied scenario are lower. Additionally, the goodput reaches higher values.

VIII. FUTURE WORK

CI-PMIPv6 network uses a P2P-based architecture. Thus, a study of the network scalability will be done. Scalability tests can verify the behavior of the CI-PMIPv6 network as a function of the domain size and under high mobility scenarios. We will also evaluate the robustness of the CI-PMIPv6 network in the presence of faulty LMAs. Another future step will be the use of the cluster as a load balancer in order to provide high availability for all domains [27]. In future studies, CI-PMIPv6 will be extended to support churn, ie., peers entering and leaving the cluster. In such a case, security aspects [28] and consistency of the information shared among entities need to be considered. Further, the application of localized routing techniques [29] may be applied to enhance the CI-PMIPv6 performance in high mobility scenarios.

REFERENCES

[1] N. C. Quental and P. A. S.Gonçalves, "CI-PMIPv6: An Approach for Inter-domain Network-based Mobility Management," in Proc. of the 16th International Conference on Networks, Venice, 2017, pp. 111–117.

[2] I. Joe and H. Lee, "An efficient inter-domain handover scheme with minimized latency for PMIPv6," in Proc. International Conference on Computing, Networking and Communications, Maui, 2012, pp. 332 – 336.

[3] N. Neumann, J. Lei, X. Fu, and G. Zhang, "I-PMIP: an inter-domain mobility extension for proxy-mobile IP," in Proc. International Conference on Wireless Communications and Mobile Computing: Connecting the World Wirelessly, Leipzig, 2009, pp. 994–999.

[4] F. Zhong, S. Yang, C. K. Yeo, and B. S. Lee, "Enabling inter-PMIPv6-domain handover with traffic distributors," in Proc. 7th IEEE CCNC, Las Vegas, 2010, pp. 1–5.

[5] S. Park, E. Lee, F. Yu, S. Noh, and S.-H. Kim, "Inter-domain roaming mechanism transparent to IPv6-node among PMIPv6 networks," in Proc. of the IEEE 71st Vehicular Technology Conference, Taipei, 2010, pp. 1–5.

[6] N. Neumann, J. Lei, X. Fu, and G. Zhang, "Kademlia with consistency checks as a foundation of borderless collaboration in open science services," in Proc. of the 5th International Young Scientist Conference on Computational Science, Krakow, 2016, pp. 304–312.

[7] H. Yokota, K. Chowdhury, R. Koodli, B. Patil, and F. Xia, "Fast Handovers for Proxy Mobile IPv6," RFC 5949, september 2011. [Online]. Available: http://tools.ietf.org/html/rfc5949

[8] A. Taghizadeh, T.-C. Wan, R. Budiarto, F. T. Yap, and A. Osman, "A performance evaluation framework for network-based IP mobility solutions," International Journal of Innovative, Computing, Information and Control, vol. 8, no. 10, 2012, pp. 7263–7288.

[9] QualNet, "QualNet - Scalable Network Technologies," 2017, Acessed: 11–18–2017. [Online]. Available: http://web.scalable-networks.com/content/qualnet

[10] T. T. Nguyen and C. Bonnet, "DMM-based inter-domain mobility support for proxy mobile IPv6," in Proc. IEEE WCNC, Shanghai, 2013, pp. 1998–2003.

[11] H. Zhou, H. Zhang, Y. Qin, H. Wang, and H. Chao, "A Proxy Mobile IPv6 based global mobility management architecture and protocol," Mobile Networks and Applications, vol. 15, no. 4, 2010, pp. 530–542.

[12] K.-W. L. et al., "Inter-domain handover scheme using an intermediate mobile access gateway for seamless service in vehicular networks," International Journal of Communication Systems, vol. 23, no. 9–10, 2009, pp. 1127–1144.

[13] P. Maymounkov and D. Mazires, "Kademlia: A Peer-to-Peer Information System Based on the XOR Metric," in Proc. of the First International Workshop on Peer-to-Peer Systems, 2002, pp. 53–65.

[14] I. Stoica, R. Morris, D. Liben-Nowell, D. R. Karger, F. F. Kaashoek, F. Dabek, and H. Balakrishnan, "Chord: A Scalable Peer-to-Peer Lookup Protocol for Internet Applications," IEEE/ACM Transactions Networking, vol. 11, no. 1, February 2003, pp. 17–32. [Online]. Available: http://portal.acm.org/citation.cfm?id=638336

[15] A. I. T. Rowstron and P. Druschel, "Pastry: Scalable, Decentralized Object Location, and Routing for Large-Scale Peer-to-Peer Systems," in Proceedings of the IFIP/ACM International Conference on Distributed Systems Platforms Heidelberg (Middleware '01). London: Springer-Verlag, 2001, pp. 329–350.

[16] B. Zhao, L. Huang, J. Stribling, S. C. Rhea, A. D. Joseph, and J. Kubiatowicz, "Tapestry: a resilient global-scale overlay for service deployment," IEEE Journal on Selected Areas in Communications, vol. 22, no. 1, 2004, pp. 41–53.

[17] D. Malkhi, M. Naor, and D. Ratajczak, "Viceroy: a Scalable and Dynamic Emulation of the Butterfly," in Proceedings of the twenty-first annual symposium on Principles of distributed computing, Monterey, 2002, pp. 183–192.

[18] D. Johnson, C. Perkins, and J. Arkko, "Mobility Support in IPv6," RFC 3775, june 2004. [Online]. Available: http://tools.ietf.org/html/rfc3775

[19] S. Gundavelli, K. Leung, V. Devarapalli, K. Chowdhury, and B. Patil, "Proxy Mobile IPv6," RFC 5213, aug 2008. [Online]. Available: http://tools.ietf.org/html/rfc5213

[20] H. Soliman, C. Castelluccia, K. E. Malki, and L. Bellier, "Hierarchical Mobile IPv6 Mobility Management (HMIPv6)," RFC 4041, aug 2005. [Online]. Available: http://tools.ietf.org/html/rfc4041

[21] V. Devarapalli, R. Wakikawa, A. Petrescu, and P. Thubert, "Network

Mobility (NEMO) Basic Support Protocol," RFC 3963, jan 2005. [Online]. Available: http://tools.ietf.org/html/rfc3963

[22] E. R. Koodli, "Mobile IPv6 Fast Handovers," RFC 5568, july 2009. [Online]. Available: http://tools.ietf.org/html/rfc5568

[23] J. McNair, I. Akyildiz, and M. D. Bender, "Handoffs for real-time traffic in mobile IP version 6 networks ," in Proc. First Global Telecommunications Conference, San Antonio, 2001, pp. 3463–3467.

[24] C. Makaya and S. Pierre, "An analytical framework for performance evaluation of IPv6-based mobility management protocols," IEEE Transactions on Wireless Communications, vol. 7, no. 3, 2008, p. 7.

[25] A. Salehan, M. Robatmili, M. Abrishami, and A. Movaghar, "A comparison of various routing protocols in mobile ad-hoc networks (MANETs) with the use of fluid flow simulation method," in Proc. 4th International Conference on Wireless and Mobile Communications, Athens, 2008, pp. 260–267.

[26] S. Molnár and M. Perényi, "On the identification and analysis of Skype traffic," International Journal of Communication Systems, vol. 24, no. 1, 2011, pp. 94–117.

[27] A. J. Jabir, "A comprehensive survey of the current trends and extensions for the proxy mobile ipv6 protocol," IEEE Systems Journal, vol. PP, no. 99, 2015, pp. 1–17.

[28] Y. Lee, H. Koo, S. Choi, B. hee Roh, and C. Lee, "Advanced Node Insertion Attack with Availability Falsification in Kademlia-based P2P Networks," in Proceedings of the 14th International Conference on Advanced Communication Technology (ICACT), PyeongChang, 2012, pp. 73–76.

[29] A. Rasem, C. Makaya, and M. St-Hilaire, "O-PMIPv6: Efficient Handover with Route Optimization in Proxy Mobile IPv6 Domain," in Proc. of the IEEE 8th International Conference on Wireless and Mobile Computing, Networking and Communications, Barcelona, 2012, pp. 47–54.

Implementation of VNF Descriptor Extensions for the Lifecycle Management of VNFs

Emanuele Miucci, Giuseppe Monteleone, Giovanni Fausto Andreotti, Paolo Secondo Crosta

ITALTEL S.p.A.
Milan, Italy
e-mail: {emanuele.miucci, giuseppe.monteleone, fausto.andreotti, paolosecondo.crosta}@italtel.com

Abstract—**This paper focuses on improvements in management and orchestration within the Network Function Virtualization (NFV) domain. The key benefits are related to automation in the Virtual Network Function (VNF) lifecycle, adaptation to different network traffic loads and new models for improving network resilience. These could be achieved by introducing some extensions of the NFV Information Model. In particular, we propose the introduction in the VNF Descriptor (VNFD) of an Information Element (IE) providing the dependencies between Virtual Deployment Units (VDUs) that allows managing the VDUs instantiation process in a more efficient way. We also suggest an extension related to the execution of script(s) - including the possibility to pass parameters - in response to particular events detected by the VNF Manager (VNFM). Since each single component of a VNF may need the execution of specific operations based on its redundancy scheme, we propose a new Information Element describing the high availability features. In addition, we give an example of how to carry information about auto-scaling rules directly in the VNFD defining a possible structure of the *autoScale* IE. Finally, in order to support the validity of the proposed approach, we provide two practical use cases related to the instantiation and scaling lifecycle events of a VNF designed by Italtel and providing Session Border Controller functionality. The main output of the paper is the definition of four extensions to the VNF Information Model - easy to fit into the ETSI specification framework - which has been used to improve the operations in the VNF lifecycle management, as demonstrated in a real implementation scenario.**

Keywords–Network Function Virtualization; Orchestration; Lifecycle Management; VNF Descriptor; User-data; Auto-scaling Rules.

I. INTRODUCTION

Network Function Virtualization (NFV), in addition to Software Defined Networking (SDN), is a rapidly emerging approach in the telecommunication field. By adopting NFV, Communication Services Providers (CSP) expect to achieve consistent cost reductions with respect to the current situation in which network equipment consists of proprietary black boxes, containing a bundle of proprietary Software (SW) and customized Hardware (HW) provided by a single Telecom Equipment Manufacturer. The adoption of the NFV concept is just the starting point to introduce in the Telco world the benefits that virtualization has brought in the Information Technology (IT) sector. Besides significant cost reductions, NFV also raises great expectations on the possibility (a) to achieve a never experienced network flexibility and service agility, (b) to introduce automation in all lifecycle of Network Functions (NFs) from deployment, installation and commissioning to operational phases [1], (c) to adapt the network to different traffic loads thanks to a novel cloud elasticity model, and (d) to develop new models for improving network resilience [2].

In fact, the objective of NFV is to allow Service Operators to achieve a high reduction in capital investments along with greater operational agility by implementing challenging architectural updates and deep changes in service models and operating procedures [3].

Virtualization is not a new technology. What is new is the way to use virtualization in Telco environments. NFV is a paradigm able to switch from manual, complex and error prone configuration processes to a new level of deployment automation, increasing flexibility, agility and the possibility to minimize complexity and errors. After the deployment, when the function is in operation it is possible to perform monitoring, scaling, healing, failover, continuous delivery and infrastructure upgrades.

In the NFV architecture, specified by the European Telecommunications Standards Institute (ETSI) NFV Industry Specification Group (ISG) [4], three main domains are identified:

- Virtualized Network Functions (VNFs), as the software implementation of network functions capable of running over the Network Functions Virtualization Infrastructure (NFVI).
- NFVI, including hardware resources (Compute, Storage, Networking) and the virtualization layer that provides Virtual resources (Virtual Compute, Virtual Storage, Virtual Networking) supporting the execution of the VNFs.
- NFV Management and Orchestration (MANO), which covers the lifecycle management of VNFs and Network Services (NS), managing the resources of NFVI and focusing on all virtualization-specific management tasks necessary in the NFV framework.

In this paper, we will focus on the Management and Orchestration domain. In particular, we propose some extensions of the NFV Information Model, specifically referring to the VNF Descriptor. These extensions can be used to increase efficiency in the lifecycle management of Network Functions and to improve the overall system reliability. Our experience as VNF provider conducted us to identify some flaws in the NFV Information Model and corresponding specific enhancements that future implementations could benefit from. In order to achieve this goal, we introduce some additional Information

Elements (IEs) in the VNF Descriptors (VNFDs) that allow a deeper control of VNFs.

The paper is organized as follows: Section II gives an overview of the ETSI standard model for NFV, with regard to the MANO architecture, including the lifecycle management of Virtual Network Functions and a general description of the NFV Information Model. Section III, the main part of the paper, provides a rationale for the extensions to VNF Descriptors, as well as some practical examples to support the validity of the proposed approach. Section IV provides insights and validation of the proposed extensions based on a real deployment. Finally, Section V draws the conclusions.

II. ETSI NFV Architectural Model

The ETSI NFV architectural framework [5] [6] is shown in Figure 1.

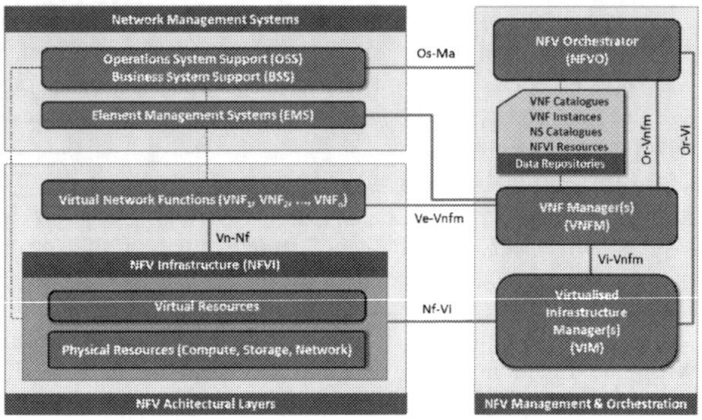

Figure 1. ETSI NFV architectural model.

The functional blocks in the framework can be grouped into three main entities:

1) NFV Architectural Layers,
2) NFV Management and Orchestration,
3) Network Management Systems.

These entities, as well their constituent functional blocks, are connected together using a set of defined reference points. The NFV Architectural Layers include the NFVI and VNFs. NFVI is the combination of both hardware and software resources, which make up the environment in which VNFs are deployed, while VNFs are implementations of NFs that are deployed on those virtual resources.

A. NFV-MANO Framework

The NFV MANO [7] consists of three functional blocks, the Virtualized Infrastructure Manager (VIM), the VNF Manager (VNFM) and the NFV Orchestrator (NFVO), and four data repositories (NS Catalogues, VNF Catalogues, VNF Instances and NFVI Resources). Each of them performs well-defined functions, in particular:

1) VIM: It manages and controls NFVI physical and virtual resources in a single infrastructure domain. This implies that an NFV architecture may contain more than one VIM, with each of them managing or controlling NFVI resources from a given infrastructure provider. In principle, a VIM may be specialized in handling a certain type of NFVI resource (e.g., compute-only or storage only), or could manage multiple types of NFVI resources (e.g., nodes in the NFVI).

2) VNFM: Each VNF instance lifecycle is associated to a VNFM. The VNFM is responsible for the management of the lifecycle of VNFs. A VNFM may manage a single or multiple VNF instances of the same or different types. It is also possible that a single VNFM handles all the active VNF instances for a certain domain.

3) NFVO: It is aimed at combining more than one virtualized network function to create end-to-end network services. To this end, the NFVO functionality can be divided into two broad categories: (a) resource orchestration, and (b) service orchestration. Resource orchestration is used to provide services that support accessing NFVI resources in an abstract manner regardless of the type of VIMs, as well as governance of VNF instances sharing resources of the NFVI infrastructure. Service orchestration deals with the creation of end-to-end services by composing different VNFs, and the topology management of the network services instances.

4) Data Repositories: These are databases that keep different types of information in the NFV MANO. Four types of repositories can be considered: (a) the NS Catalogue is a set of pre-defined templates, which define how network services may be created and how their lifecycle is managed, as well as the functions needed for the service and their connectivity; (b) the VNF Catalogue is a set of templates, which describe the deployment and operational characteristics of available VNFs; (c) the NFVI Resources repository holds information about available/allocated NFVI resources, and (d) the VNF Instances repository holds information about all function and service instances throughout their lifetime.

B. VNF Lifecycle Management

NFV is based on the principle of separating network functions from the hardware where they run on by using virtual hardware abstraction. The virtualization of network functions will change their lifecycle management by introducing automation and flexibility. Lifecycle management of VNFs is possible after a preliminary operation, the so-called VNF Package on-boarding. After that, by accessing to a VNF Catalogue it is possible to create one or more VNF instances of a VNF. A VNF instance corresponds to a run-time instance of the VNF software, i.e., all the VNF components are instantiated and the internal and external network connectivity configured.

During its lifecycle a VNF instance can be in one of the following states:

- instantiable, i.e., the on-boarded process for the VNF has been correctly performed,
- instantiated, i.e., not configured, configured & not in service, configured & in service,
- terminated.

The lifecycle is controlled by a set of operations, described in the following list:

- VNF Instantiation,
- VNF instance Scaling (horizontal/vertical),
- VNF instance Update or Upgrade,
- VNF instance Healing,
- VNF instance Termination.

It is worth mentioning that a subset of lifecycle management (LCM) operations, as VNF Instantiation and Termination, are always available for every single VNF instance.

Some other operations, such as VNF Scaling, are performed if required by the Deployment Flavour of the VNF instance. Some procedures related to VNF lifecycle management provide both manual and automatic mechanisms. Scaling, for instance, can be manually requested or automatically performed when triggered upon the occurrence of specific events defined as criteria for matching rules and actions for scaling. All the operations during the lifecycle are handled by specific workflows that are built on the basis of the tasks to perform and the associated parameters (i.e., in case of instantiation, the VNF ID, the Deployment Flavour, etc.). A workflow has a starting point and different tasks that can be performed sequentially or in parallel, in order to perform all the necessary activities.

A VNFD is used for defining workflows for the automation of specific phases. For instance, by modelling the VNFD using a description language it is possible to describe the VNF with a service template in terms of components (e.g., Virtual Deployment Units or VDUs), relationships (dependencies, connections) and management processes. The management processes can be defined as plans describing how a VNF instance is instantiated and/or terminated considering that the VNF is a complex application composed by different nodes.

C. *VNF Information Model*

In this subsection, we provide a brief description of the IEs used to carry the necessary information to manage a VNF. In fact, one of the ways the IEs can be used is as part of descriptors in a catalogue or template context.

The IEs to be handled by the NFV MANO, including the ones contained in the VNFD, need to guarantee the flexible deployment and portability of VNF instances on multi-vendor and diverse NFVI environments, e.g., with diverse computing resource generations, diverse virtual network technologies, etc. To achieve this goal, hardware resources need to be properly abstracted and VNF requirements must be described in terms of such abstractions.

With reference to Figure 1, the Vi-Vnfm reference point [8] enables the interaction between the VNFM and the VIM, providing the methods to operate cloud resources on the NFVI, in particular computing, storage and networking resources. After the upload of the VNF Package, the VNFM under operator's request or by a request coming from the Or-Vnfm reference point [9] can start to perform the lifecycle management of a VNF via the Ve-Vnfm reference point [10].

The VNF Package contains all files and artefacts needed to perform the lifecycle management for the associated VNF:

- descriptor (VNFD),
- metadata, scripts and other proprietary artefacts,
- optionally, SW images of the VNF Components (VNFCs).

Recently the Solutions working group of ETSI NFV has approved the ETSI GS NFV-SOL 004 document [11], in which are specified further practical details about the structure and format of the VNF Package.

The VNFD is a template, which describes a VNF in terms of its deployment and operational behaviour requirements. It is primarily used by the VNFM in the process of VNF instantiation and lifecycle management of a VNF instance. The information provided in the VNFD is also used by the NFVO to manage and orchestrate network services and virtualised resources on the NFVI. The VNFD also contains connectivity, interface and Key Performance Indicators (KPIs) requirements that may be used by NFV MANO functional blocks to establish appropriate virtual links within the NFVI between its VNFC instances, or between a VNF instance and the endpoint interface of the others NFs. The VNFD contains all the information needed for the lifecycle management, such as:

- basic information for VNF identification;
- internal virtual links description;
- VDUs description: these data are used to deploy the VNFCs on the NFVI (generally as Virtual Machines - VMs). For each type of VDU, it is defined the flavour of the corresponding VM, the SW image for the VM and the number of VMs to activate. Configuration scripts are also provided for the lifecycle management phases and triggered during the instantiation or by specific events;
- meters or measurements. In fact, when the VNF is in operation, measurements can be collected from the VNF itself and/or from the infrastructure, e.g., the number of session attempts per second; the contemporary active sessions; CPU, RAM, disk usage, etc.
- scaling policies. In general, they are based on the values of the measured parameters and can be used, for example, to add an instance of a VNFC when specific conditions are matched.
- alarms and associated actions. Criteria may be defined in terms of rules to check on the measurements, e.g., the value of a meter is greater than a specific threshold for a specified period of time; etc. When a rule is matched, specific actions can be performed, such as the activation of an healing policy, etc.

The ETSI GS NFV-IFA 011 [12] is the reference specification that provides requirements for the structure and the format of a VNF Package. In particular, it describes how the VNF properties and the associated resource requirements are mapped in an interoperable template, i.e, the already mentioned VNFD.

Its focus is on VNF Packaging, meta-model descriptors and package integrity and security considerations. This specification gives a holistic end-to-end view of the package lifecycle from design to runtime, thus capturing development as well as operational views. This is the result of the analysis performed by the working group aimed to use and potentially refine end-to-end VNF Package lifecycle management operations based on use cases and related actors and NFV Architectural Framework functional blocks impacted. This specification has been recently revised in order to correct errors, ambiguities, misalignments, thus applying some editorial modifications (i.e., corrections of category F and D as described in ETSI TWPs Annex L). However, this edition does not add or modify features, nor does it extend the scope of the former version we dealt with hereafter.

In the following, we describe the extensions - in terms of newly added and/or newly defined IEs - of this specification, along with some related examples of use in order to show the benefits introduced in the lifecycle management of VNFs.

III. ETSI NFV Information Model Extensions

The aim of this section is to provide a detailed description, the rationales, the relationships and the benefits of each proposed extension of the VNF Information Model.

Generally, a VNF is composed by one or more VNFCs. The VNF is described by means of its VNFD, that includes IEs for the description of the VDUs.

As an example, we describe hereafter a real implementation of a decomposed VNF. We refer to a virtualized Session Border Controller (SBC) implemented by Italtel that we will use in the description of the following use cases. This VNF provides its functionalities thanks to five different interworking VNFCs, as depicted in Figure 2:

- a front-end load balancer (FELB) that receives network traffic and distributes it to the other components;
- an operation and maintenance module (OAM);
- a control plane component managing the signalling traffic (SIG) that externalizes the states;
- a states database (States DB) for storing the information of the active signalling sessions;
- a border gateway (BGW) function engaged when audio or media transcoding is required for the incoming traffic.

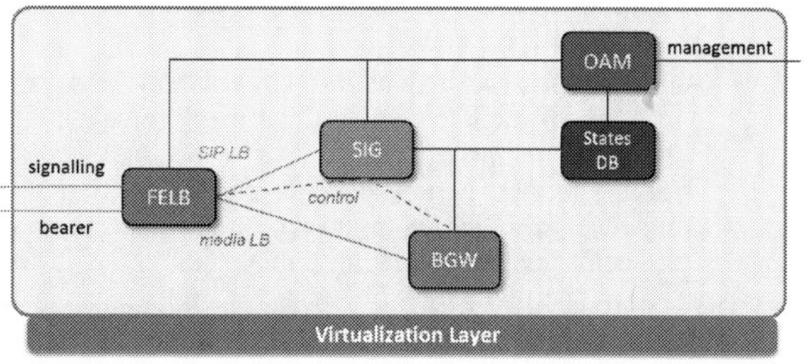

Figure 2. SBC logical components.

These components can be organized and managed to implement protection mechanisms in order to guarantee redundancy and to support high availability requirements.

TABLE I. Overview of Information Model Extensions

ETSI GS NFV-IFA 011 Specification Extensions	
dependencies	IE in the VNFD (vnfd).
metadataScript	IE in the VDU section (vnfd:vdu).
highAvailability	IE in the VDU section (vnfd:vdu).
autoScale	IE in the VNFD (vnfd).

The implementation of this decomposed VNF suggested the Information Model extensions to the ETSI GS NFV-IFA 011 [12] reference document - *dependencies*, *MetadataScript*, *highAvailability* and *autoScale* IEs -, summarized in Table I, with the relationships within the descriptor at the VNFD (vnfd) or VDU (vnfd:vdu) level. In the following, we provide a specific description for each of them.

A. Dependencies

In this subsection, we provide the description of the *dependencies* and *VduDependencies* IEs. It is possible to make use of these extensions whenever it is necessary to express dependencies among the VDUs during the instantiation process. In fact, sometimes it is necessary to coordinate the process of instantiation with information that is available - at platform level (e.g., IP addresses) or application level - at specific times. As originally proposed in the ETSI MANO specification [7], we believe it is needed to include in the VNFD an IE providing the dependencies between VDUs since it describes constraints that affect the structure of a VNF.

Table II shows the structure of the *dependencies* IE that has to be added to the VNFD standard description [12].

TABLE II. Dependencies Information Element

Attribute of the *dependencies* VNFD IE		
Attribute	**Description**	
dependencies	**Qualifier**	M
	Cardinality	0...N
	Content	VduDependencies
	Description	Describes dependencies between VDUs. Defined in terms of source and target VDU, i.e., target VDU *"depends on"* source VDU. In other words, sources VDU shall exist before target VDU can be instantiated / deployed.

The *VduDependencies* IE provides indications on the order in which VDUs associated to the same VNFD have to be instantiated. The contents of a *VduDependencies* type shall comply with the format provided in Table III.

TABLE III. VduDependencies Information Element

Attributes of the *VduDependencies* IE		
Attribute	**Description**	
vdu-id	**Qualifier**	M
	Cardinality	1...N
	Content	Identifier
	Description	The listed VDUs shall be instantiated before the VDUs listed in the target parameter.
depends-on	**Qualifier**	M
	Cardinality	0...N
	Content	0...N
	Description	The listed VDUs shall be instantiated after the VDUs listed in the source parameter have been completely instantiated.

In Figure 3, it is shown a sequence diagram based on a real implementation of the Italtel VNF SBC. It is worth to mention that in this case, all the VNFCs should be instantiated after the OAM component, since it has a central role coordinating the communications with the VNF Manager on behalf of all the other VNFCs.

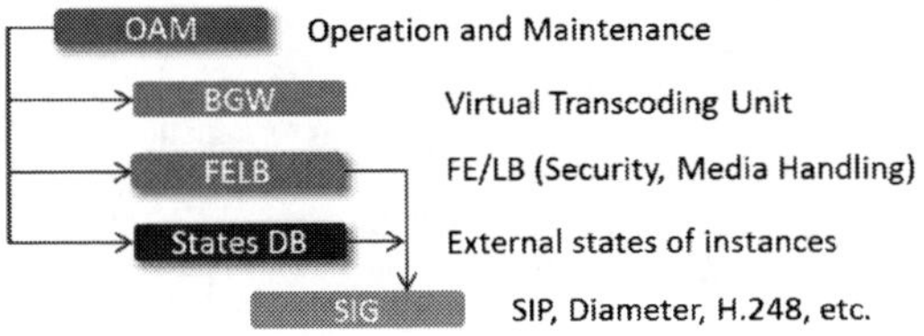

Figure 3. SBC components instantiation sequence diagram.

In Figure 4, the dependencies explained above have been expressed by using the JavaScript Object Notation (JSON) [13].

```
"dependencies": [{
   "vdu-id": "felb",
   "depends-on": "oam"
   }, {
   "vdu-id": "sig",
   "depends-on": "oam"
   }, {
   "vdu-id": "states",
   "depends-on": "oam"
   }, {
   "vdu-id": "bgw",
   "depends-on": "oam"
   }, {
   "vdu-id": "sig",
   "depends-on": "felb"
   }, {
   "vdu-id": "sig",
   "depends-on": "states"
}]
```

Figure 4. *dependencies* IE example.

Alternatively, ETSI envisages the use of a scripting language to express dependencies on virtual resources, but at the time of this writing, no consensus has been reached yet about the format to be used and the standardization process of a Domain Specific Language (DSL) is still underway.

B. *MetadataScript*

In this subsection, we provide the description of the *metadataScript* and *LifeCycleMetadataScript* IEs. These extensions are related to the execution of script(s) in response to particular events detected on a VNFM reference point. The ETSI GS NFV-IFA 011 specification [12] already supports the execution of scripts - but only at the VNF level - with the *LifeCycleManagementScript* IE. Scripts can be launched in response to lifecycle events or external stimulus detected by the VNFM. These LCM scripts should be embedded in the VNF Package and used in the LCM execution environments provided by generic VNF Managers. Although in par.6.2.6, this specification provides a list of requirements (VNF_PACK.LCM.001) for the scripting Domain Specific Language, no practical details are yet available.

Table IV shows the structure of the *MetadataScript* IE that has to be added to the VDU standard description.

TABLE IV. METADATASCRIPT INFORMATION ELEMENT

Attribute of the *metadataScript* VDU IE		
Attribute	**Description**	
dependencies	**Qualifier**	M
	Cardinality	0...N
	Content	LifeCycleMetadataScript
	Description	Includes a list of events and corresponding scripts producing metadata required during the VDU lifecycle.

A *LifeCycleMetadataScript* IE, instead of the *LifeCycleManagementScript* formerly defined in the original specification, has been defined and extended to comply with specific needs originated from practical use cases.

The attributes of the *LifeCycleMetadataScript* IE shall follow the indications provided in Table V. The advantages of this extension, compared with the existing standard specification, are (a) the possibility to execute script(s) at the VDU level, and (b) the possibility to pass parameter(s) to the script(s).

TABLE V. LIFECYCLEMETADATASCRIPT INFORMATION ELEMENT

Attributes of the *LifeCycleMetadataScript* IE		
Attribute	**Description**	
event	**Qualifier**	M
	Cardinality	1
	Content	String
	Description	Describes a VNF lifecycle event or an external stimulus detected on a VNFM reference point.
script	**Qualifier**	M
	Cardinality	1
	Content	Script
	Description	Script name.
role	**Qualifier**	M
	Cardinality	1
	Content	String
	Description	Describes the role of the VDU in redundancy scheme(s). Possible values are "Active" or "Passive".
parameter	**Qualifier**	M
	Cardinality	0...N
	Content	String
	Description	VDU specific parameters passed to the script. Each of them represents the run-time value of a NFVI resource (e.g., IP address, VNFC instance name, etc.).

In Figure 5, it is provided an example based on a real implementation of the Session Border Controller VNF. It is worth noting that this IE allows the VNFM a complete flexibility in the lifecycle management process of different VNFs/VNFCs: in this example, the script for the instantiation of the SIG component needs information from the infrastructure (i.e., the IP address of the connection point *cp_sig_int*, the *hostname* of the VNFC and the related *domain_name*), which will be available only at run-time.

According to our experience, the proposed syntax is general and can be easily adapted in order to suit different VNFM providers.

```
"LifeCycleMetadataScript": [{
   "event": "INSTANTATION",
   "script": "instantiate_sig",
   "role": "active",
   "parameters": [
     "$$param.cp_sig_int.ipaddress",
     "$$param.hostname",
     "$$param.domain_name"
   ]
}]
```

Figure 5. *LifeCycleMetadataScript* IE example.

C. HighAvailability

In this subsection, we provide the description of the *highAvailability* attribute. Availability is defined as the state to perform a required function at a given instant of time or at any instant of time within a given time interval, assuming that the external resources, if required, are provided. This attribute is important for telecom operators that want to offer their customers services that perform as expected whenever the service is requested.

Comparing the VDU IE originally proposed in the ETSI MANO specification [7] with the one described in ETSI GS NFV-IFA 011 [12], the *high_availability* IE is no longer specified. The reason provided by ETSI is based on the assumption that the VNFM alone can hardly manage the multitude of redundancy schemes: high availability policies should be performed by each single VNFC at the application level.

Instead, in our opinion, an attribute specified at the VDU level allows the VNFM to execute specific operations tailored for each single instance, thus simplifying the implementation of the VNF itself.

Table VI shows the structure of the *highAvailability* IE that has to be added to the VDU standard description.

TABLE VI. HIGHAVAILABILITY INFORMATION ELEMENT

Attribute of the *highAvailability* VDU IE		
Attribute	**Description**	
highAvailability	**Qualifier**	M
	Cardinality	0...N
	Content	Enum
	Description	Defines redundancy model to ensure high availability. Possible values are "ActiveActive" or "ActivePassive". *ActiveActive*: implies that two instance of the same VDU will co-exists with continuous data synchronization. *ActivePassive*: implies that two instance of the same VDU will co-exists without any data synchronization. If not provided: no specfic redundancy model is applied.

For example, the statement "*highAvailability*": "*ActivePassive*" implies the active part to request a set of parameters, which can be different from the configuration set, which is needed by the passive part. Furthermore, the active and passive counterparts would require a different set of instantiation/configuration scripts. As shown in Figure 5, this condition could be easily enforced by using an additional attribute defined in the *LifeCycleMetadataScript* IE, i.e., the *role* attribute, which can assume "*active*" (or "*passive*") values, as described in Table V.

D. AutoScale

An important aspect of the scaling, as VNF lifecycle operation, is that scaling may be automatically performed by the VNFM (auto-scaling) [14]. A specific attribute in the VNFD, namely *isAutoscaleEnabled* of the *VnfConfigurableProperties* IE, shall be used (set to true) in order to enable this feature for the VNF. If auto-scaling is allowed, the *autoScale* IE can be used to describe the auto-scaling rules, i.e., the conditions at which to perform a scaling operation. These rules are generally based on the values of the VNF indicators, or on the values of VDU/VL monitoring parameters defined in the VNFD, or on the combination of them. Moreover, the rules may be directly included in the VNFD or expressed using external scripts.

Recently the IFA working group, developing the IFA-023 [15] document, has proposed a stable study on how to integrate policy management in NFV MANO architecture. In this way, policies will give to MANO functions more automatic characteristics, as required in a virtualized network environment. The model adopted consists of two logical entities: a Policy Administration Point (PAP), which defines the policy, and a Policy Function (PF), which evaluates it thus making the consequent decisions. In this context, the auto-scale rules become an auto-scaling policy pre-defined in the VNFD by the VNF provider, which can be seen as the PAP, and enforced by the VNFM acting as PF. Each time the VNFM detects the occurrence of the condition(s) of the auto-scaling policy, it executes the action(s) as indicated in the policy itself.

TABLE VII. AUTOSCALE INFORMATION ELEMENT

Attribute of the *autoScale* VNFD IE		
Attribute	**Description**	
autoScale	**Qualifier**	M
	Cardinality	0...N
	Content	Rule
	Description	Rule that determines when a scaling action needs to be triggered on a VNF instance e.g., based on certain VNF indicator values or VNF indicator value changes or a combination of VNF indicator value(s) and monitoring parameter(s).

In this subsection, we provide the description of the *autoScale* IE. More precisely, we provide the description of the *Rule* attribute of this IE. In fact, the *autoScale* is already defined in IFA-011 while a detailed description of the *Rule* is missing. Table VII resumes the structure of the *autoScale* IE as specified by IFA-011 document.

As mentioned in the description of Table VII, the *Rule* (conditions and actions) may be expressed as a script: this allows to provide specific instructions using a DSL. Anyway, both IFA-011 and IFA-023 documents do not contain further information about structure or domain specific language to be used to create auto-scaling rules/policy.

In light of the above, we propose a possible structure of the Rule attribute in the *autoScale* IE.In particular, they should be expressed by indicating the following attributes:

- *ruleId*, the unique identifier for the rule within the VNFD.
- *description*, this attribute gives a human readable description of the rule itself.
- *deploymentFlavour*, an explicit reference to the Deployment Flavour(s) for which the rule will take effect. Since the cardinality can be greater than one, we make explicit reference to the Deployment Flavour(s) for which the rule will take effect.
- *conditions*: a list of *statement*, i.e., the conditions that must occur to perform the *actions* and the number of consecutive samples (*nTime* attribute) for which they have been verified (default 1). The identifiers in the *statement* are the VNF indicators and the monitoring parameters contained in the VNFD. Logical/arithmetical operators are used as defined in the specification "ISO/IEC 9899" [16].
- *actions*: attribute containing the indication of the type of scaling and a reference to the involved scaling aspect.

Figure 6 shows an example of rule to perform automatic scale out of the VDU SIG for the Italtel SBC.

```
"autoScale": [{
   "ruleId": "SIG_AUTOSCALE_OUT",
   "description": "Autoscale Rule to
      ↪ scale OUT the vdu SIG",
   "flavourId": ["dfTest"],
   "conditions": [{
      "statement": "(KPI_SIG_1 > 30)",
      "nTimes": 2
   }],
   "actions": [{
      "type": "SCALE OUT",
      "aspectId": "sig_scale"
   }]
}]
```

Figure 6. Proposed structure of the *autoScale* IE in the VNFD.

The attributes *conditions* and *actions* are the core of the auto-scaling rule/policy. The former contains a list of *statement*, i.e., the conditions that the VNFM must verify to perform the *actions* and the number of consecutive samples for which they have been verified. In this specific case the number of consecutive samples is equal to 2 to avoid an immediate reaction in case of a burst in the measured value.

Thanks to this simple data model extension, we can map, directly inside the VNFD, the details about auto-scaling in/out rules for the VNF components to be scaled (the SIG component in the specific case).

IV. Validation Use Cases

In this section we provide a description of two different use cases in order to validate the benefits introduced by the proposed extensions. The former practical example take into account *LifeCycleMetadataScript*, *highAvailability* and *dependencies* extensions showing how the information carried by those IEs can be used during the instantiation lifecycle event. The latter provides an example of the *Rule* attribute composing the *autoScale* IE, thus specifying the scripts conditions and actions applied to a real deployment.

A. Cloud-Init Use Case

In Subsection III-B, the mechanism that associates the execution of a script to a lifecycle event has been described (*LifeCycleMetadataScript*). This association, contained in the VNFD, is extremely powerful for a generic VNFM and useful for a VNF provider that needs some specific configuration in a given step of the lifecycle of its virtual network function. In particular, the instantiation phase of a VNF is a very delicate process and this mechanism shall provide all the data in order to bring the VNF in a valid state, in which all the VMs have to be up and running.

Several software tools make possible to reach the abovementioned target. Some of them consist of an agent installed in the VMs composing the VNF through which the VNFM is able to command the execution of scheduled scripts/commands [17]. Other tools, already available on recent Linux distributions, consume scripts containing user-data section. One of the most popular formats for this kind of scripts is the *cloud-config* file format while *cloud-init* is a well know Linux program designed to run these scripts [18]. They are particularly useful for initial configuration on the very first boot of a server.

Since this second solution is extremely helpful in real contexts, we decided to add it when we developed our own VNF and VNFM. As a confirmation of the goodness of our decision, recently ETSI IFA working group has started a new discussion on the possibility to introduce a user-data section in the next version of the VNF Descriptor, together with a VNFM built-in mechanism to pass real-time values as proposed in Subsection III-B.

Another important aspect related to the introduction of this feature is that, if the VIM is Openstack [19], it natively accepts user-data section as optional attribute of the VM creation command.

```
#cloud-config
users:
  - name: username#1
    <user#1 options>
  - name: username#2
    <user#2 options>
  ...
write_files:
  - content: |
      <lines to write to the file>
    path: <dir>/<filename>
  ...
runcmd:
  - command#1
  - command#2
  ...
```

Figure 7. Basic *cloud-config* file structure.

In Figure 7 we report the basic structure of a cloud-config

file that Cloud-init is able to interpret. There are several parts of this script that it worth to note:

- each cloud-config file must start with the string "*#cloud-config*" on the first line. In this way, cloud-init will be immediately aware to interpret the rest as cloud-config file;
- "*users*" key is followed by a list of items, identified by a "-" in a new indentation level, representing the different users enabled on the VM. Various options are available for this section;
- "*write_files*" key is used to open a section describing all the data, placed after the "*content*" line, that will be written in a file specified in the "*path*" line;
- "*runcmd*" key contains the list of commands that will be executed on the VM by the cloud-init process.

Note that indentation is a key aspect in a cloud-config file: it is necessary to differentiate and interpret the various levels in the script.

In the rest of the section, we will show a practical use case in which the cloud-config scripts are executed during the instantiation phase of the Italtel SBC. Furthermore, we will show how the first three IEs introduced in Section III can work together providing essential info in order to obtain a VNF running and eventually ready for service configuration. As already said, each VDU described in the VNFD of the Italtel SBC has a *LifeCycleMetadataScript* IE containing the reference to the cloud-config script associated to the "INSTANTIATION" event. The "*parameters*" attribute is the list of parameters that will be replaced in this script by the VNFM with the run-time values returned by the VIM during the instantiation of the VNF.

```
"LifeCycleMetadataScript": [{
   "event": "INSTANTATION",
   "script": "instantiate_oam_active",
   "role": "active",
   "parameters": [
      "$$param.cp_oam_int.ipaddress",
      "$$param.hostname",
      "$$param.domain_name",
      "$$param.passive.cp_oam_int.ipaddress",
      "$$param.passive.hostname"
      ]
   },{
   "event": "INSTANTATION",
   "script": "instantiate_oam_passive",
   "role": "passive",
   "parameters": [
      "$$param.cp_oam_int.ipaddress",
      "$$param.hostname",
      "$$param.domain_name",
      "$$param.active.cp_oam_int.ipaddress",
      "$$param.active.hostname"
      ]
}]
```

Figure 8. Proposed structure of the *autoScale* IE in the VNFD.

Furthermore, if a VDU has the *highAvailability* IE equal to "*ActivePassive*" it is possible to differentiate the scripts mechanism for the two instances having separate items in the JSON array describing the *LifeCycleMetadataScript* IE: one for the VNFC with the "*active*" role, and the other for the "*passive*" one.

Figure 8 shows an example of this configuration for the VDU OAM: since it has an Active/Passive redundancy model, cloud-config scripts with different commands will be executed during the instantiation of the master and the slave instance. Note that it is possible to customize the parameters lists based on what kind of information the two VMs need at their boot. In our example, for high availability purpose, the passive VNFC OAM needs to know the hostname and IP address of a connection point related to the active counterpart and vice versa. In other configurations, a VDU (e.g., VDU_A) may need some infrastructure details related to another VDU (e.g., VDU_B). In this case, the *VduDependencies* IE is extremely useful since, by defining proper dependency rules, the manager is able to instantiate the VNFC related to the VDU_B, before the component coming from the VDU_A. In this way, all the infrastructure information needed by the VDU_A will be available to the VNFM at the right time.

Once all the parameters in the cloud-config script are replaced with the run-time values, the manager will add it to the virtual resource allocation request sent to the VIM. The infrastructure manager will create the VM on the NFVI and, at the very first boot, cloud-init process will start reading the cloud-config file and performing all the tasks listed in it. Repeating this procedure for all the VNFCs, the result will be a VNF up and running, able to receive further configuration data at service level.

B. VNFD Auto-scaling Use Case

As already mentioned, the VNF Descriptor has a key role in the lifecycle management. In the last subsection we have shown how the details contained in it about architecture, virtual resources required and actions to be taken in certain conditions, are used by the VNFM in order to instantiate a VNF ready to work.

As it is depicted in Figure 9, the VNFM uses the measurement information in the VNFD to collect data and the rules to apply the consequent actions. They are the execution of workflows that can be preconfigured or expressed with lifecycle management scripts.

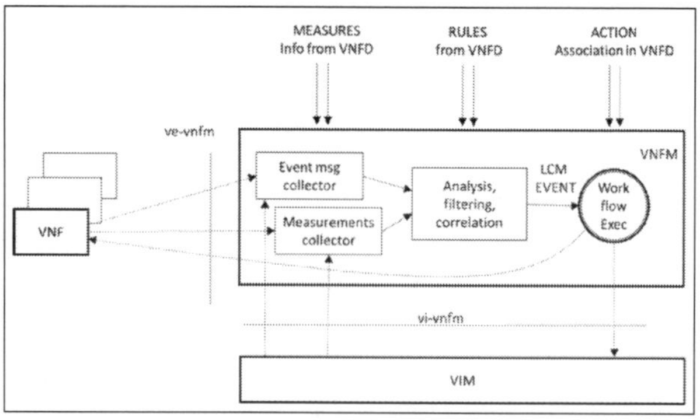

Figure 9. VNFM architecture.

A lifecycle event, that is particularly attractive in cloud environment, is the "SCALING". It represents the ability to dynamically extend or reduce resources allocated to a VNF. There are four types of scaling:

- OUT - adds new instances (e.g., VM);
- IN - removes instances;
- UP - increases resources already allocated (e.g., vCPU of a VM);
- DOWN - decreases resources already allocated.

Although not all the VNFs support these operations, they are very useful in those scenarios in which the incoming traffic increases and new components are necessary to guarantee the execution of the network function with the same level of performance. The Italtel SBC has two VNFCs that scale in/out: the SIP signaling module (SIG), and the transcoding media gateway (BGW).

In the rest of the section, we show a practical application of the auto-scaling use case. By varying the incoming signaling traffic managed by the SBC VNF, the VNFM will perform the SIG scale in/out following the info contained in the *autoScale* IE.

In Figure 10 it is reported the average vCPU load (in percentage) of the two SIG components initially instantiated by the VNFM. At this point, the VNF is fully configured, but there is no incoming traffic.

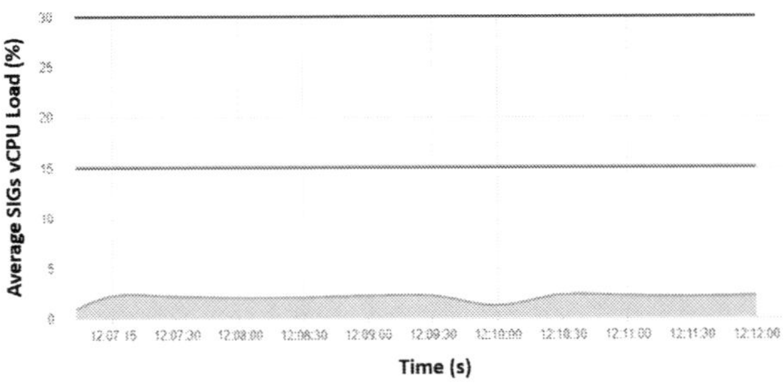

Figure 10. Average vCPU Load (%) of SIG VNFCs without incoming traffic.

In particular, the "scale out" operation, i.e., the instantiation of a new instance of a SIG component, is triggered when the vCPU load (averaged on the different instances of SIG VNFC already deployed on the NFVI) measured by the VNFM is greater than the predefined threshold of 30% (red line in Figure 10) for two consecutive sampling periods (by default scheduled every 30 seconds). On the other hand, the "scale in" operation is performed when the load goes below the threshold of 15% (blue line in Figure 10) for two consecutive samples.

This behavior is depicted in Figure 11, in which there are two aspects that are worth noting:

- after the scale out command, the VNFM will wait another two sampling periods before executing another scaling procedure: this is due to the fact that the new VM can take some time to boot and start all its applicative processes. To perform scaling without considering any guard interval would lead to an unstable system;
- once the new SIG component is up and running, the overall traffic will be distributed on an higher number of instances of this VNFC type and so, maintaining the same amount of incoming traffic, the average vCPU load will decrease remaining between the two thresholds, in the interval desired and designed as the optimal way of working of this specific VNFC.

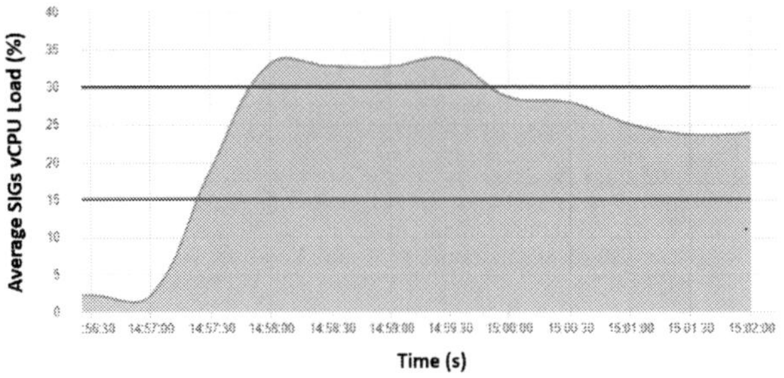

Figure 11. Average vCPU Load (%) of SIG VNFCs when incoming traffic increases.

The same threshold mechanism is defined to automatically scale in the SIG components if the selected performance metric becomes lower than 15%. This is the case reported in Figure 12, where the amount of incoming traffic decreases to such a value that the average vCPU load falls below the blue line for two consecutive sampling periods. Consequently, the VNFM commands to the VIM the termination of all the virtual resources associated to one of the VNFCs SIG instantiated on the NFVI, whose service is no longer required.

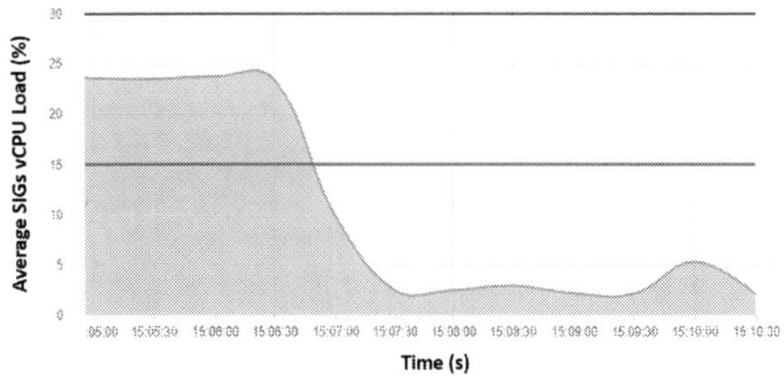

Figure 12. Average vCPU Load (%) of SIG VNFCs when incoming traffic decreases.

V. CONCLUSIONS

In this paper, some improvements have been proposed in Management and Orchestration of Virtual Network Functions, based on extensions of the Information Model specified by ETSI. The need for these additional IEs in the VNFD/VDU descriptor(s) has been originated from a real implementation of a novel NFV-compliant Session Border Controller solution. The key points addressed have been more flexibility in the management of network functions and increased reliability of virtualized systems. As a result of this work, we provided a detailed description, rationales, relationships and possible benefits coming from the new attributes, as well as practical examples to support the validity of the proposed approach. The extensions have been applied and successfully validated in two real use cases related to different lifecycle events of the Italtel SBC solution. These examples demonstrate how the proposed extensions can be very useful to improve VNF lifecycle management and easy to fit into the ETSI specification framework.

REFERENCES

[1] G. F. Andreotti, P. S. Crosta, E. Miucci, and G. Monteleone "NFV Information Model Extensions for Improved Reliability and Lifecycle Management," SOFTNETWORKING 2017, April 23 - 27, 2017 - Venice, Italy.

[2] V. Eramo, E. Miucci, M. Ammar, and F. G. Lavacca, "An Approach for Service Function Chain Routing and Virtual Function Network Instance Migration in Network Function Virtualization Architectures," in IEEE/ACM Transactions on Networking , vol.PP, no.99, pp.1-18.

[3] R. Mijumbi, J. Serrat, J. L. Gorricho, N. Bouten, F. De Turck and R. Boutaba, "Network Function Virtualization: State-of-the-Art and Research Challenges," in IEEE Communications Surveys & Tutorials, vol. 18, no. 1, pp. 236-262, Firstquarter 2016.

[4] ETSI - NETWORK FUNCTIONS VIRTUALISATION [Online]. Available: http://www.etsi.org/technologies-clusters/technologies/nfv [Nov. 28, 2017].

[5] ETSI Industry Specification Group (ISG) NFV, "ETSI GS NFV 002 V1.1.1: Network Functions Virtualization (NFV); Architectural Framework," October, 2013.

[6] ETSI Industry Specification Group (ISG) NFV, "ETSI GS NFV 003 V1.2.1: Network Functions Virtualization (NFV); Terminology for Main Concepts in NFV," December, 2014.

[7] ETSI Industry Specification Group (ISG) NFV, "ETSI GS NFV-MAN 001 V1.1.1: Network Functions Virtualization (NFV); Network Functions Virtualization Management and Orchestration," December 2014.

[8] ETSI Industry Specification Group (ISG) NFV, "ETSI GS NFV-IFA 006 V2.1.1: Network Functions Virtualization (NFV); Management and Orchestration; Vi-Vnfm reference point Interface and Information Model Specification," April 2016.

[9] ETSI Industry Specification Group (ISG) NFV, "ETSI GS NFV-IFA 007 V2.1.1: Network Functions Virtualization (NFV); Management and Orchestration; Or-Vnfm reference point Interface and Information Model Specification," October 2016.

[10] ETSI Industry Specification Group (ISG) NFV, "ETSI GS NFV-IFA 008 V2.1.1: Network Functions Virtualization (NFV); Management and Orchestration; Ve-Vnfm reference point Interface and Information Model Specification," October 2016.

[11] ETSI Industry Specification Group (ISG) NFV, "ETSI GS NFV-SOL 004 V2.3.1: Network Functions Virtualisation (NFV) Release 2; Protocols and Data Models; VNF Package specification", July 2017.

[12] ETSI Industry Specification Group (ISG) NFV, "ETSI GS NFV-IFA 011 V2.3.1: Network Functions Virtualization (NFV); Management and Orchestration; VNF Packaging Specification," August 2017.

[13] The JSON Data Interchange Format [Online]. Available: http://www.ecma-international.org/publications/files/ECMA-ST/ECMA-404.pdf [Nov. 28, 2017].

[14] P. Tang, F. Li, W. Zhou, W. Hu and L. Yang, "Efficient Auto-Scaling Approach in the Telco Cloud Using Self-Learning Algorithm," 2015 IEEE Global Communications Conference (GLOBECOM), San Diego, CA, 2015, pp. 1-6.

[15] ETSI Industry Specification Group (ISG) NFV, "ETSI GR NFV-IFA 023 V3.1.1: Network Functions Virtualisation (NFV); Management and Orchestration; Report on Policy Management in MANO," July 2017.

[16] ISO/IEC 9899, Information technology Programming languages C.

[17] Open Baton: NFV compliant MANO framework. Generic VNF Manager [Online]. Available: https://openbaton.github.io/documentation/vnfm-generic/ [Nov. 28, 2017].

[18] Cloud-init: The standard for customising cloud instances [Online]. Available: https://cloud-init.io/ [Nov. 28, 2017].

[19] Openstack: Open source software for creating private and public clouds [Online]. Available: https://www.openstack.org/ [Nov. 28, 2017].

Chimera: An Elastically Scalable High Performance Streaming System with a Shared Nothing Architecture

Pascal Lau, Paolo Maresca

Infrastructure Engineering, TSG
Verisign
1752 Villars-sur-Glâne, Switzerland
Email: {plau, pmaresca}@verisign.com

***Abstract*—On a daily basis, Internet services experience growing amount of traffic that needs to be ingested first, and processed subsequently. Technologies to streamline data target horizontal distribution as design tenet, giving off maintainability and operational friendliness. The advent of the Internet of Things (IoT) and the progressive adoption of IPv6 require a new generation of scalable data streamline platforms, bearing in mind easy distribution, maintainability and deployment. Chimera is an ultra-fast and scalable Extract Transform and Load (ETL) platform, designed for distribution on commodity hardware, and to serve ultra-high volumes of inbound data, processing in real-time while offering a simplistic fault model. It strives at putting together top performance technologies to solve the problem of ingesting huge amount of data delivered by geographically distributed agents. It has been conceived to propose a novel paradigm of distribution, leveraging a shared nothing architecture, easy to elastically scale and to maintain. It reliably ingests and processes huge volumes of data: operating at the line rate, it is able to distribute the processing among stateless processors, which can dynamically join and leave the infrastructure at any time. Experimental tests show relevant outcomes intended as the ability to systematically saturate the I/O (network and disk), preserving reliable computations (at-least-once delivery policy).**

Keywords–distributed computing; high performance computing; data systems.

I. INTRODUCTION

This paper is an extended version of the paper "Chimera, A Distributed High-throughput Low-latency Data Processing and Streaming System" presented at SOFTENG 2017, The Third International Conference of Advances and Trends in Software Engineering, held in Venice, Italy, during April 2017 [1].

With the gigantic growth of information-sensing devices (Internet of Things) [2] such as mobile phones and smart devices, the predicted quantity of data produced far exceeds the capability of traditional information management techniques. To accommodate the left-shift in the scale [3], [4], new paradigms and architectures must be considered. The big data branch of computer science defines these big volumes of data and is concerned in applying new techniques to bring insights to the data and turn it into valuable business assets.

Modern data ingestion platforms distribute their computations horizontally [5] to scale the overall processing capability. The problem with this approach is in the way the distribution is accomplished: through distributed processors, prior to vertically move the data in the pipeline (i.e., between stages), they need coordination, generating horizontal traffic. This coordination is primarily used to accomplish reliability and delivery guarantees. Considering this, and taking into account the expected growth in compound volumes of data, it is clear that the horizontal exchanges represent a source of high pressure both for the network and infrastructure: the volumes of data supposed to flow vertically are amplified by a given factor due to the coordination supporting the computations, prior to any movement. Distributing computations and reducing the number of horizontal exchanges are complex challenges. If one was to state the problem, it would sound like: *to reduce the multiplicative factor in volumes of data to fulfill coherent computations, a new paradigm is necessary and such paradigm should be able to i. provide lightweight and stateful distributed processing, ii. preserve reliable delivery and, at the same time, iii. reduce the overall computation overhead, which is inherently introduced by the distributed nature.*

An instance of the said problem can be identified in predictive analytics [6], [7] for monitoring purposes. Monitoring is all about: *i.* actively producing synthetic data, *ii.* passively observing and correlating, and *iii.* reactively or pro actively spotting anomalies with high accuracy. Clearly, achieving correctness in anomaly detection needs the data to be ingested at line rate, processed on-the-fly and streamlined to polyglot storages [8], [9], with the minimum possible delay.

From an architectural perspective, an infrastructure enabling analytics must have a pipelined upstream tier able to *i.* ingest data from various sources, *ii.* apply correlation, aggregation and enrichment kinds of processing on the data, and eventually *iii.* streamline such data to databases. The attentive reader would argue about the ETL-like nature of such a platform, where similarities in the conception and organization are undeniable; ETL-like kind of processing is what is needed to reliably streamline data from sources to sinks. The way this is accomplished has to be revolutionary given the context and technical challenges to alleviate the consequences of exploding costs and maintenance complexity.

All discussed so far settled a working context for our team to come up with a novel approach to distribute the workload on processors, while preserving determinism and reducing the coordination traffic to a minimum. Chimera (the name Chimera has been used in [10]; the work presented in this paper addresses different aspects of the data ingestion) was born as an ultra-high-throughput processing and streamlining system able to ingest and process time series data [11] at line rate, preserving a delivery guarantee of at least once with an out of the box configuration, and exactly once with a specific and tuned setup. The key design tenets for Chimera were: *i.* low-latency operations, *ii.* deterministic workload sharding, *iii.* backpropagated snapshotting acknowledgements, and *iv.*

traffic persistence with on-demand replay. Experimental tests proved the effectiveness of those tenets, showing promising performance in the order of millions of samples processed per second with an easy to deploy and maintain infrastructure.

The remainder of this paper is organized as follows. Section II focuses on the state-of-the-art and related works, with an emphasis on the current technologies and solutions meanwhile arguing why those are not enough to satisfy the forecasts relative to the advent of the IoT and the incremental adoption of IPv6. Section III presents Chimera and its architectural internals, tier by tier, with a strong focus on design, enabling algorithms and the most relevant communication protocols. Section IV presents the simple fault model Chimera achieves. Section V presents the results from the experimental campaign conducted to validate Chimera and its design tenets. Section VI concludes this work and opens to future developments on the same track, while sharing a few lessons learned from the field.

II. RELATED WORK

When it comes to assessing the state of the art of streamline platforms, a twofold classification can be approached: 1. *ETL* platforms originally designed to solve the problem of ingestion (used in the industry for many years, to support data loading into data warehouses [12]), and 2. *Analytics* platforms designed to distribute the computations serving complex queries on big data, then readapted to perform the typical tasks of ingestion too. On top of those, there are *hybrid platforms* that try to bring into play features from both categories.

The ETL paradigm [13] has been around for decades and is simple: data from multiple sources, distributed or not, is transformed into an internal format, usually more convenient to work with, then processed with the intent to correlate, aggregate and enrich with other sources; the data is eventually moved into one or multiple storages. Apart of commercial solutions, plenty of open-source frameworks have been widely adopted in the industry; it is the case of Mozilla Heka [14], Apache Flume and Apache Nifi [15], [16], [17]. Heka has been used as a primary ETL for a considerable amount of time, prior to being dismissed for its inherent design pitfalls: the single process, multi-threaded design based on green threads (Goroutines [18] are runtime threads multiplexed to a small number of system threads) had scalability bottlenecks that were impossible to fix without a complete redesign. In terms of capabilities, Heka provided valid supports: a set of customizable processors for correlation, augmentation and enrichment. Apache Flume and Apache Nifi are very similar in terms of conception, but different in the implementation: Nifi was designed with security and auditing in mind, along with enhanced control capabilities. Both Flume and Nifi can be distributed; they implement a multi-staged architecture common to Heka too. The design principles adopted by both solutions are based on data serialization and stateful processors. This require a large amount of computational resources as well as network round trips. The poor overall throughput makes them unsuited solutions for the stated problem.

On the other hand, analytics platforms adapted to ETL-like tasks are Apache Storm, Apache Spark and Apache Flink [19], [20]; all of them have a common design tenet: a task and a resource scheduler distribute computations on custom processors. The frameworks provide smart scheduling policies that invoke, at runtime, the processing logic wrapped into the custom processors. Such a design brings a few drawbacks: the most important resides in the need of heavyweight acknowledgement mechanisms or complex distributed snapshotting to ensure reliable and stateful computations. This is achieved at the cost of performance and throughput [21]. From [22], a significant measure of the message rate can be extrapolated from the first benchmark. Storm (best in class) is able to process approximately 250K messages/s with a level of parallelism of eight, meaning 31K messages/s per node with a 22% message loss in case of failure.

The hybrid category consists of platforms that try to bring the best of the two previous categories into sophisticated stacks of technologies; exemplar of this category is Kafka Streams [23], [24], a library for stream processing built on top of Kafka [25], which is unfortunately complex to setup and maintain. In distributed, Kafka heavily relies on ZooKeeper [26] to maintain the topology of brokers. Topic offset management and parallel consumers balancing depends on ZooKeeper too; clearly, a Kafka cluster needs at least a ZooKeeper cluster. However, Kafka Stream provides on average interesting levels of throughput.

As shown, three categories of platforms exist, and several authoritative implementations are provided to the community by as many open-source projects. Unfortunately, none of them is suitable to the given context and inherent needs.

III. ANATOMY OF CHIMERA

Clearly, a novel approach able to tackle and solve the weaknesses highlighted by each of the categories described in Section II is needed. Chimera is an attempt to remedy those weaknesses by providing a shared nothing processing architecture, moving the data vertically with the minimum amount of horizontal coordination and targeting *at-least-once delivery guarantee*. Chimera also offers a minimum of fault tolerance by being able to replay data in case of failures. However, as of time of writing, it is not resilient to byzantine failures.

Chimera is purely written in Java. The main reason behind this choice is because the project started as a proof of concept in the context of the first author master thesis. As such, given tight time constraints, Java has been picked as primary programming language for its higher productivity over higher performance languages. Productivity includes in particular facets such as the large amount of open-source libraries as opposed to the very proprietary aspect inherent to languages such as C and C++. The remainder of this section presents Chimera and its anatomy, intended as the specification of its key internals.

A. High Level Overview

Figure 1 presents Chimera by its component tiers. Chimera isolates three layers: *i.* queuing, *ii.* processing and *iii.* persistence. A coordinator, or cluster manager, also needs to be present for coordination purposes. To have Chimera working, it would therefore require at least three nodes, each of which assigned to one of the three layers, in addition to the cluster manager, which can by itself be a whole cluster if needed (one node is the bare minimum). Each node is focused on a specific task and only excels at that task. Multiple reasons drive such a decision. First, the separation of concerns simplifies the overall

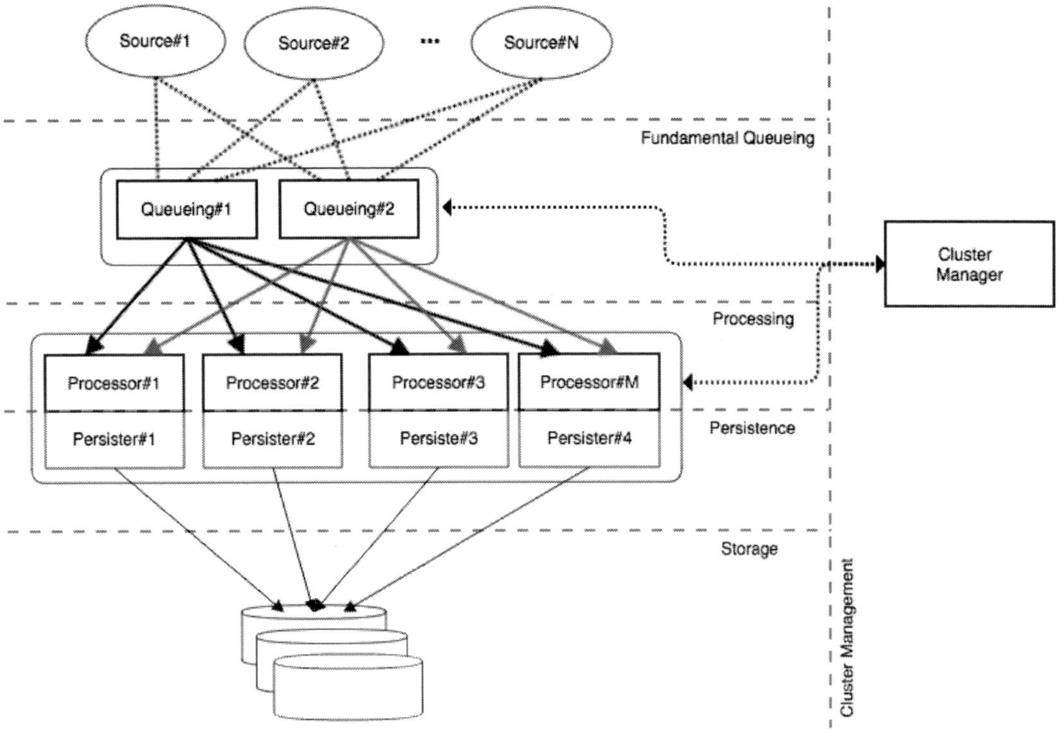

Figure 1. Chimera 10K feet view. Architectural sketch capturing the main tiers, their interactions, as well as relationships.

system, especially from an operational and maintainability perspective. Indeed, given the shared nothing architecture, joining an existing Chimera cluster only requires a handshake with the cluster manager. Secondly, in order to easily scale horizontally, organizing Chimera in a micro-service-like fashion was highly preferable. By distributing the tasks into independent nodes, scaling out only requires the addition of new nodes into the cluster, with performance expected to scale linearly with the number of nodes. Finally, this design enforces reliability by avoiding a single point of failure. Indeed, Chimera strives at providing a bare minimum in terms of fault tolerance. The whole system goes down only if there is no longer a node assigned to a particular tier, or if the coordinator goes down.

B. Internal Data Model

Data ingested by Chimera is first transformed into an internal data model. Designed for time series, the model used follows a scheme based on tags and fields, where the latter are actual metrics that provide the telemetric view for monitoring and alerting. Tags, on the other hand, can be seen as metadata. This schema is convenient for persistency, as it is a popular model used by time series databases, allowing such data to be smoothly persisted to such storages. In Chimera, tags and fields are simple key-value pairs, internally stored as ordered maps.

An important aspect of this data model is how a key is built from a data point (note that the term key here does not refer to the key from a key-value pair perspective). The key is an important component used to compute a hash, which is subsequently used for sharding. The key is obtained by concatenation of the tags, justifying the usage of ordered maps: two data points containing the same tags and values must give the same key.

C. Fundamental Queuing Tier

The fundamental queuing layer plays the central role of consistently sharding the inbound traffic to the processors (a processor refers to a node belonging to the processing tier). Consistency is achieved through a cycle-based algorithm, allowing dynamic join(s) and leave(s) of both queue nodes (a queue node refers to a node belonging to the fundamental queuing tier) and processors. To maintain statelessness of each component, the cluster manager ensures coordination between queue nodes and processors. Figure 2 gives a high-level view of a queue node.

Let $X = \{X_1, X_2, \ldots, X_N\}$ be the inbound traffic, where N is the current total number of queue nodes. X_n denotes the traffic queue node n is responsible to shard. Let $Y = \{y_{11}, y_{12}, \ldots, y_{1M}, y_{21}, \ldots y_{2M}, \ldots, y_{NM}\}$ where M is the current total number of processors. It follows that $X_n = \{y_{n1}, y_{n2}, \ldots, y_{nM}\}$, y_{nm}, $n \in [1, N]$ and $m \in [1, M]$, is the traffic directed at processor m from queue node n. Note that Y_m is all the traffic directed at processor m, i.e., $Y_m = \{y_{1m}, y_{2m}, \ldots, y_{Nm}\}$.

As suggested above, the sharding operates at two levels. The first one happens at the queue nodes. Each node n only accounts for a subset X_n of the inbound data, reducing the traffic over the network by avoiding sending duplicate data (note that each queue node still receives the totality of the traffic). X_n is determined by using a hash function on the key of the data d, i.e., $d \in X_n \iff hash(key(d))$ mod $N = n$, where the function *key()* gives the key of a data point, as described in Section III-B. The second level of sharding operates at the processor level, where $\forall d \in X_n$, $d \in Y_m \iff hash(key(d))$ mod M = m. See Algorithm 1 for a synthetic view.

N and M are variables maintained by the coordinator, and each queue node keeps a local copy of these variables (to adapt the range of the hash functions). The coordinator updates N and M whenever a queue node joins/leaves, respectively a processor joins/leaves. This event also triggers a watch, which causes the coordinator to send a notification to all the queue nodes with the new value of N or/and M. However, the local values in each queue node are not immediately updated, rather it waits for the end of the current cycle. More details will follow in Section III-F.

A cycle can be defined as a batch of messages. This means that each y_{nm} belongs to a cycle c. Let us denote y_{nm_c} the traffic directed to processor m by queue node n during cycle c. Under normal circumstances (no failure), all the traffic directed at processor m (i.e., Y_m) will be received. Queue node n will advertise the coordinator that it has completed cycle c. Upon receiving all the data and successfully flushing it to the persistent storage, processor m will also advertise that cycle c has been properly processed and stored (see Algorithm 2 for a synthetic view of the tasks accomplished by a processor). As soon as all the processors advertised that they have successfully processed cycle c, the queue nodes move to cycle $c+1$ and start over.

Let us now consider a scenario with a failure. First, the failure is detected by the coordinator, which keeps track of live nodes by the mean of heartbeats. Let us assume the case of a processor m failing. By detecting it, the cluster manager adapts $M = M - 1$, and advertises this new value to all the queue nodes. The latter do not react immediately, but wait for the end of the current cycle c. At cycle $c+1$, the data that has been lost ($\forall d \in Y_m$) is resharded and sent over again to the new set of live processors. This is possible because all the data has been persisted by the journaler (see Section III-C3). This generalizes easily to more processors failing. See Algorithm 3.

Secondly, let us consider the case where a queue node fails during cycle c. A similar process occurs: the cluster manager notices that a queue node is not responsive anymore, and therefore adapts $N = N-1$, before advertising this new value to the remaining queue nodes. At cycle $c = c+1$, $\forall d \in X_n$ are resharded among the set of live queue nodes, and the data sent over again. Similarly, this generalizes to multiple queue nodes failing.

The case of queue node(s) / processor(s) joining is trivial. The node announces itself to the coordinator (handshake), which adapts the value of N or M to $N = N+1$ or $M = M+1$. This value is then advertised to all the queue nodes, which wait for the next cycle before taking it into consideration. The new queue node or processor is therefore idle until the start of a new cycle.

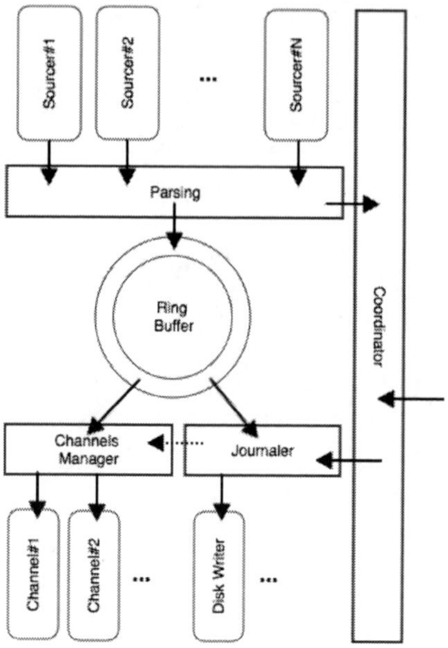

Figure 2. Fundamental queuing internals. A ring buffer disciplines the low-latency interactions between producers and consumers, respectively the sourcers that pull data from the sources, and the channels and journalers that perform the I/O for fundamental persistence and forwarding for processing.

Algorithm 1: Cyclic ingestion and continuous forwarding in the fundamental queuing tier.

```
Data: queueNodeId, N, M
Result: continuous ingestion and sharding.
initialization;
while alive do
    data = ringBuffer.next();
    n = hash(key(data)) mod N;
    if n == queueNodeId then
        m = hash(key(data)) mod M;
        push(data, m); // push in queue m
    end
    if endOfCycle then
        c = c+1;
        advertise(queueNodeId, c);
    end
end
```

Note that the approach described above guarantees that the data is delivered at least once. It however does not ensure exactly-once delivery. Section III-F3 complements the above explanations. Finally, recall that byzantine failures are out of scope and will therefore not be treated. It is worth emphasizing that introducing resiliency to such failures would most likely require a stateful protocol, which is exactly what Chimera avoids. The remainder of this section gives more details about all the components residing within the queuing layer.

1) Parser: A parser is a simple plugin component, which acts as the entry point to the pipeline. It handles the logic of transforming the input traffic into a unified internal format that is more convenient to work with. Recall from Section III-B.

2) Ring Buffer: The ring buffer is based on a multi-producers and multi-consumers scheme. As such, its design resolves around coping with high concurrency. It is an implementation of a lock-free circular buffer [27], which is able to guarantee sub-microsecond operations and, on average, ultra-high-throughput. In particular, the buffer avoids contended writes on the head of the buffer by separating producers and consumers by means of sequence numbers, where ordering is ensured by using memory barriers. Locking is avoided by using atomic operations. Furthermore, the ring buffer is backed by a constant sized pre-allocated array. The consequences of the pre-allocation is that the buffer becomes completely garbage free and mechanical sympathique. Indeed, allocating everything at once highly increases the probability of havings all the objects allocated within the same memory area, thus allowing cache striding, which highly increases cache hits. As discussed in [27], being cache friendly gives a substantial increase in performance.

3) Journaler: The journaler is a component dealing with disk I/O for durable persistence and is the first consumer from the ring buffer. Its task consists in persisting to disk the entire traffic, by consuming the data from the ring buffer. In general, I/O is a known bottleneck in high performance applications. To mitigate performance hit, the journaler, written in Java, uses memory-mapped file (MMFs) [28] and keeps garbage collection to a minimum by working off-heap.

A memory-mapped file is a segment of virtual memory that is mapped to a resouce (most of the time a file) presents on disk. In contrary to typical I/O where reading/writing from/to a file requires a system call, reading/writing from/to a memory-mapped file operates directly in main memory, by-passing the costly operations incurred by system calls (specifically context switches). Because memory-mapped files are accessed through the operating systems memory manager, the files are automatically partitioned into pages and accessed as needed: memory management is left to the operating system. From a system call perspective, creating a mapping is achieved via mmap(). The mmap() system call tells the kernel to map a parameterized amount of bytes of an object represented by a file descriptor into memory. Once a mapping is completed, the application can write into the file by the mean of the memory, rather than going through the write() system call. Using a memory-mapped file therefore avoids the extraneous copies that occurs when using the read() or write() system call, where data must be moved to and from a user-space buffer. These operations now directly operate in memory, which, from the application perspective, simply implies moving pointers, possibly avoiding fseek() calls at the same time.

On the other hand, off-heap programming particularly applies to programming languages where memory management is not handled by the programmer. Java is the most typical example, with its garbage collector. Programming off-heap simply means that objects are no longer allocated on the heap, but directly in the shared memory space. This concretely means that garbage collection will not clear these objects, leaving this task to the programmer himself (a simple analogy would be to code like in C++, but in Java: there is a need to manage memory manually). This greatly alleviates performance hits caused by garbage collection, especially during a full swipe. See [29] for detailed explanations on Java's garbage collector.

4) Channel Manager: Communications between queue nodes and processors are handled by the channel manager module, which is the second consumer from the ring buffer. This module handles the channels that are established between queue nodes and processors. It is moreover the component directly talking to the cluster manager, effectively handling the sharding of the inbound traffic. A channel is a custom implementation of a push-based client/server raw bytes asynchronous channel, able to work at line rate. It is a point to point application link and serves as an unidirectional pipe (from queue node to one instance of processor). Despite the efforts in designing the serialization and deserialization from scratch, the multi-threaded extraction module in the processor will prove to be the major bottleneck of the whole pipeline (refer to Section V).

In more details, the channel manager is a singleton intelligent unit that maintains a set of channels, each of which is connected to a processor. The unicity of the channel manager is paramount for simplicity and to keep coordination within the process to a minimum. Consumers constantly poll data from the ring buffer, and forward them to the channel manager. The latter proceeds to extract the hash from the data point, which is obtained by combining the tag from this data point (recall from Section III-B). The hash is then modded with N (number of queuing nodes) and the result compared to the current queue node ID. If the value obtained does not correspond to the one from the current queue node, the data point is simply dropped. Otherwise, the channel manager proceeds to compute the destination of this data point, consisting in modding the same hash to M, the current number of live processors. The data point is then properly forwarded to a queue, where a dispatcher will further asynchronously send it to the appropriate processor. This is extremely important for the sake of processing: data coming from a same source and that need to be aggregated together must always be sent over to the same processor. This is ensured by the determinism of the hash function. The queues are indexed and mapped directly to their respective processor ID, making it easy and fast to find the appropriate queue given the processor ID. Finally, the usage of queues here can further be justified as an application of the Half-Sync/Half-Async pattern [30], which promotes the integration of synchronous and asynchronous I/O for maximum efficiency in concurrent programming. The whole flow is synthetically summarized in Algorithm 1.

D. Shared-nothing Processing Tier

A processor is a shared-nothing process, able to perform a set of diversified lossless computations, in particular stateful aggregations. Recall that this is possible because a same processor is guaranteed to receive all the traffic matching a same key. Aggregation is an important step as one of nowadays big problems is that most databases are unable to cope with the traffic generated by modern distributed systems or infrastructures. The same applies for the querying aspect. Indeed, assuming there is somehow a way for a database to persist ten million data points per second, querying one hour worth of data would actually query $3.6 * 10^{10}$ data points, a query that would take a while time to return: unaffordable in

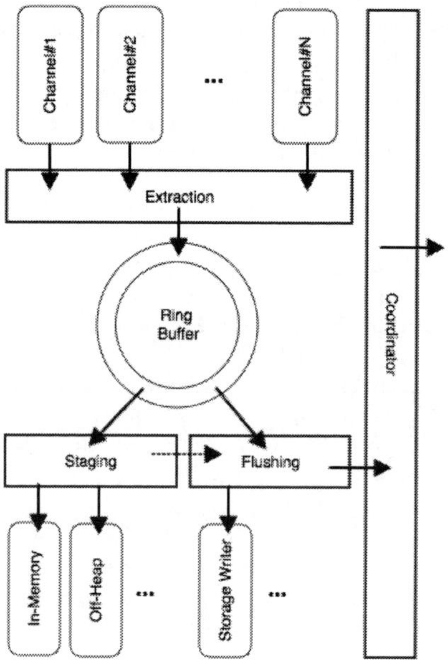

Figure 3. Processor internals. A ring buffer disciplines the interactions between producers and consumers, respectively the inbound channels receiving the data samples to process, and the staging and flushing sub-stages that store the data either for further processing or for durable persistence.

Algorithm 2: Cyclic reception, processing and flushing.

```
Data: processorId
Result: continuous processing and cyclic flushing.
initialization;
while alive do
    bytes = channel.receive();
    data = extract(bytes);
    processed = process(data);
    if to be staged then
        stage(processed);
    else
        flush();
        c = c+1;
        advertise(processorId, c);
    end
end
```

the context of monitoring where almost real-time responses are expected.

Internally, a processor is composed of three major components, which are the extractor, the stager and the flusher, as depicted on Figure 3. When joining an existing Chimera cluster, a processor only needs to advertise itself to the coordinator in order to start receiving traffic at the next useful cycle. Being stateless, it allows indefinite horizontal scaling. Details about the three main components of the processing tier are given below. The whole flow followed by a processor is synthetiacally summarized in Algorithm 2.

1) Extractor: The extractor module is a multi-threaded component that detaches asynchronous threads to rebuild the data received from the queue nodes into Chimera's internal model. It is the downstream of the channels (as per Section III-C4), which works with raw bytes for maximum efficiency.

In essence, the extractor is nothing but a big array of pre-allocated buffers. The size of the array is a static constant and is estimated by using Little's Law [31], rounded to the closest power of two for memory friendliness. The pre-allocation again favours byte continuity in memory and reduces garbage whereas the static size prevents unexpected memory exhaustion. Bytes received from the channel are sequentially allocated in the first empty buffer until completely filled, in which case the next buffer is used. If all the buffers are filled up, the extractor can effectively become a bottleneck. As soon as a buffer is completely filled up, a thread is detached and will asynchronously rebuild the data object(s) into Chimera's internal format. Upon completion of the reconstruction, the thread releases the buffer and returns it to the buffer pool, where it is made available for further bytes allocation.

2) Staging: The warehouse is the implementation of the staging area in Figure 3. It is an abstraction of an associative data structure in which the data is staged for the duration of a cycle; it is pluggable and has an on-heap and off-heap implementation. It supports various kinds of stateful processing, i.e., computations for which the output is function of a previously stored computation. In fact, as for most of the components in Chimera, the warehouse also has a pluggable side, providing flexibility, meaning any implementation fitting the needs can be used. As an example, the processor used for benchmarking Chimera has the inbound data aggregated on-the-fly for maximum efficiency; at the end of the cycle, all the data currently sitting in the warehouse get flushed to the database. However, partial data is not committed, meaning that unless all the data from a cycle c is received (i.e., Y_{m_c}), the warehouse will not flush.

In more details, the length of a cycle greatly impacts the warehouse. Indeed, the aggregation period is solely based on the length of a cycle, which can be defined by time or batch size. This is an important trade-off to make, as a longer cycle will likely means coarser data granularity, as more data will be aggregated before persisted to storage. This parameter requires fine tuning depending on the context. In the case of monitoring, a cycle will typically be fairly small, to keep maximum granularity and almost real-time data. Indeed, the longer the cycle, the later the data will be flushed to storage, which consequently means later query-able data.

3) Flusher: The flusher is an asynchronous component flushing the processed data into a storage of choice. It asynchronously consumes the data from the staging area, i.e. the warehouse, at the end of each cycle. The data is batched into a query that is submitted to the selected storage, and signals the end of a cycle to the cluster manager by acknowledging the data has been properly persisted. The flusher is a pluggable client that handle communications with the persistence layer, as queries differ depending on which database is used.

E. Persistence Tier

The persistence tier is a node of the ingestion pipeline that runs a database. This is the sole task of such kind of nodes. For the benchmarking, Chimera makes use of a time series database called KairosDB [32], which is built on top of Apache Cassandra [33]. At design time, the choice was made considering the expected throughput and the possibility to horizontally scale this tier too. Chimera offers a flexible plugin based model where selecting a different database is possible by simply providing a client talking the selected storage language (the flusher).

F. Core Protocols

The focus of this section is on the core protocols, synthetically and briefly formalized as the main algorithms implemented at the fundamental queuing and processor tiers. Their design targeted the distributed and shared nothing paradigm: coordination traffic is backpropagated and produced individually by every processor. The backpropagation of acknowledgements refers to the commit of the traffic shard emitted by the target processor upon completion of a flush operation (see Section III-D3). This commit is addressed to the coordinator only, avoiding horizontal coordination. To make sense of these protocols, the key concepts to be taken into consideration are *ingestion cycle* and *ingestion group*, as per their definitions.

1) Cyclic Operations: The ingestion pipeline works on ingestion cycles, which are configurable batching units; the overall functioning of the algorithm is independent of the cycle length, which may be an adaptive time window or any batching policy, ranging from a single unit to any number of units fitting the needs, context and type of data. Algorithm 1 presents the pseudo-code for the cyclic operations of Chimera on the fundamental queuing tier, which is mostly performed by the channel manager (Section III-C4), and Algorithm 2 presents the pseudo-code for the processing tier (Section III-D).

2) On-demand Replay: On-demand replay needs to be implemented in case of any disruptive events occurring in the ingestion group, e.g., a failed processor or queue node. In order to reinforce reliable processing, the shard of data originally processed by the faulty member needs to be replayed, and this has to happen on the next ingestion cycle. The design of the cyclic ingestion with replay mechanism allows to mitigate the effect of dynamic join and leave: the online readaptation only happens in the next cycle, without any impact on the current one. Recall from Section III-C3 that the traffic is persisted by the journaler.

Algorithm 3 presents the main flow of operations needed to make sure that any non committed shard of traffic is first re-processed consistently, and then properly flushed onto the storage. Note that this process of replaying can be nested in case of successive failures. It provides eventual consistency in the sense that the data will eventually be processed and persisted.

3) Dynamic Join/Leave: Any dynamic join(s) and leave(s) are automatically managed with the group membership and the distribution protocol. Join means any event related to a processor/queue node advertising itself to the cluster manager (or coordinator); instead, leave means any event related to a processor leaving the ingestion group and stop advertising itself to the cluster manager (e.g., a failure). Upon the arrival of a new processor, nothing happens immediately. Instead at the beginning of the next cycle, it is targeted with its shard of traffic; whenever a processor leaves the cluster, a missing commit for the cycle is detected and the on-demand replay

Algorithm 3: Data samples on-demand replay, upon failures (processor(s) not able to commit the cycle).

```
Data: cycleOfFailure, queueNodeId, prevM, M,
      failedProcessorId
Result: replay traffic according to the missing
        processor(s) commit(s).
initialization;
while alive do
    data = retrieve(cycleOfFailure);
    while data.hasNext() do
        curr = data.next();
        if hash(curr) mod N == queueNodeId then
            if (hash(curr) mod prevM) ==
             failedProcessorId then
                m = hash(curr) mod M;
                insert(curr, m);
            end
        end
    end
end
```

is triggered to have the shard of traffic re-processed and eventually persisted by one of the live processors.

IV. FAULT MODEL

This section presents a basic fault model for Chimera. The model stays shallow as the focus of this work is not security and fault resiliency, but rather scalability, performance and operational simplicity. Given a system deployed into a distributed environment, the system can be defined as a set of processes communicating between them by mean of the network. Thus, the two entities involved are the network and the processes. No distinction between the various processes is made, to stay as general as possible.

Considering three types of failures, which is reasonable given the nature of the system, the following presents whether Chimera tolerates them or not, and if yes, how. Getting inspiration from the taxonomy proposed in [34], Table I summarizes the failures (column) tolerated by Chimera, with respect to its components (row). Given the coordinator and the database are two full fledged external components, the focus will be on the queue nodes and the processors. Worth is to note that multiple failures could occur at the same time, clearly they are not mutually exclusive. Also, despite going as exhaustively as possible through all the possible failures, Chimera does not implement solutions to sustain them all. Only a small subset is addressed, as building a complete fault tolerant system was far beyond the scope of this work. Tolerance can be divided into three categories, each of which characterizes a particular dimension:

- Prevention: This dimension is concerned about ways of preventing a failure to occur. This encompasses, for example, good programming techniques and robust design.
- Detection: This deals with ways of detecting a failure occurred. It is particularly difficult in an asynchronous environment, where no assumption about time can be made.

- Mitigation: This is concerned about mitigating the damages and losses in case of failure. For example, right before failing, a process could attempt to persist its state on disk to ease the recovery.

Chimera will refer to these three dimensions to assess tolerance to given faults.

A. Process - Crash

From a process perspective, a crash could be considered the most drastic failures. Preventing a crash always start with clean coding and testing, reducing the chance of finding the process in an unexpected state. Crashes can also be induced by external events such as hardware failure, but this is irrevelant from a process perspective. Detecting that a process crashed in Chimera relies on the coordinator. Indeed, the coordinator will detect any unresponsive node(s) and act accordingly. Given the coordinator can be by itself a cluster, detecting that a coordinator node crashed is left to the coordinator itself, as ZooKeeper does it for example. In terms of mitigation, the queue nodes always persist the entirety of the traffic on disk via the journaler. In case of crash, the data is therefore recoverable with no loss. In case of the processors, they are totally stateless: there is no need to mitigate as nothing would be lost.

B. Process - Corrupted Output

A corrupted output failure can be divided into two causes: hardware or software. In the software case, preventing such a failure again starts with thorough testing to ensure the algorithms are behaving as expected. Test coverage and test generation are the difficulties here, some techniques are discussed in [35]. Input checking also plays a central role in prevention. A mean to detect a corrupted output is through data auditing. In the basic form, if an output is simply unexpected, exceptions handling should be put in place to avoid any crash.

In the case of corrupted output caused by hardware, such errors (bit flips for example) are simply assumed impossible to deal with from the application level. For example, it is discussed in [36] that CRCs are not enough to ensure error free packets.

C. Network - Crash

Network crash is completely unpredictable and very few people have control over the network (excluding malicious users). Replication and deploying Chimera in multiple independent regions would prevent a complete shut down of the system. Detecting a network crash is straightforward (no communication is possible within a certain region). Mitigating such an event consists in saving the state of each process until the network is available again. For Chimera, the queue nodes already do that, and as the processors are stateless, there is no state to save.

D. Network - Corrupted Output

A corrupted output caused by the network is in principle assumed to be prevented by TCP. This should therefore not affect the system at the application level.

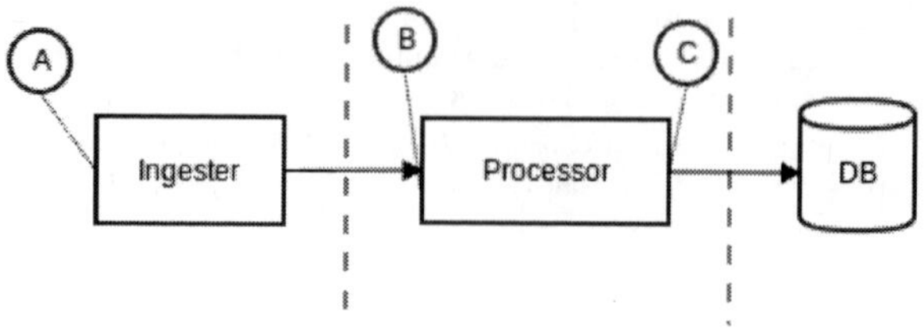

Figure 4. Graphical representation of the experimental methodology used to assess the performance of Chimera, tier by tier.

V. Experimental Campaign

In order to assess Chimera's performance with a focus to validate its design, a test campaign has been carried out. In this section, the performance figures are presented, notes are systematically added to give context to the figures and to share with the reader the observations from the implemented campaign.

A. Testbench

Performance testing has been conducted on a small cluster of three bare metal machines, each of which running with CentOS v7. Machines were equipped with two CPUs of six cores each, 48 GB of DDR3 and a HDD; they were connected by the mean of a 1 Gbit switched network. These are fairly small machines, which is perfectly aligned with one of the goals of Chimera, i.e., run on commodity hardware. Naturally, given this small cluster, one node was dedicated to the queuing tier, one node acted as a processor while the last one maintained the storage and played the role of cluster manager.

B. Experiments

The synthetic workloads were randomly generated, following a pre-defined schema reflecting the expected traffic from a production environment. The randomness might introduce slight unpredictabilities in the size of each data point, which are negligible given the load at which Chimera will operate, i.e. the unpredictabilies will be very small compared to the whole traffic. For each test scenario, a warm-up phase getting the JVM started is ran prior to running twenty iterations were results are being collected. A small idle period during each iteration is in place to clear any remaining garbage from a previous iteraiton. The results for each iteration were then averaged and summarized.

Figure 4 presents the testbench organization: probes were put in points A, B and C to capture relevant performance figures. As evident, the experiments were carried out with a strong focus on assessing the performance of each one of the composing tiers, in terms of inbound and outbound aggregated traffic.

The processor used for the tests performs a statistical aggregation of the received data points on per cycle basis; this was to alleviate the load on the database, which was not able to keep up with Chimera's average throughput. The statistical aggregation extracts typical measures such as max, min, mean and variance. The measures are extracted and aggregated on-the-fly as data points arrive [37], then flushed to storage at the

TABLE I. Summary of the faults tolerated by Chimera. The columns indicate the type of fault, the rows refer to the component involved in Chimera. Process indicate any process in Chimera, i.e. processor or queue node.

	Crash	*Corrupted Output*
Process	Yes	Yes
Network	Yes	Yes

end of a cycle, i.e. batch of datapoints. The remainder of this section presents the results with reference to this methodology.

C. Results

1) Fundamental Queuing Inbound Throughput:

a) Parsing: At the very entrance of any pipeline sits the parsing submodule, which is currently implemented following a basic scheme. This is mostly because the parsing logic highly relates to the kind of data that would be ingested by the system. As such, parsing optimizations can only be carried out when actual data is pumped into Chimera. Nevertheless, stress testing has been conducted to assess the performance of a general purpose parser. The test flow is as follow: synthetic workloads is created and loaded up in memory, before being pumped into the parsing module, which in turn pushes its output to the ring buffer. The results summarized in Table II are fairly good: a single threaded parsing submodule was able to parse 712K messages per second, on average. Clearly, as soon as the submodule makes use of multiple threads, the parser was able to saturate the ring buffer capacity.

b) Ring Buffer: The synthetic workload generator simulated many different sources pushing messages of 500 bytes (with a slight variance due to randomness) on a multi-threaded parsing module. In order to push the limits of the actual implementation, the traffic was entirely loaded in memory and offloaded to the ring buffer. The results were fair, the ring buffer was always able to go over 4M data samples ingested per second; a summary of the results as a function of the input bulks is provided in Figure 5(a);

c) Journaler: As specified in Section V, the testbench machines were equipped with HDDs, clearly the disk was a bottleneck, which systematically induced backpressure to the ring buffer. Preliminary tests using the HDD confirmed the hypothesis: the maximum I/O throughput possible was about 115 MByte/s. That was far too slow considering the performance Chimera strives to achieve. As no machine with a Solid State Drive (SSD) was available, the testing was carried out on the temporary file system (`tmpfs`, which is backed by the memory) to emulate the performance of an SSD. Running the same stress tests, a write throughput of around 1.6 GByte/s has been registered. By the time of writing, the latter is a number achieved by a good SSD [38], and which is perfectly in line with the ring buffer experienced throughput (approx. 2 GByte/s of brokered traffic data). Figure 5(b) gives a graphical representation of the results.

2) Fundamental Queuing Outbound Throughput:

a) Channel: Results from channel stress testing are shown in Figure 6(a). The testbench works on bare metal machines on a 1 Gbit switched network, which is, as for the case of the HDD, a considerable bottleneck for Chimera. Over the network, 220K data points per second were transferred (approx. 0.9 Gbit/s), maxing out the network bandwidth. Stress tests were repeated with a local setup, approaching the same reasoning as per the case of journaler. The results are reported in Figure 6(b), which demonstrates the ultra high-level of throughput achievable by the outbound submodule of the fundamental queuing tier: the channel keeps up with the ring buffer, being able to push up to 4M data points per second.

3) Processor Inbound Throughput:

a) Channel: The channel is a common component, which acts as sender on the queuing side, and as receiver on the processor side. The performance to expect has already been assessed, so for the inbound throughput of the processor the focus would be on the warehouse, which is a fundamental component for stateful processing. Note that processors operate in a stateless way, meaning that they can join and leave dynamically, but, of course, they can perform stateful processing by staging the data as needed and as by design of the custom processing logic.

b) Staging Area: Assessing the performance of this component was critical to shape the expected performance curve for a typical processor. The configuration under test made use of an on-heap warehouse (see Section III-D2), which guarantees a throughput of 3.5M operations per second, as shown on Figure 7(a). Figure 7(b) shows the result obtained from a similar test, but under concurrent writes; going off-heap was proven to be overkilling as further serialization and deserialization were needed, clearly slowing down the entire inbound stage of the processor to 440K operations per second. Note that with a decent serialization framework and an optimized writing strategy, the expected throughput of an off-heap data structure should easily outperform that of an on-heap approach.

c) Extractor: This module was proven to be the biggest bottleneck of Chimera. It has to deserialize the byte stream and unmarshal it into Chimera's domain object, using the default Java serializer. The multi-threaded implementation was able to go up to 0.9M data points rebuilt per second: a high backpressure was experienced on the channels pushing data at the line rate, producing high GC overhead on long runs. The adoption of a decent serialization framework would definitely improve the performance of the extractor by at least an order of magnitude.

4) Processor Outbound Throughput:

a) Flusher: It was very related to the specific aggregating processor and it was assessed to be approx. 85 MByte/s, which is reasonable considered the aggregation performed on the data falling into a batching on the cycle. The characteristic of this tier may variate with the support used for the storage.

D. Discussion

The test campaign was aimed at pushing the limits of each single module of the staged architecture. The setup put in

TABLE II. Summary of the experienced throughputs in millions per second. This table provides a quantitative characterization of Chimera as composed by its two main stages and inherent submodules. Parsing and extraction were multi-threaded, using a variable pool of cached workers (up to the limit of $(N * 2 + 1)$ where N was the number of CPUs available). Tests were repeated with a local processor to overcome the 1 Gbit network link saturation problem. The results involving the network are shown in the light gray shaded rows.

	Queuing [M/s]			*Processing [M/s]*		
Direction	Parsing	Ring Buffer	Journaler	Channel	Extraction	Staging
Inbound	6	4.3	4.3	0.2	0.2	0.2
Outbound	4.3	4.3	3.7	0.2	0.2	0.2
Inbound	6	4.3	4.3	4.3	0.9	0.9
Outbound	4.3	4.3	3.7	4.2	0.9	0.9

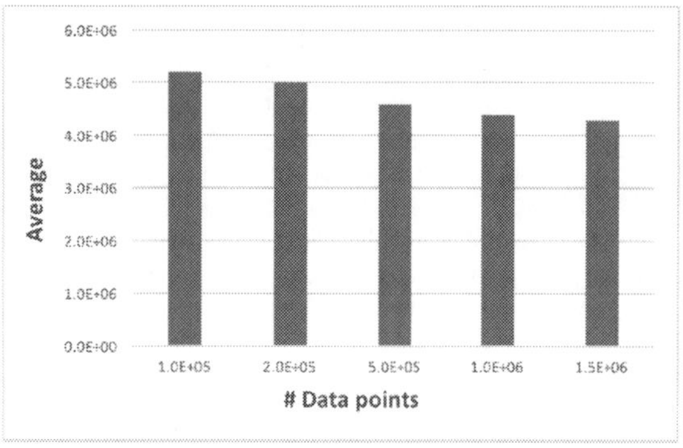

(a) Ring buffer stress test results. Synthetic traffic was generated as messages of average size 500 bytes.

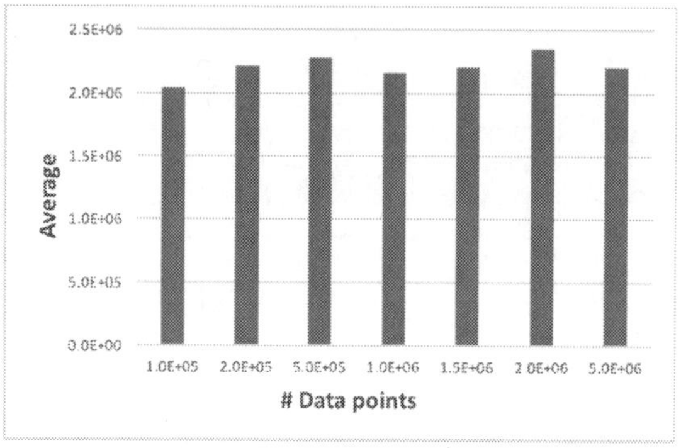

(b) Journaler stress test results. Synthetic traffic was as per ring buffer.

Figure 5. Performance of the ring buffer and journaler.

place was a single process both for the fundamental queuing and processor tiers, so the performance figures showed in the previous sections were referring to such setup.

The experimental campaign has confirmed the ideas around the design of Chimera. As per Table II, Chimera is a platform able to handle millions of data samples flowing vertically in the pipeline, with a basic setup consisting of single queuing and processing tiers. No test have been performed with scaled setups (i.e., several queuing components and many processors), but considered the almost shared nothing architecture targeted for the processing tier (slowest stage in the pipe having the bottleneck in the extraction module), a linear scalability is expected, as well as a linear increase of the overall throughput as the number of processors grows up.

During the test campaign, resource thrashing phenomenon was observed [39]. The journaler pushed the write limits of the HDD, inducing the exhaustion of the kernel direct memory pages. The HDD was only able to write at a rate of 115 MByte/s, and therefore, during normal runs, the memory gets filled up within a few seconds, inducing the operating system into a continuous swapping loop, bringing in and out virtual memory pages.

Figure 8 presents a plot of specific measurements to confirm the resource thrashing hypothesis. The tests consisted in writing over several ingestion cycles a given amount of Chimera data points to disk, namely one and three millions per cycle. The case of one million data points per batch shows resource thrashing after seven cycles: write times to HDD bump up considerably, the virtual memory stats confirmed pages being continuously swapped in and out; the case of three millions data points per batch shows resource thrashing after only two cycles, which is expected. High response times were caused by the cost of flushing the data currently in memory to the slow disk, meanwhile the virtual direct memory was filled up and swapped in and out by the kernel to create room for new data, as confirmed in [40].

VI. Conclusion

Chimera is a prototype solution implementing the proposed ingestion paradigm, which is able to distribute the queuing (intended as traffic persistence and replay) and processing tiers into a vertical pipeline, horizontally scaled, and sharing nothing among the processors (control flow is vertical, from queuing to processors, and from processors to queuing). The innovative distribution protocols allow to implement the backpropagated incremental acknowledgement, which is a key aspect for the delivery guarantee of the overall infrastructure: in case of failure, a targeted replay can redistribute the data on the live processors and any newly joining one(s). This same mechanism allows to redistribute the load, in case of backpressure, on newly joining members with a structured approach: the redistribution is implemented on a cyclic basis, meaning that a newly joined processor, once bootstrapped, starts receiving traffic only during the next useful ingestion cycle. This innovative approach solves the problems highlighted with the solutions currently adopted in the industry, keeping the level of complexity of the overall infrastructure very low: the decoupled nature of the queuing and processing tiers, as well as the backpropagation mechanism are as many design

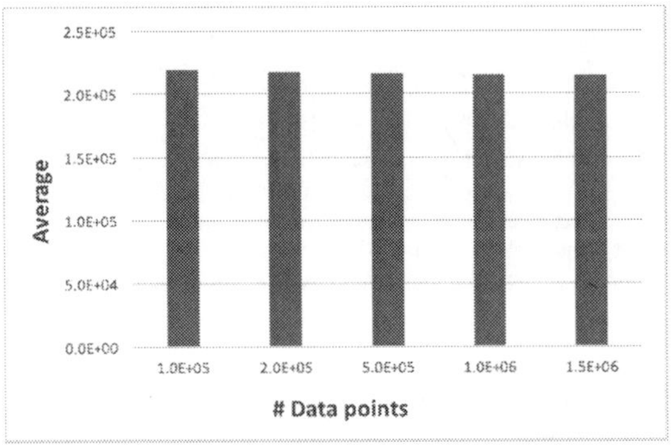

(a) Channel stress test results. Synthetic traffic was pulled from the ring buffer and pushed on the network, targeting the designated processor.

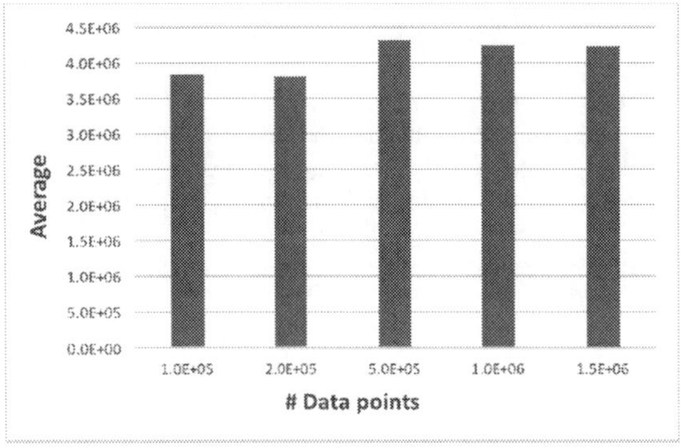

(b) Channel stress test results. Synthetic traffic was pulled from the ring buffer and pushed on the network, targeting the designated localhost processor.

Figure 6. Performance of the channel.

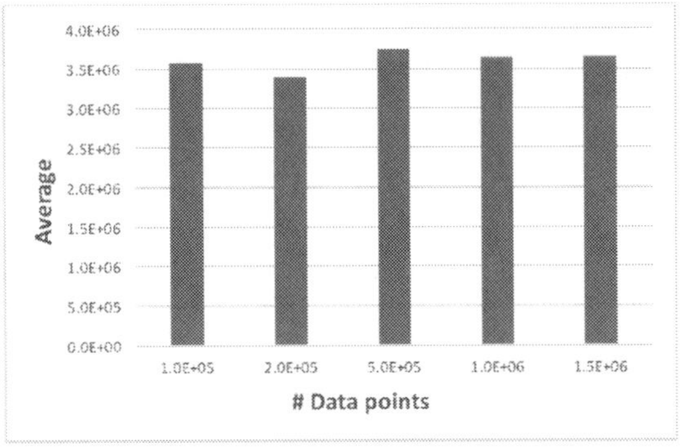

(a) Warehouse (i.e., staging area) stress test results. Scenario with non-concurrent writes.

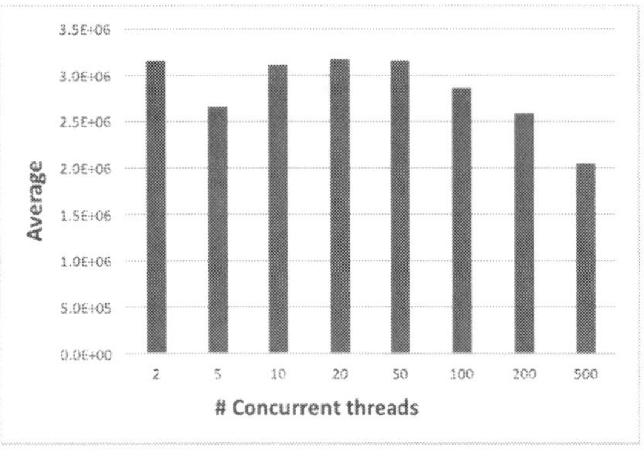

(b) Warehouse (i.e., staging area) stress test results. Scenario with concurrent writes.

Figure 7. Performance of the staging area.

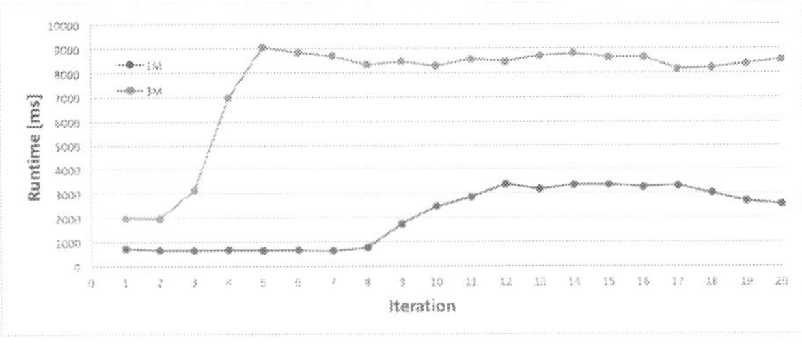

Figure 8. Experimented HDD-induced thrashing phenomenon. The I/O bottleneck put backpressure on the kernel, inducing high thrashing, which was impacting the overall functioning of the machine.

tenets that enable easy distribution and guarantee reliability despite the very high level of overall throughput.

From a performance standpoint, experimental evidences demonstrate that Chimera is able to work at line rate, maxing out the bandwidth. The queuing tier outperforms the processing tier: on average a far less number of CPU cycles is needed to first transform and second persist the inbound traffic, and this is clear if compared to the kind of processing described as example from the experimental campaign.

Finally, Chimera provides a few mechanisms to deal with failures. As explained, the queue nodes persist at maximum throughput the inboud traffic on disk for replay. The statelessness feature of the processors grant failure resiliency to Chimera out-of-the-box at this level, as the replay mechanism is all that is needed to overcome a failing processor. All in all, besides byzantine failures, Chimera yields good tolerance to failures simply by design.

A. Lessons Learned

The journey to design, implement and validate experimentally the platform was long and arduous. A few lessons have been learned by engineering for low-latency (to strive for the best from the single process on the single node) and distributing by sharing almost nothing (coordinate the computations on distributed nodes, by clearly separating the tasks and trusting deterministic load sharding). First lesson might be summarized as: *serialization is a key aspect in I/O (disk and network)*, a slow serialization framework can compromise the throughput of an entire infrastructure. Second lesson might summarized as:*memory allocation and deallocation are the evil in managed languages*, when operating at line rate, the backpressure from the automated garbage collector can jeopardize the performances, or worse, kill nodes (in the worst case, a process crash can be induced). Third lesson might be summarized as: *achieving shared nothing architecture is a chimera (i.e., something unique) by itself*, meaning that it looks almost impossible to let machines collaborate/cooperate without any sort of synchronization/snapshotting. Forth and last lesson might be summarized as: *tiering vertically allows to scale but it inevitably introduces some coupling*, this was experienced with the backpropagation and the replay mechanism in the attempt to ensure stateless and reliable processors.

B. Future Work

The first step into improving Chimera would be to work on a better serialization framework. Indeed, as shown in the test campaign, bottlenecks were found whenever data serialization comes into play. Existing open-source frameworks are available, such as Kryo [41] for Java. Secondly, in order to further assess the performance of Chimera, it would be necessary to run a testbench where multiple queue nodes and processors are live. Indeed, the test campaign has only been focused on one queue node, one processor, one storage node and a single node coordinator. This would also allow to further assess Chimera's resiliency to failures, and recovery mechanisms. Indeed, Byzantine failures have been excluded from the scope of this work, but resiliency with respect to such failures are necessary to enforce robustness and security. In particular, using Netflix Simian Army would be most interesting to assess the recovery mechanisms.

VII. Acknowledgement

This work has been carried out in collaboration with the École Polytechnique Fédérale de Lausanne (EPFL) as partial fulfillment of the first author master thesis work. A special thank goes to Prof. Katerina Argyraki for her valuable mentoring and her continuous feedback.

References

[1] L. Pascal and M. Paolo, "Chimera, a distributed high-throughput low-latency data processing and streaming system," IARIA, SOFTENG, 2017.

[2] D. Evans, "The Internet of Things," Cisco, Inc., Tech. Rep., 2011.

[3] L. Atzori, A. Iera, and G. Morabito, "The internet of things: A survey," Computer networks, vol. 54, no. 15, 2010, pp. 2787–2805.

[4] J. Gubbi, R. Buyya, S. Marusic, and M. Palaniswami, "Internet of things (iot): A vision, architectural elements, and future directions," Future generation computer systems, vol. 29, no. 7, 2013, pp. 1645–1660.

[5] B. Gedik, S. Schneider, M. Hirzel, and K.-L. Wu, "Elastic scaling for data stream processing," IEEE Transactions on Parallel and Distributed Systems, vol. 25, no. 6, 2014, pp. 1447–1463.

[6] H. Chen, R. H. Chiang, and V. C. Storey, "Business intelligence and analytics: From big data to big impact." MIS quarterly, vol. 36, no. 4, 2012, pp. 1165–1188.

[7] P. Russom et al., "Big data analytics," TDWI best practices report, fourth quarter, 2011, pp. 1–35.

[8] M. Fowler and P. Sadalage, "Nosql database and polyglot persistence," Personal Website: http://martinfowler. com/articles/nosql-intro-original. pdf, 2012.

[9] A. Marcus, "The nosql ecosystem," The Architecture of Open Source Applications, 2011, pp. 185–205.

[10] K. Borders, J. Springer, and M. Burnside, "Chimera: A declarative language for streaming network traffic analysis." in USENIX Security Symposium, 2012, pp. 365–379.

[11] D. R. Brillinger, Time series: data analysis and theory. SIAM, 2001.

[12] R. Kimball and J. Caserta, The Data Warehouse? ETL Toolkit: Practical Techniques for Extracting, Cleaning, Conforming, and Delivering Data. John Wiley & Sons, 2011.

[13] P. Vassiliadis, "A survey of extract–transform–load technology," International Journal of Data Warehousing and Mining (IJDWM), vol. 5, no. 3, 2009, pp. 1–27.

[14] "Introducing Heka," https://blog.mozilla.org/services/2013/04/30/introducing-heka/, 2017, [Online; accessed 3-March-2017].

[15] D. Namiot, "On big data stream processing," International Journal of Open Information Technologies, vol. 3, no. 8, 2015, pp. 48–51.

[16] C. Wang, I. A. Rayan, and K. Schwan, "Faster, larger, easier: reining real-time big data processing in cloud," in Proceedings of the Posters and Demo Track. ACM, 2012, p. 4.

[17] J. N. Hughes, M. D. Zimmerman, C. N. Eichelberger, and A. D. Fox, "A survey of techniques and open-source tools for processing streams of spatio-temporal events," in Proceedings of the 7th ACM SIGSPATIAL International Workshop on GeoStreaming. ACM, 2016, p. 6.

[18] R. Pike, "The go programming language," Talk given at Googles Tech Talks, 2009.

[19] P. Carbone, S. Ewen, S. Haridi, A. Katsifodimos, V. Markl, and K. Tzoumas, "Apache flink: Stream and batch processing in a single engine," Data Engineering, 2015, p. 28.

[20] S. Kamburugamuve and G. Fox, "Survey of distributed stream processing," http://dsc.soic.indiana.edu/publications, 2016, [Online; accessed 3-March-2017].

[21] S. Chintapalli, D. Dagit, B. Evans, R. Farivar, T. Graves, M. Holderbaugh, Z. Liu, K. Nusbaum, K. Patil, B. J. Peng et al., "Benchmarking streaming computation engines: Storm, flink and spark streaming," in Parallel and Distributed Processing Symposium Workshops, 2016 IEEE International. IEEE, 2016, pp. 1789–1792.

[22] M. A. Lopez, A. Lobato, and O. Duarte, "A performance comparison of open-source stream processing platforms," in IEEE Global Communications Conference (Globecom), Washington, USA, 2016.

[23] "Kafka Streams," http://docs.confluent.io/3.0.0/streams/, 2017, [Online; accessed 3-March-2017].

[24] "Introducing Kafka Streams: Stream Processing Made Simple," http://bit.ly/2nASDDw, 2017, [Online; accessed 3-March-2017].

[25] J. Kreps, N. Narkhede, J. Rao et al., "Kafka: A distributed messaging system for log processing," in Proceedings of the NetDB, 2011, pp. 1–7.

[26] P. Hunt, M. Konar, F. P. Junqueira, and B. Reed, "Zookeeper: Wait-free coordination for internet-scale systems." in USENIX annual technical conference, vol. 8, 2010, p. 9.

[27] M. Thompson, "Lmax disruptor. high performance inter-thread messaging library."

[28] S. T. Rao, E. Prasad, N. Venkateswarlu, and B. Reddy, "Significant performance evaluation of memory mapped files with clustering algorithms," in IADIS International conference on applied computing, Portugal, 2008, pp. 455–460.

[29] S. Microystems, "Memory management in the java hotspot virtual machine," 2006.

[30] D. C. Schmidt and C. D. Cranor, "Half-sync/half-async," Second Pattern Languages of Programs, Monticello, Illinois, 1995.

[31] J. D. Little, "Little's law as viewed on its 50th anniversary," Operations Research, vol. 59, no. 3, 2011, pp. 536–549.

[32] "KairosDB," https://kairosdb.github.io/, 2015, [Online; accessed 3-March-2017].

[33] A. Lakshman and P. Malik, "Cassandra: a decentralized structured storage system," ACM SIGOPS Operating Systems Review, vol. 44, no. 2, 2010, pp. 35–40.

[34] A. Avizienis, J.-C. Laprie, B. Randell, and C. Landwehr, "Basic concepts and taxonomy of dependable and secure computing," IEEE transactions on dependable and secure computing, vol. 1, no. 1, 2004, pp. 11–33.

[35] I. G. Harris, "Fault models and test generation for hardware-software covalidation," IEEE Design & Test of Computers, vol. 20, no. 4, 2003, pp. 40–47.

[36] Y. Zhou, V. Lakamraju, I. Koren, and C. M. Krishna, "Software-based failure detection and recovery in programmable network interfaces," IEEE Transactions on Parallel and Distributed Systems, vol. 18, no. 11, 2007.

[37] T. Finch, "Incremental calculation of weighted mean and variance," University of Cambridge, vol. 4, 2009, pp. 11–5.

[38] "Intel SSD Data Center Family," http://intel.ly/2nASMqy, 2017, [Online; accessed 3-March-2017].

[39] P. J. Denning, "Thrashing: Its causes and prevention," in Proceedings of the December 9-11, 1968, fall joint computer conference, part I. ACM, 1968, pp. 915–922.

[40] L. Wirzenius and J. Oja, "The linux system administrators guide," versión 0.6, vol. 2, 1993.

[41] "Kyro Serialization Framework," https://github.com/EsotericSoftware/kryo, 2017, [Online; accessed 5-April-2017].

Offline Routing and Spectrum Allocation Algorithms for Elastic Optical Networks with Survivability and Multicasting

Rana Alaskar, Anwar Alyatama, Imtiaz Ahmad
Computer Engineering Department
Kuwait University, P.O. Box 5969, Safat 13060, Kuwait
Email: rana.alaskar@hotmail.com, a.yatama@ku.edu.kw, imtiaz.ahmad@ku.edu.kw

Abstract—**Elastic Optical Network (EON) is an emerging and a promising solution for future high-speed networks, because of its ability to efficiently manage network resources and provide better spectrum utilization. The intractable routing and spectrum allocation (RSA) problem and the eventually imposed survivability and/or multicast constraints play key roles in the effective design and control of EONs. In this work, we investigate priority allocation algorithms designed to solve the offline RSA problem in protection- and/or multicast-based EONs. Our objective is to minimize the total amount of spectrum needed to serve the traffic demand, when the demand includes unicast unprotected, unicast protected, multicast unprotected, and multicast protected requests. The proposed priority allocation algorithms are based on the compact scheduling algorithm and the ordering obtained with two different metrics, both of which consider the frequency slot and required number of links of the requests presented to the network. We evaluate the performance and efficiency of the proposed algorithms across a range of demand frequency slot distributions and a set of different scenarios, in two mesh topologies, the National Science Foundation network (NSFNET) and United Kingdom (UK) Backbone. A comparative analysis of the obtained experimental results reveals that the proposed algorithms improved the results by 2% - 10% in terms of spectrum utilization compared with existing reference algorithms.**

Keywords-elastic optical networks; spectrum allocation; survivability; multicasting; spectrum utilization.

I. INTRODUCTION

Elastic Optical Network (EON) [1]-[4] is an emerging solution for the increased demand of multimedia streaming services and cloud computing applications, because it can efficiently manage network resources and provide better spectrum utilization. Many challenges have been faced by EON researchers concerning hardware development, and spectrum management. Routing and spectrum allocation (RSA) [5] is one of the key challenges to be faced. RSA includes two main functions: assigning a suitable physical path between the source and destination(s), and allocating contiguous, continuous, and non-overlapping parts of the spectrum to meet traffic demand, while minimizing the total amount of spectrum needed to serve it. RSA is considered to be an NP-hard problem, because of the continuity constraint [5]. It can be divided into offline and online RSA. In the offline RSA, the demand is known in advance, and traffic variations occur over a long period of time, whereas in the online, the traffic arrives in a random manner.

Data transmitted through the network can be of critical nature (e.g., military, medical, or financial information). Protecting the paths followed by those data is crucial, to ensure a continuous transfer of data. Survivability is an important design criterion for traditional networks in general and optical networks in particular, including EONs [6][7][8]; it describes the ability to continue providing services in the presence of a single failure, which could be caused by fiber cuts, active component failure inside the network equipment, or node failure [9][10]. Networks serve two types of requests: protected and unprotected. Protected requests are designed to overcome a single network failure, most commonly by assigning a disjoint backup path (optical path, in the context) for each working path. The commonly used protection techniques can be divided into dedicated path protection (DPP) and shared path protection (SPP) techniques. Dedicated path protection means that each working path is assigned its own dedicated backup path, to which it can switch in case of a failure. On the other hand, shared path protection means that backup spectrum subcarriers can be shared on some links, as long as their protected segments (links, subpaths, paths) are mutually disjoint. Two different channel allocation policies can be applied with the aforesaid protection schemes. The first one is a same channel (SC) policy, where the working path and the backup path share the same central frequency. The second is the different channel (DC) policy, where both the working path and the backup path can utilize any available central frequency [11].

Multicast is an important and fundamental communication style, which addresses how to distribute the data from one or many sources to a group of destinations simultaneously. Multicast instead of usual unicast can reduce the traffic sent by the sources and thus save bandwidth significantly. A wide range of applications such as file distribution, multiplayer games, and software updates, require multicast connections and can transfer petabyte-scale data [12]. Multicasting is the most effective communication technique, because it helps increasing throughput, enhancing network's performance, and saving network's resources. The high criticality and wide popularity of the applications supporting multicast services require developing effective survivable multicasting techniques in EONs, to protect critical multicast sessions from either node or link failures. Protecting multicast sessions is more sophisticated than protecting unicast sessions in both WDM and OFDM networks [13]. As reported in the literature, two different path-based protection techniques are used to protect multicast trees, self-sharing and cross-sharing. In the self-sharing, each primary path (i.e., source destination pair) in a multicast tree is protected by a link-disjoint backup path. The backup edges of a backup path can be shared with other primary or backup paths of the given multicast tree, however, they cannot be shared with its corresponding primary path. Links sharing between different multicast trees is not allowed in the self-sharing technique. In the cross-sharing, backup edges, which are not shared with any edges of the corresponding multicast tree, can be shared with other multicast trees, in addition to self-sharing with the paths of the corresponding tree. In other words, both self-sharing within a tree and cross-sharing with different trees are allowed in the cross-sharing protection technique [14][15].

As mentioned above, in the multicast tree, requests are transmitted to the leaf nodes (i.e., destination nodes). Requests passing through a non-leaf destination node are dropped locally, but a copy of the request is transmitted downstream to the next node. The multicast tree need to be protected in order to assure the delivery of the request to all destination nodes. Considering survivability in multicast trees requires taking into consideration both the primary and backup links while solving the RSA problem; in contrast with our previous work [2], which considers only the primary links. In this paper, we extend our priority allocation algorithms [1][2] to handle survivability and/or multicast in EONs with the goal of minimizing the total amount of spectrum needed to serve the traffic demand. Protecting multicast connections from a single link failure, and handling demands with different types of traffic are the contributions of this paper. In the previous work [1], we considered unicast unprotected and unicast protected requests, while in this work, we study the behavior of the priority allocation algorithms when the traffic demand includes unicast unprotected, unicast protected, multicast unprotected, and multicast protected requests. The protection technique used in this work is dedicated path protection with same channel (RSA/DPP/SC), while the multicast protection technique is path-pair protection. We consider spectrum usage as a performance metric, to show the effectiveness of the proposed algorithms.

The rest of the paper is structured as follows. Section II sheds light on the research efforts related to the problem. Section III formulates the problem. Section IV reviews the proposed algorithms, with working examples. Section V discusses the experimental results. We present our conclusions with some ideas for future work in the last section.

II. Pelated Work

In this section, we briefly present research efforts that have been proposed to handle offline RSA problem, survivability, multicasting, and survivability in multicasting for EONs. A significant amount of research has been conducted addressing the offline RSA problem [2][16]-[18]. For more details about the spectrum management techniques in EONs, readers are referred to the recent excellent surveys in [19][20].

Previous investigations have been carried out to study the issue of survivability in EONs. Some of these research efforts have been directed to the online RSA problem [21][22], whereas others considered the offline RSA problem in survivable EONs, considering the different protection techniques mentioned above. In particular, the use of DPP in EONs has been addressed in [1][11][18][23]-[26]. Alaskar et al. [1] addressed offline RSA with dedicated path protection in EONs with same channel (RSA/DPP/SC). They proposed different priority allocation mechanisms to enhance requests allocation in the network. Ruan et al. [26] studied the offline survivable multi-path RSA problem with DPP in EONs. They formulated the problem as an integer linear programming (ILP) problem, and proposed a heuristic algorithm for the static multipath routing and spectrum allocation (SM-RSA) problem. The RSA problem in EONs with DPP with static traffic demand has also been addressed in another work presented by Klinkowski [18], where the author used genetic algorithms to develop an efficient algorithm, which performs better than other reference algorithms. Concurrently, the use of SPP in EONs has been studied by many researchers [12][27]-[30]. Walkowiak et al. [29] addressed the offline RSA problem in EONs with SPP, formulating it also as an ILP problem. Another work presented by Liu et al. [31] handled spectrum fragmentation and low sharing degree in survivable EONs, by proposing an algorithm called shared path protection by reconstructing sharable bandwidth based on spectrum segmentation (SPP-RSB-SS). The aim of the algorithm was to minimize spectrum fragmentation and utilization. Recently, Goscien et al. [32] studied the survivability of EONs when the traffic demands include unicast and anycast requests, by applying multipath routing. They formulated the problem as an ILP, and proposed an algorithm called survivable multipath allocation (SMA). The problem of spectrum-aware survivable strategies with failure probability constraints has been addressed by Chen et al. [33]. They considered both dedicated and shared path protection by developing ILP models, with the goal of minimizing resource consumption. More details about the use of protection techniques in EONs can be found in [34][35], recent surveys of the topic.

Many algorithms have been introduced to solve the multicast tree problem in EONs. Kmiecik et al. [36] studied a two-layer optimization problem that combines both multicasting optimization in the application layer and the optimization of lightpaths in EONs, considering different survivability scenarios. In another work, Goscien et al. [37] addressed the routing, modulation, and spectrum allocation problem in EONs. They formulated the problem as an ILP covering both unicast and anycast traffic demands. Their proposed method is based on the standard tabu search approach. Liu et al. [38] have designed integrated multicast-capable routing and spectrum assignment (MC-RSA) algorithms by incorporating a layered approach with the aim of efficient serving of multicast requests in EONs.

Much research has been conducted to provide protection to the multicast sessions in EONs. The authors in [15] proposed a cross-sharing approach, which provides an optimal backup resources sharing between multiple multicast sessions. Their solution maximizes the sharing between multiple multicast sessions by using a link vector model. Another work proposed by Gong et al. [39] handled the problem of protecting multicast requests by proposing two ILP models. In the same context, Cai et al. [14] have evaluated both self- and cross-sharing protection schemes for distance-adaptive for multicast RSA in EONs, by formulating the problem as a mixed integer linear programming (MILP) problem. A general load balancing technique (LBT) has been proposed by Constantinou et al. [40] to be combined with any survivable multicasting approach, with the goal of balancing the distribution of the network load. The aforementioned works formulated the problem as an ILP, which is complicated, as compared with our proposed algorithms. The proposed heuristics provide a good quality solution since they are fast, and scalable.

III. Problem Formulation

In this section, we present and explain the offline RSA problem in protection/multicasting-based EONs, with an example that will be used in the priority allocation algorithms section.

A. Problem Statement

The problem to be addressed can be formulated as follows: Given: a) A directed graph $G(V, E)$, where G denotes the physical topology of an EON, V denotes the set of nodes, and E denotes the set of bidirectional optical links. b) A set of frequency slices (i.e., subcarriers) in each optical link, of cardinality sc. c) A set of requests between source-destination pairs $(s, d)_i$ of request size (i.e., the number of frequency slices needed to serve a request) sz, where $i \in I$ represents the request type. Our aim is to minimize the total amount of spectrum needed to serve the traffic demand—which includes different types of requests to the mesh network—under the following constraints:

1) Spectrum contiguity constraint: Each request should be assigned to a contiguous portion of the spectrum.

2) Spectrum continuity constraint: Each request should be assigned to a similar portion of spectrum for all the corresponding links.

3) Non-overlapping spectrum constraint: Requests that need to use similar links should be assigned to non-overlapping portions of the spectrum.

4) Same channel (applies only to RSA/DPP/SC): For each unicast protected request, the working and backup paths should be assigned to similar portions of the spectrum.

In this paper, we consider four types of requests, $I = \{1, 2, 3, 4\}$. A request can be unicast unprotected ($i = 1$), unicast protected ($i = 2$), multicast unprotected ($i = 3$), or multicast protected ($i = 4$). When the demand includes a unicast unprotected request $(s, d)_1$ from s to d, the request will be served by contiguous subcarriers on all optical links belonging to the predetermined fixed working path from s to d. However, when the demand includes a unicast protected request $(s, d)_2$ from s to d, the request will be served by contiguous subcarriers on all optical links belonging to both the predetermined fixed working and backup paths from s to d. When the demand includes a multicast unprotected request $(s, d_n)_3$ from s to $\{d_1, d_2, d_3, ..., d_n\}$, the request will be served by contiguous subcarriers on all optical links belonging to the predetermined subgraph $G(s, d_n)_3$. When the demand includes a multicast protected request $(s, d_n)_4$ from s to $\{d_1, d_2, d_3, ..., d_n\}$, the request will be served by contiguous subcarriers on all optical links belonging to both the predetermined fixed working and backup subgraphs.

B. Example

To exemplify the problem, consider the mesh network illustrated in Figure 1, with 11 nodes and 16 bidirectional links. Table I shows the requests made to the mesh network, their type (unicast protected or multicast protected), size (4, 40, or 100), and the nodes traversed by the working and backup paths.

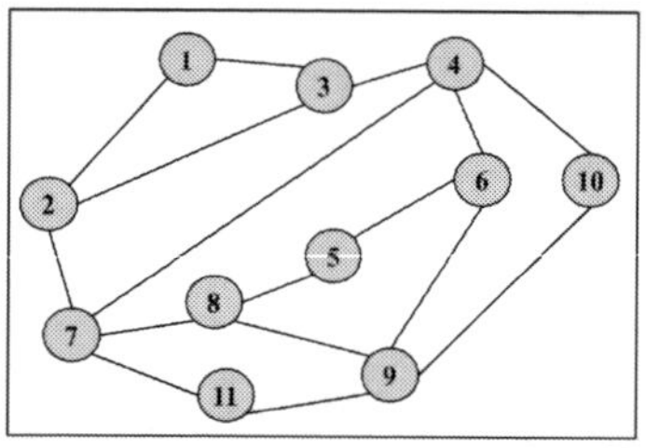

Figure 1. Mesh network with 11 nodes.

TABLE I. Requests Made to the Mesh Network

Requests	Type of request	Size (sz)	Working links	Backup links
τ_1 (8 → 5)$_2$	Unicast protected	100	8-5	8-9 9-6 6-5
τ_2 (6 → 5)$_2$	Unicast protected	100	6-5	6-9 9-8 8-5
τ_3 (3 → 2)$_2$	Unicast protected	4	3-2	3-1 1-2
τ_4 (1 → 2, 3, 4, 6)$_4$	Multicast protected	40	1-2 1-3 3-4 4-6	2-3 3-2 2-7 7-4 | 9-6 4-10 10-9
τ_5 (1 → 2, 3)$_4$	Multicast protected	100	1-2 1-3	3-2 2-3
τ_6 (4 → 1, 2)$_4$	Multicast protected	4	4-3 3-1 3-2	1-2 2-1 7-2 4-7
τ_7 (6 → 11)$_2$	Unicast protected	4	6-9 9-11	6-4 4-7 7-11
τ_8 (7 → 9)$_2$	Unicast protected	4	7-8 8-9	7-11 11-9

For the unicast protected requests, the working path is fixed and arbitrarily selected from the set of shortest paths computed with Dijkstra's algorithm; likewise, the backup path is fixed and arbitrarily selected from the set of shortest paths computed by Dijkstra's algorithm, after removing all edges belonging to the working path. For the multicast protected requests, a multicast tree is fixed and arbitrarily selected based on the minimum total number of links belonging to a rooted tree at the source *s* to the set of destination nodes $\{d_1, d_2, d_3, ..., d_n\}$. Each link in the working tree is protected separately (rather than the entire tree).

Those requests will be sorted based on the selected sorting mechanism, and the sorted list of requests will be used as an input to the compact scheduling algorithm [9]. The proposed priority allocation algorithms aim to optimize the mapping of requests to spectral resources, and minimize the total amount of spectrum needed to serve the traffic demand without violating the above-mentioned constraints.

IV. PRIORITY ALLOCATION ALGORITHMS

In this section, we evaluate the extended version of the proposed algorithms [1][2] as a solution to the offline RSA problem in survivable and/or multicast OFDM optical networks; the objective is to minimize the amount of spectrum needed to serve traffic demand when it includes unicast protected, and multicast protected requests. The RSA problem has two different dimensions: the spectrum (or bandwidth) and the links. The combination of these two dimensions plays a key role in improving the process of spectrum allocation. Therefore, the proposed solution is based on combining them in multiple ways. First, we introduce the compact scheduling algorithm [17], which has been used to show the effectiveness of the proposed algorithms. We then review the priority allocation algorithms; specifically, the sorting mechanisms. Finally, we show a working example, to demonstrate the performance of the algorithms when compared with the existing algorithms.

A. Compact Scheduling Algorithm

The proposed algorithms are based on an existing algorithm, the compact scheduling algorithm, proposed by Talebi et al. [17]. The compact scheduling algorithm is a typical list scheduling algorithm, where the quality of the solution is very sensitive to the order of requests in the list. It has a complexity of $O(n^2)$, where n is the number of requests in the list.

The input to the compact scheduling algorithm is a sorted list of requests to the mesh network. Figure 2 represents the flowchart of the compact scheduling algorithm, where *L* is the list of requests, *id* is the request location in the list, and *t* is the current execution time. The compact scheduling algorithm is constituted by the following steps:

1) Select the first request in the list and assign it to a set of consecutive links.
2) Delete the executed request from the list, and update the status (idle or busy) of the corresponding links.
3) Scan the list at the same scheduling instant to select requests that can be executed simultaneously with the currently executed requests.
4) Continue scanning the list until there are no other requests that can be executed at that scheduling instant or no available links.
5) Advance the scheduling time based on the earliest finishing request, and add the available links to the set of free links.
6) Repeat the aforementioned steps until all the requests have been satisfied.

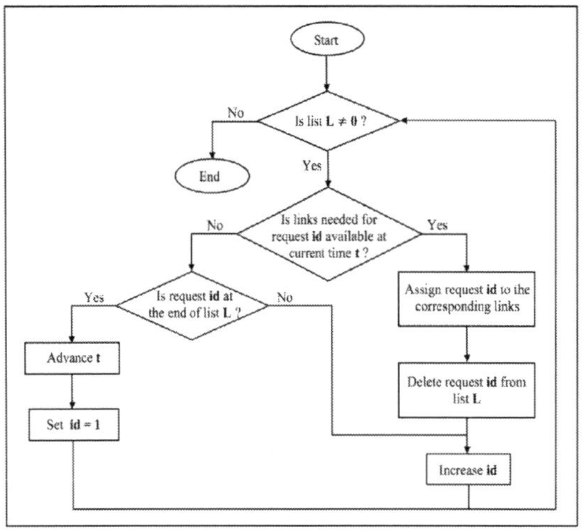

Figure 2. Compact schedulling algorithm flowchart.

B. Sorting Mechanisms

The proposed algorithms consider both dimensions of the problem: the links and the spectrum (or bandwidth). It is worth mentioning that in the present paper the link dimension is represented by the number of links used by the working path in the case of unicast unprotected requests, and by the number of links used by both the working and backup paths in the case of unicast protected requests. Similarly, in the case of multicast unprotected requests, it consists of the number of links in the working multicast tree, and the number of links in both working and backup multicast trees in the case multicast protected requests. On the other hand, in our previous work [2], the link dimension was represented by the number of links used by only the working path, because only unicast unprotected requests were being considered there. The complexity of the proposed algorithms is the same as of compact scheduling algorithm, which is $O(n^2)$, where n is the number of requests in the list. The proposed algorithms only sort the requests based on the selected criterion and pass them to the compact scheduling algorithm. The complexity of sorting algorithm is O(nlogn). Therefore, the running time of the algorithms is bounded by the complexity of the compact scheduling algorithm. The sorting mechanisms, the longest then widest compact algorithm (LWC) and the area compact algorithm (AC), are described below.

1) Longest then Widest Compact Algorithm (LWC): In the first proposed algorithm, we consider both dimensions of the problem, the links and spectrum (or bandwidth), using two levels (a primary and a secondary sorting mechanisms) to sort the requests in the demand. In the primary sorting mechanism, requests are sorted based on the amount of needed spectrum or bandwidth, from higher to lower. Then, in the secondary sorting mechanism, requests with equal bandwidth are sorted based on the required number of links from higher to lower.

2) Area Compact Algorithm (AC): In the second proposed algorithm, we also consider both dimensions of the problem, but in a different way. The amount of spectrum needed for a request and the required number of links are multiplied, thus providing a shape area. This area captures both dimensions of the problem and constitutes a better ordering metric. In this mechanism, the areas are used to sort the requests in the list, from higher to lower.

C. *Working Example*

In this subsection, we discuss the behavior of the above-mentioned algorithms, and show how different sorting mechanisms can affect the amount of spectrum needed to satisfy the demand, when it includes both unicast protected and multicast protected requests. As mentioned previously, existing algorithms [17] considered one dimension of the problem (i.e., either the bandwidth or the links), while our proposed algorithms consider both dimensions of the problem. As a result, the process of spectrum allocation is improved, and the number of needed subcarriers is decreased greatly while using our algorithms. Note that the request lists presented below are based on the demand shown in Table I in the problem formulation section.

1) Existing Algorithms:

The longest first compact algorithm (LFC) [17], sorts the requests based on the required amount of spectrum, from higher to lower. The sorted list of requests that will be used as input to the compact scheduling algorithm after applying the LFC algorithm is shown below:

$$\{\tau_2, \tau_5, \tau_1, \tau_4, \tau_3, \tau_6, \tau_7, \tau_8\}$$

Running the compact scheduling algorithm with LFC shows that 240 subcarriers are needed to serve the considered demand (which includes both unicast and multicast protected requests).

The widest first compact algorithm (WFC) [17], sorts the requests based on the required number of links used by the working and/or backup paths, from higher to lower. The sorted list of requests that will be used as input to the compact scheduling algorithm after applying the WFC algorithm is shown below:

$$\{\tau_4, \tau_6, \tau_7, \tau_8, \tau_1, \tau_2, \tau_5, \tau_3\}$$

Running the compact scheduling algorithm with WFC shows that 204 subcarriers are needed to serve the considered demand. The number of required subcarriers using WFC is therefore lower than when using LFC.

2) Proposed Algorithms (LWC):

The sorted list of requests that will be used as input to the compact scheduling algorithm after applying the LWC algorithm is shown below:

$$\{\tau_5, \tau_1, \tau_2, \tau_4, \tau_6, \tau_7, \tau_8, \tau_3\}$$

Running the compact scheduling algorithm with LWC shows that only 200 subcarriers are needed to serve the same demand. The number of subcarriers needed with LWC is therefore lower than if either LFC or WFC are used (240 and 204, respectively).

3) Proposed Algorithms (AC):

The sorted list of requests that will be used as input to the compact scheduling algorithm after applying the AC algorithm is shown below:

$$\{\tau_4, \tau_5, \tau_1, \tau_2, \tau_6, \tau_7, \tau_8, \tau_3\}$$

In Figure 3 (a), request 4 is assigned at t = 0, and it occupies 40 subcarriers from the following links: 1-2, 1-3, 3-4, 4-6, 2-3, 3-2, 2-7, 7-4, 9-6, 4-10, and10-9. Then, request 2 is assigned, and it occupies 100 subcarriers from the following links: 6-5, 6-9, 9-8, and 8-5. Last request that will be assigned at t = 0 is request 8, and it occupies 4 subcarriers from the following links: 7-8, 8-9, 7-11, and 11-9. After that, the time is advanced to t = 40, and the request list is scanned again. Figure 3 shows the spectrum utilization as time proceeds, using the AC algorithm. Running the compact scheduling algorithm with AC shows that 200 subcarriers are required for the considered demand.

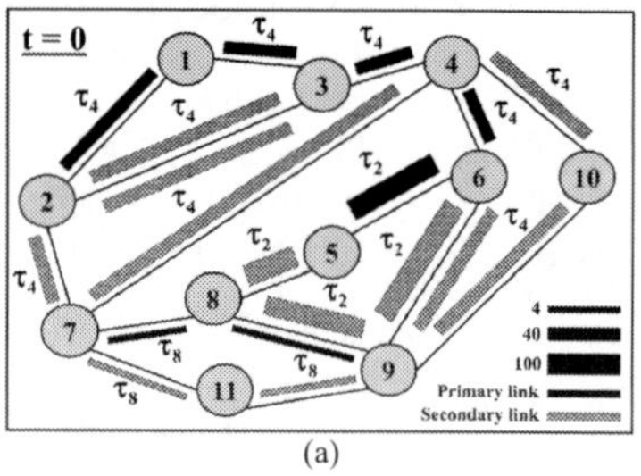

(a)

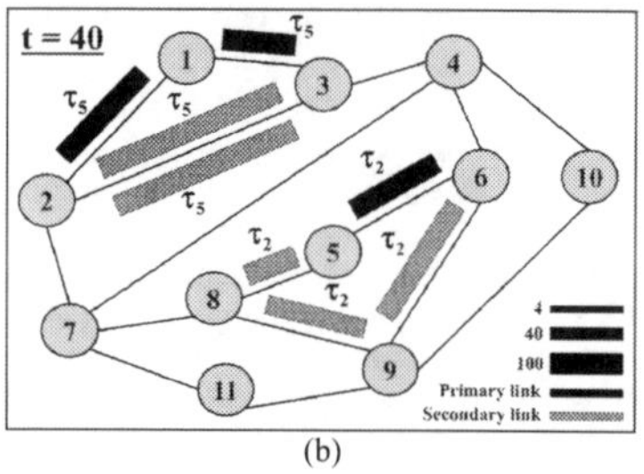

(b)

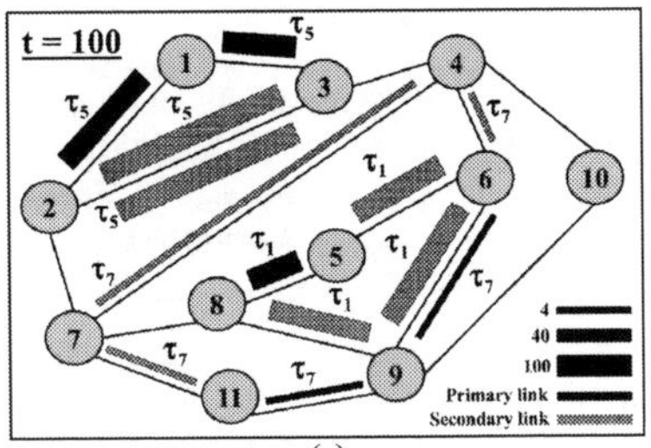

(c)

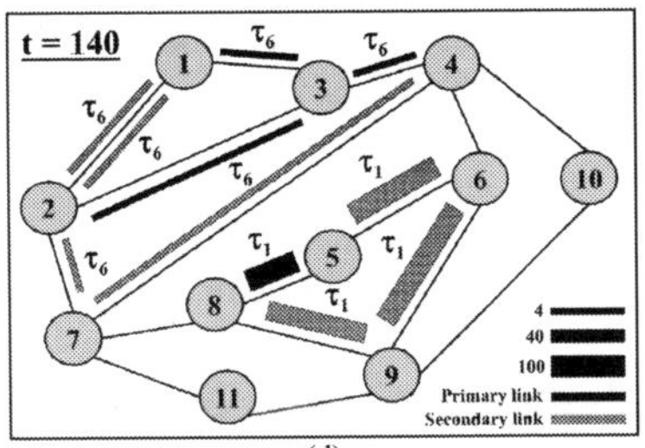

(d)

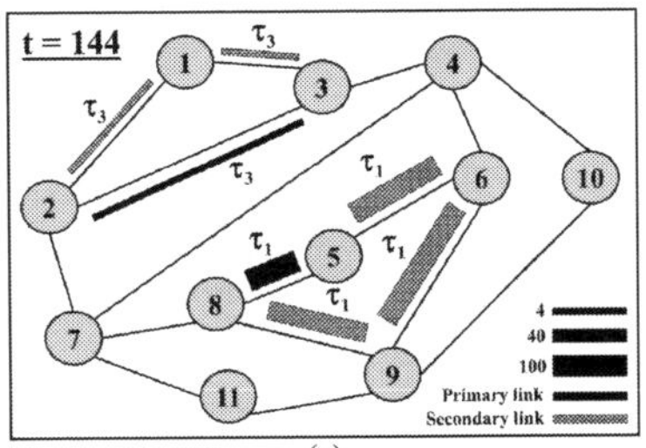

(e)

Figure 3. Area compact algorithm progression. (a) Step 1. (b) Step 2. (c) Step 3. (d) Step 4. (e) Step 5.

As obviously seen in the example, the number of subcarriers needed for the proposed algorithms (i.e., AC, and LWC) is lower than the numbers needed for the existing algorithms (LFC, and WFC (240 and 204, respectively)). Thus, both AC, and LWC strongly achieve the goal of the paper (i.e., minimize the total amount of spectrum needed to serve the traffic demand when it includes different types of requests).

Although both LWC and AC in the example require the same number of subcarriers (i.e., 200 subcarriers) to serve the demand, their behaviors are quite different. They have different request ordering mechanisms and different request allocation orders. The performance difference between them will be discussed in the experimental results and analysis section.

V. EPERIMENTAL RESULTS AND ANALYSIS

In this section, we start by presenting the comparison metric used for performance evaluation, along with the simulation environment. We examine different scenarios by varying the percentage of unicast unprotected, unicast protected, multicast unprotected, and multicast protected requests. We present a comparative evaluation between our algorithms (i.e., LWC and AC) and the heuristics recently proposed in [17] (i.e., LFC and WFC) with three traffic frequency slot distributions (discrete uniform, discrete high, and discrete low). Finally, we present the performance and analysis results. It is worth mentioning that both LFC and WFC were developed in the context of the RSA problem without additional survivability and multicasting constraints in the mesh network. Therefore, we modified the aforesaid existing algorithms to address the new constraints resulting from the use of protection and multicast.

A. Comparison Metric

We consider spectrum usage as the goal metric to evaluate the performance of our proposed algorithms. Spectrum usage is defined here as the number of subcarriers needed to serve a traffic demand including the four different types of requests (i.e., unicast unprotected, unicast protected, multicast unprotected, and multicast protected requests).

B. Simulation Setup

To test our priority allocation algorithms in terms of survivability and/or multicast EONs, we use two mesh topologies, the 14-node NSFNET and the 21-node UK Backbone as shown in Figures 4, and 5, respectively. In the case of unicast unprotected or unicast protected with dedicated path protection requests, the routing algorithm assumes an arbitrary fixed working path, selected from the set of shortest paths computed with Dijkstra's algorithm. The backup path in the unicast protected request is selected from the set of shortest paths computed with Dijkstra's algorithm, after removing all edges belonging to the working path.

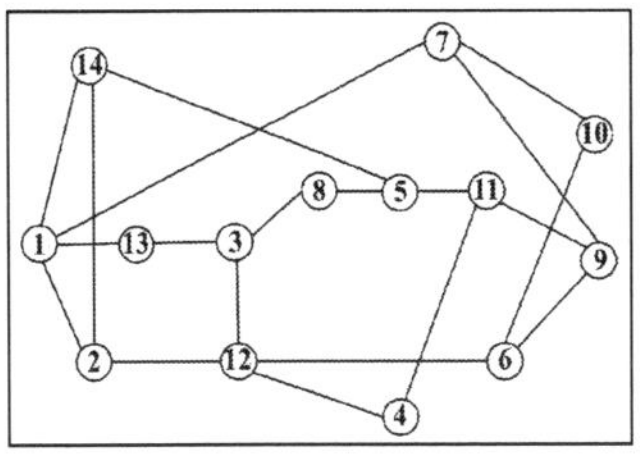

Figure 4. NSFNET-like topology.

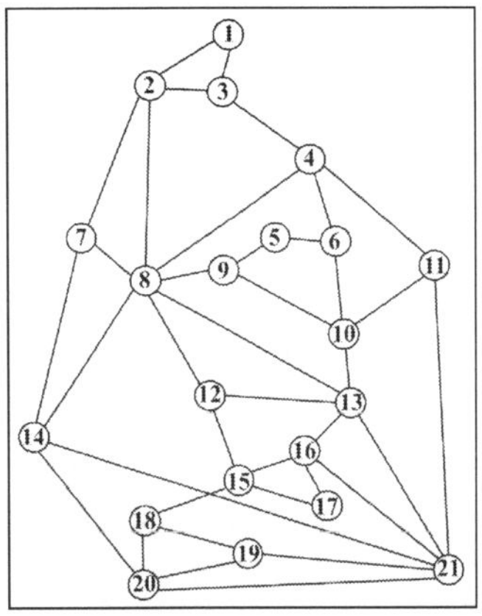

Figure 5. UK topology

For multicast unprotected and protected requests, a multicast tree is fixed and arbitrarily selected based on the minimum total number of links belonging to a rooted tree at the source s to the set of destination nodes $\{d_1, d_2, d_3, ..., d_n\}$, where the number of destinations is randomly selected from 1 to 13 in the NSFNET network, and 1 to 20 in the UK Backbone. In the NSFNET network, we arbitrarily selected 182 trees with the number of links in each tree ranging from 1 to 13. The multicast traffic is uniformly distributed between the 182 trees. In the UK Backbone, we arbitrarily selected 420 trees with the number of links in each tree ranging from 1 to 21. The multicast traffic is uniformly distributed between the 420 trees. We protect the multicast tree with path-pair protection by utilizing both the links in the working tree and a set of sharable backup links to protect from single fiber failure [41]. The sharable backup links are the outcomes of computing a backup segment for each link belonging to the working tree. That is, each link on the tree is protected by a backup segment starting at the tail node and finishing at the head node of the link it protects [42]. Therefore, we protect each link in the working tree separately (rather than the entire tree) and allow these backup segments to share links with other existing working and backup segments. Backup links are only sharable within a tree and selected based on the minimum total number of sharable backup links.

We use a distance-adaptive spectrum allocation strategy to allocate the spectrum for each traffic demand based on its needed frequency slots and the length of its path as reported in [16][17]. We assume an elastic optical network with five different types of request sizes. Each demand requests 10, 40, 100, 400, and 1000 frequency units. The size of the traffic demand is generated using three different types of frequency slot distributions. In the discrete uniform distribution case, all frequency slots have the same probability, whereas in the discrete high distribution higher frequency slots have higher probabilities, and in the discrete low distribution higher frequency slots have lower probabilities. The details of these three distributions and their frequency slot selection probabilities are listed in Table II.

We consider three scenarios to evaluate our algorithms, with different traffic demand generation patterns. These scenarios are presented below:

1) In the first scenario, the traffic demand includes both unicast unprotected and unicast protected requests; the ratio of unicast protected to unicast unprotected requests varies from 0 % to 50 %, in increments of 10 %. In the first demand type, (i.e., the first data point in the graphs), all the requests are unicast unprotected, while in the last demand type half the requests are unicast unprotected, and half are unicast protected [1].

2) In the second scenario, the traffic demand includes unicast unprotected, unicast protected, and multicast unprotected requests; the ratio of unicast protected plus multicast unprotected to unicast unprotected requests varies from 0 % to 50 %, in increments of 10 %. In the first demand, (i.e., the first data point in the graphs), all the requests are unicast unprotected, while in the last demand half the requests are unicast unprotected, one quarter are unicast protected, and one quarter are multicast unprotected.

3) In the third and last scenario, the traffic demand includes both unicast protected and multicast protected requests; the number of multicast protected to unicast protected requests varies from 0 % to 50 %, in increments of 10 %. In the first demand type, (i.e., the first data point in the graphs), all the requests are unicast protected, while in the last demand half the requests are unicast protected, and half are multicast protected.

Tables III, IV, and V present the number of unicast unprotected, unicast protected, multicast unprotected, and multicast protected requests in the above mentioned scenarios.

Our proposed algorithms are implemented in C++ using Xcode (version 8.3.2) on a MacBook Pro with macOS Sierra (version 10.12.4), a 2.2-GHz Intel Core i7 processor, and 16 GB of memory.

TABLE II. DETAILS OF THE USED TRAFFIC FREQUENCY SLOTS DISTRIBUTION

Frequency slot	Discrete uniform	Discrete high	Discrete low
10	0.2	0.1	0.3
40	0.2	0.15	0.25
100	0.2	0.2	0.2
400	0.2	0.25	0.15
1000	0.2	0.3	0.1

TABLE III. NUMBER OF REQUESTS IN THE FIRST SCENARIO

Percentage (%)	Number of requests			
	Unicast unprotected	*Unicast protected*	*Multicast unprotected*	*Multicast protected*
0	182	0	0	0
10	164	18	0	0
20	146	36	0	0
30	128	54	0	0
40	110	72	0	0
50	91	91	0	0

TABLE IV. NUMBER OF REQUESTS IN THE SECOND SCENARIO

Percentage (%)	Number of requests			
	Unicast unprotected	*Unicast protected*	*Multicast unprotected*	*Multicast protected*
0	182	0	0	0
10	164	9	9	0
20	146	18	18	0
30	128	27	27	0
40	110	36	36	0
50	91	45	46	0

TABLE V. NUMBER OF REQUESTS IN THE THIRD SCENARIO

Percentage (%)	Number of requests			
	Unicast unprotected	*Unicast protected*	*Multicast unprotected*	*Multicast protected*
0	0	420	0	0
10	0	378	0	42
20	0	336	0	84
30	0	294	0	126
40	0	252	0	168
50	0	210	0	210

C. *Performance Analysis and Results*

In this subsection, we determine the average percentual improvement in the number of needed subcarriers in the scenarios, to evaluate the performances of our proposed algorithms (LWC and AC) when compared with the two existing algorithms (LFC and WFC) [17]. For each data point in our experiment, a large number of random problem instances (up to 8000) were executed, and only the resulting average values are being reported in this research. The averaged results were obtained with 99 % confidence, with a confidence interval smaller than 1 % of the average value.

1) First Scenario:

The topology used to evaluate the first scenario, where the demand includes unicast unprotected and unicast protected requests, is 14-node NSFNET. Figures 6, 7, and 8 show the average number of needed subcarriers versus the percentage of unicast protected requests, both for our proposed algorithms (LWC and AC) and the existing LFC and WFC algorithms. Table VI presents the performance improvements of our proposed algorithms when compared to LFC and WFC, for different frequency slot distributions. As shown in Figures 6, 7 and 8, the proposed algorithms performed better than both the LFC and WFC algorithms. In other words, the number of needed subcarriers with our algorithms was less than the number of needed subcarriers with either LFC or WFC. In particular, in the case of a discrete high distribution of the requested frequency slots, LWC and AC improved the results obtained with LFC by 9.5 %, and 9.6 %, respectively; when compared with WFC, improvements of 7.1 % and 7.2 % were respectively obtained.

TABLE VI. AVERAGE PERCENTUAL IMPROVEMENTS IN THE FIRST SCENARIO

Distribution	LWC		AC	
	LFC	*WFC*	*LFC*	*WFC*
Uniform	8.5 %	6.9 %	8.5 %	6.9 %
Discrete high	9.5 %	7.1 %	9.6 %	7.2 %
Discrete low	6.3 %	6.1 %	6.3 %	6.1 %

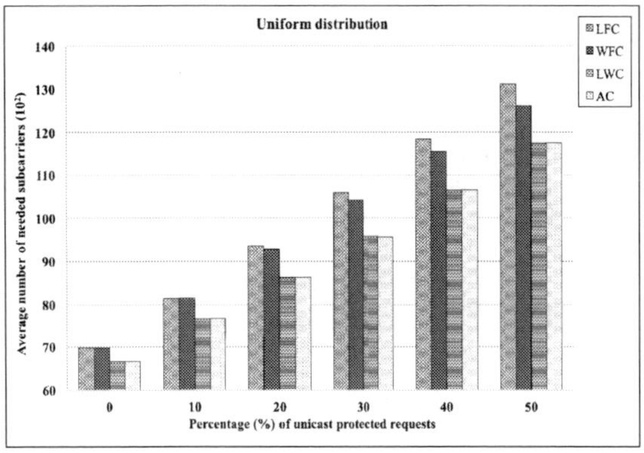

Figure 6. Average number of subcarriers as a function of the percentage of unicast protected requests; uniform frequency slot distribution.

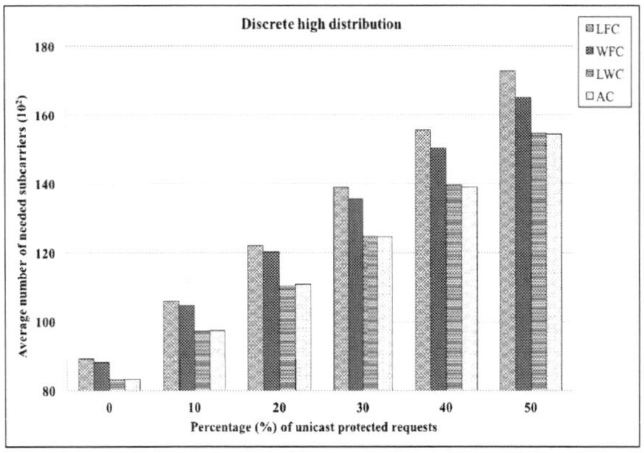

Figure 7. Average number of subcarriers as a function of the percentage of unicast protected requests; discrete high frequency slot distribution.

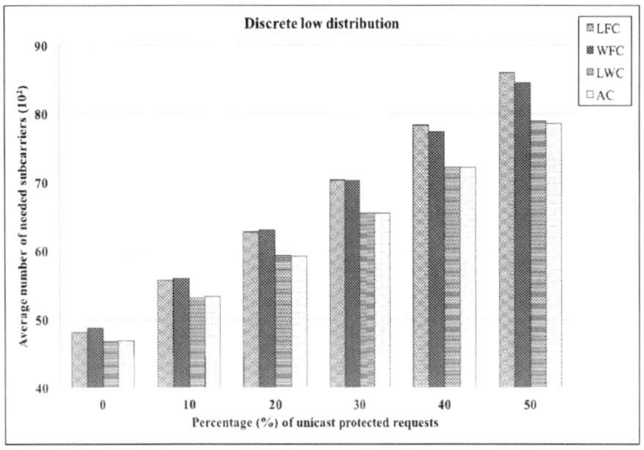

Figure 8. Average number of subcarriers as a function of the percentage of unicast protected requests; discrete low frequency slot distribution.

2) Second Scenario:

The second scenario, which has been simulated in 14-node NSFNET, considers a more varied demand, with unicast unprotected, unicast protected, and multicast unprotected requests. Figures 9, 10, and 11 show the average number of needed subcarriers versus the percentage of the sum of unicast protected and multicast unprotected requests for both our proposed algorithms (LWC and AC) and the existing LFC and WFC algorithms. Table VII presents the performance improvements of our proposed algorithms when compared to LFC and WFC, for different distributions. As shown in Figures 9, 10, and 11, both proposed algorithms perform better than either the LFC or WFC algorithms. In particular, in the case of a discrete high frequency slot distribution, LWC and AC improved the results obtained with LFC by 10.6 % and 10.7 %, respectively; when compared with WFC, improvements of 7.2 % and 7.1 % were respectively obtained.

TABLE VII. AVERAGE PERCENTUAL IMPROVEMENTS IN THE SECOND SCENARIO

Distribution	LWC		AC	
	LFC	*WFC*	*LFC*	*WFC*
Uniform	10.1 %	7.3 %	10.1 %	7.5 %
Discrete high	10.6 %	7.2 %	10.7 %	7.1 %
Discrete low	8.2 %	6.1 %	8.1 %	6.1 %

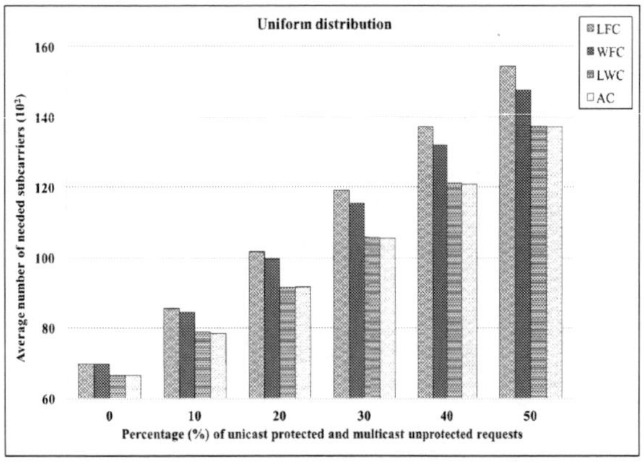

Figure 9. Average number of subcarriers as a function of the percentage of unicast protected and multicast unprotected requests; uniform frequency slot distribution.

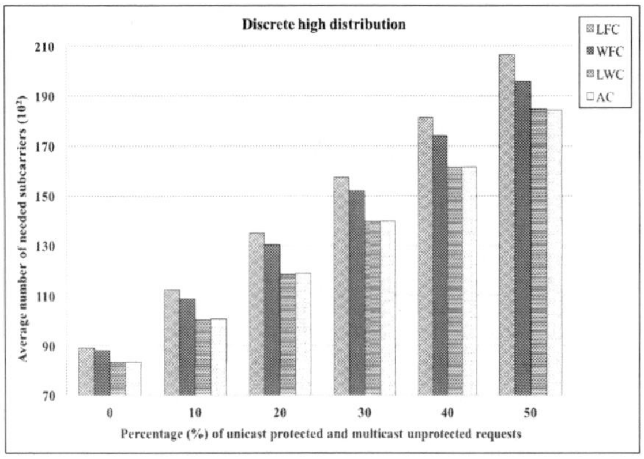

Figure 10. Average number of subcarriers as a function of the percentage of unicast protected and multicast unprotected requests; discrete high frequency slot distribution.

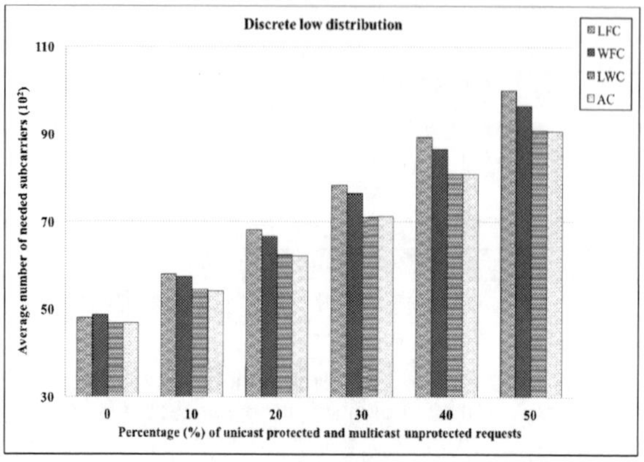

Figure 11. Average number of subcarriers as a function of the percentage of unicast protected and multicast unprotected requests; discrete low frequency slot distribution.

3) Third Scenario:

For the third and last scenario, where the demand includes unicast protected and multicast protected requests, the simulation is performed for the 21-node UK backbone. Figures 12, 13, and 14 show the average number of needed subcarriers versus the percentage of multicast protected requests for both our proposed algorithms (LWC and AC) and the existing LFC and WFC algorithms. Table VIII presents the performance improvements of our proposed algorithms when compared to LFC and WFC, for different frequency slot distributions. It can be observed that considering multicast protected requests along with unicast protected requests noticeably increases the number of needed subcarriers, especially in the discrete high distribution case. Spectrum consumption therefore increases when the traffic demand includes multicast protected requests. As shown in Figures 12, 13, and 14, both proposed algorithms performed better than either the LFC or WFC algorithms. In particular, in the case of a discrete high distribution of the requested frequency slots, LWC and AC improved the results obtained with WFC by 6.1 % and 6.3 %, respectively; when compared with LFC, even higher improvements of 4.6 % and 4.8 % were respectively obtained.

As mentioned previously, considering both dimensions; the amount of spectrum and the number of links (both primary and backup links); while sorting the requests, affects the number of subcarriers needed to serve the traffic demand. Therefore, the proposed sorting mechanisms outperform the existing mechanisms, and require less number of subcarriers.

TABLE VIII. AVERAGE PERCENTUAL IMPROVEMENTS IN THE THIRD SCENARIO

Distribution	LWC		AC	
	LFC	*WFC*	*LFC*	*WFC*
Uniform	4.5 %	5.5 %	4.6 %	5.6 %
Discrete high	4.6 %	6.1 %	4.8 %	6.3 %
Discrete low	2.8 %	3.8 %	2.8 %	3.7 %

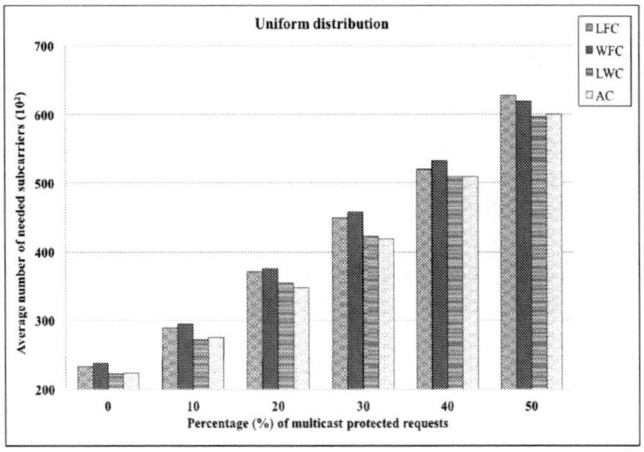

Figure 12. Average number of subcarriers as a function of the percentage of multicast protected requests; uniform frequency slot distribution.

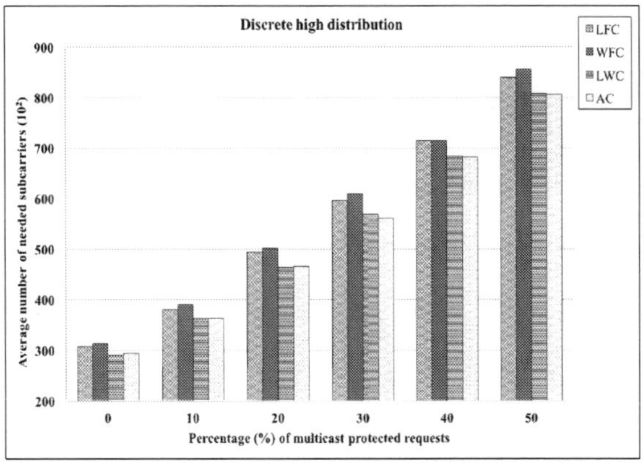

Figure 13. Average number of subcarriers as a function of the percentage of multicast protected requests; discrete high frequency slot distribution.

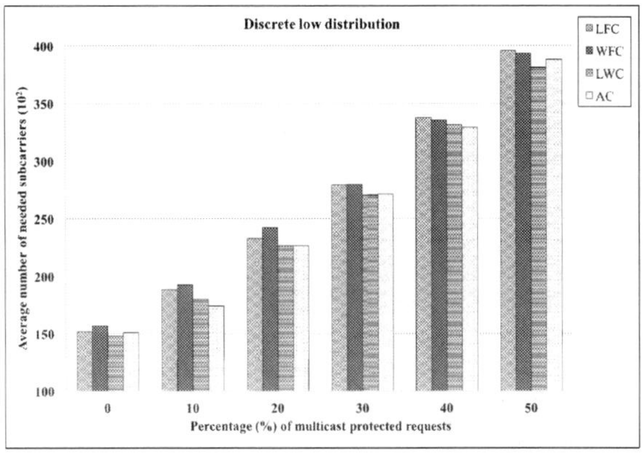

Figure 14. Average number of subcarriers as a function of the percentage of multicast protected requests; discrete low frequency slot distribution.

Overall, the simulation results demonstrate the viability and effectiveness of the proposed algorithms in serving different traffic demands (i.e., with different fractions of unicast unprotected, unicast protected, multicast unprotected, and multicast protected requests) using a smaller number of subcarriers than the existing algorithms, across a range of demand frequency slot distributions.

VI. Conclusion and Future Work

In this paper, we addressed the intractable offline RSA problem in protection- and/or multicast-based EONs, with the objective of minimizing the total amount of spectrum needed to serve traffic demand when this demand includes unicast unprotected, unicast protected, multicast unprotected, and multicast protected requests. We investigated the efficiency of priority allocation algorithms based on the compact scheduling algorithm and the ordering obtained with two different metrics, both of which consider the frequency slot and required number of links of the requests presented to the network, albeit in slightly different ways. We evaluated the performance of the algorithms across a range of demand frequency slot distributions, and for a set of different demand composition scenarios, in two mesh topologies, the 14-node NSFNET and the 21-node UK backbones. The obtained experimental results have shown that the proposed algorithms outperformed other reference algorithms in term of spectrum utilization. The proposed algorithms are robust, and can be used in EONs with different setups.

This work can be extended in several interesting directions. For instance, it would be enlightening to investigate the online RSA problem in protection- and/or multicast-based EONs, in what concerns the reduction of blocking and/or fragmentation obtainable by combining multiple bin packing algorithms (e.g., first fit, best fit, and worst fit). Moreover, the algorithms can be extended to achieve the power saving in the survivable EONs with an energy-efficient hybrid protection scheme (i.e., shared and dedicated) [43], while serving the maximum amount of traffic [44]. Additionally, it would also be very interesting to study the trade-off between the energy consumption and fragmentation [45].

References

[1] R. Alaskar, A. Alyatama, and I. Ahmad, "Offline Routing and Spectrum Allocation Algorithms for Elastic Optical Networks with Survivability," *16th Int. Conf. on Networks*, Venice, 2017, pp. 8-14.

[2] R.W. Alaskar, I. Ahmad, and A. Alyatama, "Offline routing and spectrum allocation algorithms for elastic optical networks," *Opt. Switch. Netw.*, vol. 21, pp. 76-92, July 2016.

[3] M. Jinno et al., "Spectrum-efficient and scalable elastic optical path network: architecture, benefits, and enabling technologies," *IEEE Commun. Mag.*, vol. 47, no. 11, pp. 66-73, Nov. 2009.

[4] O. Gerstel, M. Jinno, A. Lord, and S.J. Yoo, "Elastic optical networking: a new dawn for the optical layers?," *IEEE Commun. Mag.*, vol. 50, no. 2, pp. s12-s20, Feb. 2012.

[5] M. Klinkowski and K. Walkowiak, "Routing and spectrum assignment in spectrum sliced elastic optical path network," *IEEE Commun. Lett.*, vol. 15, no. 8, pp. 884-886, Aug. 2011.

[6] C. Politi et al., "Dynamic operation of flexi-grid OFDM-based networks," *Optical Fiber Communication Conf. and the Nat. Fiber Optic Engineers Conf.*, Los Anglos, CA, 2012, pp. 1-3.

[7] S. Ramamurthy and B. Mukherjee, "Survivable WDM mesh networks, Part I – Protection," *18th Annu. Joint Conf. IEEE Computer and Communications Societies*, New York, 1999, pp. 744-751.

[8] R. Ramaswami, K. Sivarajan, and G. Sasaki, Optical Networks: A Practical Perspective, CA (2001).

[9] L. Ruan and Y. Zheng, "Dynamic survivable multipath routing and spectrum allocation in OFDM-based flexible optical networks," *J. Opt. Commun. Netw.*, vol. 6, no. 1, pp. 77-85, Jan. 2014.

[10] G. Shen and Q. Yang, "From coarse grid to mini-grid to gridless: How much can gridless help contentionless?," *Optical Fiber Communication Conf. and Expo. and the Nat. Fiber Optic Engineers Conf.*, Los Anglos, CA, 2011, pp. 1-3.

[11] M. Klinkowski and K. Walkowiak, "Offline RSA algorithms for elastic optical networks with dedicated path protection consideration," *4th Int. Congress on Ultra-Modern Telecommunications and Control Systems and Workshops*, St. Petersburg, 2012, pp. 670-676.

[12] T. Takagi et al., "Algorithms for maximizing spectrum efficiency in elastic optical path networks that adopt distance adaptive modulation," *13th European Conf. and Exhibition on Optical Communication*, Torino, 2010, pp. 1-3.

[13] D. Din and L. Lai, "Multicast protection problem on elastic optical networks using segment-base protection," *Int. Conf. on Informatics Electronics and Vision*, Fukuoka, 2015, pp. 1-6.

[14] A. Cai, M. Zukerman, R. Lin, and G. Shen, "Survivable multicast routing and spectrum assignment in light-tree-based elastic optical networks," *Asian Communication and Photonics Conf.*, Hong Kong, 2015.

[15] N. Singhal, C. Ou, and B. Mukherjee, "Cross-sharing vs self-sharing trees for protecting multicast sessions in mesh networks," *Comput. Netw.*, vol. 50, no. 2, pp. 200-206, Feb. 2006.

[16] M. Jinno et al., "Distance-adaptive spectrum resource allocation in spectrum-sliced elastic optical path network," *IEEE Commun. Mag.*, vol. 48, no. 8, pp. 138-145, Aug. 2010.

[17] S. Talebi, E. Bampis, G. Lucarelli, I. Katib, and G. Rouskas, "Spectrum assignment in optical networks: a multiprocessor scheduling perspective," *IEEE/OSA J. Opt. Commun. Netw.*, vol. 6, no. 8, pp. 754-763, Aug. 2014.

[18] M. Klinkowski, "A genetic algorithm for solving RSA problem in elastic optical networks with dedicated path protection," *Adv. Intell. Syst. Comput*, vol. 189, pp. 167-176, 2013.

[19] S. Talebi et al., "Spectrum management techniques for elastic optical networks: a survey," *Opt. Switch. Netw.*, vol. 13, pp. 34-48, July 2014.

[20] B. Chatterjee, N. Sarma, and E. Oki, "Routing and spectrum allocation in elastic optical networks: a tutorial," *Commun. Surv. Tuts.*, vol. 17, no. 3, pp. 1776-1800, May 2015.

[21] A. Alyatama, "Dynamic spectrum allocation for orthogonal frequency-division multiplexing optical networks with survivability and multicasting," *J. High Speed Netw.*, vol. 22, no. 1, pp. 1-13, Feb. 2016.

[22] A. Tarhan and C. Cavdar, "Shared path protection for distance adaptive elastic optical networks under dynamic traffic," *5th Int. Congr. on Ultra-Modern Telecommunications and Control Systems and Workshops*, Almaty, 2013, pp. 62-67.

[23] M. Klinkowski, "An evolutionary algorithm approach for dedicated path protection problem in elastic optical networks," *Cybern. Syst.*, vol. 44, no. 6-7, pp. 589-605, Aug. 2013.

[24] K. Walkowiaka, M. Klinkowskib, B. Rabiegaa, and R. Gościeńa, "Routing and spectrum allocation algorithms for elastic optical networks with dedicated path protection," *Opt. Switch. Netw.*, vol. 13, pp. 63-75, July 2014.

[25] J. López, Y. Ye, V. López, and F. Jimenez, "Traffic and power-aware protection scheme in elastic optical networks," *15th Int. Telecommunications Network Strategy and Planning Symposium*, Rome, 2012, pp. 1-6.

[26] S. Shirazipourazad, C. Zhou, and A. Sen, "On routing and spectrum allocation in spectrum-sliced optical networks," *IEEE INFOCOM*, Turin, 2013, pp. 385-389.

[27] C. Yang, N. Hua, and X. Zheng, "Shared Path Protection based on Spectrum Reserved Matrix Model in Bandwidth-Variable Optical Networks," *7th Int. ICST Conf. Communications and Networking in China*, Kun Ming, 2012, pp. 256-261.

[28] M. Liu, M. Tornatore, and B. Tornatore, "Survivable Traffic Grooming in Elastic Optical Networks—Shared Protection," *J. Lightw. Technol.*, vol. 31, no. 6, pp. 903-909, March 2013.

[29] K. Walkowiak and M. Klinkowski, "Shared Backup Path Protection in Elastic Optical Networks: Modeling and Optimization," *9th Int. Conf. Design of Reliable Communication Networks*, Budapest, 2013, pp. 187-194.

[30] B. Chen et al., "Spectrum-block consumption for shared-path protection with joint failure probability in flexible bandwidth optical networks," *Opt. Switch. Netw.*, vol. 13, pp. 49-62, July 2014.

[31] H. Liu, M. Zhang, P. Yi, and Y. Chen, "Shared path protection through reconstructing shareable bandwidth based on spectrum segmentation for elastic optical networks," *Opt. Fiber Technol.*, vol. 32, pp. 88-95, Dec. 2016.

[32] R. Goścień, K. Walkowiak, and M. Tornatore, "Survivable multipath routing of anycast and unicast traffic in elastic optical networks," *IEEE/OSA J. Opt. Commun. Netw.*, vol. 8, no. 6, pp. 343-355, June 2016.

[33] B. Chen et al., "Spectrum aware survivable strategies with failure probability constraints under static traffic in flexible bandwidth optical networks," *J. Lightw. Technol.*, vol. 32, no. 24, pp. 4823-4836, Dec. 2014.

[34] G. Shen, G. Guo, and S.K. Bose, "Survivable elastic optical networks: survey and perspective," *Photonic Netw. Commun.*, vol. 31, no. 1, pp. 71-87, Feb. 2016.

[35] R. Goscien, K. Walkowiak, M. Klinkowski, and J. Rak, "Protection in elastic optical networks," *IEEE Network*, vol. 29, no. 6, pp. 88-96, Dec. 2015.

[36] W. Kmiecik, R. Goścień, K. Walkowiak, and M. Klinkowski, "Two-layer optimization of survivable overlay multicasting in

elastic optical networks," *Opt. Switch. Netw.*, vol. 14, no. 2, pp. 164-178, Aug. 2014.

[37] R. Goscien, K. Walkowiak, and M. Klinkowski, "Tabu search algorithm for routing, modulation, and spectrum allocation in elastic optical network with anycast and unicast traffic," *Comput. Netw.*, vol. 79, pp. 148-165, March 2015.

[38] X. Liu, L. Gong, and Z. Zhu, "Design integrated RSA for multicast in elastic optical networks with a layered approach," *IEEE Global Comuunication Conf.*, Atlanta, 2013, pp. 2346-2351.

[39] L. Gong et al., "Efficient resource allocation for all-optical multicasting over spectrum-sliced elastic optical networks," *IEEE/OSA J. Opt. Commun. Netw.*, vol. 5, no. 8, pp. 836-847, Aug. 2013.

[40] C. Constrantinou and G. Ellinas, "A load balancing technique for efficient survivable multicasting in mesh optical networks," *Opt. Switch. Netw.*, vol. 22, pp. 1-8, Nov. 2016.

[41] N. K. Singhal, L. H. Sahasrabuddhe, and B. Mukherjee, "Provisioning of survivable multicast sessions against single link failures in optical WDM mesh networks," *J. Lightw. Technol.*, vol. 21, no. 11, pp. 2587-2594, Nov. 2003.

[42] L. Long and A. Kamal, "Tree-based protection of multicast services in WDM mesh networks," *IEEE Global Telecomuunication Conf.*, Honolulu, 2009, pp. 1-6.

[43] N. Anoh et al., "An affection hybrid protection scheme with shared/ dedicated backup paths on elastic optical networks," *Digital Commun. and Netw.*, vol. 3, no. 1, pp. 11-18, Feb. 2017.

[44] R. Ren et al., "Spectrum and energy-efficient survivable routing algorithm in elastic optical network," *Optik*, vol. 127, no. 20, pp. 8795-8806, Oct. 2016.

[45] J. Vizcaino et al., "Protection in optical transport networks with fixed and flexible grid: cost and energy efficiency evaluation," *Opt. Switch. Netw.*, vol. 11, pp. 55-71, Jan. 2014.

Cross-Layer Design for Caching Scheme by using Successive Interference Cancellation in Information-Centric Network-based Wireless Sensor Network

Shintaro Mori
Department of Electronics Engineering and Computer Science
Fukuoka University
8-19-1, Nanakuma, Jonan-ku, Fukuoka 814-0180, Japan
e-mail: smori@fukuoka-u.ac.jp

***Abstract*—Advanced wireless sensor network technologies, such as the Internet of Things and Machine to Machine, have recently been widely applied to various fields. The network protocol of future wireless networks, however, requires sensing data from the various monitoring values in the large-scale wireless sensor network and, hence, may not be effectively built if based on the current host-centric scheme. We must therefore redesign based on a content-centric concept. From this perspective, we focus on an information-centric network-based wireless sensor network framework. We propose a novel, efficient caching scheme using overhearing phenomena, and boost the proposed caching mechanism by using the successive interference cancellation technique. Moreover, we propose protocol stacking and signal processing based on a cross-layer design. Our numerical result reveals that the amount of stored sensing data can be increased, the number of multi-hops reduced, and the distance of data transfer between the publisher and subscriber nodes improved by using the exhaustive computer simulation.**

***Keywords*—wireless sensor network; information-centric network; caching scheme; successive interference cancellation; cross-layer design.**

I. INTRODUCTION

New WSNs (Wireless Sensor Networks), such as IoT (Internet of Things) and M2M (Machine to Machine), play a primary role in providing global access by using billions of various devices. In general, a WSN system is constructed based on vast amounts of resource-constrained sensor nodes, e.g., a low-performance processor, low-capacity memory, and limited battery. However, we expect that the hardware limitations of current WSN devices will lessen in the near future. Therefore, we believe that it is necessary to redesign not only the radio transmission procedure, but also the network architecture and technologies for an advanced WSN framework. On the other hand, most users are interested in accessing the same contents or information sources, such as Google, Facebook, YouTube, Amazon, and Dropbox, despite the availability of numerous other web services over the last few years. This epidemic trend has led to a new paradigm shift in which the network architecture is designed from a content-oriented aspect. In view of the evolving network framework, the ICN (Information-Centric Network) scheme promotes a new communication model [2][3]. We note that the current WSN's network protocol is founded upon the host-centric and IP-based network architecture, such as the traditional Internet infrastructure. In short, the ICN architecture is fundamentally different from the host-centric network, i.e., the major concept of ICN is an ability to retrieve data independently from the current location where the required sensing data are provided.

ICN design has been investigated not only for wired networks, such as the post/next Internet architecture, but also for wireless and mobile networks. For example, in a cellular telecommunications system, popular content is copied onto several intermediate servers called middle-box gateways or routers [4][5]. As a result, frequent requests for the same content data can be effectively provided without requiring the content providers to transfer the redundant data, thus reducing the number of data transmissions. The concept of an improvement mechanism for the ICN scheme resembles the CDN (Content Delivery Network) technique. In the CDN scheme, mirrored content data are stored and provided by using the in-network content servers of service providers; whereas, in the ICN scheme, the copied content data are cached and distributed by using the cache memory of the individual network node.

As another related topic, for content flow, Higuchi and Hirotsu [6] proposed a novel verification-based flow space management based on the OpenFlow method that is a form of SDN (Software Defined Networking) technology. On the other hand, Zhang et al. and Amadeo et al. [7][8] investigated and surveyed emerging and hot trends in ICN-based and IoT/M2M-oriented WSNs, e.g., naming formulation, name resolution technique, data routing formula, caching mechanism, mobility support, and security protection. In addition, Wang et al. [9] examined two promising technologies: the wireless network virtualization and ICN scheme for the D2D (Device to Device)-assisted cellular network. Based on the above, in this paper, we place particular focus on the caching mechanism in order to share duplicated content data effectively. In general, there are two common principles for caching methodologies: the on-path caching scheme and the off-path caching scheme [10]. In short, in the on-path caching scheme, content data are copied along with the routing path by name resolution requests, whereas, in the off-path caching scheme, the network node located outside the routing path actively and positively executes the caching transaction.

In related studies of the caching mechanism, in the traditional ICN architecture, the DONA (Data-oriented Network Architecture) framework [11] and the NDN (Named

Data Networking) framework [12] support natively based on the on-path caching scheme. On the other hand, Sourlas et al. [13] proposed four online intra-domain cache management algorithms with different levels of automaticity and compared them with respect to performance, complexity, execution time, and message exchange overhead to achieve both the on-path and off-path caching schemes. Wang et al. [14] proposed a collaborative in-network caching scheme that users both the content-space partitioning method and hash-routing technique in order to exploit the built-in caching capability of the ICN framework fully. Hajimirsadeghi et al. [15] investigated joint caching and pricing strategies based on duplicated content popularity with the game theoretic approach. Li et al. [16] proposed a modern dynamic caching mechanism for video streaming in order to guarantee QoS (Quality of Service) in terms of average throughput.

In general, most researchers have utilized an exclusive and additive mechanism for replication of the frequently referred content data, which is undoubtedly a proper solution in a wired network. However, in this paper, we adopt a different approach for WSN; we effectively utilize the specific wireless feature. In our previous study [1], we proposed a novel scratch and blueprint strategy of the efficient caching scheme for the ICN-based WSN. We proposed a new off-path caching mechanism using overhearing phenomena and the SIC (Successive Interference Cancellation) technique [17] in order to boost caching capability. We note that, for the overhearing phenomena, when a sensor node wirelessly transmits any content data, its neighbor sensor nodes located in the transmitter sensor node's coverage area can watch the forwarding content data due to free-space radio propagations, regardless of whether it is necessary. In other words, by using the overhearing phenomena, the proposed scheme can achieve an off-path caching scheme without using alternative exclusive control packets and without introducing additional and sophisticated wireless communication systems.

As another key element technology of the proposed scheme, the SIC technique has been extensively studied as a familiar interference reduction mechanism at the physical layer [18]. SIC application technologies have already appeared as industry solutions for cellular and mobile communication systems, such as Qualcomm's CSM6850 chipset [19]. With the SIC method, the SIC-based receiver decodes the strongest signal in the parallel received signals from several various transmitters. If the strongest signal is successfully recovered, the correct decoded signal is encoded again and the re-encoded signal is subtracted from the received signal. As a result, the decoding performance of the remaining signal can be improved by removing the strongest interference; however, its performance and behavior in the ICN-based WSN remain unknown. Hence, our study can provide significant preliminary evaluations.

Furthermore, for introducing the SIC technique into the ICN-based WSN system, it is important to consider the protocol layers holistically and integratively, and the protocol stack must be optimized. To the best of our knowledge, this optimization problem can be solved in a cross-layer design manner [20][21]. Cross-layer design is a new paradigm in network architecture that involves the interaction and sharing of significant information among layers. If we optimize the protocol stack by using the cross-layer design concept, several layers with different functionality performance can collaboratively work together.

Consequently, we summarize the contributions of our paper as follows:

- We formulate an ICN-based WSN framework for adopting the proposed caching mechanism.
- We propose a novel caching scheme based on both the overhearing phenomena and SIC technique.
- We propose a protocol design and procedure of signal processing for the proposed caching mechanism based on the cross-layer design concept.
- We demonstrate the effectiveness of the proposed scheme via exhaustive computer simulation.

The remainder of our paper is organized as follows: Section II describes the manner of the proposed scheme; Section III provides the computer simulation results; and finally, we conclude with our acknowledgments and conclusions.

II. PROPOSED SCHEME

In the ICN-based WSN, the proposed scheme is constructed based on the overhearing phenomena and SIC technique in order to construct an efficient caching mechanism. In this chapter, after presenting our network model and the proposed caching mechanism based on the above two key technologies, we will provide the protocol stack and signal processing procedure for the proposed caching mechanism based on the cross-layer design concept.

A. Network Model of Information-Centric Network Based Wireless Sensor Network

In the network model of the proposed scheme, as shown in Figure 1, sensor nodes are distributed on the surface of the observation area and these sensor nodes measure the environmental monitoring values as the sensing data. Unlike the traditional host-centric network model in which the sensing data are gathered in a fusion center or cloud server, in the proposed scheme, the sensing data are managed in the WSN devices and stored among sensor node devices. As a common policy of the ICN-based system, when a sensor node acquires sensing data that have been already requested from other nodes, there is no difference between the original sensing data and the duplicated caching data. Therefore, in the proposed scheme, as shown in Figure 1, the sensor nodes copy and store the sensing data in their cache memories as much as possible.

As the caching transaction trigger, the proposed scheme executes when the sensing data are transferred from the publisher node (source) to the subscriber node (destination). Specifically, when a user wants to acquire the sensing data, the user accesses any nearest and acceptable sensor node located in the proposed WSN system; that is, the sensor node

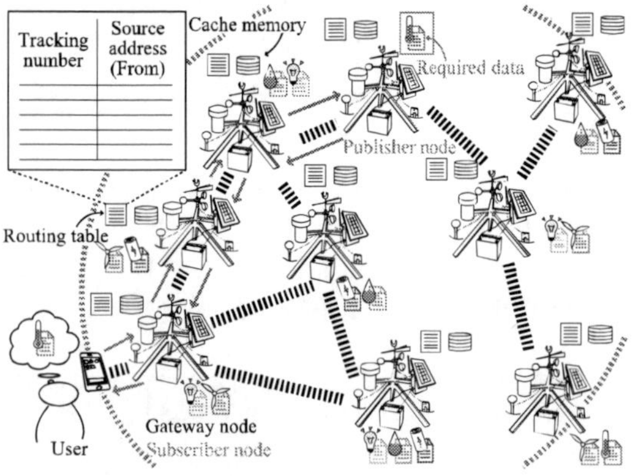

Figure 1. Network model of the proposed ICN-based WSN framework.

works as a gateway node between the proposed WSN system and the users. In addition, the gateway node behaves as the subscriber node instead of the users; that is, the gateway node broadcasts the request message of the sensing data acquisition among the proposed WSN member nodes. When the request message arrives at the sensor node, the sensor node searches for the requested sensing data in its cache memory. If the sensor node finds the target sensing data, the sensor node holding the desired data replies to the subscriber node with its data as the publisher node in the response transaction. Therefore, the proposed scheme establishes a routing path from the publisher node to the subscriber node to transfer the required sensing data, the detailed procedure for which will be described later. In addition, a benefit of the proposed scheme is that the popular sensing data frequently requested by users are cached because of the above procedure. Thus, the proposed scheme promotes effective sensing data acquisition.

As shown in Figure 2, we define and utilize three kinds of packets: the sensing data packet, the find packet, and the response packet. Especially, as shown in Figure 2 (a), the sensing data packet consists of two components—the header section and payload section. In the sensing data packet, the header part contains extra information, e.g., time, location, and sensor node identifier, that operates as searching tags when the subscriber requests their desired sensing data, whereas the payload part should be defined depending on the usage environment of the proposed WSN framework. Moreover, the find packet and the response packet have an identifier number, source/destination address, and the sensing data for the searching transaction, and the response packet also has the replied sensing data, as shown in Figures 2 (b) and (c). On the other hand, every sensor node has not only the cache memory, but also a routing table, as shown in Figure 1. Therefore, since the sensor nodes record both the tracking identifier and the source and destination node information into the routing table when the request messages are flooding in and passing through, we can determine the proper routing path between the publisher node and the subscriber node.

As an addressing rule, the sensor node identifier must be assigned a unique physical address. In typical ICN-based

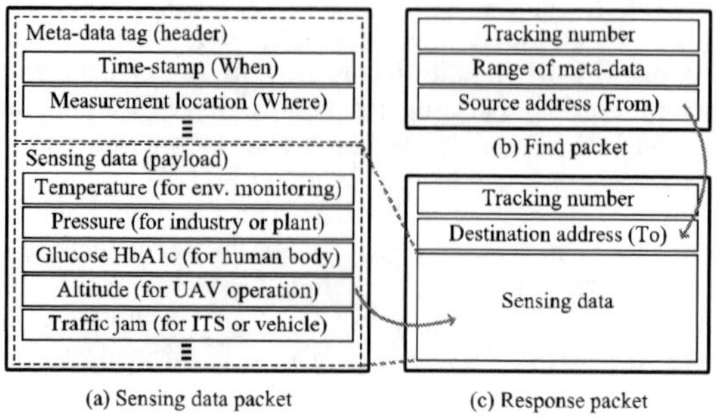

Figure 2. Structure of the sensing data, find, and response packets.

systems, there are two types of naming rules, specifically, the hierarchical and flat naming formula. In the hierarchical naming rule, an individual sensor node is managed based on a hierarchical URI (Uniform Resource Identifier), such as an HTTP (Hyper Text Transfer Protocol)-based website. On the other hand, in the flat naming rule, all sensor nodes are assigned the same and unique namespace. The hierarchical addressing method has the advantage of eliminating the overhead of the aggregations among sensor nodes; hence, the hierarchical naming rule achieves scalable routing. However, if the network structure must be dynamically changed when the sensor node is moved, appended, removed, and renewed, it is hard to adopt hierarchical addressing. As a result, if we define the sensor node that must transfer the sensing data as forwarding content data along the routing path as the relay node, we believe that the relay node can transmit and/or receive from/to the next relay node via the mechanism described above.

B. *Effective Caching Scheme with Overhearing Phenomena*

In this section, after describing the aim of the caching mechanism and the on-path caching scheme in the proposed scheme, we present the proposed off-path caching scheme based on the overhearing phenomena. Since there is no difference between the original data and the duplicated data from the subscriber node viewpoint, as mentioned above, if lots of sensor nodes have the required data, the hit probability of meeting the target data is improved. As a result, we can eliminate the number of wireless communications; thus, we expect that the proposed caching scheme will reduce energy consumption and radio frequency resources.

Figure 3 shows the proposed caching methods, specifically, the on-path caching scheme and the off-path caching scheme, and the relationship of the overhearing phenomena. For the on-path caching scheme, as with traditional schemes, the proposed scheme is copied and stored along the routing path; i.e., when the response packet is generated and forwarded, the relay node completes the on-path caching transaction. In greater detail, when the relay node receives the response packet, the relay node extracts the sensing data from the received response packet and stores it into the cache memory. After execution of the on-path caching transaction, the relay node sends the response packet to the

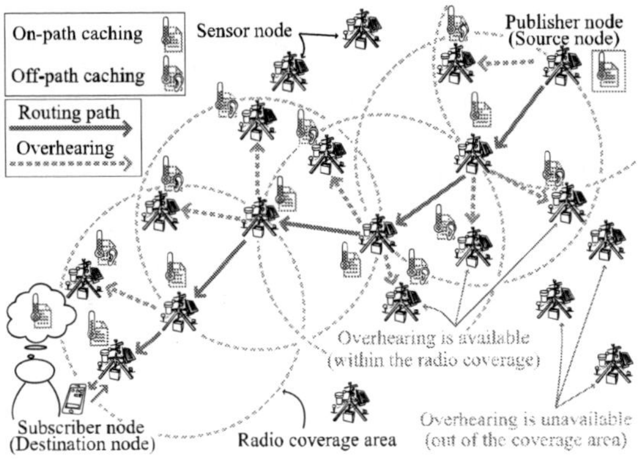

Figure 3. Comparison between on-path caching and off-path caching transactions in the proposed scheme, and the relationship between the off-path caching method and the overhearing phenomena.

neighbor sensor nodes, and the relay node updates the destination address from the current address to the next sensor node's address based on its routing table depending on the tracking identifier. For the off-path caching scheme, we introduce the overhearing phenomena into the proposed scheme without the extra overhead cost of a sophisticated hardware module. Unlike the wired network system, in the wireless network system, the neighbor sensor nodes located within the relay node's radio coverage area receive and acquire the sensing data, which is called the overhearing phenomena, as shown in Figure 3. When the relay node transfers the sensing data, the proposed scheme proactively watches and gathers the cross-talked and surrounded sensing data as the overhearing sensing data. The detailed procedure of the signal processing will be described later on.

In the proposed scheme, the neighbor sensor nodes of the relay node need not communicate with the relay node because of the overhearing phenomena. However, there are two major and considerable drawbacks when the overhearing mechanism works effectively, specifically, an increase in energy consumption of the signal processing for the wireless receiving (overhearing) transaction and additional cache memory capacity for the overhearing sensing data. Formerly, even if the computational energy consumption, e.g., micro-controller processing, memory access, and circuit power loss, is increasing, it is significantly (extremely) smaller than that of the radio transmission. Therefore, the proposed scheme reduces the total energy consumption depending on the decrease the number of wireless communications. On the other hand, for the latter issue, we (and everyone) will expect and experienience a decline in the RAM (Random Access Memory) hardware price under the influence of mass production, broad usage, and price competition, whereas, a shortage in the limited, common, and valuable radio resource will continue infinitely.

Consequently, the proposed scheme has significant and sufficient benefits, such as reduced energy consumption and the effective utilization of radio resources, even with the above two costs.

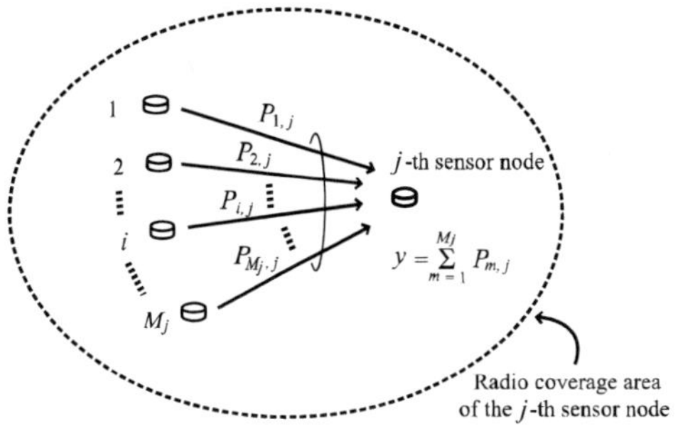

Figure 4. A received signal, $\mathbf{y}$, from the neighbor sensor nodes with $\boldsymbol{M_j}$ concurrent transmitter, and its fundamental model.

C. Effective Caching Scheme with Successive Interference Cancellation

As mentioned above, the sensor node receives from its neighbor nodes, which is a double-edged sword. In other words, this circumstance is positively applicable as the overhearing phenomena; however, it causes significant interferences, that is, the probability of successful reception is negatively degraded. Therefore, in the proposed scheme, we will not only execute the off-path caching scheme but also reduce the interference by using the cached sensing data based on the overhearing phenomena. Specifically, we utilize the SIC technique in order to eliminate interference. The beauty of the SIC technique resides in its simplicity; it is a purely received-based interference management scheme that does not require sophisticated coordination among sensor nodes. Figures 4 and 5 show the fundamental SIC model. In short, the SIC-based receiver decodes in order of high-power among several received signals. If the strongest signal can be successfully decoded, its decoded signal is encoded again, and then this re-encoded signal is subtracted from the received signals in order to remove the greatest interference; i.e., the SINR (Signal to Interference and Noise Ratio) for the remaining signals is improved. Then, the SIC-based receiver continues to decode the second strongest signal, and so forth, until all signals are decoded or the remaining signals are no longer decodable.

As shown in Figure 4, let $P_{i,j}$ denote the signal strength at the j-th sensor node that is a destination relay node or neighbor nodes based on the overhearing processing from the i-th sensor node that is a source relay node. In addition, let $\mathcal{M}_j$ denote the set of concurrent transmitting sensor nodes that can be heard by the j-th sensor node. As with the traditional wireless reception model, the j-th sensor node treats all interfering signals from other concurrent and non-intended transmissions as a noise signal. When the i-th sensor node transmits the required signal, if its SINR at the j-th sensor node is greater than or equal to a threshold value Λ, the j-th sensor node can be successfully recovered. In other words, let $P_{i,j}$ denote the power level from the i-th sensor node to the j-th sensor node; if the signal from the i-th sensor node to the j-th sensor node can be correctly decoded, $P_{i,j}$ is satisfied with

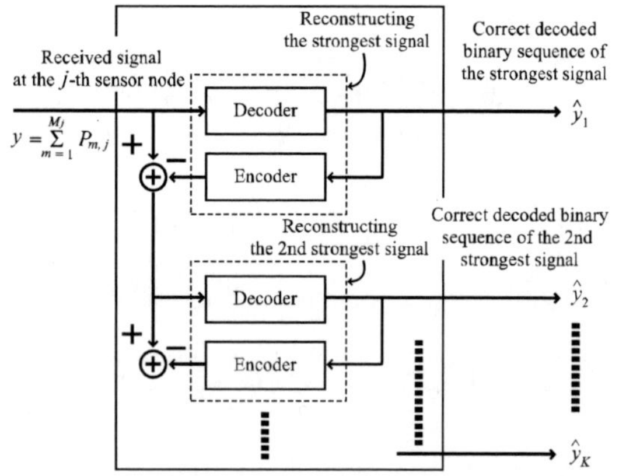

Figure 5. Schematic procedure of the proposed SIC-based receiver side transaction at the j-th sensor node.

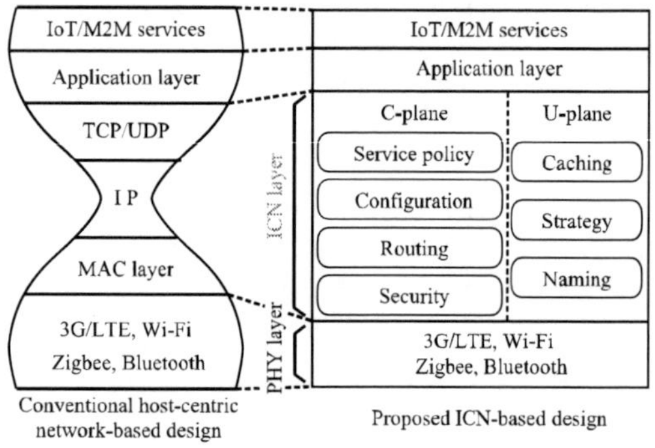

Figure 6. Protocol-stack design of the proposed ICN-based WSN scheme in comparison with the host-centric network architecture.

$$\mathcal{H}: \frac{P_{i,j}}{\sum_{k \in \mathcal{M}_j}^{k \neq i} P_{k,j} + \sigma^2} \geq \Lambda \qquad (1)$$

where Λ is the power level of the required received signal threshold and σ^2 is the power of the ambient noise, respectively. In short, (1) indicates that the j-th sensor node can store the replicated data of the i-th sensor node, if the SINR is sufficiently large.

In Figures 4 and 5, let y denote the received signal strength of the j-th sensor node, which is expressed as

$$y = \sum_{m=1}^{M_j} P_{m,j} \qquad (2)$$

where M_j is the amount of $\mathcal{M}_j$'s elements.

As shown in Figure 5, in the proposed scheme, the decoder works to recover the strongest signal among the input signals of y, such as the received signal in the first transaction. Based on (1), if the strongest signal can be successfully decoded, that is, its SINR is no less than threshold Λ, the decoded signal is subtracted from the aggregate signal. Following this procedure, the j-th sensor node decodes the second strongest signal and so forth until all signals are correctly decoded or the SINR criterion is no longer satisfied. Therefore, when the j-th sensor node decodes the signals based on (1), the received signal can be decoded correctly if and only if

$$\begin{aligned} &\text{Step 1:} && \frac{\hat{y}_1}{y} = \frac{P_{1,j}}{\sum_{m=1}^{M_j-1} P_{m,j} + \sigma^2} \geq \Lambda \\ &\text{Step 2:} && \frac{\hat{y}_2}{y - \overline{y}_1} = \frac{P_{2,j}}{\sum_{m=1}^{M_j-2} P_{m,j} + \sigma^2} \geq \Lambda \\ &\vdots && \vdots \\ &\text{Step } K: && \frac{\hat{y}_K}{y - \sum_{k=1}^{K-1} \overline{y}_k} = \frac{P_{K,j}}{\sum_{m=1}^{M_j-K} P_{m,j} + \sigma^2} \geq \Lambda \end{aligned} \qquad (3)$$

where K denotes the number of correct decoded signals, $\hat{y}_k (k = 1, 2, \cdots, K)$ denotes the correct decoded signal, and $\overline{y}_k (k = 1, 2, \cdots, K)$ denotes the re-constructed transmission signal based on the decoded signal of $\hat{y}_k$, respectively.

In (2) and (3), we assume that both $\overline{y}_k$ and $P_{m,j}$ are in non-decreasing order as $\overline{y}_1 \geq \overline{y}_2 \geq \cdots, \overline{y}_K$ and $P_{1,j} \geq P_{2,j} \geq \cdots \geq P_{K,j}$, respectively. If we achieve the SIC technique as shown in Figure 5, we can formulate the detailed protocol design, which we will describe in the next section.

D. Cross-Layer Design for Protocol Stack

In the proposed scheme, as shown in Figure 6, the ICN-layer is constructed by summarizing the middle layers, which is Srivastava and Motani's cross-layer design concept of 'merging of adjacent layers' [21]. We note that, as mentioned in reference [21], the aim of 'merging of adjacent layers' is to design two or more adjacent layers together and a new super-layer to provide the union services of the constituent layers. Namely, the ICN layer of the proposed scheme corresponds to this super-layer. In addition, this design concept should not require any new interface to be created in the protocol stack; that is, architecturally speaking, the super-layer should be constructed based on the rest of the layers by using interfaces that already exist in the original architecture. Therefore, the proposed scheme inherits the protocol stack of the host-centric network-based framework from the physical (PHY) layer, the application (APP) layer, and the IoT/M2M services layer, as shown in Figure 6.

Regarding the ICN layer's functionality, we examine and implement the separated data aspect, such as the C-plane for the control signal and the U-plane for the sensing data, respectively. As shown in Figure 6, there are lots of key technologies for the ICN-layer feature, and their elemental techniques, e.g., service policy, configuration, routing, security, strategy, naming, and caching, are essential to creating the proposed framework. However, we do not take into account their considerations without the caching scheme

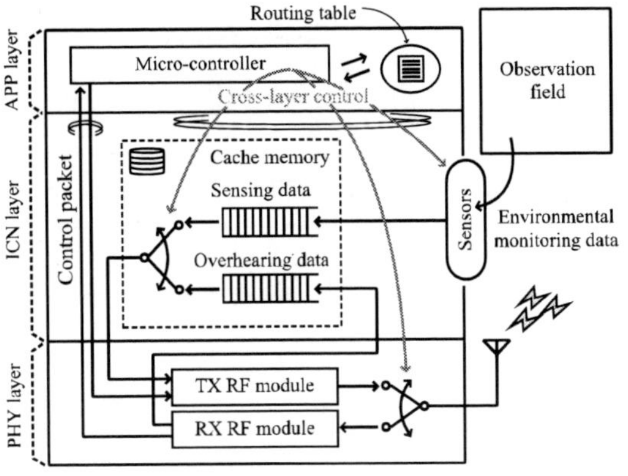

Figure 7. Signal processing procedure of the proposed sensor node device.

as this is outside the scope of this manuscript and will be the focus our future work.

E. Cross-Layer Design of Signal Processing Procedure

Figure 7 shows our proposed sensor node device's signal processing procedure. The routing table and cache memory in Figure 7 are the same components as in Figure 1. From a data flow viewpoint, the environmental monitoring data are observed from the target observation area. The micro-controller digitizes them as sensing data via the various sensors; then, the sensing data are stored in the cache memory. Two types of preserving data accumulate data: the self-sensing data that was previously mentioned and the overhearing sensing data that is acquired based on the procedure of the previous section. When the sensor node transmits the stored data, the micro-controller encourages the TX RF module to send the sensing data. On the other hand, when the sensor node carefully watches the radio propagation space at the RX RF module, the adequately received sensing data is stored in the cache memory as much as possible. We note that it is necessary to determine which sensing data should be stored because the cache memory capacity of the sensor node is limited, the consideration of which is outside the scope of this manuscript. However, we believe this decision rule poses a significant problem; in fact, we feel that the frequently requested data should be preferentially stored, and the old and worthless data should be removed.

On the other hand, the micro-controller should not only generate the sensing data and manage the database of the routing table, but also control the cache memory and the RF TX/RX modules. Notably, when the sensor node works as a publisher node for response transactions, the micro-controller produces the response packet and then the generated packet is adaptively transmitted. To achieve this, the proposed scheme constructs and optimizes based on Srivastava and Motani's cross-layer design concept of 'downward information flow' [21]. In short, in the 'downward information flow,' the setting parameters at the lower layer are adaptively controlled depending on the upper layer's information as a notification and hint.

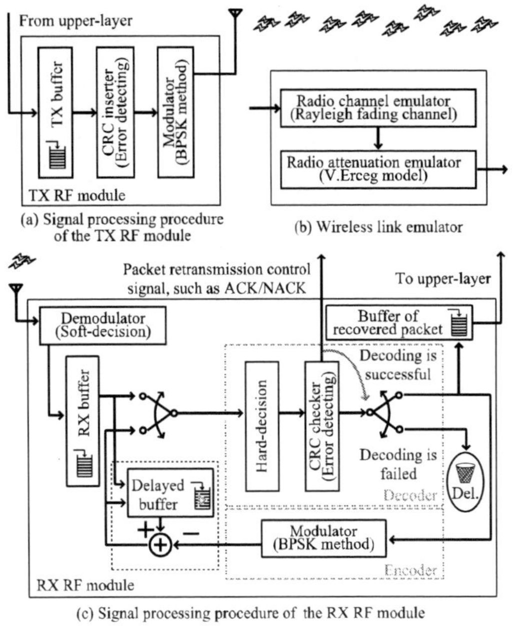

Figure 8. Procedure of signal processing at the transmitter device, the receiver device, and the wireless link emulator.

Figure 8 shows the procedure of the signal processing for the transmitter, receiver, and wireless link in the proposed scheme. In Figure 8, the TX RF module (see Figure 8 (a)) and the RX RF module (see Figure 8 (c)) have the same components as in Figure 7. A detailed description of the wireless link model (see Figure 8 (b)) is provided in the next section. In addition, as shown in Figure 8 (c), the RX RF module has an encoder and decoder, which corresponds to the SIC-based encoder and decoder in Figure 5.

As shown in Figure 8 (a), in the TX RF module, the transmission packets—the sensing data packet and the control signal packet—are streamed from the upper layers and buffered in the TX buffer in order to adjust the data transmission rate. The CRC inserter appends a sequence based on the CRC code to every packet to detect the packet errors. Then, the transmission bit-stream is modulated by using the modulator based on the BPSK (Binary Phase Shift Keying) method. The transmission signal, i.e., the output signal of the TX RF module, is wirelessly transmitted via radio propagation space. Its model is shown in Figure 8 (b). In the proposed scheme, the wireless link emulator is designed based on radio attenuation model of Erceg et al. [22] and the Rayleigh fading channel model, which are described in the next section.

As shown in Figure 8 (c), in the RX RF module, the demodulator recovers based on the soft-decision decoding formula in order to conduct a signal processing based on the SIC technique, and the demodulated soft-decision information temporarily queues in the RX buffer. The received and detected signal is sent not only to the decoder, but also to the delayed buffer, for which the buffered signal is utilized for the interference removal stage in the SIC technique. In the decoder, the soft-decision information is judged based on the hard-decision metric, i.e., the hard-decision-based detector decides the estimated bit-stream. We note that, if we adopt the FEC (Forward Error Correction) mechanism, we need to add the error control decoder before the hard-decision. After that, the CRC checker verifies the estimated bit-stream sequence in order to detect bit errors and then the correct decoded bit-stream sequence is stored in the recovered packet's buffer. The verification result of the CRC checker can be utilized for the packet retransmission control signal, such as ACK and NACK, if we adopt the ARQ (Automatic Repeat reQuest) mechanism. The properly recovered packet is sent to not only the upper layers, i.e., the cache memory in the ICN-layer, but also the encoder. This is because, for interference reduction based on the SIC technique, the re-encoded signal of the recovered packet in the encoder is subtracted from the buffered signal in the delayed buffer, the detailed mechanism and procedure of which are described in Section II-C.

F. Wireless Link Model

In the wireless channel, as shown in Figure 8 (b), the packet error probability is related to the received signal strength, RSSI (Received Signal Strength Indication), and the received signal strength can be calculated based on the distance between the sensor nodes. Hence, the goal of this section is to expose this relationship. Let P_{TX} and P_{RX} denote the electrical power, let G_{TX} and G_{RX} denote the antenna gain of the wireless communication module, and let L_{TX} and L_{RX} denote the circuit attenuation loss at the transmitter side and the receiver side, respectively. The circuit attenuation loss of L_{TX} and L_{RX} is caused not only by the thermal noise due to the electric-resistive components, but also the impedance mismatching and transmission power losses of high-frequency signals. In addition, let L_P denote the radio-wave attenuation over the wireless channel. In general, the relationship among the parameters of P_{TX}, P_{RX}, G_{TX}, G_{RX}, L_{TX}, L_{RX}, and L_P are calculated based on

$$P_{RX} = P_{TX} - L_{TX} + G_{TX} - L_P + G_{RX} - L_{RX} \text{ (dB)} \quad (4)$$

where the constant parameters of P_{TX}, P_{RX}, G_{TX}, G_{RX}, L_{TX}, and L_{RX} are provided by the wireless module specification.

For the radio-attenuation parameters, to determine the parameter of L_P in (4), we use model of Erceg et al. [22], which can be calculated based on

$$L_P = \alpha + 10 \cdot \beta \cdot \log_{10} (d/d_0) \quad (5)$$

and

$$\alpha = 20 \log_{10} (4\pi d_0/\lambda) \quad (6)$$

and

$$\beta = a - bh_0 + c/h_0 \quad (7)$$

TABLE I. Simulation parameters.

Terms		Values
Number of simulation trials		10,000 trials average
Observation area (in rectangular shape)		1,000 m × 1,000 m
Packet length		ℓ = 1,000 bit
Number of publisher/subscriber node pairs		N_{PS} = 100
Sensor node based on XBee [25]	Transmission power	R_{TX} = 0 dBm (1 mW)
	Antenna gain	$G_{TX} = G_{RX}$ = 0 dBi
	Circuit power loss	$L_{TX} = L_{RX}$ = 0 dB
	Antenna height	h_0 = 0.5 m
	Radio frequency	2.4 GHz (λ = 0.125 m)
	Modulation method	BPSK
Thermal noise (Device temperature)		N_0 = -171.94 dBm (τ_o = 1,600 K)
Parameters in reference [22] (Flat ground surface/light tree density)		d_0 = 100, a = 3.6, b = 0.005, and c = 20
Channel model		Rayleigh fading
Probability of correct recovery		p_e = 1% (Req. $p_b = 10^{-5}$)

where d denotes the distance between the sensor nodes, λ denotes the radio wavelength, h_0 is the antenna height, and d_0, a, b, and c denote the constant parameters depending on the surrounding environment given by Erceg et al. [22].

In our computer simulation, we calculate the packet error probability based on the signal to noise ratio (SNR) and the theoretical equation of bit error probability. If we utilize the BPSK method for the modulation scheme, we can calculate the SNR, γ, based on

$$\gamma = P_{RX} / \kappa \tau_o \quad (8)$$

where κ (= 4.0×10^{-21} W/Hz) is the Boltzmann's constant parameter and τ_o (K) is the absolute temperature of the system device, respectively.

On the other hand, the bit error probability, p_b, under the Rayleigh fading channel that is utilized for familiar wireless communication system evaluation, can be theoretically calculated [23] based on

$$p_b = \frac{1}{2} \cdot \left(1 - \sqrt{\gamma/(\gamma + 1)} \right) \quad (9)$$

Let ℓ denotes the packet length. We can calculate the packet error probability, p_e, using (9) based on

$$p_e = 1 - (1 - p_b)^{\ell} \quad (10)$$

III. COMPUTER SIMULATION

In this chapter, we evaluate the fundamental performance using computer simulation in terms of three benchmarks—the amount of stored sensing data, the number of multi-hops, and the data transfer distance between the publisher and subscriber nodes.

A. Simulation Setting

In the computer simulation, we implemented the computer simulator by using C++ computer programming language. We

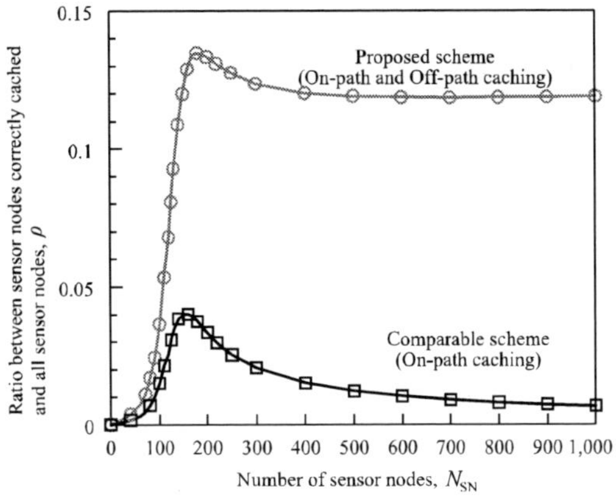

Figure 9. Number of sensor nodes, N_{SN}, versus ratio between sensor nodes correctly cached and all sensor nodes, ρ.

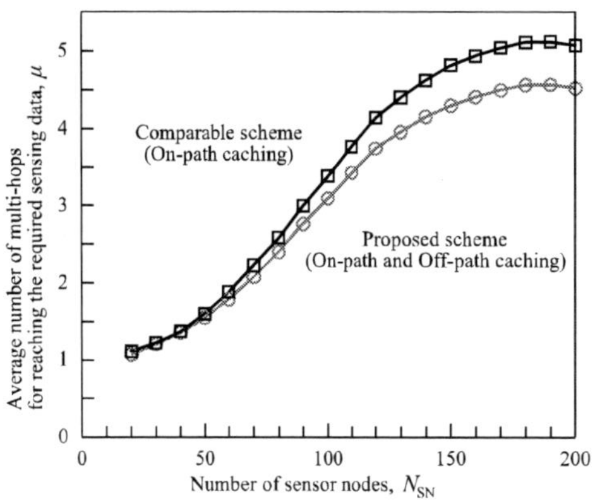

Figure 10. Number of sensor nodes, N_{SN}, versus average number of multi-hops for forwarding the required sensing data, μ.

will evaluate the TX/RX RF module, wireless link, and cache memory as shown in Figures 7 and 8. Table I shows the parameter settings of our computer simulation. In the simulation scenario, the sensor nodes are randomly scattered, i.e., the position of the sensor node is distributed based uniformly. The publisher node and the subscriber node pair is randomly selected; that is, their identifier numbers are distributed based uniformly, and their identifier numbers are different. Let N_{SN} and N_{PS} denote the number of sensor nodes and the number of publisher and subscriber node pairs, respectively, which are provided in Table I. For the routing path decision and calculation, we introduce Dijkstra's algorithm [24]. Dijkstra's algorithm can calculate the optimal path while minimizing the physical distance as a metric of weight links in order to reduce the computational time complexity of our simulation.

In the channel model, the constant parameters of P_{TX}, P_{RX}, G_{TX}, G_{RX}, L_{TX}, and L_{RX} in (4) and the RF wavelength, λ, in (6) are determined based on the familiar XBee RF module [25]. On the other hand, in the radio attenuation model, the constant parameters of a, b, and c in (7) are provided by Erceg et al. [22] when the observation area is assumed to be a suburban area with trees and buildings standing sparsely on flat ground. These detailed parameter settings are shown in Table I. In addition, we assume that the control signal is ideally exchanged and we ignore the shadowing for the wireless communications to avoid system complexity.

B. Simulation Result

The numerical result reveals how the proposed scheme improves the caching capability. The proposed scheme reduces the number of multi-hops and the distance of data transfer between the publisher node and the subscriber node.

Figure 9 shows how many sensor nodes hold the duplicated sensing data in the proposed sensor network. Namely, for the evaluation benchmark, we illustrate the ratio between the sensor nodes that are correctly copied and stored as cached sensing data, ρ, and all sensor nodes, as expressed as

$$\rho = \frac{N_{SN}^*}{N_{SN}} \tag{11}$$

where N_{SN}^* denotes the number of sensor nodes that can copy and store the overhearing sensing data into the cache memory.

As shown in Figure 9, from the qualitative viewpoint, ρ can be improved with increasing N_{SN}, because of the increase in sensor nodes that can store with the overhearing transactions due to increasing dense deployment. In the proposed and comparable schemes, ρ reaches its maximum value at $N_{SN} = 180$ and ρ is degraded in the case of $N_{SN} > 180$ region. This is because ρ reaches its upper limitations in the case of $N_{SN} = 180$ and then decreases depending on N_{SN} when N_{SN} is sufficiently large. However, in the proposed scheme, N_{SN}^* significantly increases in proportion to N_{SN}, which does not increase as dramatically as when $N_{SN} < 180$ region; hence, ρ maintains a constant value when $N_{SN} > 500$ region. On the other hand, from the quantitative viewpoint, the proposed scheme can be improved 1.42, 2.61, 8.85, and 17.0 times over the comparable scheme with any off-path caching mechanism in the cases of N_{SN} = 100, 180, 500, and 1,000.

Figure 10 shows how many multi-hops the response packet transmits from the publisher node to the subscriber node, namely, the number of sensor nodes, N_{SN}, versus the average number of multi-hops for wirelessly forwarding the response packet among the relay nodes, μ. From a qualitative viewpoint, in the proposed scheme, μ is improved in comparison with the comparable scheme. This is because the hit probability of the required sensing data increases depending on if ρ is large; hence, μ can be improved. In addition, when $N_{SN} < 50$ region, the difference of μ between the proposed and comparable schemes is significantly small because of the small ρ difference, and μ reaches its maximum value at $N_{SN} = 180$ by reaching upper limitation, the same as for ρ, as shown in Figure 9. On the other hand, the curve of μ gradually increases depending on N_{SN}, since the multi-hop transmission promotes by increased sensor nodes. From a

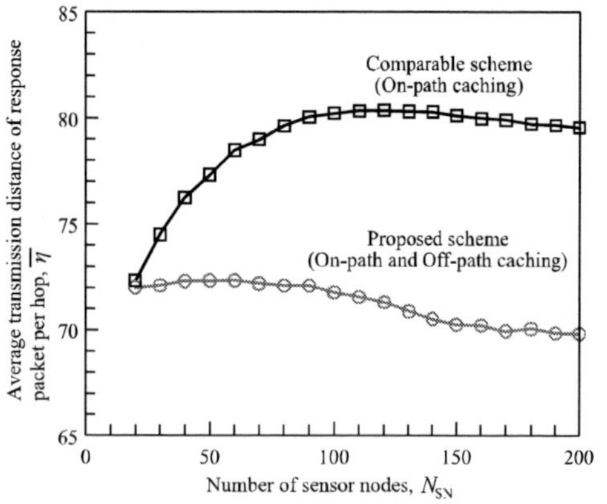

Figure 11. Number of sensor nodes, N_{SN}, versus average transmission distance of response packet per hot, $\overline{\eta}$.

quantitative viewpoint, the proposed scheme can be improved by 3.35%, 8.51%, 10.8%, and 10.9% when N_{SN} = 50, 100, 150, and 200, respectively.

Figure 11 shows how long the response packet takes to transfer from the publisher node to the subscriber node; i.e., the number of sensor nodes N_{SN} versus the average transmission distance of the response packet per hop, $\overline{\eta}$, which is calculated based on

$$\overline{\eta} = \frac{\eta}{\mu} \tag{12}$$

where η denotes the transmission distance of the overall routing path between the publisher and subscriber nodes. In our computer simulation, we utilize Dijkstra's algorithm to obtain the routing path while minimizing η, as mentioned above. Hence, we can calculate η based on the distance metric, which is the summation of the linked weights when the optimal routing path is decided.

As shown in Figure 11, from a qualitative viewpoint, when $N_{SN} < 100$ region, the $\overline{\eta}$ of the comparable scheme worsens, whereas the proposed scheme prevents an increase of $\overline{\eta}$. This is because the probability of holding the target sensing data in the near sensor node becomes large due to the proposed caching mechanism, hence, $\overline{\eta}$ improves. From a quantitative viewpoint, the proposed scheme is improved by 6.46%, 10.5%, 12.3%, and 12.2% when N_{SN} = 50, 100, 150, and 200, respectively.

Consequently, since the proposed scheme improves ρ, as shown in Figure 9, the proposed scheme reduces the number of multi-hops and the data transfer distance between the publisher and subscriber nodes as shown in Figures 10 and 11, respectively. In particular, for the numerical result of Figures 10 and 11, the target sensing data is randomly decided. However, the requested sensing data must have several biases; therefore, we demonstrate our computer simulations in the worst condition, such as an upper (or lower) limitation, and thus expect that the evaluation metrics of ρ, μ, and $\overline{\eta}$ will be significantly more improved in the practical environment.

IV. Conclusion

In this paper, we addressed an effective caching mechanism and its cross-layer-design protocol construction for an ICN-based WSN. We proposed a novel caching scheme using the overhearing phenomena and the SIC technique. We also proposed the protocol-stack and mechanism procedure based on the cross-layer design. The numerical result demonstrated that the proposed scheme is improved 2.61 times that of the comparable scheme (without adopting an off-path caching scheme) when $N_{SN} = 180$ for the caching capability. In addition, the proposed scheme can maximally reduce the number of multi-hops and data transfer distance between the publisher and subscriber nodes by 10.9% and 12.3%, respectively. In our future research, we will demonstrate and discuss our work further in a realistic environment using a hardware testbed-based experiment.

Acknowledgment

A part of this work is supported by the TAF (Telecommunications Advancement Foundation).

References

[1] S. Mori, "A Study on Off-path Caching Scheme by using Successive Interference Cancellation for Information-Centric Network-based Wireless Sensor Network," *Proc. IARIA the 16-th Int. Conf. Networks (ICN'17)*, Apr. 2017, pp. 42–45.

[2] J. Choi, J. Han, E. Cho, T. Kwon, and Y. Choi, "Survey on Content-Oriented Networking for Efficient Content Delivery," *IEEE Commun. Mag.*, vol. 49, no. 3, pp. 121–127, Mar. 2011.

[3] B. Ahlgren, C. Dannewitz, C. Imbrenda, D. Kutscher, and B. Ohlman, "Survey of Information-Centric Networking," *IEEE Commun. Mag.*, vol. 50, no. 7, pp. 26–36, July 2012.

[4] X. Wang, M. Chen, T. Taleb, A. Ksentini, and V. C. M. Leung, "Cashe in the Air: Exploiting Content Caching and Delivery Techniques for 5G Systems," *IEEE Commun. Mag.*, vol. 52, no. 2, pp. 131–139, Feb. 2014.

[5] C. Liang, F. R. Yu, and X. Zhang, "Information-Centric Network Function Virtualization over 5G Mobile Wireless Networks," *IEEE Network*, vol. 29, no. 3, pp. 68–74, May–June 2015.

[6] S. Higuchi and T. Hirotsu, "A Verification Based Flow Space Management Scheme for Multi-Tenant Virtualized Network," *Proc. IARIA the 11-th Int. Conf. Digital Society and eGovernments (ICDS'17)*, Apr. 2017, pp. 24–29.

[7] Y. Zhang, D. Raychadhuri, L. Grieco, E. Baccelli, J. Burke, R. Ravindran, and G. Wang, "ICN Based Architecture for IoT-Requirements and Challenges," *IETF Internet Draft*, Nov. 2014.

[8] M. Amadeo, C. Campolo, J. Quevedo, D. Corujo, A. Molinaro, A. Iera, R. L. Aguiar, and A. V. Vasilakos, "Information-Centric Networking for the Internet of Things: Challenges and Opportunities," *IEEE Network*, vol. 30, no. 2, pp. 92–100, Mar. –Apr. 2016.

[9] K. Wang, F. R. Yu, H. Li, and Z. Li, "Information-Centric Wireless Networks with Virtualization and D2D Communications," *IEEE Wireless Commun.*, vol. 24, no. 3, pp. 104–111, June 2017.

[10] M. Zhang, H. Luo, and H. Zhang, "A Survey of Caching Mechanisms in Information-Centric Networking," *IEEE*

Commun. Surveys and Tutorials, vol. 17, no. 3, pp. 1473–1499, Third-quarter 2015.

[11] T. Koponen, M. Chawla, B. Chun, A. Ermoliskiy, K. H. Kim, S. Schenker, and I. Stoica, "A Data-Oriented (and beyond) Network Architecture," *Proc. ACM Annual Conf. Special Interest Group on Data Commun. (SIGCOM'07)*, Aug. 2007, pp. 181–192, doi:10.1145/1282427.1282402.

[12] http://www.named-data.net/ [retrieved: Nov. 2017]

[13] V. Sourlas, L. Gkatzikis, P. Flegkas, and L. Tassiulas, "Distributed Cache Management in Information-Centric Networks," *IEEE Trans. Network and Service Management*, vol. 10, no. 3, pp. 286–299, Sept. 2013.

[14] S. Wang, J. B. J. Wu, and A. V. Vasilakos, "CPHR: In-network Caching for Information-Centric Networking with Partitioning and Hash-routing," *IEEE/ACM Trans. Networking*, vol. 24, no. 5, pp. 2742–2755, Oct. 2016.

[15] M. Hajimirsadeghi, N. B. Mandayam, and A. Reznik, "Joint Caching and Pricing Strategies for Popular Content in Information Centric Networks," *IEEE J. Sel. Areas in Commun.*, vol. 35, no. 3, pp. 654–667, Mar. 2017.

[16] W. Li, S. M. A. Oteafy, and H. S. Hassanein, "Rate-Selective Caching for Adaptive Streaming over Information-Centric Networks," *IEEE Trans. Computers*, vol. 66, no. 9, pp. 1613–1628, Sept. 2017.

[17] S. Sen, N. Santhapuri, R. R. Choudhury, and S. Nelakuditi, "Successive Interference Cancellation: A Back-of-the-Envelope Perspective," *Proc. ACM Annual Conf. Special Interest Group on Data Commun. (SIGCOM'10) WS Hot Topics in Networks*, Oct. 2010, pp. 1–6, doi:10.1145/1868447.1868464.

[18] J. G. Andrews, "Interference Cancellation for Cellular Systems: A Contemporary Overview," *IEEE Wireless Commun.*, vol. 12, no. 2, pp. 19–29, Apr. 2005.

[19] S. Sambhwani, W. Zhang, and W. Zeng, "Uplink Interference Cancelation in HSPA: Principles and Practice," *QUALCOMM Inc. White Paper*, 28 pages, San Diego, CA, USA, 2009.

[20] S. Shakkottai, T. S. Rappaport, and P. C. Karlsson, "Cross-Layer Design for Wireless Networks," *IEEE Commun. Mag.*, vol. 41, no. 10, pp. 74–80, Oct 2003.

[21] V. Srivastava and M. Motani, "Cross-Layer Design: A Survey and the Road Ahead," *IEEE Commun. Mag.*, vol. 43, no. 12, pp. 112–119, Dec. 2005.

[22] V. Erceg, L. J. Greenstein, S. Y. Tjandra, S. R. Parkoff, A. Gupta, B. Kulic, and A. A. Julius, "An Empirically based Path Loss Model for Wireless Channels in Suburban Environments," *IEEE J. Sel. Areas in Commun.*, vol. 17, no. 7, pp. 1205–1211, July 1999.

[23] J. G. Proakis, *Digital Communications 5-th Edition*, McGraw-Hill, Jan. 2008.

[24] E. W. Dijkstra, "A Note on Two Problems in Connection with Graphs," *J. Numerische Mathematik*, vol. 1, no. 1, pp. 269–271, Dec. 1959.

[25] http://www.digi.com/ [retrieved: Nov. 2017]

Design and Implementation of Verification Based OpenFlow Hypervisor for Multi-Tenant Virtualized Network

Shun Higuchi

Graduate School of Computer and Information Science
Hosei University
Tokyo, Japan
Email: shun.higuchi.6j@stu.hosei.ac.jp

Toshio Hirotsu

Faculty of Computer and Information Science
Hosei University
Tokyo, Japan
Email: hirotsu@hosei.ac.jp

***Abstract*—Cloud services that virtualize existing IT infrastructures in data centers are widely used by governments, universities, and companies. Multi-tenancy is an indispensable feature for data centers to provide a large number of isolated networks to different organizations. OpenFlow is a core technology of software defined networking (SDN) and is useful for centrally managing and controlling these networks; however, SDN is used only at the management level. It is desirable to make the flexible features of SDN/OpenFlow available to users' virtual networks. FlowVisor provides virtualized multi-tenant OpenFlow networks by coordinating multiple controllers, but it is unable to prevent conflicts among the control rules of individual virtual networks. Administrators of each tenant thus need to design the specifications of each virtual network carefully. In this paper, we propose a verification-based scheme for coordinating multiple tenants' OpenFlow networks. The scheme enables administrators to design their own virtual networks without considering conflicts with other tenants. A flow space manager manages overlaps of the address spaces and resolves conflicts between rules of different tenants; in so doing, isolation is preserved transparently for each tenant.**

Keywords–OpenFlow; Virtualization; Multi-tenant Network.

I. INTRODUCTION

With the development of server virtualization technology, cloud computing services, such as Infrastructure as a Service (IaaS), have become popular. Here, an organization's IT infrastructure is consolidated in a data center by using server virtualization and is provided through the Internet. In multi-tenant networks, one physical network is divided into many virtual tenant networks. The traffic in each virtual network needs to be isolated from the traffic in other networks. Virtual LAN (VLAN) is a popular isolation technology. IaaS providers define many virtual layer 2 tenant networks by assigning VLAN-IDs to each tenant; the tenants' administrators then construct their own layer 3 networks by using the VLANs. On an IaaS cloud using VLAN technology, the IaaS administrator needs to change the configuration of the VLAN on all related network devices in order to modify the virtual tenant networks. However, in such environments, demand is growing for an efficient means of changing, i.e., creating, modifying and destroying, virtual networks; what is required is a more flexible virtual network construction and management method.

OpenFlow [3], which is a core technology of software-defined networking (SDN) [2], enables flexible routing control and centralized management of networks by separating the control plane from the data transfer plane. A controller defines the routing of packet forwarding, and the data plane switches transfer packets in accordance with the instructions of the controller. Since this technology has the ability to recognize and rewrite the VLAN-ID of each packet, IaaS providers can aggregate VLAN management functionalities into one controller. The OpenFlow based network architecture enables flexible virtual network management for IaaS providers; however, a tenant network is not allowed to use OpenFlow functionalities to avoid confusion with cloud management level controls. This means administrators of tenant networks can not gain the benefits of OpenFlow even if the provider uses OpenFlow technology to manage its IaaS platform. In contrast, effectively coordinating multiple OpenFlow networks would enable all tenants to manage their own virtual tenant networks by using OpenFlow on a physical network.

FlowVisor [4] is one idea for handling requests from multiple OpenFlow controllers. In FlowVisor, a proxy is placed between the OpenFlow controller and the switches, and it exchanges and manages each tenant's control messages sent between the controllers and switches. OpenFlow switches on physical networks work properly under the control of FlowVisor, which coordinates multiple tenant controllers. In FlowVisor, each isolated virtual network space is expressed as a flow space. The administrator of a flow space needs to regulate the OpenFlow controller to write flow entries under the restrictions of the allocated flow space definition. This mechanism can be used to construct a plurality of virtual OpenFlow networks, and it enables each tenant controller to control their virtual tenant networks individually; however, FlowVisor does not avoid overlaps between flow spaces. When using FlowVisor to isolate multiple OpenFlow tenant networks, each tenant network is expected to obey the flow space definition provided by the IaaS provider. This problem becomes more complicated because the flow specifications used in the networks are not always exclusive. In the case of monitoring one tenant's network from another management network, the flow specifications allocated to each network's flow space must overlap. The IaaS provider needs to define them very carefully so as not to cause unintended traffic control.

In this research, we propose a verification-based OpenFlow network virtualization based on OpenFlow hypervisor that enables the network to be freely designed by each tenant. To guarantee isolation of tenant networks, we introduce a conflict management system that uses verification of flow space definitions. When a conflict occurs, the management system detects it and resolves the conflict by rewriting a flow entry. Our approach verifies and manages overlapping parts of the flow spaces defined by individual tenants, detects conflicts between flow spaces and flow entries, and rewrites the entries to avoid conflicts in the FlowVisor. This paper describes the method of flow space verification and its implementation based on our proposed mechanisms [1]. Section II is an overview of OpenFlow/SDN technology. Section III explains the mechanism and problems of FlowVisor. Section IV outlines the proposed virtualization method based on flow entry verification, and Section V describes the method for avoiding flow entry conflicts in more detail. Section VI describes our prototype implementation and its performance evaluation. Section VII discusses our method in relation with other research. Section VIII is a conclusion that mentions future work.

II. OpenFlow/SDN

OpenFlow is a representative architecture of software-defined networking, and it is currently being standardized. It is a next-generation network technology for cloud computing environments. An OpenFlow network consists of an OpenFlow controller responsible for routing control and an OpenFlow switch for transferring packets according to flow entries written by the controller. Hence, it is a centralized control architecture that enables centralized management of networks by separating the traditional network system into a control plane and data plane.

The controller is software, and a pair of matching fields, such as a MAC address, an IP address, a transport number, a VLAN-ID, and the actions to be performed on a packet are defined as a flow entry. Flexible routing control is enabled by transferring packets according to flow entries in the switch. If the switch has to be reconfigured in response to a change in the network configuration, the change is applied to all the switches by describing the change settings as new flow entries in the controller. This improves the manageability of the network. The controller and switch are connected by an OpenFlow channel, which is a control network using TCP/IP that is constructed separately from the data network, and they exchange control messages called OpenFlow messages through it. Through OpenFlow messages, the controller controls switches such as for writing the flow entry. In OpenFlow, since the controller controls all the switches and knows the network topology, it is possible for it to control routing flexibly such as through source routing and multi-path forwarding. Virtualizing a physical network by using OpenFlow makes it possible not only to improve the manageability of VLAN-IDs but also to ensure logical division of the network by using the packet headers of layers 1 to 4 that can be specified as a match field. OpenFlow enables its users to create a number of virtual networks beyond the usual limits of VLAN-IDs by dividing up the used address space in advance.

However, the conventional OpenFlow technology has some problems when it comes to virtualizing and controlling the OpenFlow network itself. For example, it is not possible to control each switch individually from multiple controllers in one OpenFlow network. Moreover, there is no mechanism to logically divide one OpenFlow network into multiple virtual OpenFlow networks. These problems make it impossible for a tenant to construct and control each controller or devise a virtual OpenFlow network in a multi-tenant data center that provides IaaS.

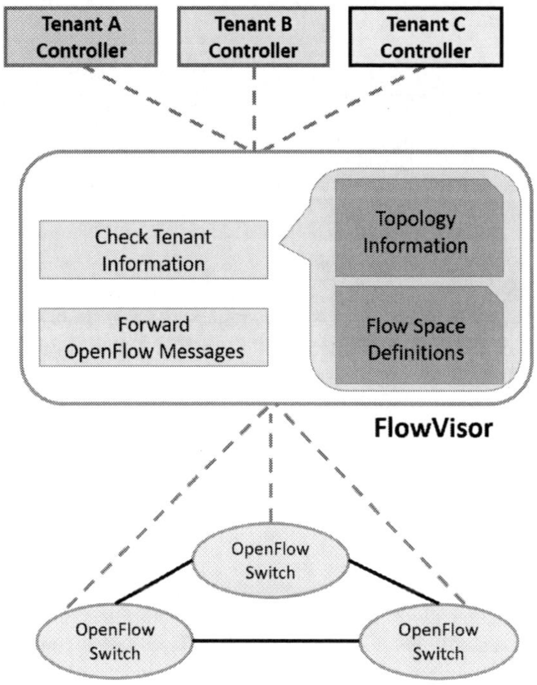

Figure 1. FlowVisor

III. FlowVisor

A FlowVisor is placed in the controller and switches, as shown in Figure 1. It operates as a proxy that transfers the OpenFlow messages necessary to control the switch from the controller. The administrator of FlowVisor defines the available network space to each tenant as a flow space and presents a flow space definition to each tenant user in some way. Tenant users create their own controllers that write flow entries in accordance with the network topologies and flow space definitions of the tenants' OpenFlow networks presented to them by the FlowVisor administrator. A tenant user can control the tenant network by connecting his/her controller to FlowVisor.

A. *Flow Space*

The administrator of FlowVisor defines a network space called a "flow space" that expresses the ranges of network parameters allowed to each tenant beforehand. Table I shows an example of a flow space. The flow space definition holds a slice name indicating the name of the tenant network, a DPID that indicates the OpenFlow switch ID, and a MAC address, IP address, transport number, etc., as an available match field from layer 1 to 4 in a flow entry and priority. In addition, each flow space is based on the premise that the defined network space is independent and has no overlaps. Therefore, there is no mechanism in FlowVisor for checking whether flow space conflicts exist; hence, the administrator needs to define each flow space carefully.

TABLE I. EXAMPLES OF FLOW SPACE

Slice	DPID	Priority	VLAN	Src MAC	Dst MAC	Src IP	Dst IP	Src TCP	Dst TCP
Tenant A	1	100	50	*	*	*	*	80, 22	*
Tenant B	1	100	50	*	*	10.0.1.0/24	*	80	*
Tenant C	1	100	50	*	*	10.0.2.0/24	*	80	*

B. FlowVisor Mechanism

FlowVisor functions as a proxy on the OpenFlow channel and controls the transfer of OpenFlow messages between multiple controllers and switches. This function differs between the case of transferring messages from the switch to the controller, such as when sending Packet-In and Port-Status messages, and the case of forwarding messages from the controller to the switch, such as when sending the Flow-Mod message.

First, we describe the messages that are transferred from the switch to the controller. In this case, it is necessary to specify the controller to which the message pertains before transferring the message to it. As an example, a Port-Status message notifying that the physical port state of the switch has changed will affect all the tenant controllers using that port. Accordingly, FlowVisor searches for all target controllers from the topology information of each tenant network and transfers the Port-Status message to all of them. In the case of a Packet-In message, FlowVisor searches the flow space definition to specify which tenant network the packet belongs to and forwards the message to the tenant controller of the corresponding flow space.

Next, we describe the messages that are transferred from the controller to the switch. In this case, FlowVisor refers to the topology information of all the tenant networks; then it transfers the message to the target switch; it performs the same operation on every message. If a tenant user tries to send a message to a switch that does not belong to its own tenant network, the send operation fails and a message transfer error is returned to the controller.

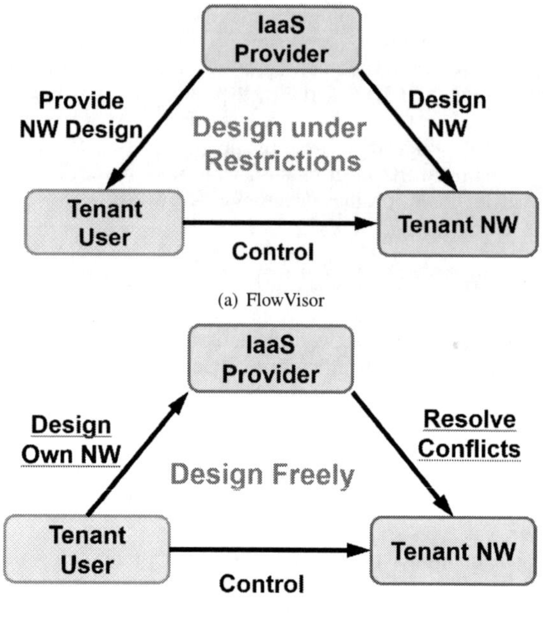

(a) FlowVisor

(b) Ideal for IaaS

Figure 2. Network Design Policy

C. FlowVisor Problem

FlowVisor is based on the premises that the flow spaces allocated to each tenant network are independent and the tenant controller sets flow entries within the allocated flow space. If a FlowVisor administrator defines an unintended or incorrect flow space content, an unexpected network control will be executed. This problem can be discussed from a different viewpoint that the IaaS provider forces each tenant to restrict his/her network design, as shown in Figure 2(a). In contrast, if IaaS providers want to enable each tenant user to freely design their own tenant network, as shown in Figure 2(b), each tenant user should be able to define their flow space freely. This, however, leads to a problem that unintended traffic control can occur when a flow entry is written that conflicts with the flow space of another tenant. Hence, it is necessary to implement a mechanism that can check for conflicts in flow spaces and flow entries in a multi-tenant network.

Table I shows an example of conflicting flow entries, wherein tenant user A tries to write a flow entry that prohibits the SSH session such as by sending"*Src TCP = 22, action = DROP*" to the switch with DPID = 1. In the table, the match fields of tenant A are defined as wildcard values " * " with the exception of Src TCP; thus, tenant user A can freely use this value. However, if a flow entry such as what is mentioned above is written, it will be applied to all packets transferred through this switch with the source TCP port number 22. Since all the packets are dropped, all SSH connections are closed, even in the other tenant networks. In this case, the packet was dropped unintentionally, however, it is possible to rewrite the packet header as a specified action and transfer it in OpenFlow. It is also possible to act in dubious or illegal ways, such as eavesdropping by transferring traffic of other tenants that are not permitted to use a server on their tenant network. In particular, it is possible to transfer the traffic of other tenants to a server on one's own tenant network for the purpose of sniffing packets.

If a FlowVisor administrator allows each tenant user to freely design their tenant network and flow space definition, a flow space that has overlaps will cause unintended behaviors because the flow entries conflict. This is due to OpenFlow's ability to flexibly set values such as wildcards about the L1-L4 headers in the match field. In the example mentioned above, since the tenant user can write a flow entry with wildcards other than the source TCP port number to the switch, s/he can control the traffic in unassigned flow spaces.

IV. Virtualization Based on Flow Entry Verification

We propose a new scheme to manage the virtualization of an OpenFlow network that allows each tenant to freely design his/her own network. It coordinates the controllers of the tenants' networks to make their designs work properly on a physical OpenFlow network (Figure 2(b)). The core tasks of the coordination are verification and conflict resolution. The management system verifies duplications of flow spaces assigned to each tenant, then resolves the conflict by rewriting the flow entries received from the tenant controllers. Figure 3 shows the verification process in OpenFlow Hypervisor. First, this system verifies and manages the overlapping address spaces in the owned flow space. A tenant administrator defines the combination of address spaces that is used in each tenant network as a "flow space". In addition, when a flow entry in a flow space includes address spaces overlapping those of other flow spaces, it checks for conflicts in the flow entries and rewrites the match field to guarantee separation of traffic of each tenant network. This minimizes the amount of rewriting of flow entries by applying verification and management to the flow space in advance.

The flow space of our system has a different definition from that of FlowVisor. Our definition of a flow space is a set of specific elements of OpenFlow match fields. In the existing work, there is no mechanism to check for violations of the flow space definition; thus, each tenant network is able to set arbitrary values for all match field elements. In this case, a tenant user controller may cause unintended traffic controls, such as using wildcards. On the other hand, our method restricts tenants to using only the range of match fields' values that each tenant defined as a flow space previously. If the tenant controller tries to set erroneous match fields in the flow entry, our system verifies and rewrites them to fit to the flow space definition. Our system also resolves the conflict ranges of the match fields by rewriting and writing back the values of the match fields.

A. Flow Space Definition

This flow space is different from the definition of FlowVisor in Section III-A. In previous work, a flow space was defined for each switch that the tenant can control; however, here, a new flow space is defined as a combination of address spaces that the tenant can use for one tenant network. A flow space is composed of multiple rules, where each rule consists of rule IDs, flow space names, and a matching field that is available to the tenant, as shown in Table II. In the matching field, it is possible to set five kinds of header information of L2 to L4, i.e., VLAN ID, Src/Dst IP address, and Src/Dst TCP port, which are necessary for network operations. These definitions are described in JSON format, as shown in Figure 4. Each flow space has a flow space name and a set of flow definitions. A flow definition is described for each element of a match field, and it is defined as a conjunction of fields. Since one flow space is represented by one or more flow definitions, multiple flow definitions are defined as disjunctions to allow flow entries that match any one. Each tenant uses only the combination of address spaces specified in this flow space. Definition example 2 in Table II, which summarizes the examples of Figure 4, shows the following address space:

- VLAN ID = 100, Src IP = 192.168.64.0/20, Dst IP = 192.168.64.0/20, Src TCP = 80
- VLAN ID = 101, Src IP = 192.168.64.0/20, Dst IP = 192.168.64.0/20, Src TCP = 80

The tenant assigned this flow space can control the network by using these two different combinations as a match field of the flow entry. The top row of Table II shows the available address space as the match field, but the upper limit of the VLAN ID is half the original limit of 4096. This is due to securing independent address space as management space for managing duplications of flow spaces and resolving conflicts in advance. VLAN-IDs are allocated from this management space to the flow space when necessary.

B. Duplicate Flow Space Verification and Flow Entry

Now let us explain the overlap verification between flow spaces and conflicts of flow entries on the basis of the definition in the previous section. Table III lists examples of flow spaces defined for three tenants A, B, and C. Since the flow space definition of tenant A on the top row completely includes the flow spaces of tenants B and C, the flow space of A overlaps those of B and C and is not independent. On the other hand, in the flow spaces of tenants B and C are independent in Table II, and independent values are specified for any of the match fields, such as Src IP address. Since only a combination of the address spaces is used as a match field in our flow space definition, we can detect duplications by verifying the inclusion relation for each combination of address spaces.

If the flow spaces have a complete inclusion relation, one must detect and avoid conflicts of flow entries after managing any flow space duplication. In flow spaces such as in Table III, the flow entry at the top of the Table IV written from tenant A's controller will collide with the flow entries of other tenants. Table IV shows two examples, i.e., one that conflicts with other flow space definitions and another that does not conflict with any other. In the example flow entry on the upper row, the value of Src IP is 192.168.64.0/20, and it is based on the flow space of tenant A. Since it includes the range of the flow spaces of the other tenants B and C, it conflicts with their flow entries, and their traffic is also controlled by this conflicting flow entry. On the other hand, in the example flow entry on the lower row, VLAN-ID = 101, which is an independent value from the flow space of the other tenants, is set in the match field. This flow entry does not cause a conflict. As mentioned above, we must verify the inclusion relation of the value specified in the match field for each flow space. If the value includes other tenant's flow spaces, it is possible to verify and avoid conflict by allocating a new value from the free independent address space and setting it in the conflicting flow entry.

V. Conflict Verification of Flow Entry

To avoid conflicts between flow entries, we propose a two-step conflict resolution method. The first step involves checking the consistency between the address space defined in the match field of the flow entry and its own flow space. In the second step, the OpenFlow hypervisor rewrites the match field of the conflicting flow entries that overlap with the address spaces in another tenant's flow space. Only switches under the common topology of the tenants' network are targets of this operation. Part of the match field of the flow entry is

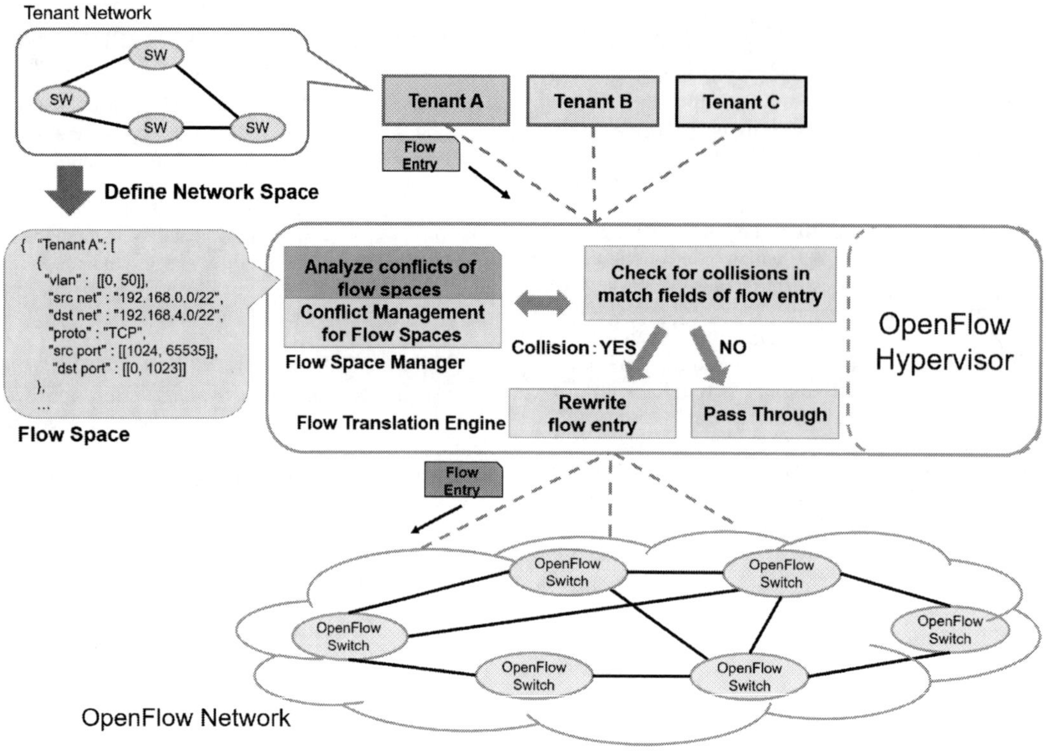

Figure 3. Proposed Architecture

TABLE II. FLOW SPACE LIMIT AND DEFINITION EXAMPLES

Rule ID	Space Name	VLAN	Src IP	Dst IP	Src TCP	Dst TCP
1	Maximum usage	0∼2047	0.0.0.0∼255.255.255.255	0.0.0.0∼255.255.255.255	0∼65535	0∼65535
2	Example 1	0∼50	192.168.0.0/22	192.168.4.0/22	1024∼65535	0∼1023
3	Example 2	0∼50	192.168.4.0/22	192.168.0.0/22	0∼1023	1024∼65535
4	Example 3	100, 101	192.168.64.0/20	192.168.64.0/20	80	*

TABLE III. EXAMPLES OF DUPLICATE FLOW SPACES

Rule ID	Space Name	VLAN	Src IP	Dst IP	Src TCP	Dst TCP
1	Tenant A	100, 101	192.168.64.0/20	192.168.64.0/20	80, 22	*
2	Tenant B	100	192.168.64.0/24	192.168.64.0/24	80	*
3	Tenant C	100	192.168.65.0/24	192.168.65.0/24	80	*

TABLE IV. EXAMPLES OF FLOW ENTRIES IN TABLE III

Entry	Match Field	Action
Conflicting Flow Entry	VLAN ID = 100 Src IP = 192.168.64.0/24 Dst IP = 192.168.64.0/24 Src TCP = 80	Output: port 2
Non-Conflicting Flow Entry	VLAN ID = 101 Src IP = 192.168.64.0/24 Dst IP = 192.168.64.0/24 Src TCP = 80	Output: port 2

converted into an independent value by using an address space not used by other tenants. At this time, the rewriting method will vary depending on the type of overlap in the topology. As a result, conflicts due to flow entries are automatically detected and avoided, while at the same time, different flow entries are prohibited in the defined flow space. These measures guarantee that the traffic of different tenant networks stays separated.

A. Consistency Check with Flow Spaces

When the OpenFlow hypervisor receives a Flow-Mod message from a tenant controller, it check whether the match field included in the message deviates from the tenant's flow space definition. To do so, it simply checks the range of the address space for values other than wildcards in the match field to see if they go beyond the range defined in the flow space. If a flow entry with a value beyond that of the flow

```
{
  "Example 1"   : [
    {
      "vlan" :  [[0, 50]],
      "src net" : "192.168.0.0/22",
      "dst net" : "192.168.4.0/22",
      "proto" : "TCP",
      "src port" : [[1024, 65535]],
      "dst port" : [[0, 1023]]
    },
    {
      "vlan" :  [[0, 50]],
      "src net" : "192.168.4.0/22",
      "dst net" : "192.168.0.0/22",
      "proto" : "TCP",
      "src port" : [[0, 1023]],
      "dst port" : [[1024, 65535]]
    }
  ],
  "Example 2"   : [
    {
      "vlan" : [[100], [101]]
      "src net" : "192.168.64.0/20",
      "dst net" : "192.168.64.0/20",
      "proto" : "TCP",
      "src port" : [[80]],
      "dst port" : [[80]]
    }
  ]
}
```

Figure 4. JSON Format for Flow Space

space definition is written, the OpenFlow hypervisor discards the Flow-Mod message and sends an error for the message to the tenant controller.

Subsequently, for flow entries that have passed the consistency check, the possibility of conflicting flow entries is checked by using the flow space management information. If the flow entry has no conflicts, the Flow-Mod message is simply transferred to the OpenFlow switch. By contrast, when flow entries conflict, our OpenFlow hypervisor rewrites the flow entry according to the rules discussed in the next section and forwards the rewritten Flow-Mod message.

B. Rewriting Flow Entries

If two tenants have common areas in their network topologies and address spaces in the flow definitions of their flow spaces, the flow entries may conflict on the switches in the common topology. In this case, it is necessary to rewrite a tenant's flow entry and to inject a flow entry to convert the packet header into one that resolves the conflict. When rewriting the flow entries so as not to conflict with other tenants' flow spaces, the hypervisor needs to determine an address space without the conflict. Two rewriting methods can be used; the choice is based on the size of the common area of the topology with other tenants. Below, we explain these methods using the flow spaces of Tables III and the topology of Figure 5 as an example.

1) Partial Case: If the common area covers only part of the topology, we resolve the conflict by using NAT (Network Address Translation) with unused IPv4 address blocks. First, NAT flow entries with unused IPv4 address blocks are set at the edge switch of the common part of the tenant network. These NAT entries convert the collision addresses of all packets in the tenant network temporarily into different address blocks at the edge of the common area. All of the original flow entries from the tenant controller need to be modified to fit the NAT address blocks before they are transferred to the switches.

In Figure 5, SW2 is located in the common area of the topologies of tenant A and tenant B. When the controller of tenant B tries to write a flow entry that conflicts with tenant A to SW2, the OpenFlow hypervisor sets the NAT flow entry to SW3 and SW6 in advance. An example of a NAT flow entry installed in the switches is shown in Table V(a). In this example, the IPv4 address block of tenant B collides with the one of tenant A and is converted into an unused IPv4 address block. In this example, for the packet header of tenant B, the IPv4 address described in the flow space of Table III is rewritten to an unused address 10.168.64.0/24. In SW3 and SW6, this flow entry and a flow entry to convert back to the original packet header are set to each. The match fields of all subsequent OpenFlow messages for the switches in the tenant network are rewritten in order to use the VLAN-ID to determine the tenant's traffic.

2) Overall Case: If the topology of a tenant network is fully included in one of another network, the OpenFlow hypervisor rewrites the flow entry which uses the VLAN-ID reserved for the management address space, as explained in Section IV-A. First, the flow entry for assigning or converting the VLAN-ID is installed in the switches in the common area. This flow entry assures that a different VLAN-ID is assigned to each tenant on the basis of the ingress physical port number. Subsequently, we rewrite the VLAN-ID of the match field for the flow entry that the tenant writes and forward it to the switch.

In Figure 5, the topology of tenant C is entirely included in the one of tenant A. In this case, a flow entry for rewriting the VLAN-ID is installed in SW1 and SW4, that are in the included tenant network, where the flow entries may conflict. If the flow space of tenant C, which is the included tenant network, uses VLAN, the flow entry that converts the value of the VLAN-ID is installed. If it does not use VLAN, a flow entry which pushes a VLAN-ID is installed. The first row of Table V(b) shows the former case, and the second row shows the latter. The OpenFlow hypervisor converts all OpenFlow messages received from the controller of tenant C into ones that use the VLAN-ID assigned for tenant C before transferring them to SW1 and SW4.

VI. Implementation

We implemented an OpenFlow hypervisor prototype. The core modules of the system were the flow space manager and flow translation engine. We measured and evaluated simple benchmarks individually for each of these prototypes. In this section, we describe the implementation of each module of the

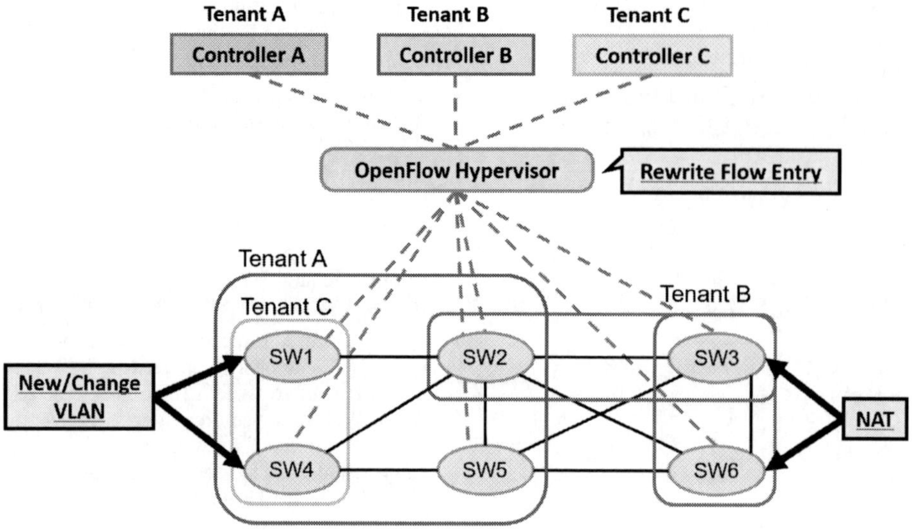

Figure 5. Rewriting Flow Entry

TABLE V. EXAMPLES OF FLOW ENTRIES FOR REWRITING

(a) NAT Flow Entry

Entry	Match Field	Action
NAT Flow Entry	VLAN-ID = 100 Src IPv4 = 192.168.64.0/24 Dst IPv4 = 192.168.64.0/24 Src TCP = 80	Set Field: Src IPv4 = 10.168.64.0/24, Dst IPv4 = 10.168.64.0/24

(b) VLAN Flow Entry

Entry	Match Field	Action
New VLAN Flow Entry	In_Port = 2	Push VLAN: 2049
Change VLAN Flow Entry	In_Port = 2 VLAN ID = 100 Src IP = 192.168.65.0/24 Dst IP = 192.168.65.0/24 Src TCP = 80	Set Field: VLAN-ID: 2049

prototype system and the preliminary performance evaluation for each.

A. Flow Space Manager

The flow space manager holds definitions of the given flow space and investigates in advance where flow entries can collide in it. Here, the flow space is defined as shown in Figure 4; the manager analyzes it and holds flow definitions for each flow space. At this time, in each flow definition, an address space that has overlapping address blocks with one of the other flow spaces in all match fields may cause a conflict.

The flow definition is managed using the hash of the source IP address space with the network address of a 24-bit prefix as the key. In this case, if the source IP address space of the flow definition is smaller than /24, the network address of the /24 network including it is used as the key. If it is larger than /24, the network addresses of all /24 networks are registered as multiple entries.

The manager prototype was implemented in Ruby 2.3, and the overhead of flow registration was measured. In particular, we measured the overhead of flow registration of 5000 flow spaces to the manager. Figure 6 shows the results of the evaluation measured for an Intel Core-i7 3.6GHz with 16GB memory. The graph with the plus signs (+) shows the case of 5000 flow spaces without any conflicts, while the one with the cross signs (x) shows that of 5000 flow spaces containing one conflict for each. Considering that the flow space registration is relatively infrequent, this result indicates an acceptable level of performance.

B. Flow Translation Engine

The flow translation engine receives flow entries that tenant controllers try to write to the OpenFlow switch and rewrites them to avoid conflicts by using the algorithm described in Section V-B. In OpenFlow, the controller sends a Flow-Mod message to an OpenFlow switch for changing the flow entry on each switch. The flow translation engine parses this Flow-Mod message and transfers it after rewriting the packet data such as the match field of the flow entry.

The flow translation engine was implemented in Python 3.6

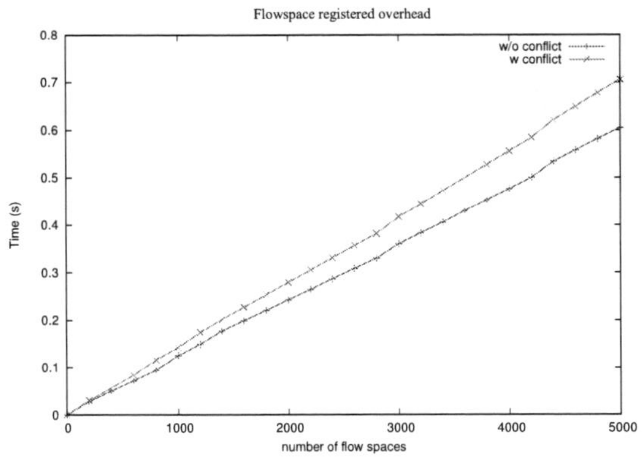

Figure 6. Execution Time of Flow Registration

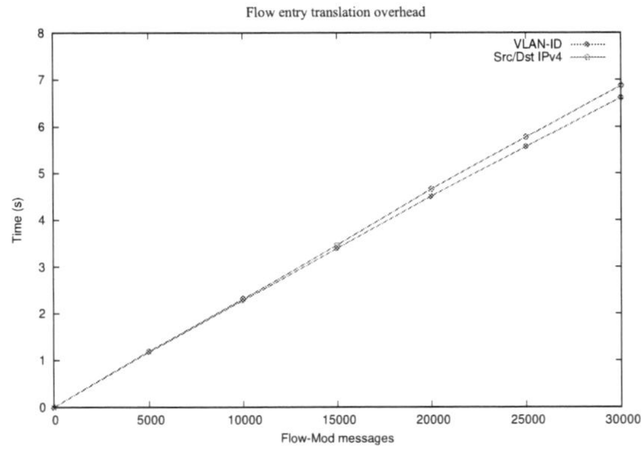

Figure 7. Overhead of Flow Translation

and Ryu SDN Framework 4.16, and the overhead of rewriting the match field of the flow entries was measured. In particular, we measured the execution time of translation for two rewriting patterns with 30000 Flow-Mod messages. The first pattern worked to evaluate the overhead for rewriting the original VLAN-ID to a different value, while the second pattern worked to evaluate rewriting the source and destination IPv4 addresses. The results, as measured by a computer with an Intel Core-i7 3.6GHz and 16 GB memory are shown in Figure 7. This engine could rewrite 30000 Flow-Mod messages in about 13 seconds for both patterns. This means that the average flow translation overhead was 0.22 ms per Flow-Mod message. This overhead is required only when a new flow space is added. Therefore, these results show that this engine has sufficient performance.

VII. Discussion

We proposed an OpenFlow network virtualization scheme that allows each tenant to freely use OpenFlow technology in a multi-tenant network environment. The core module of our scheme is the verification-based virtualization management of OpenFlow networks. The proposed OpenFlow hypervisor manages the flow spaces defined by each tenant beforehand, detects overlaps of the flow space definitions, resolves conflicts by rewriting the match fields' values, and monitors for erroneous control messages violating the flow space definitions. The designers of tenant networks can use it to freely design their own networks by defining network address ranges such as the IP address.

FlowVisor expects that the individual flow spaces never overlap; thus, it does not verify whether conflicts occur between flow spaces. This means that conflict avoidance among flow spaces is left to the responsibility of the tenant's administrators. From this point of view, it seems reasonable to view it as a network partitioning technique rather than a virtualization. Sköldström [5] et al. propose a virtualization method that uses FlowVisor as a relay network of a wide area network. They focus on resource management, whereas our research mainly deals with mapping to lower-layer network separation technology such as MPLS. The virtualization method of Yamanaka et al. [6] works by assigning and tagging a specific MAC address for each virtual network at the edge of the network. This method restricts flow definitions to those that can be described by each tenant.

Our method enables each tenant to define its virtual networks freely and guarantees isolation of the tenant networks automatically. Using our scheme, established TCP/IP networks can be migrated to a datacenter where flexible controls can easily be introduced using OpenFlow technology. Even when the backend of the IT infrastructure of the current organization is moved to the cloud environment, it will be possible to provide both flexible network control and ease of design like that of a conventional network.

VIII. Conclusion

We proposed a virtual network management system that maximizes the ability of OpenFlow virtualization by using verification of the flow space definition. The method enables individual tenant networks to be freely designed in a multi-tenant network environment and ensures isolation among them. This makes it possible for IaaS providers to provide a flexible tenant network in which OpenFlow technology is freely used for and by each tenant user. A preliminary evaluation of a prototype shows that the proposed flow space management has sufficient performance.

Acknowledgment

This work was supported by the Japan Society for the Promotion of Science (JSPS KAKENHI Grant Number JP15K00138).

References

[1] S. Higuchi and T. Hirotsu, "A Verification Based Flow Space Management Scheme for Multi-Tenant Virtualized Network," The Eleventh International Conference on Digital Society and eGovernments (ICDS), pp. 24-29, March 2017.

[2] N. McKeown, "Software-defined networking," INFOCOM keynote talk, vol. 17, no. 2, pp. 30-32, 2009.

[3] N. McKeown et al., "OpenFlow: enabling innovation in campus networks," ACM SIGCOMM Computer Communication Review, vol. 38, Issue 2, pp. 69-74, April 2008.

[4] R. Sherwood et al., "FlowVisor: A Network Virtualization Layer," Tech. Rep. OPENFLOW-TR-2009-01, OpenFlow Consortium, October 2009.

[5] P. Sköldström and K. Yedavalli, "Network Virtualization and Resource Allocation in OpenFlow-based Wide Area Networks," IEEE International Conference on Communications (ICC), pp. 6622-6626, June 2012.

[6] H. Yamanaka, S. Ishii, and E. Kawai, "Realizing Virtual OpenFlow Networks by Flow Space Virtualization," IEICE Technical Report, Network Systems, vol. 112, no. 85, pp. 67-72, June 2012.

Data Mining for Forecasting Fog Events and Comparing Geographical Sites

Designing a novel method for predictive models portability

Gaetano Zazzaro, Gianpaolo Romano
Italian Aerospace Research Centre, CIRA
Capua (CE), Italy
email: g.zazzaro@cira.it
email: g.romano@cira.it

Paola Mercogliano
Euro-Mediterranean Center on Climate Change, CMCC,
Italian Aerospace Research Centre, CIRA
Capua (CE), Italy
email: paola.mercogliano@cmcc.it

***Abstract*— Fog represents high impact atmospherical phenomena especially for aviation. Low visibility conditions severely affect air traffic operations especially during the landing and take-off phases and thereby reducing the capacity of an airport. In particular, in 2001 the Linate Airport in Milan was hit by a disaster, the deadliest air disaster to ever occur in Italian aviation history, due to un-forecasted thick fog. For this reason, improvement of fog monitoring and forecast tool is a challenge topic for the aviation community. Moreover, forecasting fog is an important issue for air traffic safety because adverse visibility conditions represent one of the major causes of traffic delay and of the economic loss associated with such phenomena. In such context, the present work illustrates a Data Mining application for the fog forecasting on a short time range (1 hour) on Linate airport. Indeed two predictive models have been trained using an historical dataset of 18 years of fog observations including many meteorological parameters collected in the Synop message. These models have been made up by applying BayesNet and Neural Network algorithms. The performances evaluation highlights that the complete model shows 90% of instances correctly predicted. Moreover, in order to discover whether predictive models trained on Milan can also be used for forecasting fog events on other geographic sites, a new method to characterize fog events and compare different airport areas is described. Thus, a novel metric is defined, aimed at comparing different sites. This metric is based on the Euclidean distance between performance vectors that are also here defined. Thanks to this metric, we can determine whether a new set of fog observations is compatible or not with Linate fog observations and whether, formally, the predictive models are portable to the new site. Furthermore, we are able to group geographical locations that can be also many kilometers distance away. This work represents a first design step to define the comparative metric. It has been carried on according to the standard process (CRISP-DM) for Knowledge Discovery in Database Process.**

Keywords-Data Mining; Forecast Fog; Bayesian Networks, Artificial Neural Networks; Inductive Decision Trees; Model Portability; CRISP-DM.

I. INTRODUCTION

This paper is an extended version of the conference paper [1]. With respect to the conference version, in this paper we expand the description of the methodology adopted for the creation of fog predictive models on Linate Airport in Milan, including more details of Data Understanding and statistical exploratory charts. Moreover, a new descriptive model of fog events is explained and the design of an its innovative use is introduced, aimed at comparing different geographical sites; in addition, we discuss the portability of predictive models to other sites that are similar (or compatible, with a meaning that will be detailed in this paper) with the Milan Linate site.

The effort spent by aeronautic research on this topic is due to the importance to reduce the impact on the different flight phase (e.g., taxing, landing, take off) on the atmospherical phenomena. This requirement is obtained improving the current capability to forecast (on different time range) adverse weather condition.

Fog forecast and its characterization represent a challenging topic due to the local condition causing this phenomena. Moreover, low visibility conditions severely affect air traffic operations especially during the landing and take-off phases and thereby reduce the capacity of an airport. This leads to the built-up of a wave of delayed flights in case demand exceeds the reduced capacity, which is especially critical at major hubs, such as, for Italy, Milan Linate during peak times. Since these hubs are central nodes in the air traffic network, the effect also spreads causing the event to be of much more than just local importance. Indeed the occurrence of low ceilings and/or poor visibility conditions restricting the flow of air traffic into major airport terminals is one of the major causes of traffic delay and of the economic loss associated with such phenomena [2]. For these reasons, a fast forecasting tool is crucial to adequately manage the occurrence of these events and to mitigate their impact over the whole airport system. Consequently, it is important to deeply understand the process leading to the formation of fog and justifies the efforts made by meteorologists to forecast such events.

In this paper, a method for fog nowcasting (short-range forecasting of 1 hour) on Linate Airport in Milan based on Data Mining techniques is presented. Indeed Data Mining (DM) [3] – also called "Knowledge Discovery in Databases" – refers to the process of extraction or "Mining" useful knowledge from large amounts of data. DM draws upon ideas, such as sampling, estimation, and hypothesis testing from statistics and search algorithms, modeling techniques, and learning theories from artificial intelligence, pattern recognition, and machine learning.

DM can represent a useful analysis method for this complex meteorological phenomenon because it has the ability to work with many data described by a high number of variables.

In order to obtain DM models for fog prediction, we used an historical dataset consisting of 164.352 meteorological SYNOP observations collected at Milan's Linate airport station from January 1996 until September 2014.

Knowledge Discovery in Database Process, that we carried on in order to predict fog events, has been conducted according to the standard process conceived from the Cross-Industry Standard Process for DM (CRISP-DM) [4]. CRISP-DM is structured in six steps (Figure 1).

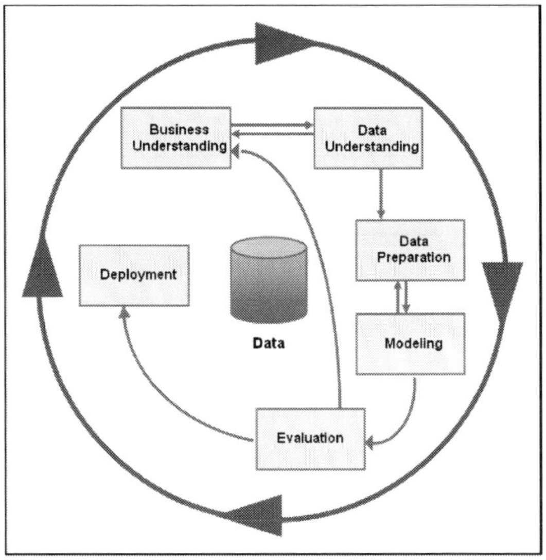

Figure 1. CRISP-DM Steps

Every step of the process has been supported by the validation of domain experts. In this work, we used the Weka tool (Version 3.8.0) (Waikato Environment for Knowledge Analysis) [5] to carry on DM analysis. In particular, we used the Weka Explorer interface to mine data by applying Bayesian Nets, Artificial Neural Networks, and Inductive Decision Trees algorithms.

A. *Structure of the paper*

The paper is organized by describing all the CRISP phases one by one. In Section II, the Business Understanding is carried on in order to understand the fog phenomenon and its development, to explore the state of the art from meteorological and DM points of view, and to fix DM goals. In Section III, we illustrate the data collection, the data sources, the variables and statistics of the attributes. In Section IV, we explain all the activities of the Data Preparation phase aimed at constructing the final datasets to be mined; in particular, the preprocessing phase and the hold-out method. In Section V, we provide details about the Modeling phase: from the identification of target functions to model testing. Moreover, we illustrate a descriptive model by which we are able to better understand the fog phenomenon and to define a measure of similarity between meteorological stations (or geographic locations). In Section VI, we present the Evaluation phase including the analysis of the misclassified fog events. In Section VII we design how to use the descriptive model and its future investigations ad applications. Finally, in Section VIII, we show our considerations.

II. Business Understanding

This first step of the CRISP-DM process includes fixing of the business objectives, Data Mining goals and assess situation.

A. *Fog Formation and State of the Art of Fog Nowcasting*

Fog is basically a cloud of small water droplets near ground level and sufficiently dense to reduce horizontal visibility to less than 1 km (3281 feet). The word fog also may refer to clouds of smoke particles, ice particles, or mixtures of these components. Under similar conditions, but with visibility greater than 1000 m, the phenomenon is termed a mist or haze, depending on whether the obscurity is caused by water drops or solid particles. The formation of fog is due to the condensation of water vapor on condensation nuclei (non-gaseous solid particles) to form water droplets, near the ground. Fog usually develops when relative humidity is near 100% and when the air temperature and dew point temperature are close to each other or less than 4˚F (2.5˚C). When air reaches 100% of relative humidity, its dew point is said to be saturated and can thus hold no more water vapor. As a result, the water vapor condenses to form water droplets and fog. The formation of fog is a complex process involving highly non-linear interactions between surface and sub-surface processes, atmospheric radiation, turbulence and flows. Such interactions are not adequately described by the current operational Numerical Weather Prediction (NWP) [6], because the vertical and horizontal resolutions are larger than the corresponding fog scales [7] that are of the order of 1 km on the horizontal scale and up to few ten meters on the vertical scale. For these reasons these models [2] [8] [9] are unable to treat complex three-dimensional flows due to their poor representation of horizontal heterogeneities [7].

In order to overcome such limitations, dedicated NWP models have been implemented [10] in order to predict the formation of fog in regions of complex terrain and reach horizontal grid resolution of 1km or better. The disadvantage of such models lies on the computational costs required to run them [6]. For this reason, they can be applied only on small domains and on high speed computer [6].

Finally, the statistical methods [11] can overcome the above-mentioned problems but they require long time series of homogeneous data and they can be used only for specific locations for which the fog events can be correlated to the local conditions. In fact fog events can be triggered by different physical causes and their characteristic strongly depends on the specific geographical location [12].

Traditional data analysis techniques (including statistical and physical driven techniques) have been often faced with practical difficulties in meeting the challenges posed by new datasets including meteorological datasets (with a high number of records, variables, sources, etc.). DM techniques can represent useful analysis methods because they are able to investigate different meteorological variables coming from numerous datasets. DM techniques provide a high level of prediction in terms of consistency and frequency of correct predictions.

Prediction is the most used DM task in meteorology domain. DM has been applied successfully to predict different weather elements like wind speed [13] [14], rainfall [15] [16], cloud [17] and temperature [18] [19].

DM description task is carried on in [20] and [21] by using Decision Trees and Bayesian Networks in order to create some fog local indices, based on the post-processing of meteorological variables. The same methods were used in [22] for creation of some basic neural network structures that were further adapted to local prediction models. This approach was implemented and tested in various conditions of major Australian airports.

The fog formation and its important parameters were identified based on collected historical dataset from the International Airport of Rio de Janeiro [23]. In [24] the authors describe three short-range fog-forecasting models by applying Bayesian Networks in order to predict fog events between 0-3 hours on Paris Charles De Gaulle airport.

The availability of a long time series data set (SYNOP data) together with the necessity to describe such phenomenon in a specific site (Milan's Linate airport), make the DM approach one of the best solutions in describing and short range forecasting fog phenomena.

B. Business Objectives and Data Mining Goals

The Business objective is to develop an algorithm, which is able to describe, and nowcast fog phenomenon over Milan's Linate Airport, using DM techniques and Synop data. In particular, the objective is to forecast a fog event on the time range of 1 hour, associating a prediction probability. Classification models will be trained in order to forecast fog events.

Of course, probabilities can be transferred into crisp event forecasts, but since developments in air traffic management systems point towards more and more automation and decision support, direct use of probabilities will be favored because it enables detailed cost benefit analysis for triggering decisions

III. Data Understanding

This step of the CRISP-DM includes the initial data collection, data description, data exploration, and the verification of data quality.

A. Data Collection

In order to build a predictive model using DM techniques for fog forecast, a historical dataset made up of fog observations and relevant meteorological parameters needs to be built.

Data have been collected from ECMWF MARS Archive [25] containing the surface Synoptic observations (SYNOP) provided by Linate meteorological station.

SYNOP observations are recorded every hour. A list of the meteorological variables used for DM and selected from the SYNOP message is reported in TABLE I.

B. Fog Event Description

Each fog event can be defined as a sequence of SYNOP records with a visibility attribute value less or equal than 1000 meters. Each record describes the weather conditions observed.

TABLE I. List of Meteorological Variables (Features)

#	Name	Description	Units
1	Date	Date of the observation	Date
2	Pressure	Force per unit area exerted against a surface by the weight of the air above that surface	Pa
3	three hour pressure change	Change of the pressure with respect to three hours ago	Pa
4	char pressure tendency	Coded values indicating how the pressure has changed during one hour	-
5	wind direction	Wind direction at 10 m	Deg
6	wind speed	Wind speed at 10 m	kn
7	Visibility	It represents the greatest distance at which a black object of suitable dimensions (located on the ground) can be seen and recognized when observed against the horizon sky during daylight or could be seen and recognized during the night if the general illumination were raised to the normal daylight level. Visibility values below 1 km can indicate the presence of fog	m
8	present weather	Coded values describing the weather phenomena present at the time of the observation. Values between 40-49 indicate the presence of fog	-
9	past weather1	Coded values describing weather phenomena occurring during the preceding hour	-
10	past weather2	Coded values describing weather phenomena occurring during the two preceding hours	-
11	cloud cover	Values between 0 and 8 indicating the fraction of the celestial dome covered by all clouds visible. It is estimated in eighths (okta) of sky covered by clouds. Clear sky is indicated with 0 okta, overcast with 8	okta
12	height of base of cloud	Height of bases of clouds above ground level	m
13	cloud type	Coded values reporting the type of cloud and the state of sky	-
14	Dewpoint	Temperature at which moist air saturated with respect to water at a given pressure has a saturation mixing ratio equal to the given mixing ratio (ratio between the mass of water vapour and the mass of dry air)	°C
15	Drybulb	Temperature of the air measured with a thermometer shielded to radiation and humidity	°C

Fog events are characterized by an initial and final SYNOP message: the first recording is the head of the event; the last one is the end of fog event; one or more persistences of YES are between the head and ending in the single fog event.

In Figure 2, two examples of fog events are reported: the first event lasts three hours and the second one lasts two hours (the second event has no persistence of YES because it lasts only two hours and the first hour is the head while the last one is the end).

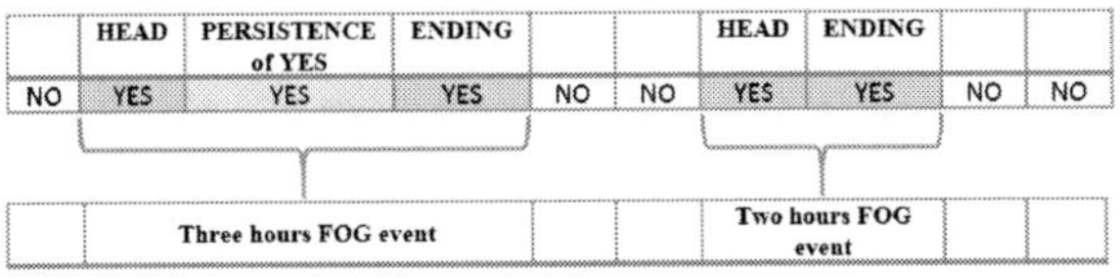

Figure 2. Sequences of recordings

C. Data Exploration

The collected dataset contains 164.352 instances belonging to the period from 1st January 1996 until 30th September 2014. Using the Weka's explorer interface [5] [29] we are easily able to view histograms for each attribute in TABLE I and plot matrices of different attribute combinations. Weka also displays basic statistics for each numeric attribute. In the following, some histograms are reported in order to investigate data and variables. For example, Figure 3 reports the number of instances of Dewpoint variable in the considered dataset. Dewpoint histogram presents a distribution similar to a Gaussian one.

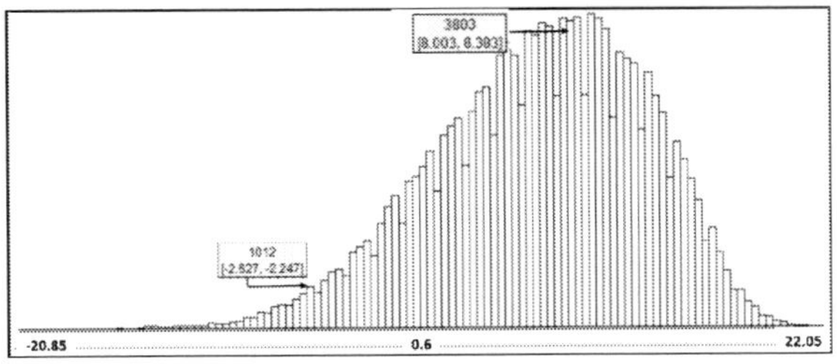

Figure 3. Histogram of instances by Dewpint attribute.

In TABLE II some basic statistics of Dewpoint attribute are reported.

TABLE II. STATISTICS OF DEWPOINT ATTRIBUTE

Statistic	Value
Minimum	-20.85
Maximum	22.05
Mean	8.001
StdDev	5.636
Missing	10741 (6.53%)
Distinct	375

The dewpoint temperature has a very low minimum value. This indicates that there are some outliers in the data set, which are removed in the next CRISP step.

Figure 4 reports the number of instances of Pressure variable in the dataset considered. Also Pressure histogram presents a distribution similar to a Gaussian one. In addition, table of basic statistics is reported in TABLE III.

IV. DATA PREPARATION

In order to obtain the final dataset that can be used in the modeling phase, data have been preprocessed to report them in a format usable by DM algorithms. In the original dataset there are 10676 missing records corresponding to the same number of missing hours. For these recordings, we have only date and time variables. The other attributes are all null. These missing records are removed from the original dataset, obtaining a new dataset with 153.676 instances.

TABLE III. STATISTICS OF PRESSURE ATTRIBUTE

Statistic	Value
Minimum	94950
Maximum	102750
Mean	100194.228
StdDev	882.571
Missing	51 (0%)
Distinct	669

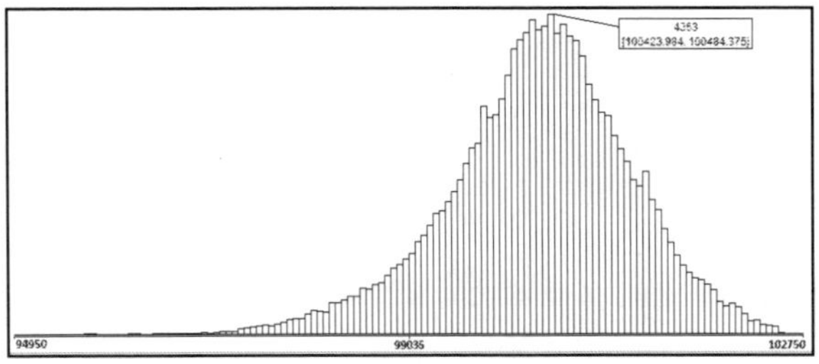

Figure 4. Histogram of instances by Pressure attribute

A. Variables Transformation and Target Class Creation

The meteorological parameters coded according to the World Meteorological Organization (WMO) code tables [26] have been converted from numeric to nominal type in order to report them in a format usable by DM algorithm. Such conversion is also required for a clearer reading of data and results. After the conversion, the target attribute has been identified according to the domain expert indications. Indeed the presence of fog is detected if visibility is less than or equal to 1 km [27].

Moreover, *Date* variable is splitted into two new attributes: *Month* and *Hour*.

The histogram of target class of Figure 5 shows how fog is a quite rare meteorological event on Linate airport: fog occurs about once every 53 events. Target class is unbalanced.

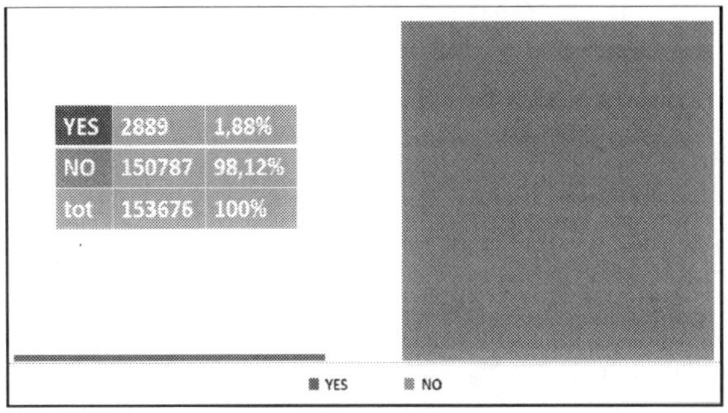

Figure 5. Histogram of instances by class target attribute

In order to visualize the distribution of FOG according to the variation of variables, the graph of Figure 6 shows that fog events, which are represented in blue color, occur mostly from October to March. In addition, from the histogram of instances by Hour attribute (not reported), fog events occur in the early hours of the morning and in the late evening.

Figure 7 shows the scatter plot for Dewpoint and Drybulb variables with the line bisector. Fog events are in blue color. Since the points of the line bisector have Dewpoint=Drybulb, in the area close to the upper side of the line bisector where the fog events are mostly distributed, fog events have a small positive value of (drybulb–dewpoint).

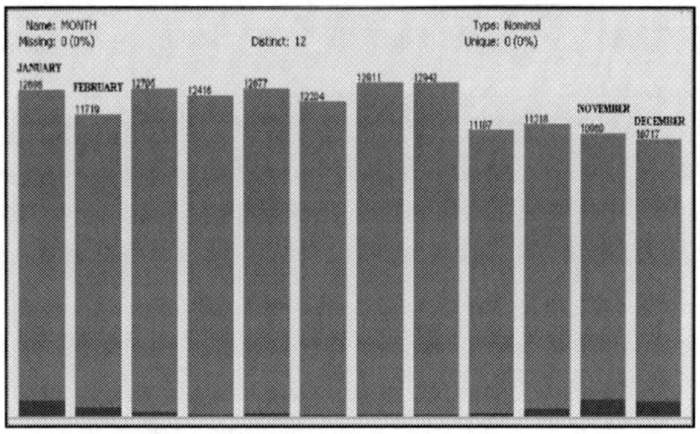

Figure 6. Histogram of instances by Month attribute, from Jan. to Dec.

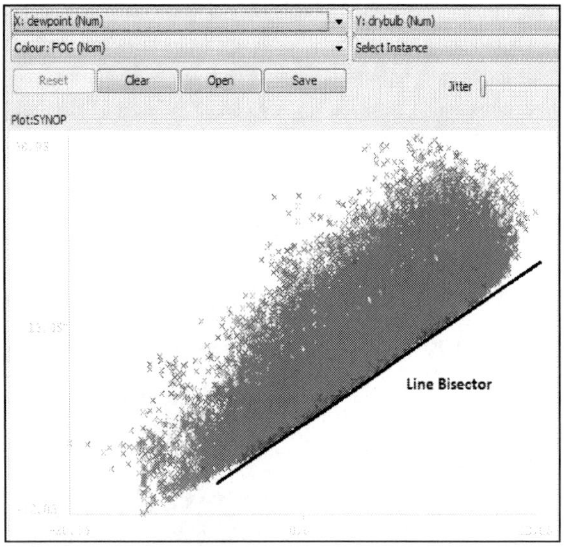

Figure 7. Scatter plot for Dewpoint and Drybulb variables with Line Bisector

In total, the Linate weather dataset has 17 (16+1) attributes, including FOG target class.

B. *Hold-Out Method and Forecast Sets Preparation*

For DM goal, we adopted the working strategy named hold-out method [28]. In this method, the original data with labeled examples is partitioned into two disjoint sets, called training and test sets, respectively. A classification model is induced from the training set and its performances are evaluated on the test set. The accuracy of the classifier can be estimated based on the accuracy of the induced model on the test set.

As test set we choose the records belonging to the last 13 months of meteorological observations, from 1st September 2013 until 30th September 2014. This test set is called 1_YEAR, it has 9314 full weather observations and it has roughly the same target class distribution of whole dataset.

FOG and 1_YEAR are useful to train and test a descriptive model, called *F-model*, as described in the next section.

V. MODELING

Modeling follows Data Preparation; in Modeling phase descriptive and forecast models are trained and tested.

A. *The F-model*

In order to better understand the fog phenomenon on Milan Linate airport, a descriptive Data Mining model is realized. This model, called *F-model*, takes into account the actual weather conditions and it is able to recognize whether the measured weather conditions are related to Milan fog events or not:

$$F: (feat_1, feat_2, \dots, feat_{14}, t_0) \rightarrow \{YES, NO\}_{t_0} \in FOG$$

Input variables are 14 (and not 16) because *Visibility* and *present weather* attributes are obviously removed (they are directly and closely correlated to FOG class).

Thus, F is a system of classification rules that has at least two main uses:

1. describe fog events at the Linate airport;
2. provide a "similarity metric" able to determine whether the fog meteorological conditions of an airport are similar to those at Milan Linate airport. Thanks to F we can determine whether a new set of fog observations is compatible or not with Linate fog observations.

FOG set is used to training the *F-model* while 1_YEAR set is used to test it. FOG set has got 152971 full weather observations, 1_YEAR has got 9314 records.

In the current section, *F-model* is described in order to understand data, explore fog events and recognize them at Linate airport; whilst in Section VII, a novel use of the descriptive model is suggested in order to compare fog events at different airports and to group geographic locations that can be also very distance away (from the spatial point of view).

The descripted *F-model* is an Ensemble model trained combining different classifiers by using a majority voting strategy [30] [31]. A combined classifier often shows better performance than individual classification models (component classifiers). An optimal set of classifiers is first selected and then combined by a specific fusion method, in order to obtain the *F-model*.

Furthermore, the improvement of the generalization performance of such ensemble model will be demonstrated experimentally (TABLE XI).

The *F-model* is 10-cross folds validated, and it is obtained by combining 4 Bayesian Nets (BN) [29] and 9 Inductive Decision Trees (IDT) [28] [32], by changing the values of the parameters of BayesNet and J48 Weka algorithms. The choice of BN and IDT is due to [20] [21].

The BayesNet algorithm of Weka allows to define such components by means of the following parameters:

- *searchAlgorithm* selects the method for searching network topology; we fixed it to K2.
- *Estimator* selects the algorithm for calculating the conditional probability tables. We chose the SimpleEstimator algorithm. This algorithm has a parameter, called A = alpha parameter, which sets the starting value for the calculation of conditional probability.

Four models have been produced, by changing the values of the following P parameter:

- P = maxNrOfParents parameter of K2 algorithm which sets the maximum value of the number of parents (maximum number of edge arrows) of each node in the net topology.

In particular, A is fixed to 0.5 and P ranges from 1 to 4 in order to obtain 4 Bayesian networks.

The J48 algorithm of Weka allows to generate a pruned or unpruned C4.5 decision tree. Its main parameter is N = "NumOfFolds", that determines the amount of data used for reduced-error pruning (one fold is used for pruning, the rest for growing the tree). Moreover, the "reducedErrorPruning" J48 parameter is fixed to "True" value (whether reduced-error pruning is used instead of C4.5 pruning).

By changing N from 2 to 9 and fixing one time "reduceErrorPruning" = "False", 9 Inductive Decision Trees are trained. TABLE IV summarizes the 13 trained models.

TABLE IV. 13 DESCRIPTIVE MODELS

BayesNet	J48	Total
P = 1, ..., 4	N = 2, ..., 9 +	
A = 0.5	reduceErrorPruning = "False"	
4 BN	9 IDT	13 models

As reported in Figure 4, target class FOG is imbalanced; the Weka filter SpreadSubsample under-samples the dataset in order to obtain the same number of FOG = "YES" and FOG = "NO" instances. This balancing technique is used in order to overcome the class unbalance problem. In particular, the balanced Training set has 5502 instances (2751 FOG="NO" + 2571 FOG="YES"). Another way to overcome the class unbalance problem is the cost-sensitive technique [21].

All obtained descriptive models of fog events have been compared and the achieved results have been evaluated by means of adequate performance metrics able to highlight the classifying ability with respect to the fog events and the no-fog events separately (e.g., confusion matrix, AUC) [28] [29].

Finally, the Ensemble *F-model* has the performances of TABLE V, TABLE VI, and TABLE VII, considering 10-cross folds validation as test mode:

TABLE V. *F-MODEL* EVALUATION

Total Number of Instances	5502	
Correctly Classified Instances	5367	(97.5463 %)
Incorrectly Classified Instances	135	(2.4537 %)

TABLE VI. *F-MODEL* DETAILED ACCURACY BY CLASS

=== Detailed Accuracy By Class ===				
Class	TP Rate	FP Rate	Precision	ROC Area
YES	0.976	0.025	0.975	0.975
NO	0.975	0.024	0.976	0.975

TABLE VII. CONFUSION MATRIX OF *F-MODEL*

Forecast		← Classified as	
YES	NO		
2684	67	YES	Observed
68	2683	NO	

F-model shows the performances on 1_YEAR Test Set included in TABLE VIII, TABLE IX, and TABLE X. FOG class target in 1_YEAR test set has, roughly, the original unbalanced distribution of the whole dataset.

TABLE VIII. *F-MODEL* EVALUATION ON *1_YEAR*

Total Number of Instances	9314	
Correctly Classified Instances	9198	(98.7546 %)
Incorrectly Classified Instances	116	(1.2454 %)

TABLE IX. *F-MODEL* DETAILED ACCURACY BY CLASS

=== Detailed Accuracy By Class ===				
Class	TP Rate	FP Rate	Precision	ROC Area
YES	0.977	0.012	0.535	0.983
NO	0.988	0.023	1	0.983

TABLE X. CONFUSION MATRIX OF *F-MODEL* ON *1_YEAR*

Forecast		← Classified as	
YES	NO		
130	3	YES	Observed
113	9068	NO	

The Ensemble model has better performance than its single components. The following TABLE XI shows some metrics of the components of *F-model* on 1_YEAR test set, including *F-model*.

TABLE XI. *PERFORMANCES OF THE COMPONENTS OF F-MODEL ON 1_YEAR TEST SET*

#	Model	True Positive Rate (TPR)	True Negative Rate (TNR)	AUC
1	BN_1	0.887	0.992	0.981
2	BN_2	0.962	0.985	0.982
3	BN_3	0.97	0.989	0.989
4	BN_4	0.962	0.988	0.99
5	IDT_2	0.977	0.986	0.985
6	IDT_3	0.962	0.984	0.987
7	IDT_4	0.977	0.983	0.98
8	IDT_5	0.977	0.985	0.985
9	IDT_6	0.977	0.984	0.984
10	IDT_7	0.977	0.986	0.991
11	IDT_8	0.977	0.981	0.99
12	IDT_9	0.97	0.981	0.99
13	IDT_false	0.97	0.98	0.98
14	***F-model***	**0.977**	**0.988**	**0.983**

The best component model is the Inductive Decision Tree trained fixing N=7 (called IDT_7). In particular, IDT_7 has the highest TPR (0.977) and the highest TNR (0.986). The *F-model* exceeds IDT_7 because *F* has an higher TNR than IDT_7.

B. A and B Models Design

The DM models should be able to predict fog after one hour from the recording of the last available SYNOP data. So, in order to easily forecast fog events, a new dataset is released starting from the dataset available after Data Preparation step. Shifting upwards of a position the time series of FOG variable, we obtain a new target attribute (FOG+1) describing the condition of fog at time $t_{0+1hour}=t_1$, while the meteorological attributes remains at time t_0. Such elaboration allows getting a new training set, called FOG+1, and a new test set, called 1_YEAR+1.

The one-hour prediction model has to be able to recognize both the beginning and the end of a fog event. Therefore, two models have been trained, *A-model* and *B-model*:

3. *A-model* is used in order to predict the persistence of NO and the discontinuities from NO to YES (heads of new fog events).
4. *B-model* is used in order to predict the persistence of YES and the discontinuities from YES to NO (endings of fog events that are heads of NO-fog events), instead.

As a consequence, *A-model* is used when the occurring visibility (visibility at time t_0) is greater than 1000 m and *B-model* in the other cases. A summary of this criterion is reported in TABLE XII.

TABLE XII. RULE FOR MODELS APPLICATION

if visibility at time t_0 > 1000m then *A-model* else *B-model*

DM models are simple predictors for time series, where the prediction of outputs for time t_1 is based on the sequence of historical data observed at time t_0.

In order to obtain two predicting models (*A-model* and *B-model*), each one of two datasets (FOG+1 and 1_YEAR+1) has been splitted in two subsets.

*A*_FOG+1, *B*_FOG+1 aim at train the *A-model* and the *B-model*, respectively, *A*_1YEAR+1 is useful to evaluate the performances of *A-model*, while *B*_1YEAR+1 is useful to evaluate the performances of *B-model*. The next schema of Figure 8 summarizes the steps of the Data Preparation phase.

In particular, after the step I, detailed in Figure 7, the original dataset has been cleaned and splitted in two subsets; after the step II the label class of the two datasets has been upward shifted for one hour.

Finally, in order to obtain the training and the test sets for A-model we have selected FOG="NO", and to obtain the training and test sets for B-model we have selected FOG="YES".

Therefore, we have applied the rules of TABLE XIII and TABLE XIV.

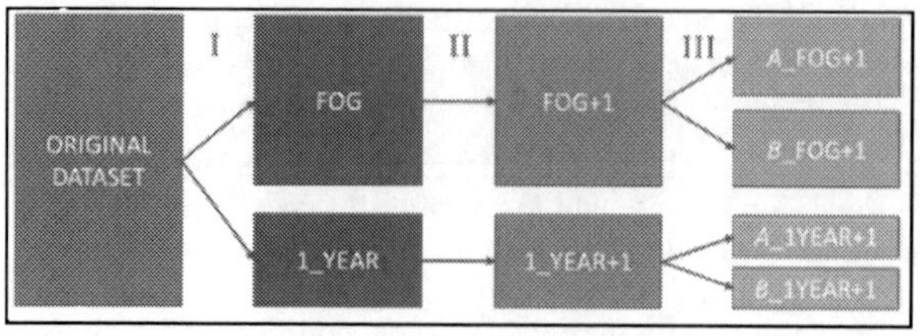

Figure 8. Forecast Sets Preparation Schema

TABLE XIII. RULE FOR *A_FOG+1* AND *A_1YEAR+1* SETS

FOG	FOG+1	
NO	NO	← Persistence of NO
NO	YES	← Head of fog event

TABLE XIV. RULE FOR *B_FOG+1* AND *B_1YEAR+1* SETS

FOG	FOG+1	
YES	YES	← Persistence of YES
YES	NO	← Ending of fog event

In addition, in order to overcome the class imbalance problem (Figure 4), the class labels of training sets have been under sampled, obtaining the same numbers of records with FOG+1="NO" and FOG+1="YES". However, the two test sets retain the original class target distributions. Finally, the Data Preparation produces the four datasets presented in TABLE XV, including their sizes.

TABLE XV. DATASETS ROLES AND DIMENSIONS

	A-model	*B-model*
Training	*A*_FOG+1 1380	*B*_FOG+1 1392
Test	*A*_1YEAR+1 9046 records	*B*_1YEAR+1 135 records

Starting from the two new datasets *A*_FOG+1 and *B*_FOG+1, we are able to train forecast models by using DM techniques. Indeed a forecast model is a function that takes into account the meteorological variables measured at time t_0 and computes a binary variable FOG+1 that indicates the presence or absence of fog at time t_1 and the respective probabilities.

In the next sections, the best obtained models are described but, for the sake of clarity, in our project many predictive models have been trained and only the performances of a Bayesian Net and an Artificial Neural Network are highly satisfactory for one-hour fog predictions on Linate airport database. The testing of the two 1-hour classification models show good performances, as follows.

C. The A-model

The *A-model* is a Bayesian Network classifier. It has been trained on the *A*_FOG+1 dataset (obtained from FOG+1 set using the instances tagged by FOG="NO"). For the sake of clarity, the training set *A*_FOG+1 is obtained by balancing the target class FOG+1, using the filter SpreadSubsample of Weka tool.

In this way, A-set presents 690 records tagged by FOG+1="NO" and 690 records tagged by FOG+1="YES". The *A-model* is trained by using BayesNet Weka algorithm.

Fixing P=3 and A=0.25, the *A-model* performs on 10-fold cross-validation and it shows the performances included in TABLE XVI, TABLE XVII, and TABLE XVIII.

TABLE XVI. *A-MODEL* EVALUATION

Total Number of Instances	1380	
Correctly Classified Instances	1214	(87.971 %)
Incorrectly Classified Instances	166	(12.029 %)

TABLE XVII. *A-MODEL* DETAILED ACCURACY BY CLASS

=== Detailed Accuracy By Class ===				
Class	TP Rate	FP Rate	Precision	ROC Area
YES	0.884	0.125	0.876	0.932
NO	0.875	0.116	0.883	0.932

TABLE XVIII. CONFUSION MATRIX OF *A-MODEL*

Forecast		← Classified as	
YES	NO		
610	80	YES	Observed
86	604	NO	

TABLE XIX. *A-MODEL* EVALUATION ON *A_1YEAR+1*

Total Number of Instances	9046	
Correctly Classified Instances	8480	(93.7431 %)
Incorrectly Classified Instances	566	(6.2569 %)

TABLE XX. *A-MODEL* DETAILED ACCURACY BY CLASS

=== Detailed Accuracy By Class ===				
Class	TP Rate	FP Rate	Precision	ROC Area
YES	0.732	0.062	0.051	0.934
NO	0.938	0.268	0.999	0.934

TABLE XXI. CONFUSION MATRIX OF *A-MODEL* ON *A_1YEAR+1*

Forecast		← Classified as	
YES	NO		
30	11	YES	Observed
555	8450	NO	

The *A-model* shows the performances on A_1YEAR+1 Test Set included in TABLE XIX, TABLE XX, and TABLE XXI. This test analyzes the capability of the *A-model* to predict the persistence of the condition FOG="NO" or the presence of the head of the fog events (FOG="YES").

D. The B-model

The B-classifier is an Artificial Neural Network (ANN) [28] trained on the balanced *B*_FOG+1 dataset (obtained from FOG+1 set using the instances tagged by FOG="YES" and balancing the target class FOG+1 by using the Weka filter SpreadSubsample). In this way, *B*_FOG+1 presents 696 records tagged by FOG+1="NO" and 696 records tagged by FOG+1="YES".

TABLE XXII. THE *B-MODEL* EVALUATION

Total Number of Instances	1392	
Correctly Classified Instances	1207	(86.71 %)
Incorrectly Classified Instances	185	(13.29%)

TABLE XXIII. THE *B-MODEL* DETAILED ACCURACY BY CLASS

=== Detailed Accuracy By Class ===				
Class	TP Rate	FP Rate	Precision	ROC Area
YES	0.888	0.154	0.852	0.891
NO	0.846	0.112	0.883	0.891

The *B-model* is trained by using the MultilayerPerceptron [29] algorithm of Weka tool, with 10 hidden layers (H=10) and N=1000 that is the number of epochs to train through. It performs on 10-fold cross-validation and it shows the performances included in TABLE XXII, TABLE XXIII, and in TABLE XXIV.

TABLE XXIV. CONFUSION MATRIX OF THE *B-MODEL*

Forecast		← Classified as	
YES	NO		
618	78	YES	Observed
107	589	NO	

B-model shows the performances on *B*_1YEAR+1 of TABLE XXV, TABLE XXVI, and TABLE XXVII.

TABLE XXV. THE *B-MODEL* EVALUATION ON *B_1YEAR+1*

Total Number of Instances	135	
Correctly Classified Instances	109	(80.74%)
Incorrectly Classified Instances	26	(19.259%)

TABLE XXVI. THE *B-MODEL* DETAILED ACCURACY BY CLASS

=== Detailed Accuracy By Class ===				
Class	TP Rate	FP Rate	Precision	ROC Area
YES	0.828	0.25	0.881	0.814
NO	0.75	0.172	0.614	0.814

TABLE XXVII. MATRIX OF THE *B-MODEL* ON *B_1YEAR+1*

Forecast		← Classified as	
YES	NO		
82	17	YES	Observed
9	27	NO	

This test analyzes the capability of the *B-model*, when the instances FOG="YES" is present, to predict in the following hour the persistence of the condition FOG="YES" or the presence of the end of the fog events.

VI. MODEL EVALUATION

Evaluation of the performance of a classification model is based on the number of test records correctly and incorrectly predicted by the model. Good results correspond to large numbers along the main diagonal of the confusion matrix and small, ideally zero, off-diagonal elements.

The confusion matrix of the *A-model* on *A*_1YEAR+1 Test Set shows 555 records incorrectly classified as "YES" (TABLE XII), corresponding to 555 false positives instances (555 recordings without fog incorrectly predicted as heads of fog events).

TABLE XXVIII shows the distribution of such False Positives by Month attribute. The 74% of False Positive instances occur in [September, January].

TABLE XXVIII. DISTRIBUTION OF FALSE POSITIVES BY MONTH

# of records	Month	Total number of hours in the month
100	September 2013	720
49	October 2013	744
102	November 2013	720
99	December 2013	744
62	January 2014	744
12	February 2014	672
73	March 2014	744
18	April 2014	720
15	May 2014	744
5	June 2014	720
15	July 2014	744
5	August 2014	744
Tot=555		

Figure 9 shows the histogram of False Positives by Hour attribute. About 80% of False Positive instances occur in [00:00, 09:00] (range of Hour attribute).

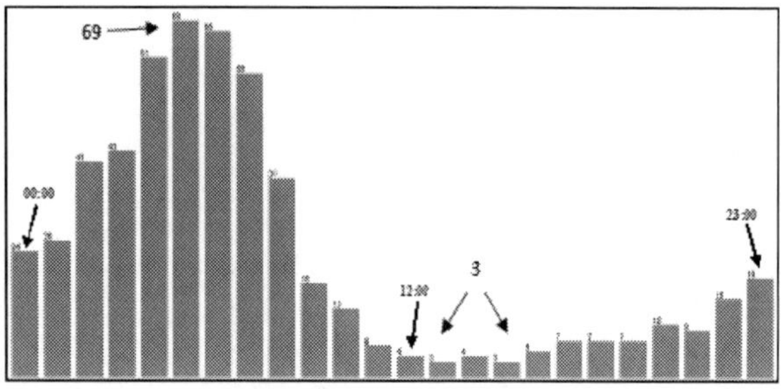

Figure 9. Histogram of false positives by Hour attribute

In addition, about 75% of False Positive instances occur when visibility ranges within [1200m, 4500m] (range of Visibility attribute). About 70% of False Positives occur when the 'Height of base of cloud' attribute is within [30m, 1000m] range and about 81% in [0kn, 7.77kn] range of 'Wind speed'. Therefore, False Positives have higher occurrence when these favorable meteorological conditions for fog presence are recorded, as low wind speed intensity and low cloud.

TABLE XXIX shows the distribution of False Positives by 'Present Weather' attribute.

The histograms and the statistic distributions prove that most of predicted false positives occur when the observed visibility conditions are below 5 km due to the presence of meteorological conditions that can reduce visibility (mist, drizzle, rain or fog). It has been considered that the present model considers only prediction of low visibility due to fog presence, while there are also other physical sources causing the reduction of the visibility. Therefore, even if these events are classified as false positives for fog event presence (because the observed visibility is greater than 1000 m), they correctly classify the events being physically characterized by low visibility conditions.

TABLE XXIX. FALSE POSITIVES DISTRIBUTION BY 'PRESENT WEATHER'

# of records	Present weather
56	Drizzle
17	Rain
9	Fog
305	Mist
136	No Meteors
25	Fog or Ice Fog
7	Patches
Tot=555	

Furthermore, most of the incorrectly predictions occur during months and hours often interested by fog events (autumn and winter seasons, night and early hours of the day), and during which a reduction of visibility conditions occur.

In conclusion, the *B-model* performs worse than the *A-model*. However, this evaluation does not worry us considering the significant increase of flight safety.

Anyway, considering the difficulty of the prediction of this atmospherical phenomenon results can be considered very promising for further investigation.

VII. HOW TO USE THE LINATE DESCRIPTIVE MODEL

In this section, a novel and alternative use of the *F-model* obtained in Section V is described.

A. Portability

A-model and *B-model*, built using Data Mining techniques applied to the weather data of Milan Linate airport site, are hardly able to predict fog events in other geographic locations without a meaningful loss of performance; in other words they are not "portable" to other different sites.

This inability has at least two explanations, the former in the meteorological field and the latter in the statistical field:

1. Meteorological inability: the geo-physical conditions of the various sites can be very different. Local classical forecast models, though they may have a similar analytical structure, are usually tailored to the geographic area using different known parameters.
2. Statistical inability: a model built with Data Mining techniques has a satisfactory accuracy only if it is tested on a set "compatible" with the set used for training; for example, it occurs when the test set is a random subset of the training set. Distributions of weather variables of data sets coming from different sites can be very "discordant". Obviously, "concordant" statistical distributions are a

necessary but not sufficient condition for model applicability in other different sites.

Getting a general purpose model able to predict fog events irrespective of the site being monitored is a very complex undertaking and may even fail if adequate methods are not taken into account and specific techniques are not applied.

A useful strategy for obtaining a "general purpose" model could be to consider a broader training set, obtained by merging the weather data sets of the various sites. Training such a model could approach too different situations and several attempts have led to an increase of the classification error.

In this section a novel strategy is described, which takes into account a single analytical model that exceeds the critical issues of points 1 and 2. A criterion is defined to determine whether the predictive model previously made at the Milan airport is portable or not on a different site, based on an automatic comparison among sites by defining a distance (a metric) by which to establish a "similarity" criterion among databases and then geographic locations.

In particular, this strategy has various corollaries, aimed at enhancing knowledge of the domain and meteorological phenomenon of fog.

B. Procedure Design

The algorithmic scheme developed for the prediction model portability is based on the idea that the predictive models of Milan Linate are also applicable to another site S if S is compatible (or similar) with the Milan site.

This paper describes the procedure for comparing a new geographic site S with the Milan Linate site using the descriptive model F.

The application and testing of the procedure is not here reported, but there is only the procedure design.

TABLE XXX. PERFORMANCE VECTOR MEASURES

1.	CCR	Correctly Classified instances Rate	0.987
2.	KS	Kappa Statistic	0.686
3.	TPR	True Positive Rate	0.977
4.	FPR	False Positive Rate	0.012
5.	PR	Precision	0.535
6.	MCC	Matthews Correlation Coefficient	0.718
7.	AUC	Area Under the ROC Curve	0.983
8.	PRCA	Area under Precision Recall Curve	0.471

The *F-model* has a performance vector *REFP* that summarizes its behavior on 1_YEAR test set. The chosen metrics [28] [29] [33] [34] [35] of *REFP* are in TABLE XXX, where also their values are reported. This *REFP* vector can be considered as a reference point for calculating the similarity measure of other geographical sites.

Considering now a new site S, the performance vector, *T_S_V*, derived from the *F-model* testing on the *S* set, is calculated. *S* is a set of meteorological observations recorded in the same time period of 1_YEAR test set, and its variables have been prepared in the same way as the Milan Linate weather variables.

The Euclidean distance, $ED(S)$, between *T_S_V* and *REFP*, can be considered as a similarity measure between S and Milan Linate. This measure of similarity, or compatibility, causes sorting between the various sites: the S_1 site is more compatible (or more similar) than the S_2 site, with respect to Milan Linate, (and you write $S_1 >_c S_2$), if $ED(S_1) < ED(S_2)$.

After finding the closest sites (more similar) to Milan Linate using the descriptive model *F*, you can try exporting predictive models *A-model* and *B-model* to these new geographical sites as well. If the tests are good, predictive models are portable on new geographic locations. Another alternative predictive model may be [24].

C. Compatibility Schema

Next TABLE XXXI summarizes the symbols used and useful for the Compatibility Schema.

TABLE XXXI. SYMBOLS OF COMPATIBILITY SCHEMA

Name	Description
F-model	A descriptive model trained on Milan Linate dataset [01/01/1996, 08/31/2013]
1_YEAR	Milan Test Set [09/01/2013, 09/30/2014]
REFP	The Performance Vector of *F*, with metrics calculated on 1_YEAR
S	A new geographical Site S is a dataset of weather observations
T_S	*S* Test Set [01/09/2013, 30/09/2014]
T_S_V	The Performance Vector, with metrics calculated on *T_S*
$ED(S)$	The Euclidean distance between *T_S_V* and *REFP*

The Compatibility Schema is the procedure useful to easily understand if a new geographical site *S* is "compatible" with Milan Linate. In the case of compatibility, *A-model* and *B-model* may also be applied to predict fog events on the new *S* site. For the sake of clarity, obviously, a small value of $ED(S)$ is a necessary but not sufficient condition for model portability.

The scheme in TABLE XXXII aims at comparing S_1 and S_2 sites, calculating their distances with Milan Linate separately. $S_1 >_c S_2$ only means that S_1 is closer to Milan than S_2, but S_1 may not be close enough to Milan. It is important to analyze an adequate number of sites, to determine a proximity threshold (that is an Euclidean distance), under which predictive models are portable.

Figure 10 summarizes the compatibility schema for predictive models portability, extended to n geographical sites.

The descriptive *F-model* is evaluated on 1_YEAR (=T_MIL) and on the other test sets $T\_S_1, , T\_S_2, \dots, T\_S_n$; the $n+1$ descriptive performance vectors are calculated, where the first one is *REFP*; all the n Euclidean distances $(ED(S_1), ED(S_2), \dots, ED(S_n))$ are measured; and finally these distances are sorted, in order to discover the sites more similar (or compatible) to Milan and to study the portability of the predictive models to these sites.

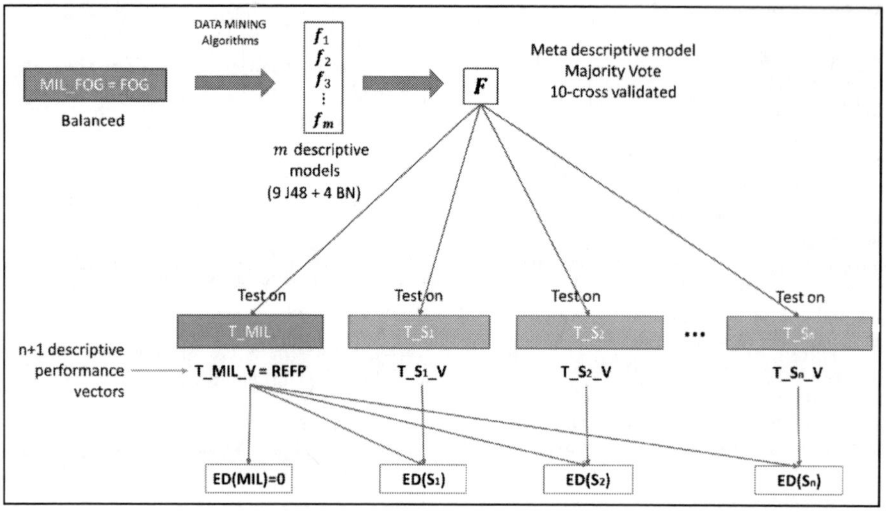

Figure 10. Compatilibility Schema for n Sites

TABLE XXXII. COMPATIBILITY SCHEMA

#	Step	Note
1	Data Preparation	Preparation of S_1 and S_2 datasets, including outliers detection and cleaning, and Target Variable creation. Selecting of test sets T_S_1 and T_S_2. This Data Preparation steps are the same steps of Milan Linate preparation steps (FOG and 1_YEAR)
2	Modeling	Training of the Linate descriptive *F-model*
3	Evaluation	Calculation of performance vectors *REFP*, $T\_S_1\_V$ and $T\_S_2\_V$, by considering 8 metrics: $(CCR, KS, TPR, FPR, PR, MCC, AUC, PRCA)$
4	Evaluation	Calculation of Euclidean distances d: $ED(S_1) = d(T\_S_1\_V, REFP)$ $ED(S_2) = d(T\_S_2\_V, REFP)$
5	Evaluation	Comparison of distances $ED(S_1) < ED(S_2)$ and then $S_1 >_c S_2$
6	Testing	Testing of *A-model* and *B-model* on T_S_1 to decide if models are portable to S_1

D. Future Investigations

Of course, the next steps will be dedicated to testing the compatibility procedure between geographical sites, calculating performance vectors and their distances to Milan, and also validating predictive models on the other sites. The predictive models can be the *A-model* and *B-model* of this paper but also the Bayesian Networks illustrated in [24].

The Euclidean distance among the performance vectors obtained on many geographic sites thanks to the F function, can be used as a measure of distance in a clustering algorithm (for example, k-means clustering), useful for obtaining homogeneous groupings of geographical sites. These sites can be colored on a map depending on whether they belong to a cluster, obtaining, for example, a new layer in a GIS.

VIII. CONCLUSIONS

This paper reports the main features of a statistical tool implemented for the forecast, in a very rapid time, the occurrence of low visibility events (or fog events) over the airport area. This method is essentially based on the use of an historical time series of SYNOP data available over Milan Linate airport and on the Data Mining techniques. SYNOP are a meteorological data message available in many airports, therefore the method can potentially be extended easily to different other airports. Two different classifiers have been trained in order to obtain two models that together are able to predict fog events on 1 hour time range. In order to reach this aim, the Data Understanding, Data Preparation, Modeling and Evaluation phases of CRISP-DM have been carried out.

Data Understanding phase includes the collection, description and exploration of data used for DM. Data Preparation phase allowed to elaborate data in order to obtain the dataset to be used for Modeling phase. In the Modeling phase, two different forecasting models (*A-model*, *B-model*) have been produced by applying BayesNet and Neural Network algorithms. Preliminary results show that the two models encourage the forecast of fog events on 1-hour time range. The *A-model* presents a percentage of correct classified instances of 93.74% and a percentage of true positive rate of about 73.2% corresponding to heads of fog events correctly predicted. Additionally the *B-model* presents a percentage of correct classified instances of 80.74% and a percentage of true positive rate of 75% corresponding to ends of fog events correctly predicted. Furthermore, both models have a very high percentage of correct classification of persistences of FOG="NO" and FOG="YES".

In addition to A and B models, this work has also illustrated how a descriptive model F was trained. F is an Ensemble meta-model, based on Bayesian Networks and Inductive Decision Trees. It is useful for better understanding the fog phenomenon and as a preliminary step to define new method for fog forecast. It can be mainly used to apply the Milan predictive models in other sites. Thus, *F* is useful to define a new similarity measure between different geographical sites, useful for determining the portability of the predictive models in future applications. In this way, the geographic locations space can be clustered, in order to identify the sites that are more compatible or more similar to the Linate site.

In addition, future investigations could quantify the performances for detecting sharp transients, i.e., change of status from no-fog to fog and vice versa.

ACKNOWLEDGMENT

The authors would express their gratitude for funding part of this work in equal parts to the SESAR programme (www.sesarju.eu) funded by the European Union, Eurocontrol and its industrial members and to Selex ES GmbH. This work have contributed to the design of an integrated Ground Weather Monitoring System (GWMS) in SESAR project 15.04.09.c lead by Selex ES. Moreover, the authors would also mention the project TECVOL II founded by the Italian PRORA where the upgrade of the tool has been developed.

REFERENCES

[1] G. Zazzaro, P. Mercogliano, and G. Romano, "Bayesian and Artificial Neural Network for Nowcasting Rare Fog Events," in The Ninth International Conference on Advances in Databases, Knowledge, and Data Applications (DBKDA), 2017, pp. 84-90.

[2] T. Bergot, D. Carrer, J. Noilhan, and P. Bougeault, "Improved Site-Specific Numerical Prediction of Fog and Low Clouds: A Feasibility Study," Weather and Forecasting 20, 627–646, 2005.

[3] P. Tan, M. Steinbach, and V. Kumar, "Introduction to Data Mining," Pearson Addison Wesley, 2005.

[4] P. Chapman et al., "CRISP DM 1.0. Data Mining guide," 2000.

[5] M. Hall, E. Frank, G. Holmes, B. Pfahringer, P. Reutemann, and I.H. Witten (2009), "The WEKA Data Mining Software: An Update," SIGKDD Explorations, Volume 11, Issue 1.

[6] R. Capon, Y. Tang, R. Forbes, and P. Clark, "A very high resolution model for local fog forecasting," Cost Action 722 Report, 2008.

[7] T. Bergot et al., "Intercomparison of single-column numerical models for the prediction of radiation fog," Cost Action 722 Report, 2008.

[8] B.W. Golding, "Nimrod: a system for generating automated very short range forecasts," Meteorol. Appl. 5, 1-16, 1998.

[9] I. Gultepe and J. Milbrandt, "Microphysical observations and mesoscale model simulation of a warm fog case during FRAM project," Pure Appl. Geophys., vol. 164, 6/7, pp. 1161–1178, 2007.

[10] R. Capon, "Fog forecasting at very high resolution with the Met Office Unified Model," Met Office Forecasting Research Technical Report 444, JCMM Report 149 (available at http://www.metoffice.gov.uk), 2004.

[11] Pasini, V. Pelino, and S. Potestà, "A neural network model for visibility nowcasting from surface observations: results and sensitivity to physical input variables," J. Geophys. Res.106, 14951–14959, 2001.

[12] W. Jacobs and V. Nietosvaar, Foreword. Cost Action 722 Final Report, 2008.

[13] M.F. Al-Roby and A.M. El-Halees, "Data Mining Techniques for Wind Speed Analysis," Journal of Computer Eng., Vol. 2, No. 1, 2011.

[14] G. Li and J. Shi, "On comparing three artificial networks for wind speed forecasting," Applied Energy, vol. 87, no. 7, pp. 2313-2320, Jul. 2010.

[15] C.T. Dhanya and D.N. Kumar, "Data Mining for Evolving Fuzzy Association Rules for Predicting Monsoon Rainfall of India," Journal of Intelligent Systems, Vol. 18, No. 3, 2009.

[16] S. Dong-Jun and J.P. Breidenbach, "Real-Time correction of Spatially Nonuniform Bias in Radar Rainfall Data Using Rain Gauge Measurements," Hydrometeorology, Vol. 3, no. 2, pp. 93-111, 2002.

[17] L. Hluchy et al, "Prediction of significant meteorological phenomena using advanced data Mining and integration methods," Fuzzy Systems and Knowledge Discovery (FSKD), vol. 6. pp. 2998-3002, 10-12 Aug. 2010.

[18] S.N. Kohail and A.M. El-Halees, "Implementation of Data Mining Techniques for Meteorological Data Analysis," Int. Journal of Information and Communication Technology Res., Vol. 1, No. 3, 2011.

[19] S. Kotsiantis, A. Kostoulas, S. Lykoudis, A. Argiriou, and K. Menagias, "Using Data Mining Techniques for Estimating Minimum, Maximum and Average Daily Temperatures Values," International Journal of Mathematical, Physical and Engineering Sciences, pp. 16-20, 2007.

[20] G. Zazzaro, "An index for local fog forecast by applying Data Mining techniques," Fog Remote Sensing and Modeling (FRAM) Workshop, Dalhousie University, Halifax, Nova Scotia, 21-22 May, 2008.

[21] G. Zazzaro, P. Mercogliano, and F.M. Pisano, "Data Mining to Classify Fog Events by applying Cost-Sensitive Classifier," CISIS 2010, The Fourth International Conference on Complex, Intelligent and SW Intensive Systems, Krakow, Poland, 15-18 February 2010.

[22] G.T. Weymouth, "Dealing with uncertainty in fog forecasting for major airports in Australia," In 4thConference on Fog, Fog Collection and Dew, La Serena, Chile, pp. 73-76, 2007.

[23] F.F. Ebecken, "Fog Formation Prediction in Coastal Regions Using Data Mining Techniques," in International Conf. On Environmental Coastal Regions, Cancun, Mexico, vol. 2, pp. 165-174, 1998.

[24] G. Zazzaro, P. Mercogliano, G. Romano, V. Rillo, and S. Kauczok, "Short Range Fog Forecasting by applying Data Mining Techniques," 2nd IEEE International Workshop on Metrology for Aerospace, at Benevento, Italy, June 3-5 2015, vol. 1, pp. 469-474.

[25] ECMWF. Mars User Guide. User Support. Operations Dep. 2013.

[26] World Meteorological Organization, 2011. Manual on Codes. WMO-No. 306. Volume I.2.

[27] W.T. Roach, "Back to basics: Fog: Part 1—Definitions and basic physics," Weather 49.12, pp. 411-415, 1994.

[28] J. Han and M. Kamber, "Data Mining: Concepts and Techniques," Morgan Kaufmann Publishers, 2001.

[29] I.H. Witten and E. Frank, "Data Mining. Practical Machine Learning Tools and Techniques," Morgan Kaufmann, 2005.

[30] L.I. Kuncheva, "Combining Pattern Classifiers: Methods and Algorithms," John Wiley and Sons, Inc., 2004.

[31] J. Kittler, M. Hatef, R.P.W. Duin, and J. Matas, "On combining classifiers," IEEE Transactions on Pattern Analysis and Machine Intelligence, vol. 20(3), pp. 226-239, 1998.

[32] R. Quinlan, "C4.5: Programs for Machine Learning," Morgan Kaufmann Publishers, 1993, San Mateo, CA.

[33] B.W.Matthews, "Comparison of the predicted and observed secondary structure of T4 phage lysozyme," Biochimica et Biophysica Acta, vol. 405, pp. 442-451, 1975.

[34] D.M.W. Powers, "Evaluation: From Precision, Recall and F-Factor to ROC, Informedness, Markedness & Correlation," Technical Report SIE-07-001, 2007.

[35] C. Sammut, G.I. Webb, "Encyclopedia of Machine Learning and Data Mining. II Ed.," Springer, 2017.